T0221113

BUILDING SOFTWARE FOR SIMULATION

BUILDING SOFTWARE FOR SIMULATION
Theory and Algorithms, with Applications in C++

JAMES J. NUTARO
Oak Ridge National Laboratory

WILEY

A JOHN WILEY & SONS, INC., PUBLICATION

Library of Congress Cataloging-in-Publication Data:

Nutaro, James J.
 Building software for simulation: theory and algorithms with applications in C++ / James J. Nutaro
  p. cm.
 Includes bibliographical references and index.
 ISBN 978-0-470-41469-9 (cloth)

Printed in the United States of America

10 9 8 7 6 5 4 3 2 1

CONTENTS

PREFACE

Building Software for Simulation is different from many other books on simulation because its focuses on the design and implementation of simulation software; by culminating in a complete system for simulation, this book makes itself unique. The design and construction of simulation software has been a topic persistently absent from textbooks even though many, if not most, simulation projects require the development of new software. By addressing this important topic, *Building Software for Simulation* will, I hope, complement other excellent textbooks on modeling and simulation. This book is intended as both an introduction to simulation programming and a reference for experienced practitioners. I hope you will find it useful in these respects.

This book approaches simulation from the perspective of Zeigler's theory of modeling and simulation, introducing the theory's fundamental concepts and showing how to apply these to problems in engineering. The original concept of the book was not so ambitious; its early stages more closely resembled a cookbook for building simulators, focusing almost exclusively on algorithms, examples of simulation programs, and guidelines for the object-oriented design of a simulator. The book retains much of this flavor, demonstrating each concept and algorithm with working code. Unlike a cookbook, however, concepts and algorithms discussed in the text are not disembodied; their origins in the theory of modeling and simulation are made apparent, and this motivates and provides greater insight into their application.

Chapters 3, 4, and 5, are the centerpiece of the text. I begin with discrete-time systems, their properties and structure, simulation algorithms, and applications. Discrete-time system will be familiar to most readers and if not, they are easily grasped. Discrete-time systems are generalized to introduce discrete event systems; this approach leads naturally to Zeigler's discrete-event system specification, its properties and structures, and simulation procedures. The central three chapters conclude with methods for modeling and simulating systems that have interacting continuous and discrete-event dynamics.

The three main chapters are bracketed by applications to robotics, control and communications, and electrical power systems. These examples are more complicated than might be expected in a textbook; three examples occupy two complete chapters. They are, however, described in sufficient detail for a student to reproduce the printed results and to go a step further by exploring unanswered questions about the example systems. The book's appendixes discuss technical problems that do not fit cleanly into the narrative of the manuscript: testing and design, parallel computing, and a brief review of mathematical topics needed for the examples.

Many people contributed advice and guidance as the book evolved. I am particularly grateful to Vladimir Protopopescu at Oak Ridge National Laboratory for his review of and critical commentary on my rough drafts; his advice had a profound impact on the organization of the text and my presentation of much of the material. I'm also grateful to Angela, who reviewed very early drafts and remarked only rarely on the state of the yard and unfinished projects around the house. Last, but not least, thanks to Joe and Jake, who, in the early morning hours while I worked, quietly (for the most part) entertained themselves.

JIM NUTARO

Oak Ridge, Tennessee
December 2009

CHAPTER 1

INTRODUCTION

Simulation has made possible systems that would otherwise be impracticable. The sophisticated controls in modern aircraft and automobiles, the powerful microprocessors in desktop computers, and space-faring robots are possible because simulations reduce substantially the need for expensive prototypes. These complicated systems are designed with the aid of sophisticated simulators, and the simulation software itself has therefore become a major part of most engineering efforts. A project's success may hinge on the construction of affordable, reliable simulators.

Good software engineering practices and a serviceable software architecture are essential to building software for any purpose, and simulators are no exception. The cost of a simulator is determined less by the technical intricacy of its subject than by factors common to all software: the clarity and completeness of requirements, the design and development processes that control complexity, effective testing and maintenance, and the ability to adapt to changing needs. Small software projects that lack any of these attributes are expensive at best, and the absence of some or all of these points is endemic to projects that fail.[1]

It is nonetheless common for the design of a complicated simulator to be driven almost exclusively by consideration of the objects being simulated. The project begins with a problem that is carefully circumscribed: for example, to calculate the time-varying voltages and currents in a circuit, to estimate the in-process storage requirements of a manufacturing facility, or to determine the rate at which a disease

---

[1]Charette's article on why software fails [22] gives an excellent and readable account of spectacular software failures, and Brooks' *The Mythical Man Month* [14] is as relevant today as its was in the 1970s.

Building Software for Simulation: Theory and Algorithms, with Applications in C++, By James J. Nutaro
Copyright © 2011 John Wiley & Sons, Inc.

will spread through a population. Equipped with an appropriate set of algorithms, the scientist or engineer crafts a program to answer the question at hand. The end result has three facets: the model, an algorithm for computing its trajectories, and some means for getting data into and out of the simulator. The first of these are the reason why the simulator is being built. The other two, however, often constitute the majority of the code. Because they are secondary interests, their scope and size are reduced by specialization; peculiarities of the model are exploited as the simulator is built, and so its three aspects become inextricably linked.

If the model is so fundamental as to merit its exact application to a large number of similar systems, then this approach to simulation can be very successful.[2] More likely, however, is that a simulator will be replaced if it does not evolve in step with the system it mimics. A successful simulator can persist for the lifetime of its subject, changing to meet new requirements, to accommodate new data and methods of solution, and to reflect modifications to the system itself. Indeed, the lifetime cost of the simulator is determined primarily by the cost of its evolution. A simulation program built solely for its immediate purpose, with no thought to future uses and objectives, is unlikely to flourish. Its integrated aspects are costly to reengineer and replacement, probably after great expense, is almost certain when new requirements exceed the limits of an architecture narrowly conceived. Conversely, a robust software architecture facilitates good engineering practices and this, in turn, ensures a long period of useful service for the software, while at the same time reducing its lifetime cost.

1.1 ELEMENTS OF A SOFTWARE ARCHITECTURE

Four elements are common to nearly all simulation frameworks meant for general use: a concept of a dynamic system, software constructs with which to build models, a simulation engine to calculate a model's dynamic trajectories, and a means for control and observation of the simulation as it progresses. The concept a dynamic system on which the framework grows has a profound influence on its final form, on the experience of the end user, and on its suitability for expansion and reuse.

Monolithic modeling concepts, which were employed in the earliest simulation tools, rapidly gave way to modular ones for two reasons: (1) the workings of a large system can not be conceived as a whole. Complex operations must be broken down into manageable pieces, dealt with one at a time, and then combined to obtain the desired behavior; and (2) to reuse a model or part of a model requires that it and its components be coherent and self-contained. The near-universal adoption by commercial and academic simulation tools of modular modeling concepts, and the simultaneous growth of model libraries for these tools, demonstrates the fundamental importance of this idea.

---

[2] Arrillaga and Watson's *Computer Modelling of Electrical Power Systems* [6] provides an excellent example of how and where this approach can succeed. In that text, the authors build an entire simulation program, based on the principles of structured design, to solve problems that are relevant to nearly all electrical power systems.

The simulation engine produces dynamic behavior from an assemblage of components. Conceptually, at least, this is straightforward. A simulator for continuous systems approximates the solution to a set of differential equations, the choice of integration method depending on qualitative features of the system's trajectories and requirements for accuracy and precision. A discrete-event simulation executes events scheduled by its components in the order of their event times. Putting aside the details of the event scheduling algorithm and procedure for numerical integration, these approaches to simulation are quite intuitive and any two, reasonably constructed simulators provided with identical models will yield essentially indistinguishable results.

In models with discrete events—the opening and closing of switches, departure and arrival of a data packet, or failure and repair of a machine—simultaneous occurrences are often responsible for simulators that, given otherwise identical models, produce incompatible results (see, e.g., Ref. 12). This problem has two facets: intent and computational precision. The first is a modeling problem: what is the intended consequence of distinct, discrete occurrences that act simultaneously on a model? By selecting a particular solution to this problem, the simulation tool completes its definition of a dynamic system. This seemingly obscure problem is therefore of fundamental importance and, consequently, a topic of substantial research (a good summary can be found in Wieland [146] and Raczynski [113]). Simultaneous interactions are unavoidable in large, modular models, and the clarity with which a modeler sees their implications has a profound effect on the cost of developing and maintaining a simulator.

The issue of how simultaneous events are applied is distinct from the problem of deciding whether two events occur at the same time. Discrete-event systems measure time with real numbers, and so the model itself is unambiguous about simultaneous occurrences; events are concurrent when their scheduled times are equal. The computer, however, approximates the real numbers with a large, but still finite, set of values. Add to this the problem of rounding errors in floating-point arithmetic, and it becomes easy to construct a model that, in fact, does not generate simultaneous events, but the computer nonetheless insists that it does. The analysis problems created by this effect and the related issue of what to do with simultaneous actions (real or otherwise) are widely discussed in the simulation literature (again, see the article by Wieland [146] and the text by Raczynski [113]; see also Refs. 10, 107, and 130).

The concept of a dynamic system and its presentation as object classes and interfaces to the modeler are of fundamental importance. Effort expended to make these clear, consistent, and precise is rewarded in proportion to the complexity and size of the models constructed. In very small models the benefit of organization is difficult to perceive for the same reasons that structure seems unimportant when experience is confined to 100-line computer programs. For large, complicated models, however, adherence to a well-conceived structure is requisite to a successful outcome; organizing principles are important for the model's construction and its later reuse.

The modeling constructs acted on by the simulation engine are reflected in the interface it presents to the outside world. Large simulation projects rarely exist in isolation. More often, the object under study is part of a bigger system, and when the simulator satisfies its initial purpose, this success creates a desire to reuse it in the larger context. Simulators for design can, for example, find their way into training and testing equipment, component-based simulations of a finished system, and even into the operational software of the machine that it models.

Looking beyond the very difficult problems of model validation and reuse (see, e.g., Ref. 32), issues common to the reuse of software in general can prevent an otherwise appropriate simulator from being adapted to a new context. The means for control and observation of a simulation run, and in particular the facilities for control of the simulation clock, for extracting the values of state variables, for receiving notification of important events, and for injecting externally derived inputs are of prime importance. The cost of retrofitting a simulator with these capabilities can be quite high, but they are invariably needed to integrate with a larger application.

1.2   SYSTEMS CONCEPTS AS AN ARCHITECTURAL FOUNDATION

Systems theory, as it is developed by various authors such as Ashby [7], Zeigler et al. [157], Mesarovic and Takahara [86], Wymore [149, 150], and Klir [68], presents a precise characterization of a dynamic system, two aspects of which are the conceptual foundation of our simulation framework. First is the state transition model of a dynamic system, particularly its features that link discrete-time, discrete-event, and continuous systems. Of specific interest is that discrete-time simulation, often described as a counterpart to discrete event simulation, becomes a special case of the state transition model. This fact is readily established by appeal to the underlying theory.

Second is the uniform notion of a network of systems, whereby the components are state transition models and the rules for their interconnection are otherwise invariant with their dynamics. This permits models containing discrete and continuous components to be constructed within a single conceptual framework. The consistent concept of a dynamic system—unvarying for components and networks, for models continuous and discrete—is also reflected in the facilities provided by the simulation engine for its control and observation. The conceptual framework is thereby extended to reuse of the entire simulator, allowing it to serve as a component in other simulation tools and software systems.

The small number of fundamental concepts that must be grasped, and the very broad reach of those same concepts, makes the simulation framework useful for a tremendous range of applications. It can also be used as an integrating framework for existing simulation models and as a tool for expanding the capabilities of a simulation package already in hand. Moreover, a simulation framework grounded in a broad mathematical theory can reveal fundamental relationships between simulation models and other representations of dynamic systems; the close relationship between hybrid automata, which appear frequently in the modern literature on control, and discrete-event systems is a pertinent example.

The approach taken here is not exclusive, nor is it unrelated to the established worldviews for discrete event simulation. For instance, Cota and Sargent's process interaction worldview [29, 125] incorporates key elements of Zeigler's discrete-event system specification [152], from which the simulation framework in this book is derived. The activity-scanning worldview is apparent in models containing discrete events that are contingent on continuous variables reaching specific values. Discrete-event models constructed with any of the classic views can be components in a large model, and conversely models described within our framework can be components in other simulations. This capacity for composing a complex model from pieces in a variety of forms is, perhaps, the most attractive part of this book's approach.

1.3 SUMMARY

The modeling and simulation concepts developed in this book are illustrated with Unified Modeling Language (UML) diagrams and code examples complete enough to very nearly constitute a finished simulation engine; a finished product in C++ can be obtained by downloading the *adevs* software at http://freshmeat.net/projects/adevs. Implementing these simulation concepts in other programming languages is not unduly difficult.[3]

If this specific framework is not adopted, its major elements can still be usefully adapted to other simulation packages. The approach, described in Chapter 5, to continuous components can be used to build a hybrid simulator from any discrete-event simulator that embodies a modular concept of a system. Continuous system simulation tools can likewise make use of the separation of discrete-event and continuous components to integrate complex discrete-event models into an existing framework for continuous system modeling.

A programmer's interface to the simulation engine, by which the advance of time is controlled and the model's components are accessed and influenced, should be a feature of all simulation tools. Its value is attested to by a very large body of literature on simulation interoperability, and by the growing number of commercial simulation packages that provide such an interface. The interface demonstrated in this text can be easily adapted for a new simulator design or to an existing simulation tool.

Taken in its entirety, however, the proposed approach offers a coherent worldview encompassing discrete time, discrete event, and continuous systems. Two specific benefits of this worldview are its strict inclusion of the class of discrete-time systems within the class of discrete-event systems and the uniformity of its coupling concept, which allows networks to be built independent of the inner workings of their components. This unified world view, however, offers a more important, but less easily quantified, advantage to the modeler and software engineer. The small set of very expressive modeling constructs, the natural and uniform handling of simultaneity, and the resulting simplicity with which large models are built can greatly reduce the cost of simulating a complex system.

---

[3]Implementations in other programming languages can be found with a search for discrete-event (system) simulation (DEVS) and simulation on the World Wide Web.

1.4 ORGANIZATION OF THE BOOK

Chapter 2 motivates major aspects of the software design, the inclusion of specific numerical and discrete simulation methods, and other technical topics appearing in the subsequent chapters. The robotic tank developed in Chapter 2 has three important facets: (1) it is modeled by interacting discrete-event and continuous subsystems, (2) the parts are experimented with individually and collectively, and (3) its simulator is used both interactively and for batch runs.

Chapter 3 introduces state transition systems, networks of state transition systems, and builds from these concepts the core of a simulation engine. This is done in the simple, almost trivial, context of discrete-time systems, where fundamental concepts are most easily grasped and applied. The software is demonstrated with a simulator for cellular automata.

Chapter 4 builds on this foundation, introducing discrete-event systems as a generalization of discrete-time systems. Using these new concepts, the simulation engine is expanded and then demonstrated with a simulator for the computer that controls the robotic tank introduced in Chapter 2. Chapter 4 also revisits the cellular automata from Chapter 3 to show that they are a special case of asynchronous cellular automata, which are conveniently described as discrete-event systems.

Chapter 5 completes the simulation framework by introducing continuous systems. Numerical techniques for locating state events, scheduling time events, and solving differential equations are used to construct a special class of systems having internal dynamics that are continuous, but that produce and consume event trajectories and so are readily incorporated into a discrete-event model. The simulation framework from Chapter 4 is expanded to include these new models, and the whole is demonstrated with a complete simulator for the robotic tank. The cellular automata are again revisited, and it is shown that the asynchronous cellular automata of Chapter 4 are, in fact, a special case of differential automata, which have attracted considerable attention in recent years.

Chapter 6 has examples of engineering problems that exemplify different aspects of the simulation technology. The book concludes with a discussion of open problems and directions for future research. The appendixes contain supplemental material on the design and test of simulation models, the use of parallel computers for simulating discrete-event systems, and a brief introduction to system homomorphisms as they are used in the running discussion of cellular automata.

CHAPTER 2

FIRST EXAMPLE: SIMULATING A ROBOTIC TANK

This example serves two purposes. First, it illustrates how hybrid dynamics can appear in engineering problems. The model has three main parts: the equations of motion, a model of the propulsion system, and a model of the computer. The first two are piecewise continuous with discontinuities caused by step changes in the motor voltage and the sticking friction of the rubber tracks. The third model is a prototypical example of a discrete-event system; the tank's computer is modeled with an interruptible server and queue. The equations of motion, propulsion system, and computer are combined to form a complete model of the tank.

Second, this example illustrates the basic elements of a software architecture for large simulation programs. The simulation engine is responsible solely for calculating the dynamic behavior of the model; other functions (visualization and interactive controls, calculation of performance metrics, etc.) are delegated to other parts of the software. This approach is based on two patterns or principles: model–view–control and the experimental frame.

Model–view–control is a pattern widely used in the design of user interfaces (see, e.g., Refs. 47 and 101); the simulation engine and model are treated as a dynamic document and, with this perspective, the overarching design will probably be familiar to most software engineers. The experimental frame (as described, e.g., by Daum and Sargent [31])[1] is a logical separation of the model from the components of the program that provide it with input and observe its behavior. These principles simplify

---

[1]Be aware, however, of its broader interpretation [152, 157].

Building Software for Simulation: Theory and Algorithms, with Applications in C++, By James J. Nutaro
Copyright © 2011 John Wiley & Sons, Inc.

reuse; programs for two experiments illustrate how they are applied and the benefit of doing so.

The entirety of this example need not be grasped at once, and its pieces will be revisited as their foundations are established in later chapters. Its purpose here is to be a specific example of how the simulation engine is used, and to motivate the software architecture and algorithms that are discussed in the subsequent chapters of this book.

2.1 FUNCTIONAL MODELING

Fishwick [42] defines a functional model as a thing that transforms input into output. This view of a system is advantageous because it leads to a natural decomposition of the simulation software into objects that implement precisely defined transformations. Distinct functions within the model are described by distinct functional blocks which are connected to form a complete model of the system. The software objects that implement the functional blocks are connected in the same way to build a simulator.

There are numerous methods for designing models. Many of them are quite general: bond graphs and state transition diagrams, for instance. Others are specific to particular problems: the mesh current method for electric circuits and the Lagrangian formulation of a rigid body. The majority of methods culminate in a state space model of a system: a set of state variables and a description of their dynamic behavior. Mathematical formulations of a state space model can take the form of, for example, differential equations, difference equations, and finite-state machines.

To change a state space model into a functional model is simple in principle. The state variables define the model's internal state; state variables or functions of state variables that can be seen from outside the system are the model's output; variables that are not state variables but are needed for the system to evolve become the model's input. In practice, this change requires judgment, experience, and a careful consideration of sometimes subtle technical matters. It may be advantageous to split a state space model into several interacting functional models, or to combine several state space models into a single functional model. Some state space models can be simplified to obtain a model that is easier to work with; simplification might be done with precise mathematical transformations or by simply throwing out terms. The best guides during this process are experience building simulation software, familiarity with the system being studied, and a clear understanding of the model's intended use.

Functional models and their interconnections are the specification for the simulation software. For this purpose, there are two types of functional model: atomic and network. An atomic model has state variables, a state transition function that defines its internal response to input, and an output function that transforms internal action into observable behavior. A network model is constructed from other functional models, and the behavior of the network is defined by the collective behavior of its interconnected components. The simulator is built from the bottom up by implementing atomic models, connecting these to form network models, combining

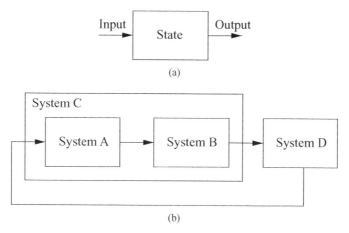

FIGURE 2.1   Bottom–up construction of a model from functional pieces: (a) input, output, and internal state of an atomic model; (b) a network model constructed from three atomic models.

these network models to create larger components, and repeating until the software is finished. This bottom–up approach to model construction is illustrated in Figure 2.1.

The simulation engine operates on software objects that implement atomic and network models. To build a simulator therefore requires the parts of a dynamic system to be expressed in this form. Functional models need not be built in a single step. Atomic and network models are more easily obtained by a set of steps that start with an appropriate modeling technique, proceed to a state space description of the model's fundamental dynamics, combine these to create more sophisticated components, and end with a—possibly large—functional model that can be acted on by the simulation engine.

2.2   A ROBOTIC TANK

The robotic tank is simple enough to permit a thorough discussion of its continuous and discrete dynamics, but sufficiently complicated that it has features present in larger, more practical systems. The robot's operator controls it through a wireless network, and the receipt, storage, and processing of packets is modeled by a discrete event system. An onboard computer transforms the operator's commands into control signals for the motors. The motors and physical motion of the tank are modeled as a continuous system. These components are combined to create a complete model of the tank.

Our goal is to allocate the cycles of the tank's onboard computer to two tasks: physical control of the tank's motors and processing commands from the tank's operator. The tank has four parts that are relevant to our objective: the radio that receives commands from the operator, the computer and software that turn these commands into control signals for the motors, the electric circuit that delivers power to the motors, and the gearbox and tracks that propel the tank. The tank has two tracks, left and right, each driven by its own brushless direct-current (DC) motor. A gearbox connects each motor to the sprocket wheel of its track. The operator drives the tank by setting the duty ratio of the voltage signal at the terminals of the motors. The duty ratio are set using the control sticks on a gamepad and sent via a wireless network to the computer.

The computer generates two periodic voltage signals, one for each motor. The motor's duty ratio is the fraction of time that it is turned on in one period of the signal (i.e., its ON time). Because the battery voltage is fixed, the power delivered to a motor is proportional to its duty ratio. Driving the tank is straightforward. If the duty ratio of the left and right motors are equal then the tank moves in a straight line. The tank spins clockwise if the duty ratio of the left motor is higher than that of the right motor. The tank spins counterclockwise if the duty ratio of the right motor is higher than that of the left motor. A high duty ratio causes the tank to move quickly; a low duty ratio causes the tank to move slowly.

If the voltage signal has a high frequency, then the inertia of the motor will carry it smoothly through moments when it is disconnected from the batteries; the motors operate efficiently and the tank handles well. If the frequency is too low, then the motor operates inefficiently. It speeds up when the batteries are connected, slows down when they are disconnected, and speeds up again when power is reapplied. This creates heat and noise, wasting energy and draining the batteries without doing useful work. Therefore, we want the voltage signal to have a high frequency.

Unfortunately, a high-frequency signal means less time for the computer to process data from the radio. If the frequency is too high, then there is a noticeable delay as the tank processes commands from the operator. At some point, the computer will be completely occupied with the motors, and when this happens, the tank becomes unresponsive.

Somewhere in between is a frequency that is both acceptable to the driver and efficient enough to give a satisfactory battery life. There are physical limits on the range of usable frequencies. It cannot be so high that the computer is consumed entirely by the task of driving the motors. It cannot be so low that the tank lurches uncontrollably or overheats its motors and control circuits. Within this range, the choice of frequency depends on how sensitive the driver is to the nuances of the tank's control.

An acceptable frequency could be selected by experimenting with the real tank; let a few people drive it around using different frequencies and see which they like best. If we use the real tank to do this, then we can get the opinions of a small number of people about a small number of frequencies. The tank's batteries are one constraint on the number of experiments that can be conducted. They will run dry after a few trials and need several hours to recharge. That we have only one tank is another constraint. Experiments must be conducted one at a time. If, however, we build a simulation of the tank, then we can give the simulator to anyone who cares to render an opinion, and that person can try as many different frequencies as time and patience permit.

TABLE 2.1   Value of Parameters Used in the Tank's Equations of Motion

Parameter	Value	Description
m_t	0.8 kg	Mass of the tank
J_t	5×10^{-4} kg · m^2	Angular mass of the tank
B	0.1 m	Width of the tank from track to track
B_r	1.0 N · s / m	Mechanical resistance of the tracks to rolling forward
B_s	14.0 N · s / m	Mechanical resistance of the tracks to sliding forward
B_l	0.7 N · m · s / rad	Mechanical resistance of the tracks to turning
S_l	0.3 N · m	Lateral friction of the tracks

2.2.1 Equations of Motion

The model of the tank's motion is adapted from Anh Tuan Le's PhD dissertation [74]. The model's parameters are listed in Table 2.1, and the coordinate system and forces acting on the tank are illustrated in Figure 2.2. The model assumes that the tank is driven on a hard, flat surface and that the tracks do not slip. The position of the tank is given by its x and y coordinates. The heading θ of the tank is measured with respect to the x axis of the coordinate system and the tank moves in this direction with a speed v.

The left track pushes the tank forward with a force F_l; the right track, with a force F_r; and B_r is the mechanical resistance of the tracks to rolling. The tank uses skid steering; to turn, the motors must collectively create enough torque to cause the tracks to slide sideways. This requires overcoming the sticking force S_l. When sufficient torque is created, the vehicle begins to turn. As it turns, some of the propulsive force is expended to drag the tracks laterally; this is modeled by an additional resistance B_l to its turning motion and B_s to its rolling motion.

The tank's motion is described by two sets of equations, one for when the tank is turning and one for when it is not. The switch from turning to not turning (and vice

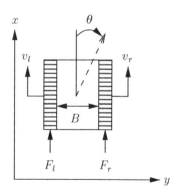

FIGURE 2.2 Coordinate system, variables, and parameters used in the tank's equations of motion.

versa) has two discrete effects: (1) the angular velocity ω changes instantaneously to and remains at zero when the tracks stick and the turn ends, and (2) the rolling resistance of the tank changes instantaneously when the tank starts and ends a turn. The Boolean variable *turning* is used to change the set of equations. The equations that model the motion of the tank are

$$turning = \begin{cases} true & \text{if } \dfrac{B}{2}|F_l - F_r| \geq S_l \\ false & \text{otherwise} \end{cases} \tag{2.1}$$

$$\dot{v} = \begin{cases} \dfrac{1}{m_t}\Big(F_l + F_r - (B_r + B_s)v\Big) & \text{if } turning = true \\ \dfrac{1}{m_t}\Big(F_l + F_r - B_r v\Big) & \text{if } turning = false \end{cases} \tag{2.2}$$

$$\dot{\omega} = \begin{cases} \dfrac{1}{J_t}\Big(\dfrac{B}{2}(F_l - F_r) - B_l\omega\Big) & \text{if } turning = true \\ 0 & \text{if } turning = false \end{cases} \tag{2.3}$$

$$\dot{\theta} = \omega \tag{2.4}$$

$$\dot{x} = v\sin(\theta) \tag{2.5}$$

$$\dot{y} = v\cos(\theta) \tag{2.6}$$

$$\text{If } turning = false \text{ then } \omega = 0 \tag{2.7}$$

When *turning* changes from false to true, every state variable evolves from its value immediately prior to starting the turn, but using the equations designated for *turning* = true. When *turning* changes from true to false, every state variable except ω evolves from its value immediately prior to ending the turn, but using the equations designated for *turning* = false; ω changes instantaneously to zero and remains zero until the tank begins to turn again.

These differential equations describe how the tank moves in response to the propulsive force of the tracks. The track forces F_l and F_r are inputs to this model, and we can take any function of the state variables—v, ω, θ, x, and y—as output. For reasons that will soon become clear, we will use the speed with respect to the ground of the left and right treads; Figure 2.2 illustrates the desired quantities. The speed v_l of the left tread and speed v_r of the right tread are determined from the tank's linear speed v and rotational speed ω by

$$v_l = v + B\omega/2 \tag{2.8}$$

$$v_r = v - B\omega/2 \tag{2.9}$$

The dependence of the input on the output is denoted by the function

$$\begin{bmatrix} v_l(t) \\ v_r(t) \end{bmatrix} = M \left(\begin{bmatrix} F_l(t) & F_r(t) \end{bmatrix}^T \right) \tag{2.10}$$

This function accepts the left and right tread forces as input and produces the left and right tread speeds as output.

How were the values in Table 2.1 obtained? Two of them were measure directly: the mass of the tank with a postal scale and the width of the tank with a ruler. The angular mass of the tank is an educated guess. Given the width w and length l of the tank's hull, which were measured with a ruler, and the mass, obtained with a postal scale, the angular mass is computed by assuming the tank is a uniformly dense box. With these data and assumptions, we have

$$J_t = \frac{m_t}{12}(w^2 + l^2)$$

This is not precise, but it is the best that can be obtained with a ruler and scale.

The resistance parameters are even more speculative. The turning torque S_l was computed from the weight W of the tank and length l_t of the track, which were both measured directly, a coefficient of static friction μ_s for rubber from Serway's *Physics for Scientists and Engineers* [133], and the approximation

$$S_l = \frac{W l_t \mu_s}{3}$$

from Le's dissertation [74]. The resistances B_r and B_s to forward motion and resistance B_l to turning were selected to give the model reasonable linear and rotational speeds.

This mix of measurements, rough approximations, and educated guesses is not uncommon. It is easier to build a detailed model than to obtain data for it. The details, however, are not superfluous. The purpose of this model is to explore how the tank's response to the driver changes with the frequency of the power signal sent to the motors. For this purpose it is necessary to include those properties of the tank that determine its response to the intermittent voltage signal: specifically, inertia and friction.

2.2.2 Motors, Gearbox, and Tracks

The motors, gearbox, and tracks are an electromechanical system for which the method of bond graphs is used to construct a dynamic model (Karnopp et al. [61] give an excellent and comprehensive introduction to this method). The bond graph model is coupled to the equations of motion by using Equation 2.10 as a bond graph element. This element has two ports, one of which has the effort variable F_l and flow variable v_l, and the other, the effort variable F_r and flow variable v_r. The causality of this element is determined by the functional form of Equation 2.10: it is supplied with the effort variables and produces the flow variables. This was the reason for selecting the track speeds as output.

The model of the motors, gearbox, and tracks accounts for the inductance and internal resistance of the electric motors, the angular mass and friction of the gears, and the compliance of the rubber tracks. The electric motors are Mabuchi FA-130 Motors, the same type of DC motor that is ubiquitous in small toys. One motor drives each track. The motors are plugged into a Tamiya twin-motor gearbox. This gearbox has two sets of identical, independent gears that turn the sprocket wheels. The sprocket wheels and tracks are from a Tamiya track-and-wheel set; the tracks stretch when the tank accelerates (in hard turns this causes the tracks to come off the wheels!), and so their compliance is included in the model.

To drive the motors, the computer switches a set of transistors in an Allegro A3953 full-bridge pulsewidth-modulated (PWM) motor driver. When the switches are closed, the tank's batteries are connected to the motors. When the switches are open, the batteries are disconnected from the motors. The transistors can switch on and off at a rate three orders of magnitude greater than the rate at which the computer can operate them, and power lost in the circuit is negligible in comparison to inefficiencies elsewhere in the system. The batteries and motor driver are, therefore, modeled as an ideal, time varying voltage source.

A sketch of the connected motors, gearbox, and tracks and its bond graph are shown in Figure 2.3. Table 2.2 lists the parameters used in this model. The differential

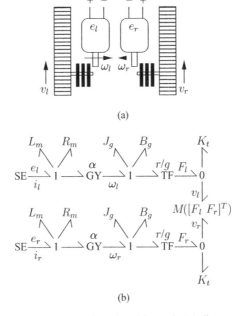

(a)

(b)

FIGURE 2.3   Motors, gears, and tracks of the tank: (a) diagram; (b) bond graph.

TABLE 2.2   Parameters of the Motors, Gearbox, and Tracks

Parameter	Value	Description
L_m	10^{-3} H	Inductance of the motor
R_m	3.1 Ω	Resistance of the motor
J_g	1.2×10^{-6} kg $\cdot$ m^2	Angular mass of the gears
B_g	6.7×10^{-7} N $\cdot$ m $\cdot$ s / rad	Mechanical resistance of the gears to rotation
g	204	Gear ratio of the gearbox
α	10^{-3} N $\cdot$ m / A	Current–torque ratio of the electric motor
r	0.015 m	Radius of the sprocket wheel
K_t	10^{-3} m / N	Compliance of the track

equations are read directly from the bond graph:

$$\dot{i}_l = \frac{1}{L_m}(e_l - i_l R_m - \alpha \omega_l) \qquad (2.11)$$

$$\dot{\omega}_l = \frac{1}{J_g}\left(\alpha i_l - \omega_l B_g - \frac{r}{g}F_l \right) \qquad (2.12)$$

$$\dot{F}_l = \frac{1}{K_t}\left(\frac{r}{g}\omega_l - v_l \right) \qquad (2.13)$$

$$\dot{i}_r = \frac{1}{L_m}(e_r - i_r R_m - \alpha \omega_r) \qquad (2.14)$$

$$\dot{\omega}_r = \frac{1}{J_g}\left(\alpha i_r - \omega_r B_g - \frac{r}{g}F_r \right) \qquad (2.15)$$

$$\dot{F}_r = \frac{1}{K_t}\left(\frac{r}{g}\omega_r - v_r \right) \qquad (2.16)$$

where e_l and e_r are the motor voltages and v_l and v_r are the track speeds given by Equations 2.8 and 2.9.

Values for the parameters in Table 2.2 were obtained from manufacturers' data, from measurements, and by educated guesses. The gear ratio g and current–torque ratio α are provided by the manufacturers. The gear ratio is accurate and precise (especially with respect to the values of other parameters in the model). The current–torque ratio is an average of the two cases supplied by Mabuchi, the motor's manufacturer. The first case is the motor operating at peak efficiency, and the second case is the motor stalling. The difference between these two cases is small, suggesting that α does not vary substantially as the load on the motor changes. The estimate of α is, therefore, probably very reasonable.

The radius r of the sprocket wheel and the resistance R_m and inductance L_m of the motor were measured directly. A ruler was used to measure the radius of the sprocket wheel. To determine R_m and L_m required more effort. The current i through the unloaded motor is related to the voltage e across the motor by the differential equation

$$\dot{i} = \frac{1}{L_m}(e - i R_m) \tag{2.17}$$

The parameters L_m and R_m were estimated by connecting a 1.5-V C battery to the motor and measuring, with an oscilloscope, the risetime and steady state of the current through the motor. Let i_f be the steady-state current, t_r the risetime, and $0.9i_f$ the current at time t_r (i.e., the risetime is the amount of time to go from zero current to 90% of the steady-state current). At steady state $\dot{i} = 0$ and the resistance of the motor is given by

$$R_m = \frac{e}{i_f}$$

The transient current is needed to find L_m. The transient current is given by the solution to Equation 2.17:

$$i(t) = \frac{e}{R_m}\left(1 - \exp\left(-\frac{R_m}{L_m}t\right)\right) \tag{2.18}$$

Substituting $0.9i_f$ for $i(t)$ and t_r for t in Equation 2.18 and solving for L_m gives

$$\frac{1}{L_m} = -\frac{1}{R_m t_f}\ln\left(1 - 0.9\frac{R_m}{e}i_f\right) = -\frac{i_f}{e t_f}\ln(0.1) \approx 2.3\frac{i_f}{e t_f}$$

or, equivalently

$$L_m \approx 0.652\frac{t_f}{i_f}$$

A similar experiment was used to obtain B_g. In this experiment, the motor was connected to the gearbox. As before, an oscilloscope was used to measure the risetime and steady-state value of the current through the motor. The rotational velocity $\tilde{\omega}$ of the motor is given by

$$\dot{\tilde{\omega}} = \frac{1}{J_g}(\alpha i - \tilde{\omega} B_g)$$

The manufacturer gives the speed of the motor when operating at peak efficiency as $\tilde{\omega} = 731.6$ radians per second (rad/s). At steady state $\dot{\tilde{\omega}} = 0$. The steady state current

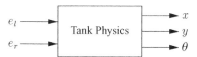

FIGURE 2.4   Input and output of the model of the tank's physics.

i_f is measured with the oscilloscope. With i_f and the motor speed, the mechanical resistance of the gearbox is given by

$$B_g \approx \frac{\alpha i_f}{\tilde{\omega}} = 1.37 \times 10^{-6} \, i_f$$

The angular mass J_g of the gearbox was estimated from its mass m_{gb}, radius of the gears r_{gb}, and the assumption that the mass is uniformly distributed in a cylinder. With this set of measurements and assumptions, the angular mass is

$$J_g = m_{gb} r_{gb}^2$$

The compliance of the tracks is an order-of-magnitude approximation. The tracks can be stretched by only a few millimeters before they slip off the wheels. The maximum propulsive force of the track is about a newton. The order of magnitude of the track compliance is, therefore, estimated to be 10^{-3} meters/10^0 newtons, or about 10^{-3} m/N.

2.2.3   Complete Model of the Tank's Continuous Dynamics

Equations 2.1–2.9 and 2.11–2.16 collectively describe the physical behavior of the tank. The equations of motion and the equations for the motors, gearbox, and tracks were developed separately, but algorithms for solving them work best when coupled equations are lumped together. Consequently, these are put into a single functional model called "tank physics," which is illustrated in Figure 2.4. The inputs to the tank are the voltages across its left and right motors; these come from the computer. The output of the tank is its position and heading; these are observed by the tank's operator. The complete state space model of the tank's physical dynamics is

$$turning = \begin{cases} true & \text{if } \frac{B}{2}|F_l - F_r| \geq S_l \\ false & \text{otherwise} \end{cases} \tag{2.19}$$

$$\dot{v} = \begin{cases} \dfrac{1}{m_t}\left(F_l + F_r - (B_r + B_s)v \right) & \text{if } turning = \text{true} \\[2mm] \dfrac{1}{m_t}\left(F_l + F_r - B_r v \right) & \text{if } turning = \text{false} \end{cases} \tag{2.20}$$

$$\dot{\omega} = \begin{cases} \dfrac{1}{J_t}\left(\dfrac{B}{2}(F_l - F_r) - B_l\omega\right) & \text{if } turning = \text{true} \\ 0 & \text{if } turning = \text{false} \end{cases} \tag{2.21}$$

$$\dot{\theta} = \omega \tag{2.22}$$

$$\dot{x} = v\sin(\theta) \tag{2.23}$$

$$\dot{y} = v\cos(\theta) \tag{2.24}$$

If $turning = \text{false}$ then $\omega = 0$ \hfill (2.25)

$$\dot{i_l} = \frac{1}{L_m}(e_l - i_l R_m - \alpha\omega_l) \tag{2.26}$$

$$\dot{\omega}_l = \frac{1}{J_g}\left(\alpha i_l - \omega_l B_g - \frac{r}{g}F_l\right) \tag{2.27}$$

$$\dot{F}_l = \frac{1}{K_t}\left(\frac{r}{g}\omega_l - \left(v + \frac{B\omega}{2}\right)\right) \tag{2.28}$$

$$\dot{i_r} = \frac{1}{L_m}(e_r - i_r R_m - \alpha\omega_r) \tag{2.29}$$

$$\dot{\omega}_r = \frac{1}{J_g}\left(\alpha i_r - \omega_r B_g - \frac{r}{g}F_r\right) \tag{2.30}$$

$$\dot{F}_r = \frac{1}{K_t}\left(\frac{r}{g}\omega_r - \left(v - \frac{B\omega}{2}\right)\right) \tag{2.31}$$

This model has 11 state variables—v, ω, θ, x, y, i_l, ω_l, F_l, i_r, ω_r, and F_r; two input variables—e_l and e_r; and three output variables—x, y, and θ.

2.2.4 The Computer

The computer, a TINI microcontroller from Maxim, receives commands from the operator through a wireless network and transforms them into voltage signals for the motors. The computer extracts raw bits from the Ethernet that connects the computer and the radio, puts the bits through the Ethernet and User Datagram Protocol (UDP) stacks to obtain a packet, obtains the control information from that packet, and stores that information in a register where the interrupt handler that generates voltage signals can find it. The interrupt handler runs periodically, and it has a higher priority than the thread that processes commands from the operator. Therefore, time spent in the interrupt handler is not available to process commands from the operator.

The frequency of the voltage signal is determined by the frequency of the interrupt handler. Frequent interrupts create a high-frequency voltage signal; infrequent interrupts, a low-frequency signal. Figure 2.5 illustrates how the interrupt handler works. It is executed every N machine cycles and at each invocation adds 32 to a counter stored in an 8-bit register. The counter is compared to an ON time that is set,

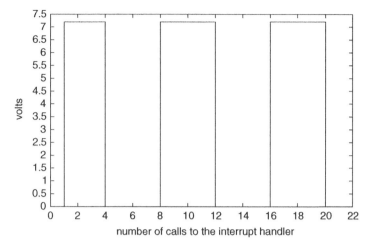

FIGURE 2.5 Generating a voltage signal with the interrupt handler.

albeit indirectly, by the operator. If the counter is greater than or equal to the ON time, then the motor is turned off. If the counter is less than the ON time, then the motor is turned on. If, for example, the tank is operating at full power, then the ON time for both motors is 255 and the motors are always on; if the motors are turned off, then the ON time is zero.

In Figure 2.5, the counter is initially zero and the motors are turned off. The ON time is 128. The first call to the interrupt handler adds 32 to the counter, compares $32 < 128$, and turns the motor on by connecting it to the tank's 7.2-V battery pack. At call 4, the counter is assigned a value of 128, which is equal to the ON time, and the motor is shut off. At call 8, the counter rolls over and the motor is turned on again.

The code in the interrupt handler is short; it has 41 assembly instructions that require 81 machine cycles to execute. According to the computer's manufacturer, there are 18.75×10^6 machine cycles per second, which is one cycle every 0.0533×10^{-6}s (0.0533 μs). The interrupt handler, therefore, requires 0.432×10^{-6} s (0.432 μs) to execute. The frequency of the voltage signal is determined by how quickly the interrupt handler rolls the counter over. On average, eight calls to the interrupt handler complete one period of the voltage signal. The length of this period is $8 \times (0.432 \times 10^{-6} + 0.0533 \times 10^{-6} \times N)$. We can choose N and thereby select the period of the voltage signal; the frequency f_e due to this selection is

$$f_e \approx \frac{10^6}{3.46 + 0.426N} \tag{2.32}$$

The discrete-event model of the interrupt handler has two types of events: *Start interrupt* and *End interrupt*. The *Start interrupt* event sets the interrupt indicator to true and schedules an *End interrupt* to occur 0.432×10^{-6} s later. The *End interrupt* event increments the counter, sets the motor switches, sets the interrupt indicator to

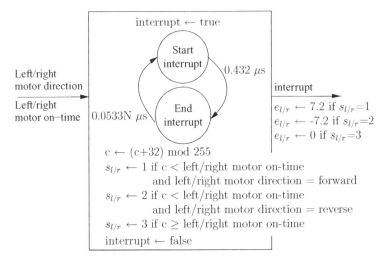

FIGURE 2.6   Event graph for the interrupt handler.

false, and schedules a *Start interrupt* event to occur $0.0533 \times 10^{-6} N$ s later. There are two software switches, one for each motor, and each switch has three positions. If the software switch is in the first position, then the motor is connected to the tank's 7.2-V battery pack. If the switch is in the second position, then the motor is connected to the batteries but the positive and negative terminals are reversed and the motor runs backward. In the third position, the motor is disconnected from the batteries. At any given time, a new ON time and direction for either motor can be given to the interrupt handler, and it acts on the new settings when the next *End interrupt* event occurs.

An event graph for the interrupt handler is shown in Figure 2.6 (event graphs were introduced by Schruben [131]; Fishwick [42] describes their use in functional models). The model has nine state variables. Four of these are apparent in the diagram: the 8-bit counter c, the *interrupt* indicator, and the switches s_l and s_r for the left and right motors. Events that change the ON time and direction of a motor are inputs to the model; these input variables are stored as the *left motor ON time*, *left motor direction*, *right motor ON time*, and *right motor direction*, bringing the count of state variables to eight. Implicit in the edges that connect the events is the time until the next event occurs, which is the ninth and final state variable for this system. The outputs from this model are the interrupt indicator and the left and right motor voltages. The output variables change immediately after the corresponding state variables. In the case that an event is scheduled at the same time that an input variable is changed, the event is executed first and then the corresponding variables are modified.

When the computer is not busy with its interrupt handler, it is processing commands from the operator. Every command arrives as a UDP packet with 10 bytes: two floating-point numbers that specify the direction and duty ratio of the left and right motors, and 2 bytes of information that are not relevant to our model. The computer can receive data at a rate of about 40 kilobytes per second (kB). This estimate, which comes from the jGuru forum [120], agrees reasonably well with, but is slightly lower than, the maximum data rate given by the manufacturer. The computer talks to the 802.11b radio through an Ethernet (the radio is controlled by a separate microprocessor) that has a minimum packet size of 64 bytes, much larger than the 10-byte payload. Consequently, we can optimistically estimate that processing a packet takes 0.0016 s (1.6 ms, or 1600 μs). We will ignore packet losses and assume that the computer (or, at least, the radio) can store any number of unprocessed packets. This is modeled with a server that has a fixed service time and an infinite queue. When the interrupt handler is executing, the server is forced to pause. The server produces ON times and directions for the motors when it finishes processing a packet.

Figure 2.7 is a DEVS graph (described by Zeigler et. al. [159] and, more recently, by Schulz et. al. [132]; these are sometimes called *phase graphs* [42]) for this model. It has three state variables: the packet queue q; the time σ remaining to process the packet at the front of the queue; and the model's phase, which is *interrupted* or *operating*. It responds to two types of input: the interrupt indicator from the interrupt handler and packets from the network. The interrupt indicator moves the system into its *interrupted* phase where it remains until a second interrupt indicator is received, and this moves the system back to its *operating* phase. When the computer finishes processing a packet, it sets the ON time and direction for the left and right motors and begins to process the next packet or, if there are no packets left, becomes idle. Each edge in the phase graph is annotated with the state variables that change when the phase transition occurs. Each phase contains its duration and the output value that is generated when the phase is left because its duration has expired.

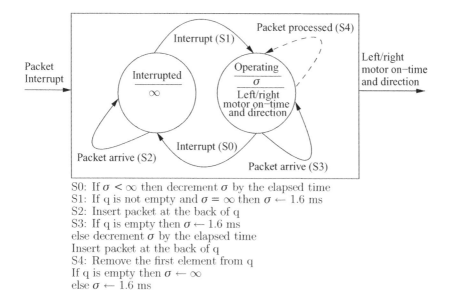

S0: If $\sigma < \infty$ then decrement σ by the elapsed time
S1: If q is not empty and $\sigma = \infty$ then $\sigma \leftarrow 1.6$ ms
S2: Insert packet at the back of q
S3: If q is empty then $\sigma \leftarrow 1.6$ ms
else decrement σ by the elapsed time
Insert packet at the back of q
S4: Remove the first element from q
If q is empty then $\sigma \leftarrow \infty$
else $\sigma \leftarrow 1.6$ ms

FIGURE 2.7 Phase graph showing how the computer processes a packet.

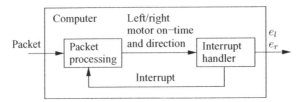

FIGURE 2.8 Block diagram of the tank's computer.

The models of the interrupt handler and thread that processes packets are connected to create a model of the computer. The interrupt handler receives the motor ON times from the thread that processes packets; the thread receives interrupt indicators from the interrupt handler and packets from the network. The output from the computer sets the voltage at the left and right motors. Figure 2.8 shows a block diagram of the computer with its inputs, outputs, and internal components.

The event graph and phase diagram are informative but not definitive. They do not specify when, precisely, output is produced or how to treat simultaneous events. These issues are deferred to Chapter 4, where state space models of discrete-event systems are formally introduced.

2.2.5 Complete Model of the Tank

The complete model of the tank comprises the computer and the tank's physics. The output of the computer is connected to the input of the tank's physics. The position and orientation of the tank are displayed for the driver. The driver closes the loop by sending packets with control information to the computer. This arrangement is shown in Figure 2.9. The tank's operator is not a model; the operator controls the simulated tank with the same software and hardware that are used to control the real tank.

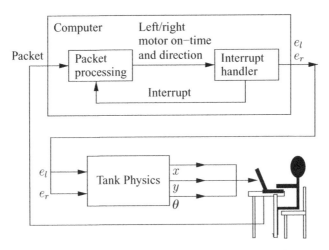

FIGURE 2.9 Block diagram of the simulated tank and real operator.

2.3   DESIGN OF THE TANK SIMULATOR

The simulator has four parts: the simulation engine, the model of the tank, the driver's interface, and the network interface. Figure 2.10 shows the classes that implement these parts and their relationships. The simulation engine and tank, which are our main concern, are implemented by the *Simulator* class and *SimEventListener* interface and the *Tank* class, respectively. The user interface is implemented by the *Display* class and *DisplayEventListener* interface, which take input from the user and display the motion of the tank. The *UDPSocket* class implements the network interface by which the simulator receives commands from the driver.

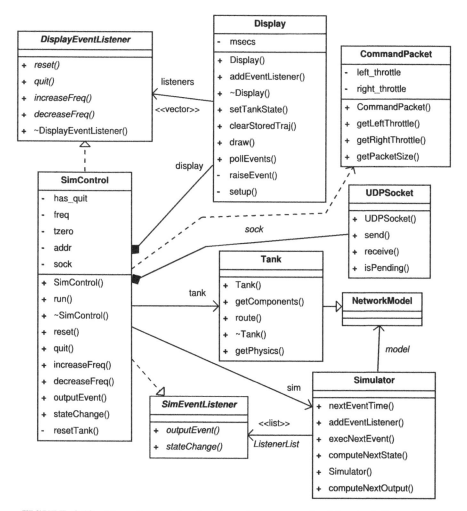

FIGURE 2.10   Class diagram showing the major components of the simulation software.

The *SimControl* class implements the main loop of the application in its *run* method. This method advances the simulation clock in step with the real clock, updates the *Display*, and polls the *Simulator*, *Display*, and *UDPSocket* for new events. The *SimControl* class implements the *SimEventListener* interface by which it is notified when components of the model change state and produce output. These callbacks are received when the *SimControl* object calls the *Simulator*'s *computeNextState* method. The *SimControl* also implements the *DisplayEventListener* class by which it is notified when the user does something to the display: for instance, pressing the quit key "q" or pressing the simulation reset key "r". These callbacks are received when the *SimControl* calls the *Display*'s *pollEvents* method. The *SimControl* object extracts *CommandPackets* from the network by polling the *UDPSocket*'s *pendingInput* method at each iteration of the main loop.

The *Simulator* has six methods. The constructor accepts a model—it can be a multilevel, multicomponent model or a single atomic model—that the simulator will operate on. The method *nextEventTime* returns the time of the simulator's next event: the next time at which some component will produce output or change state in the absence of an intervening input. The method *computeNextOutput* provides the model's outputs at the time of its next event without actually advancing the model's state. The method *computeNextState* advances the simulation clock and injects into the model any input supplied by the caller. Objects that implement the *SimEventListener* interface and register themselves by calling the *addEventListener* method are notified by the *Simulator* when a component of the model produces an output or changes its state. These notifications occur when *computeNextState* or *computeNextOutput* is called.

Missing from Figure 2.10 are the details of how the *Tank* is implemented; its major components are shown in Figure 2.11. The relationship between the *Tank* and *Simulator* is important. The *Simulator* is designed to operate on a connected collection

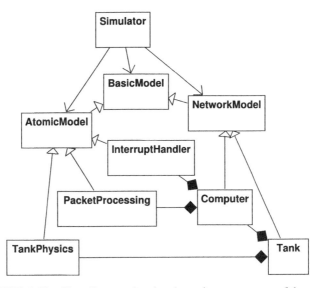

FIGURE 2.11 Class diagram showing the major components of the model.

of state space models; the *Tank* is a specific instance of such a model. The parts of the tank are derived, ultimately, from two fundamental classes: the *AtomicModel* class and the *NetworkModel* class. The *Tank* and *Computer* classes are derived from *NetworkModel* and they implement the block diagrams shown in Figures 2.8 and 2.9. The *TankPhysics* class, derived from *AtomicModel*, implements Equations 2.19–2.31. The *PacketProcessing* and *InterruptHandler* classes, also derived from *AtomicModel*, implement the models shown in Figures 2.6 and 2.7.

This design separates the three aspects of our simulation program. The *SimControl* class coordinates the primary activities of the software: rendering the display, receiving commands from the network, and running the simulation. It uses the *Simulator*'s six methods to control the simulation clock, inject input into the model, and obtain information about the model's state and output.

The *Simulator* and its myriad supporting classes (which are not shown in the diagrams) implement algorithms for event scheduling and routing, numerical integration, and other essential tasks. These algorithms operate on the abstract *AtomicModel* and *NetworkModel* classes without requiring detailed knowledge of the underlying dynamics.

Models are implemented by deriving concrete classes from *AtomicModel* and *NetworkModel*. Models derived from the *AtomicModel* class implement state space representations of the continuous and discrete-event components. Models derived from the *NetworkModel* class describe how collections of state space and network models are connected to form the complete system.

2.4   EXPERIMENTS

Before experimenting with the simulated tank, we must establish the range of frequencies that are physically feasible. An upper limit can be derived without simulation. Suppose that the computer does nothing except execute the interrupt handler. With zero instructions between invocations of the interrupt handler, Equation 2.32 gives a maximum frequency of 289 kHz for the voltage signal. At this frequency, the computer has no time to process commands from the driver and, consequently, the tank cannot be controlled.

To determine a lower limit we simulate the tank running at half-throttle and measure the power dissipated in the motors. After examining the power lost at several frequencies, we can pick the lowest acceptable frequency as the one for which higher frequencies do not significantly improve efficiency. The software for this simulation is much simpler than for the interactive simulation, but it uses all of the classes shown in Figure 2.11 and the *SimEventListener* and *Simulator* classes shown in Figure 2.10. The classes that implement the model of the tank do not change: Figure 2.11 is precisely applicable. The remainder of the program, all of the new code that must be implemented to conduct this experiment, has fewer than 100 lines.

The main function creates a *Tank*; a *Simulator* for the *Tank*; and a *TankEventListener*, which computes the power lost in the motors. The *TankEventListener* is derived from the *SimEventListener* class. After registering the *TankEventListener* with the *Simulator*, the program injects a *SimPacket* into the tank at time zero. This packet contains the duty ratio for the left and right motors. Now the simulation is run for 3 s, long enough for the tank to reach is maximum speed of approximately 0.2 m/s and run at that speed for a little over 2 s. The power P lost in the motors is

$$P = \frac{1}{3} \int_0^3 i_l(t)^2 R_m + i_r(t)^2 R_m \, dt$$

$$\approx \frac{1}{t_M} \sum_{k=0}^{M-1} (t_{k+1} - t_k)(i_{l,k}^2 R_m + i_{r,k}^2 R_m) \tag{2.33}$$

where the t_k are the times at which the *stateChange* method of the *TankEventListener* is called and $i_{l,k}$ and $i_{r,k}$ are the currents at time t_k. Note that $t_0 = 0$ and t_M may be slightly less than 3, depending on how the simulator selects timesteps for its integration algorithm (it could be made to update the state of the tank at $t = 3$, but was not in this instance).

The *stateChange* method of the *TankEventListener* is called every time the *Simulator* computes a new state for an atomic component of the *Tank*. When this occurs, the *TankEventListener* calculates one step of the summation in Equation 2.33. The *getPowerLost* method computes the lost power by dividing the lost energy by the elapsed time. The C++ code that implements the *TankEventListener* is shown below.

―――――――――――――――― ***TankEventListener*** ――――――――――――――――

```
1   #ifndef TankEventListener_h
2   #define TankEventListener_h
3   #include "Tank.h"
4   #include "SimEvents.h"
5   #include "SimEventListener.h"
6   #include <fstream>
7
8   class TankEventListener: public SimEventListener
9   {
10      public:
11          TankEventListener(const Tank* tank):
12              SimEventListener(),
13              tank(tank),fout("current.dat"),
14              E(0.0), // Accumulated energy starts at zero
15              tl(0.0), // First sample is at time zero
16              il(tank->getPhysics()->leftMotorCurrent()), // i_l(0)
17              ir(tank->getPhysics()->rightMotorCurrent()) // i_r(0)
18          {
19              fout << tl << " " << il << " " << ir << std::endl;
20          }
21          // Listener does nothing with output events
22          void outputEvent(ModelInput, double){}
23          // This method is invoked when an atomic component changes state
```

```
24      void stateChange(AtomicModel* model, double t)
25      {
26          // If this is the model of the tank's physics
27          if (model == tank->getPhysics()) {
28              // Get the current and motor resistance
29              double Rm = tank->getPhysics()->getMotorOhms();
30              // Update the enery dissipated in the motors
31              E += (t-tl)*(il*il*Rm + ir*ir*Rm);
32              // Remember the last sample
33              il = tank->getPhysics()->leftMotorCurrent();
34              ir = tank->getPhysics()->rightMotorCurrent();
35              tl = t;
36              fout << tl << " " << il << " " << ir << std::endl;
37          }
38      }
39      // Get the power dissipated in the left and right motors
40      double getPowerLost() const { return E/tl; }
41  private:
42      const Tank* tank;
43      std::ofstream fout;
44      double E, tl, il, ir;
45  };
46
47  #endif
```

A shell script calls the main program repeatedly to conduct the simulation experiment. Each invocation of the simulation program computes the power dissipated in the motors at one frequency and pair of duty ratios. The first argument to the simulation program is the frequency of the voltage signal sent to the motors, the second argument is the duty ratio for the left motor, and the third argument is the duty ratio for the right motor. (The zeroth argument is the name of the executable itself.) The program prepares the experiment, runs it, prints the result to the console, cleans up, and exits. The C++ code for the main function is listed below.

_____ *Main Program for the Power Dissipation Experiment* _____

```
1   #include "Tank.h"
2   #include "SimEvents.h"
3   #include "TankEventListener.h"
4   using namespace std;
5
6   int main(int argc, char** argv)
7   {
8       // Get the parameters for the experiment from the command line
9       if (argc != 4) {
10          cout << "freq left_throttle right_throttle" << endl;
11          return 0;
12      }
```

```
13   // Get the frequency of the voltage signal from the first argument
14   double freq = atof(argv[1]);
15   // Create a command from the driver that contains the duty ratios from
16   // the second and third arguments.
17   SimPacket sim_command;
18   sim_command.left_power = atof(argv[2]);
19   sim_command.right_power = atof(argv[3]);
20   // Create the tank, simulator, and event listener. The arguments to the
21   // tank are its initial position (x = y = 0), heading (theta = 0), and
22   // the smallest interval of time that will separate any two reports of
23   // the tank's state (0.02 seconds).
24   Tank* tank = new Tank(freq,0.0,0.0,0.0,0.02);
25   Simulator* sim = new Simulator(tank);
26   TankEventListener* l = new TankEventListener(tank);
27   // Add an event listener to compute the power dissipated in the motors
28   sim->addEventListener(l);
29   // Inject the driver command into the simulation at time zero
30   ModelInputBag input;
31   SimEvent cmd(sim_command);
32   ModelInput event(tank,cmd);
33   input.insert(event);
34   sim->computeNextState(input,0.0);
35   // Run the simulation for 3 seconds
36   while (sim->nextEventTime() <= 3.0) sim->execNextEvent();
37   // Write the result to the console
38   cout << freq << " " << l->getPowerLost() << endl;
39   // Clean up and exit
40   delete sim; delete tank; delete l;
41   return 0;
42 }
```

Simulations are executed for a set of frequencies with the shell script

```
for ((i=50;i<=7000;i+=50)); do ./a.out \$i 0.5 0.5; done
```

where a.out is the name of the simulation program (this is the default name of the executable produced by the GNU C++ compiler). This script computes the power dissipated in the motors at frequencies in the range [50, 7000] at 50 Hz increments. The result is plotted in Figure 2.12. This graph suggests 3000 Hz as a reasonable lower limit for the frequency. The interactive experiments will start at 3000 Hz and proceed to higher frequencies until we discover the highest that permits effective control.[2]

---

[2]What happens to this lost power? It becomes heat and noise. The frequencies shown in Figure 2.12 are in the range of human hearing. Consequently, the motors emit a distinct high-pitched hum. This is accompanied by a grumbling and grinding from the gears and, if the motors are running near full power, a faint smell of ozone.

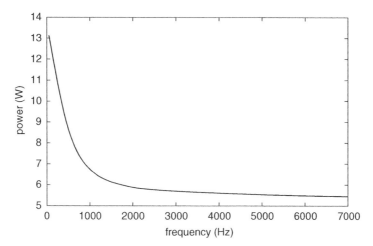

FIGURE 2.12 Total power dissipated in the motors as a function of the frequency of the voltage signal at the motor terminals.

The track shown in Figure 2.13 was used for the interactive experiments. The tank started in the center of the leftmost leg of the track, and was steered around the track to return to the starting position. If the tank left the track, that run was discarded. After several practice runs, the experimental runs were conducted at 2 kHz increments. At each frequency, the tank raced around the track until three circuits were completed. The author recorded the time to complete each circuit and the number of failed attempts at each frequency. The results are tabulated in Table 2.3.

The tradeoff between efficiency and control is immediately apparent on comparison of the data for lost power, time to complete a round of the track, and the number of failed runs. At low frequencies, the tank is very responsive and the experimental course can be safely navigated in about a minute. At higher frequencies, the driver

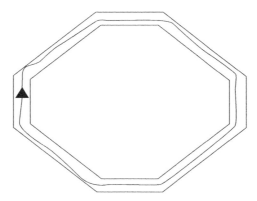

FIGURE 2.13 The test track and one path followed by the tank in a successful run.

TABLE 2.3   Data from the Interactive Experiment

Frequency (kHz)	Time (s)			Average	Failed
	T_1	T_2	T_3		
3	68.7	68.3	69.1	68.7	0
5	68.9	68.3	70.8	69.3	0
7	69.8	70.0	67.9	69.2	0
9	68.3	68.5	88.4	75.1	2
11	67.6	84.4	113.0	88.3	0
12	104.0	101.7	No data	103.2	2

must be more cautious and at 9 kHz and above the track is very difficult to negotiate. As the frequency is increased, the motors run more efficiently but the tank is more difficult to control.

From these data and the data in Figure 2.12, we can conclude that a frequency between 7 and 8 kHz is the best choice. In this range, the motors run efficiently and the computer processes commands from the driver in a timely manner. The real tank operates at about 7.4 kHz: 310 machine cycles separate invocations of the interrupt handler.

2.5 SUMMARY

This example has demonstrated the three main features of the simulation engine that is developed in the remainder of this book: modular, bottom–up construction of models, separation of the model and its simulator, and the inclusion of discrete-event and continuous components. Modular, bottom-up construction allows large simulators to be built and tested piecewise. Atomic models encapsulate basic behaviors, and if a large model is judiciously decomposed, then these smallest pieces can be built, tested, and maintained in isolation. As pieces are combined to create larger components, these, too, can be built, tested, and debugged independently of one another. This principle of encapsulation extends to the entire simulator, ultimately allowing the whole to be used as a self-contained component within a larger software system.

The separation of the model and its simulator serves a similar purpose. The algorithms contained within the simulation engine are designed for a specific class of systems. They can therefore be built, tested, and maintained without reference to any particular system. Test cases for the simulation engine will consist chiefly of simple models with behavior that can be deduced by hand calculations or with another simulator that is known to be correct. This is also an advantage for the modeler; the definition of the class of systems presumed by the simulator is a guarantee of how it will function. Improvements in the simulation engine are therefore transparent to the models, and this greatly simplifies the long-term maintenance of a simulation program.

Inclusion of discrete-event and continuous components is indispensable to modeling many engineered systems; the robotic tank is one example. This must be done accurately and with precision, but it is accuracy that presents the greatest challenge. To say that a simulation is accurate with respect to an idealized model is to say that the model's behavior can, in principle, be deduced without recourse to the simulator: there must be a correct outcome against which accuracy can be gauged. Consequently, separation of the model and the algorithms that compute its behavior is essential. These two concepts, therefore, are central to the study of modeling and simulation.

CHAPTER 3

DISCRETE-TIME SYSTEMS

The simulation engine is a collection of C++ classes that are used to build a simulator. Models are constructed by extending classes that encapsulate structure and dynamics. These are given to objects implementing the simulation algorithms that calculate the model's dynamic behavior. The classes that encapsulate the simulation algorithms have methods for monitoring and controlling the progress of the simulator.

Large models are built with two types of components. Atomic models describe things that are fundamental. They encapsulate the dynamic behavior of components that, as the name suggests, are not subjected to further decomposition. The tank's interrupt handler, packet-processing model, and the differential equations that describe the tank's motion are atomic models. Network models are composed of interacting parts: atomic models and other networks. They encapsulate structure: the components and linkages in a multicomponent system. The tank's computer and the tank itself are network models.

The simulation engine operates on the interfaces provided by these two types of components. An atomic model has methods for computing its output from its current state and for computing its next state from its current state and input. A network model has methods for retrieving its set of components, for transforming output from its components to inputs for its other components and outputs from itself, and for transforming its inputs into input for its components. Algorithms for event scheduling, numerical integration, and other necessary tasks are contained in the classes that implement the simulation engine.

Visualization, live interaction, interfaces to simulation networks, and other similar functionality is implemented by the software that uses the simulation engine. This

Building Software for Simulation: Theory and Algorithms, with Applications in C++, By James J. Nutaro
Copyright © 2011 John Wiley & Sons, Inc.

software, called in the parlance of software engineering a *client* of the simulation engine, interacts with it in three ways. The client controls the rate at which time in the simulation advances. Time can be advanced as rapidly as the simulation engine is able, coordinated with the passage of time in the real world, or in any other way that is needed. The client is notified when any component, atomic or network, produces an output and when any atomic component changes its state. These notifications can be used to drive a display in an interactive simulation, to collect statistics, or to create a file that logs information for later display or for debugging. The client can also inject input into a running simulation. This is required for interactive simulations and can be used to feed the simulator a scripted trajectory.

The simulation engine is simplest for discrete-time systems. Once the essential concepts and software artifacts are established, extending them to discrete-event and continuous systems is straightforward. The structure, if not the details, of the simulation engine persists in the general case; models continue to be derived from *Atomic* and *Network* classes, and the *Simulator* computes their dynamic behavior. The discrete-time, discrete-event, and continuous simulations differ mainly in the algorithms that are used to advance the simulation clock. A simulation engine for discrete-time systems is, therefore, a useful foundation.

3.1 ATOMIC MODELS

An *atomic model* is a dynamic system that changes in response to its environment and affects its environment as it changes. The variables that affect the system are its input, and these are described with a set X. The variables by which the system affects its environment are its output, and these are described with a set Y. The variables that constitute the system are its state, and these are described with a set S.

The dynamic behavior of the system is described by functions from time to the sets of input, output, and states. The set of times used by the system is called its *time base*; for discrete-time systems this is the set $\mathbb{N}$ of natural numbers. An *input trajectory* is a function from the set $\mathbb{N}$ of times to the set X of input; an output trajectory is a function from $\mathbb{N}$ to Y; and a state trajectory is a function from $\mathbb{N}$ to S.

3.1.1 Trajectories

The value of a trajectory z (it can be an input, output, or state trajectory) at a specific time t is written $z(t)$. A trajectory defined on an interval from t_0 to t_n is denoted generically by $z < t_0, t_n >$. When specific endpoints are desired, the $<$ and $>$ are replaced with [and] for inclusion or (and) for exclusion, specifically

$$t \in [t_0, t_n] \iff t_0 \leq t \leq t_n$$

$$t \in (t_0, t_n] \iff t_0 < t \leq t_n$$

$$t \in [t_0, t_n) \iff t_0 \leq t < t_n$$

$$t \in (t_0, t_n) \iff t_0 < t < t_n$$

A set of trajectories whose domain is the time base T and range is the set Z is denoted by $< T, Z >$. Each member $z \in< T, Z >$ is a function $T \rightarrow Z$. Two trajectories $z_a < t_1, t_2 >$ and $z_b < t_1, t_2 >$ are equal if, for all $t \in< t_1, t_2 >$, $z_a(t) = z_b(t)$: succinctly

$$z_a < t_1, t_2 >= z_b < t_1, t_2 > \iff (\forall t \in< t_1, t_2 >)(z_a(t) = z_b(t)) \tag{3.1}$$

and, if the domains are understood, we can simply write $z_a = z_b$. When describing the sets of input, output, and state trajectories for a discrete-time system, we use the notation $< \mathbb{N}, X >$, $< \mathbb{N}, Y >$, and $< \mathbb{N}, S >$, respectively.

Trajectories that begin and end at compatible times can be concatenated to create a new trajectory. Concatenating $z_a[t_0, t_n)$ and $z_b[t_n, t_m)$ creates $z_{ab}[t_0, t_m)$ defined by

$$z_{ab}(t) = \begin{cases} z_a(t) & \text{if } t \in [t_0, t_n) \\ z_b(t) & \text{if } t \in [t_n, t_m) \end{cases}$$

The symbol $\cdot$ denotes concatenation; in this particular example

$$z_{ab}[t_0, t_m) = z_a[t_0, t_n) \cdot z_b[t_n, t_m)$$

or, more briefly

$$z_{ab} = z_a \cdot z_b$$

if the domains are understood. Concatenation of trajectories is illustrated in Figure 3.1. This definition covers the specific case that is relevant to us. More generally, two trajectories $z_a < t_0, t_n >$ and $z_b < t_n, t_m >$ can be concatenated if there is not a conflict at the time t_n where the trajectories are joined. Trajectories can also be torn apart. For example, $z < t_0, t_3 >$ can be dissected into $z_a < t_0, t_2 >$ and $z_b < t_2, t_3 >$ such that $z = z_a \cdot z_b$.

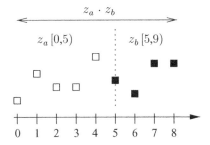

FIGURE 3.1   Concatenating two trajectories.

The time-shifting operator τ moves the starting and ending times of the trajectory by equal distances. For example, applying τ with the argument 1 to a trajectory $z_a[0, 2]$ gives $\tau(1, z_a[0, 2]) = z_b[1, 3]$. The new trajectory z_b is the same as z_a but is defined over a different interval; in this example, $z_a(0) = z_b(1)$, $z_a(1) = z_b(2)$, and $z_a(2) = z_b(3)$. The definition of τ is a generalization of this example:

$$\tau(h, z_a < t_1, t_2 >) = z_b < t_1 + h, t_2 + h > \quad \text{such that} \quad z_a(t) = z_b(t + h) \quad (3.2)$$

For brevity, the $\bullet$ operator combines $\cdot$ and τ to concatenate two trajectories $z_a[t_1, t_2)$ and $z_b[t_3, t_4)$ that do not necessarily begin and end at the same time. This operation is very common, and the separate notation for shifting and concatenation quickly becomes tiresome. The $\bullet$ operator is defined by

$$z_a[t_1, t_2) \bullet z_b[t_3, t_4) = z_a[t_1, t_2) \cdot \tau(t_2 - t_3, z_b[t_3, t_4)) \quad (3.3)$$

Shifting z_b by $t_2 - t_3$ translates its domains from $[t_3, t_4)$ to $[t_3 + (t_2 - t_3), t_4 + (t_2 - t_3)) = [t_2, t_4 + t_2 - t_3)$, giving the two trajectories a common time at which to join.

3.1.2 The State Transition and Output Function

The total state transition function Δ moves the system from a state s to a state s' in response to the input trajectory $x[t_0, t_n)$:

$$s' = \Delta(s, x[t_0, t_n)) \quad (3.4)$$

Not all such functions are total state transition functions; Δ must satisfy

$$\Delta(s, x_1 \bullet x_2) = \Delta(\Delta(s, x_1), x_2) \quad (3.5)$$

$$\Delta(s, x[t, t)) = s \quad (3.6)$$

Equation 3.6 requires that the system not change its state over an empty interval of time. Equation 3.5 is the semigroup property. It states that feeding the system a series of input trajectories $x_1, x_2, \ldots, x_n$ has the same effect as feeding it the single trajectory $x_1 \bullet x_2 \bullet \cdots \bullet x_n$. It is very common in practice to also require

$$\Delta(s, \tau(h, x)) = \Delta(s, x) \quad (3.7)$$

Equation 3.7 states that the response of the system to an input does not depend on the time at which it is applied. A system that satisfies this property is called *time-invariant*.

These three properties are mathematical expressions of everyday experience. Of central importance is the semigroup property. To illustrate it, imagine an experiment with a lock and key. If the lock is closed, in a state *locked*, and the key k is turned, then we can expect the lock to be opened, in a state *unlocked*. Mathematically, *unlocked* = $\Delta(locked, x[0, 1))$ where $x(0) = k$. If we can turn the key again, we expect the lock to close: *locked* = $\Delta(unlocked, x[0, 1))$. If the lock is closed and we turn the key twice, we expect it to be closed when we are done: *locked* = $\Delta(locked, x \bullet x)$. To summarize, we expect *locked* = $\Delta(locked, x \bullet x) = \Delta(\Delta(locked, x), x)$.

It is also significant that Δ is a function and not some weaker construct. Suppose that we make a copy, call it k_2, of the original key k_1. These keys are indistinguishable, so $k_1 = k_2$. If the lock is closed and we turn the second key, we expect the lock to open: exactly the same outcome that we obtained with the first key. Letting $x_2[0, 1)$, with $x_2(0) = k_2$, be the input trajectory that turns the key k_2 in the lock, we can write $x_1[0, 1) = x_2[0, 1)$ and, consequently, $\Delta(locked, x_1[0, 1)) = \Delta(locked, x_2[0, 1))$. Turning the key again so that $x_1 \bullet x_1 = x_2 \bullet x_2$, we expect $\Delta(locked, x_1 \bullet x_1) = \Delta(locked, x_2 \bullet x_2)$. The same lock; the same experiment; identical keys; identical outcomes.

Finally, consider Equation 3.7. If the lock is closed and we turn the key, then the lock will open, regardless of when this is done. Similarly, if the lock is open and we turn the key, then the lock will close, regardless of when we take this action. What, you might ask, if the lock has a timer? If it is an internal timer, then its value is determined by the time that has elapsed since we last reset it. The elapsed time is a state variable that can be set to zero by an input to the system.

If the lock uses an external timer, perhaps a signal received from a global positioning system or atomic clock, then the value of the external clock is an input to the lock. If, to test the lock, it is given a timing signal that is too fast, or too slow, or runs in the wrong direction, the response of the lock will depend only on the value of the timing signal and not when it is applied. This test will, if conducted once in the morning and once in the evening, produce the same result both times. We expect Equation 3.7 to hold.

The semigroup property is of fundamental importance because iterative algorithms for simulation are derived from it. The requirement that Δ be a function is likewise essential; it plays a critical role in the handling of simultaneous actions. Time invariance is not essential to the simulation algorithms, but to require it is not restrictive and very convenient. If time invariance is not required, then the simulation engine must be supplied with an initial time and provide a means for accessing the simulation clock. In this way, a model can incorporate time directly into its state transition function. It is just as reasonable, and ultimately much simpler, to incorporate any dependence on time into the state of the model by making it a state variable. From here on, it is assumed that our models are time-invariant.

Suppose that we apply an input trajectory that is defined at a single point. For example, the trajectory $x[t_0, t_1) = x(t_0)$. The system is begun in state s_0 and its state s_1 at time t_1 is

$$s_1 = \Delta(s_0, x[t_0, t_1)) = \delta(s_0, x(t_0)) \tag{3.8}$$

where the function δ is the single-step state transition function or just the state transition function. The function δ maps a single state and a single input into a new state; it has the form

$$\delta : S \times X \to S$$

We could write Equation 3.8 without referring to time at all. Given the current state s and an input x the next state s' is

$$s' = \delta(s, x) \tag{3.9}$$

This function gives us a convenient way to define the total state transition by describing how the system responds to any single input. The total state transition function Δ is defined by recursive application of δ to the values in an input trajectory $x[t_0, t_n)$. The trajectory is decomposed into segments $x_0, x_1, \ldots, x_{n-1}$ of unit length such that

$$x[t_0, t_n) = x_0[t_0, t_1) \cdot x_1[t_1, t_2) \cdots \cdot x_{n-1}[t_{n-1}, t_n)$$

Using the semi-group property, we write

$$
\begin{aligned}
s_n &= \Delta(\Delta(s_0, x_0), x_1 \cdot x_2 \cdots x_{n-1}) \\
&= \Delta(\delta(s_0, x_0(t_0)), x_1 \cdot x_2 \cdots x_{n-1})
\end{aligned}
$$

Repeated application of this formula lets us compute s_n entirely by application of δ. This calculation, carried out in detail, is

$$
\begin{aligned}
\Delta(s_0, x) &= \Delta(\Delta(s_0, x_0), x_1 \cdot x_2 \cdots \cdot x_{n-1}) \\
&= \Delta(\delta(s_0, x_0(t_0)), x_1 \cdot x_2 \cdots \cdot x_{n-1}) \\
&= \Delta(s_1, x_1 \cdot x_2 \cdots \cdot x_{n-1}) \\
&= \Delta(\Delta(s_1, x_1), x_2 \cdots \cdot x_{n-1}) \\
&= \Delta(\delta(s_1, x_1(t_1)), x_2 \cdots \cdot x_{n-1}) \\
&= \Delta(s_2, x_2 \cdots \cdot x_{n-1}) \\
&= \ldots \\
&= \Delta(\Delta(s_{n-2}, x_{n-2}), x_{n-1}) \\
&= \Delta(\delta(s_{n-2}, x_{n-2}(t_{n-2})), x_{n-1}) \\
&= \Delta(s_{n-1}, x_{n-1}) \\
&= \delta(s_{n-1}, x_{n-1}(t_{n-1})) \\
&= s_n
\end{aligned}
$$

```
1  s ← s₀
2  for tₖ ∈ [t₀, tₙ) do
3       print time tₖ and state s
4       s ← δ(s, x(tₖ))
5  end
```

Algorithm 3.1   Iterative procedure for computing the total state transition function of a discrete-time system.

This recursive procedure consumes the input trajectory one segment at a time. The state s_1, resulting from the input $x_0(t_0)$ applied to the state s_0, is computed first. The state s_2 is computed by $\delta(s_1, x_1(t_1))$. The state s_3 is computed next by $\delta(s_2, x_2(t_2))$, and this is repeated until we reach s_n. This definition of the total state transition function is tail-recursive, and so it can be easily rewritten as the iterative procedure in Algorithm 3.1.

The output function λ describes how the state of the system appears to an observer. It maps the current state s to an output y and has the form

$$\lambda : S \to Y$$

The output trajectory $y < t_0, t_n >$ produced by a state trajectory $s < t_0, t_n >$ is defined by

$$y(t_k) = \lambda(s(t_k)) \tag{3.10}$$

for every $t_k \in < t_0, t_n >$. To accommodate the output function in our simulation, only a small change to Algorithm 3.1 is needed; this gives us Algorithm 3.2.

Figure 3.2 illustrates the roles of the state transition function and output function in defining the dynamic behavior of a system. In summary, the state transition function defines the internal response of the system to input; the output function projects a view of the internal state for an outside observer.

```
1  s ← s₀
2  for tₖ ∈ [t₀, tₙ) do
3       print time tₖ, state s, and output λ(s)
4       s ← δ(s, x(tₖ))
5  end
```

Algorithm 3.2   Iterative algorithm for simulating an atomic, discrete-time system.

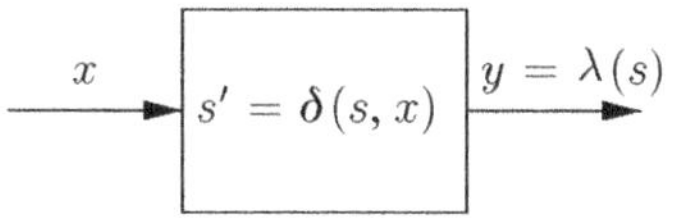

FIGURE 3.2 The dynamic parts of an atomic model.

3.1.3 Two Examples of Atomic, Discrete-Time Models

For our first example, consider a system with state s, input x, and output y that are real numbers, and state transition and output functions

$$\delta(s, x) = \frac{s}{2} + x \tag{3.11}$$

$$\lambda(s) = 10s \tag{3.12}$$

Two simulations of this system are shown in Table 3.1. The first row contains the initial state and first output. The input trajectories $x_1[0, 4)$ and $x_2[0, 4)$ are written in their respective columns. The state and output columns in each row after the first are filled in two steps: (1) the state s is computed by putting the state and input from the previous row into Equation 3.11, and (2) the output y is computed by putting the new state into Equation 3.12. This procedure is repeated until the input trajectory ends.

Note that the second experiment begins in the same state in which the first experiment ends. If we had continued the first experiment by feeding the second input trajectory into the system (i.e., by feeding it $x_1 \bullet x_2$), then the outcome would have been identical, with the final state and output the same as in the second experiment.

For our second example, consider a vending machine that sells coffee but accepts only nickels, dimes, and quarters. When \$1 has been inserted in the solt, the machine dispenses a cup of coffee. When the CHANGE button is pressed, the machine returns any unspent coins. To construct a model of this machine, we take time to be the number of inputs provided to it. Time is incremented when coins are inserted, the CHANGE button is pushed, or both. Several coins can be inserted and the CHANGE button pressed simultaneously. Time is also incremented when the customer waits for the machine to respond to a previous input.

TABLE 3.1   Two Simulations of the System Described by Equations 3.11 and 3.12

	Experiment 1				Experiment 2		
t	s	x_1	y	t	s	x_2	y
0	1	1	10	0	0.5	0	5
1	1.5	1	15	1	0.25	−0.125	2.5
2	1.75	0	17.5	2	0	1	0
3	0.875	0.0625	8.75	3	1	0	10
4	0.5	—	5	4	0.5	—	5

The model accepts any combination of inputs from the set

$$X = \{nickel, dime, quarter, cancel, wait\}$$

and produces combinations of output from the set

$$Y = \{nickel, dime, quarter, coffee, nothing\}$$

Inputs to the model are bags of values from X and outputs are bags of values from Y. A bag (sometimes called a *multiset*) is an unordered collection. For example, the bag $\{nickel, nickel, dime\}$ contains two nickels and a dime, a total value of 25 cents. The empty bag, like the empty set, is denoted by $\emptyset$. The union of two bags is the same as the union of two sets except that duplicates are permitted. For example, $\{nickel, nickel, dime\} \cup \{dime\} = \{nickel, nickel, dime, dime\}$. The empty bag is an identity for the union operator: for any bag X, $X \cup \emptyset = X$.

The order in which items are listed does not matter. For example, $\{nickel, dime, nickel\}$ is equal to $\{nickel, nickel, dime\}$. Consequently, the machine must produce an identical result if, when in any particular state s, it is provided with either of these values. It is necessary, for example, that

$$\delta(s, \{nickel, nickel, dime\}) = \delta(s, \{nickel, dime, nickel\})$$

The inventory of coins, the value of the coins inserted by the current customer, and the status of the CANCEL button constitute the state of the model. The variables n, d, and q are the number of nickels, dimes, and quarters in the inventory. The variable v is the total value of the coins put into the machine by the current customer. The variable *cancel* is true if the CANCEL button is depressed and false otherwise.

The state transition function for this machine is defined by Algorithm 3.3, which is written in the form of a method for an object whose member variables are the machine's state variables. The method's single argument is a bag x^b of inputs in X. The method *getCoins*, which is implemented by Algorithm 3.4, returns a bag of coins selected from the machine's inventory and with a total value equal to its argument. The state transition function begins by deducting, if possible, a dollar from the value of the unspent coins previously inserted by the customer. Any new coins are then added to the customer's total value and the inventory of the machine. The status of the CANCEL button is established last.

Algorithm 3.5 defines the model's output function, and it is in the same form. This method returns a bag y^b of elements in the output set Y. If there is at least \$1 in the machine then it produces a cup of coffee. If the CANCEL button has been pressed, then the machine returns the customer's change. If a cup of coffee was also sold, then only the unspent coins are returned.

Table 3.2 shows two experiments with this model. Once again, we see the semigroup property in action. That the state transition function is in fact a function can be verified by checking that a change in the order of the items in the input bags does not change the outcome of the simulation.

1 **method** $\delta(x^b)$
2   Sell a cup of coffee
3   **if** $v \geq 100$ **then** $v \leftarrow v - 100$
4   If cancel is pressed, clear it and return any change
5   **if** $cancel = true$ **then**
6       $cancel \leftarrow false$
7       $C \leftarrow getCoins(v)$
8       $n \leftarrow n -$ number of nickels in C
9       $d \leftarrow d -$ number of dimes in C
10      $q \leftarrow q -$ number of quarters in C
11      $v \leftarrow 0$
12   **end**
13   Add the coins inserted by the customer
14   $n_c \leftarrow$ number of nickels in $x^b, n \leftarrow n + n_c$
15   $d_c \leftarrow$ number of dimes in $x^b, d \leftarrow d + d_c$
16   $q_c \leftarrow$ number of quarters in $x^b, q \leftarrow q + q_c$
17   $v \leftarrow v + 5n_c + 10d_c + 25q_c$
18   Check the cancel button
19   $cancel \leftarrow$ cancel is in x^b
20 **end method**

Algorithm 3.3   State transition function for the coffee-vending machine.

1 **method** getCoins(*cents*) returns C
2   Initialize the bag of coins
3    $C \leftarrow \emptyset$
4   Copy the inventory of the machine
5    $q_c \leftarrow q, d_c \leftarrow d, n_c \leftarrow n$
6   Pick quarters first
7   **while** $q_c > 0$ *and cents* ≥ 25 **do**
8       $q_c \leftarrow q_c - 1, cents \leftarrow cents - 25$
9       $C \leftarrow C \cup \{quarter\}$
10   **end**
11   Pick dimes next
12   **while** $d_c > 0$ *and cents* ≥ 10 **do**
13      $d_c \leftarrow d_c - 1, cents \leftarrow cents - 10$
14      $C \leftarrow C \cup \{dime\}$
15   **end**
16   Pick nickels last
17   **while** $n_c > 0$ *and cents* ≥ 5 **do**
18      $n_c \leftarrow n_c - 1, cents \leftarrow cents - 5$
19      $C \leftarrow C \cup \{nickel\}$
20   **end**
21   return C
22 **end method**

Algorithm 3.4   Definition of the *getCoins* method.

```
1  method λ() returns y^b
2    Initialize the output bag
3    y^b ← ∅
4    How much money has the customer put into the machine?
5    cash ← v
6    Sell a cup of coffee
7    if cash ≥ 100 then
8        y^b ← {coffee}
9        cash ← cash − 100
10   end
11   Expel any change that remains after the sale
12   if cancel = true then  y^b ← y^b ∪ getCoins(cash)
13   If the bag is still empty, then the output is nothing
14   if y^b = ∅ then  y^b ← {nothing}
15   return y^b
16 end method
```

Algorithm 3.5   Output function for the coffee-vending machine.

3.1.4 Systems with Bags for Input and Output

Bags are so useful as the basic type of input and output to a model that we will include them in the definition of a system. The set of bags with elements in X is denoted X^b. Similarly, the set of bags with elements in Y is denoted Y^b. For example, if $Y = \{nickel, dime, quarter\}$, then $\{nickel\} \in Y^b$, $\{nickel, nickel\} \in Y^b$, and so is $\{dime, nickel\}$. The state transition function computes the next state of the model from its current state s and a bag x^b of inputs in X; it has the form

$$\delta : S \times X^b \rightarrow S \tag{3.13}$$

The output function maps the current state s to a bag y^b of outputs in Y; its form is

$$\lambda : S \rightarrow Y^b \tag{3.14}$$

These new forms do not change the definition of the total state transition function or the simulation algorithm for atomic models. Their significance is chiefly in how network models are defined and simulated, a topic that is addressed in Section 3.2.

3.1.5 A Simulator for Atomic Models

The simulation engine for atomic models has four classes: *Atomic*, *Simulator*, *EventListener*, and *Bag*. The *Bag* is a generic class for unordered collections of objects. It is used to supply input to and obtain output from the *Atomic* model. The *Bag* is a partial implementation of a multiple associative container as defined in the

TABLE 3.2 Two Simulations of the Vending Machine

		Experiment 1					Experiment 2	
t	s	x_1	y		t	s	x_2	y
0	$q = d = n = 10$ $cancel = false$ $v = 0$	{quarter, quarter, quarter, nickel, dime}	{nothing}		0	$q = 14, d = n = 10$ $cancel = false$ $v = 0$	{quarter, quarter, quarter, dime, dime}	{nothing}
1	$q = 14, d = n = 11$ $cancel = false$ $v = 115$	{wait}	{coffee}		1	$q = 17, d = 13, n = 10$ $cancel = false$ $v = 105$	{cancel}	{coffee}
2	$q = 14, d = n = 11$ $cancel = false$ $v = 15$	{cancel}	{nothing}		2	$q = 17, d = 13, n = 10$ $cancel = true$ $v = 5$	{wait}	{nickel}
3	$q = 14, d = n = 11$ $cancel = true$ $v = 15$	{wait}	{dime, nickel}		3	$q = 17, d = 13, n = 9$ $cancel = false$ $v = 0$		{nothing}
4	$q = 14, d = n = 10$ $cancel = false$ $v = 0$		{nothing}					

C++ Standard Template Library (STL) (see, e.g., Ref. 60). It has methods to insert and remove objects, iterate through the contained objects, and determine the number of objects in the container.

The *EventListener* can be registered with the *Simulator*, which will notify the listener when the model produces output and changes its state. The *EventListener* has two abstract methods: *stateChange* and *outputEvent*. The *stateChange* method is called by the *Simulator* when the model changes its state. The *outputEvent* method is called when the model produces an output.

The *Simulator* has four methods: *addEventListener*, *getTime*, *computeNextState*, and *computeOutput*. The *addEventListener* method puts an *EventListener* into the list of listeners that are notified of changes to the model. The *getTime* method returns the simulation time at which the state was last computed. The *computeNextState* method does four things: (1) computes the model's output function if this has not already been done, (2) computes the model's next state, (3) notifies listeners of these actions, and (4) tells the model to clean up objects created by its output function. The *computeOutput* method invokes the model's output function and informs registered *EventListeners* of the consequent output values; it does not change the state of the model.

Atomic models are derived from the abstract *Atomic* class, which defines the interface needed by the simulation algorithm. This class has two abstract methods: *delta* and *output_func*. The method *delta* implements the state transition function, and *output_func*[1] implements the output function. The member variables of the derived class are the state variables of the model, and these are initialized by its constructor.

The *computeOutput* method is effective just once at each simulation time. Subsequent calls at the same simulation time have no effect. This design decision has two practical motivations: (1) it simplifies the management of output objects by cleaning them up just once at the end of the *computeNextState* method, and (2) the model's *output_func* method is called just once at each simulation time; in practice, modelers often collect statistics, drive output devices, and perform other tasks in the *output_func* or in response to output that must be done just once at each simulation time.

The type of object in the model's input–output set is specified with a template parameter. The decision to use a template class for building atomic models is strongly motivated by use of the C++ programming language. C++ is a strongly typed language and it lacks a built-in base class. Consequently, the simulation engine must know at compile time what types of objects will be produced and consumed by the model. A generic base class for atomic models, with a template for specifying the type of input and output, solves this problem and gives the programmer explicit control over how

---

[1] Why not *lambda*? The symbol (or word) *delta* is commonly used to represent change. This usage is introduced in first- and second-year calculus and physics courses. Use of the symbol (or word) lambda for output is relatively uncommon. The method name *output_func* seemed, therefore, less likely to confuse the programmer.

input and output objects are managed. This, however, forces every class that uses the *Atomic* interface to be a generic class, and therefore the entire simulation engine must be implemented as a set of generic classes.

Other programming languages will prompt other solutions to this problem. Typeless languages and dynamically typed languages, Tcl and Python, for example, solve this problem implicitly. For languages with a built-in, universal superclass—Java and its *Object* class is an example—it is natural to use the language's superclass as the basic type of input to and output from *Atomic* models. When the language has an intrinsic garbage collector, this solution is particularly attractive.

Consider, for a moment, how a universal base class might be used in a C++ implementation of the simulation engine. We could force the programmer to use a base class, provided by the simulation engine, for all input and output, but this is awkward in practice. Small simulation projects become cluttered with objects that encapsulate simple data types: doubles, integers, and strings. Large simulation projects are pushed into a design that invariably forces models to exchange pointers to objects, rather than the objects themselves (or copies of the objects). The memory allocated to input and output objects must, therefore, be carefully managed and this becomes a source of errors. Pointers to objects are sometimes necessary, and the use of templates permits this, but it can often be avoided and templates provide a way of doing so.

Nonetheless, some simulators need to use objects that are allocated dynamically as the basic type of input and output for their models. For this reason, the *Atomic* class has an abstract *gc_output* method for managing objects created by the *output_func* method. This is necessary because the model that created the object cannot know when the simulator is finished with it. "Finished," in this case, means that all the models within the simulator and the event listeners outside the simulator have had an opportunity to access the object. Only the *Simulator* knows when this condition is satisfied, and so only it can safely invoke the *gc_output* method, at which time the *Atomic* model may destroy any output objects that is has created.

The classes that constitute the simulation engine are in the *adtss* namespace to prevent conflicts with classes, functions, and variables that are not part of the simulation engine. The name *adtss* describes what the collection of classes is: a discrete-time system simulator. Figure 3.3 shows the classes in the simulation engine, and their methods, attributes, and primary relationships. The *Simulator* and *Bag* classes are the only ones with concrete methods. All of the other classes are (almost) purely abstract. The only exception is the *Atomic* class, which has one member variable. This variable, the *Bag* y, is used by the *Simulator* when it invokes the model's *output_func* method and, subsequently, the *gc_output* method. Even though this *Bag* belongs to the *Atomic* class, it is private and, consequently, inaccessible by derived classes. Only the *Simulator*, which is a friend of the *Atomic* class, has access to it.

The *Bag* class can be implemented with any suitable data structure. It might be a simple alias for an STL *multiset*, a dynamically sized array, or something optimized for use in the simulation engine. Regardless, the name *Bag* is retained to remind the

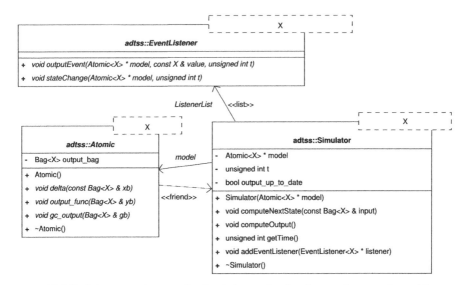

FIGURE 3.3 Class diagram of a simulation engine for discrete-time atomic models.

programmer that it is an unordered collection of objects. The simulation algorithm does not attach any importance to the order of elements in the *Bag*, and neither should the model.

The *Simulator* class is the most complicated part of the simulation engine. It implements the basic simulation algorithm, implements the interface that makes this algorithm available to clients of the *Simulator*, and assists the *Atomic* model with cleaning up its garbage. The source code for the *Simulator* is listed below. This simulator implementation, an implementation for the *Bag* class, and the abstract *EventListener* and *Atomic* classes constitute a complete library of classes for simulating discrete-time, atomic models. These classes are defined in the file `dtss_atomic.h` that the simulator includes.

Simulator for a Discrete-Time Atomic Model

```
1   #ifndef _dtss_simulator_h_
2   #define _dtss_simulator_h_
3   #include "dtss_atomic.h"
4
5   namespace adtss
6   {
7
8   template <typename X> class Simulator
9   {
10     public:
11       // Create a simulator for the supplied model
12       Simulator(Atomic<X>* model):
13         model(model),t(0),output_up_to_date(false){}
```

```
14      // Compute the next state of the model and invoke stateChange
15      // and outputEvent callbacks as appropriate
16      void computeNextState(const Bag<X>& input);
17      // Compute the model's output and make outputEvent callbacks
18      void computeOutput();
19      // Get the simulation time.
20      unsigned int getTime() { return t; }
21      // Add an event listener
22      void addEventListener(EventListener<X>* listener)
23      {
24          listeners.push_back(listener);
25      }
26    private:
27      Atomic<X>* model; // The model to simulate
28      unsigned int t; // Simulation clock
29      bool output_up_to_date; // Is the model output up to date?
30      // List of event listeners
31      typedef std::list<EventListener<X>*> ListenerList;
32      ListenerList listeners;
33  };
34
35  template <typename X>
36  void Simulator<X>::computeNextState(const Bag<X>& input)
37  {
38      computeOutput(); // Compute the output at time t
39      t++; // Advance the simulation clock
40      model->delta(input); // Compute the new state of the model
41      // Notify listeners that the state has changed
42      for (typename ListenerList::iterator iter = listeners.begin();
43              iter != listeners.end(); iter++)
44          (*iter)->stateChange(model,t);
45      // Cleanup
46      model->gc_output(model->output_bag);
47      model->output_bag.clear();
48      output_up_to_date = false;
49  }
50
51  template <typename X>
52  void Simulator<X>::computeOutput()
53  {
54      // Return if the output function has been evaluated
55      if (output_up_to_date) return;
56      // Compute the output
57      output_up_to_date = true;
58      model->output_func(model->output_bag);
59      // Tell listeners about the output
60      for (typename Bag<X>::iterator yiter = model->output_bag.begin();
61              yiter != model->output_bag.end(); yiter++) {
62          for (typename ListenerList::iterator iter = listeners.begin();
```

```
63        iter != listeners.end(); iter++) {
64      (*iter)->outputEvent(model,*yiter,t);
65    }
66  }
67 }
68
69 } // end of namespace
70
71 #endif
```

An interactive simulation of the vending machine described in Section 3.1.3 will illustrate how the simulator is used. The model is implemented by the *CoffeeMachine* class, which is derived from the *Atomic* class. The input–output for this model is an enumeration, and so the garbage collection method isn't necessary. The state variables of the vending machine model are member variables of the *CoffeeMachine* class. The state transition function is implemented in the *delta* method and the output function, in the *output_func* method. The initial state of the model is set by the constructor. The code for the *CoffeeMachine* class is listed below. Note that the coffee machine is started in the initial state from Table 3.2.

_____ ***Definition of the CoffeeMachine Class*** _____

```
1  #ifndef _CoffeeMachine_h_
2  #define _CoffeeMachine_h_
3  #include "adtss.h"
4
5  // Input and output values
6  typedef enum {
7    NICKEL, DIME, QUARTER,
8    CANCEL, WAIT, COFFEE, NOTHING
9  } IO_Type;
10
11 // Definition of the coffee machine
12 class CoffeeMachine: public adtss::Atomic<IO_Type>
13 {
14   public:
15     // Constructor puts the model into its initial state
16     CoffeeMachine();
17     // State transition function
18     void delta(const adtss::Bag<IO_Type>& xb);
19     // Output function
20     void output_func(adtss::Bag<IO_Type>& yb);
21     // Garbage collection method does not do anything
22     void gc_output(adtss::Bag<IO_Type>&){}
23     // Get the amount of money in the machine
24     int getInventoryValue() const { return 5*n+10*d+25*q; }
25     // Get the amount of money left to the customer
26     int getCustomerValue() const { return v; }
```

```
27    private:
28        int n, d, q; // Numbers of nickels, dimes, and quarters
29        int v; // Value left to the customer
30        bool cancel; // Status of the cancel button
31        // Find coins in the inventory.
32        void getCoins(int cents, int& nout, int& dout, int& qout);
33    };
34
35    #endif
```

_____ **Implementation of the CoffeeMachine Class** _____

```
1    #include "CoffeeMachine.h"
2    using namespace adtss;
3
4    void CoffeeMachine::getCoins(int cents, int& nout, int& dout, int& qout)
5    {
6        int qc = q, dc = d, nc = n;
7        nout = dout = qout = 0;
8        // Pick quarters
9        while (qc > 0 && cents >= 25) {
10           qout++; qc--; cents -= 25;
11       }
12       // Pick dimes
13       while (dc > 0 && cents >= 10) {
14           dout++; dc--; cents -= 10;
15       }
16       // Pick nickels
17       while (nc > 0 && cents >= 5) {
18           nout++; nc--; cents -= 5;
19       }
20   }
21
22   CoffeeMachine::CoffeeMachine():
23       adtss::Atomic<IO_Type>(),
24       n(10),d(10),q(10), // Start with ten of each type of coin
25       v(0),cancel(false){}
26
27   void CoffeeMachine::delta(const Bag<IO_Type>& xb)
28   {
29       // Sell a cup of coffee
30       if (v >= 100) v -= 100;
31       // Remove change if the cancel button is pressed
32       if (cancel) {
33           // Clear the cancel signal
34           cancel = false;
35           // Return the coins
36           int nc, dc, qc;
37           getCoins(v,nc,dc,qc);
```

```
38      q -= qc; d -= dc; n -= nc;
39      v = 0;
40    }
41    // Add change that was inserted by the customer
42    // and check the state of the cancel button
43    for (Bag<IO_Type>::const_iterator iter = xb.begin();
44          iter != xb.end(); iter++) {
45      if ((*iter) == NICKEL) { n++; v += 5; }
46      else if ((*iter) == DIME) { d++; v += 10; }
47      else if ((*iter) == QUARTER) { q++; v += 25; }
48      else if ((*iter) == CANCEL) cancel = true;
49    }
50  }
51
52  void CoffeeMachine::output_func(Bag<IO_Type>& yb)
53  {
54    // How much cash is in the machine?
55    int cash = v;
56    // If there is enough money for a cup of coffee, then pour a cup
57    if (cash >= 100) {
58      yb.insert(COFFEE);
59      cash -= 100;
60    }
61    // Return any remaining change if the cancel button is pressed
62    if (cancel) {
63      int nreturn, dreturn, qreturn;
64      getCoins(cash,nreturn,dreturn,qreturn);
65      for (int i = 0; i < nreturn; i++) yb.insert(NICKEL);
66      for (int i = 0; i < dreturn; i++) yb.insert(DIME);
67      for (int i = 0; i < qreturn; i++) yb.insert(QUARTER);
68    }
69    // If no output was produced then put NOTHING into the output bag
70    if (yb.empty()) yb.insert(NOTHING);
71  }
```

The *CoffeeMachineListener* class, which is derived from the *EventListener* class, reports output from the *CoffeeMachine* and reports the change remaining to the customer whenever the *CoffeeMachine* changes its state. The code for the *CoffeeMachineListener* is shown below.

The CoffeeMachineListener Class

```
1  #ifndef _CoffeeMachineListener_h_
2  #define _CoffeeMachineListener_h_
3  #include "CoffeeMachine.h"
4  #include <iostream>
5
6  class CoffeeMachineListener: public adtss::EventListener<IO_Type>
```

```
7   {
8       public:
9           // Listen for events from a coffee machine
10          CoffeeMachineListener(CoffeeMachine* m):m(m){}
11          // This is invoked by the simulator when the model produces output
12          void outputEvent(adtss::Atomic<IO_Type>* model,
13                  const IO_Type& value, unsigned int t)
14          {
15              std::cout << "output @ t = " << t << ", ";
16              if (value == NICKEL) std::cout << "nickel\n";
17              else if (value == DIME) std::cout << "dime\n";
18              else if (value == QUARTER) std::cout << "quarter\n";
19              else if (value == COFFEE) std::cout << "Coffee!\n";
20              else std::cout << "nothing\n";
21          }
22          // This is invoked by the simulator when the model changes state
23          void stateChange(adtss::Atomic<IO_Type>* model, unsigned int t)
24          {
25              std::cout << "You have " <<
26                  m->getCustomerValue() << " cents @ t = "
27                  << t << std::endl;
28          }
29      private:
30          CoffeeMachine* m;
31  };
32
33  #endif
```

The program's main function has two parts. The first part creates a *CoffeeMachine*, a *CoffeeMachineListener*, and a *Simulator*. The *CoffeeMachine* is passed to the *Simulator*'s constructor, and the *CoffeeMachineListener* is registered to receive output and state change notifications from the *Simulator*. The second part runs the simulation until the user types "quit." Each line of input to the program is parsed into quarter (q), dime (d), nickel (n), cancel (c), and wait (w) inputs for the model. These are applied to the *CoffeeMachine* via the *Simulator*'s *computeNextState* method. When the user types "quit," the profit made by the machine is printed, the program cleans up, and then it exits.

_____ Main Function for the Coffee Machine Simulation _____

```
1   #include "CoffeeMachine.h"
2   #include "CoffeeMachineListener.h"
3   #include <iostream>
4   using namespace std;
5
6   int main()
7   {
8       // Create the model
```

```
 9    CoffeeMachine* m = new CoffeeMachine();
10    // Create the simulator and register a listener to report changes to
11    // the model
12    CoffeeMachineListener* l = new CoffeeMachineListener(m);
13    adtss::Simulator<IO_Type>* sim = new adtss::Simulator<IO_Type>(m);
14    sim->addEventListener(l);
15    // Look for input and apply it to the simulator
16    while (true) {
17        // Get a command from the user
18        string command;
19        adtss::Bag<IO_Type> input;
20        cout << sim->getTime() << " > ";
21        cin >> command;
22        // Is it time to stop?
23        if (command == "quit") break;
24        // Otherwise process the input string
25        for (int i = 0; i < command.length(); i++) {
26            if (command[i] == 'q') input.insert(QUARTER);
27            else if (command[i] == 'd') input.insert(DIME);
28            else if (command[i] == 'n') input.insert(NICKEL);
29            else if (command[i] == 'c') input.insert(CANCEL);
30            else if (command[i] == 'w') input.insert(WAIT);
31        }
32        // Apply the input to the model. This invokes the listener's
33        // callback methods
34        sim->computeNextState(input);
35    }
36    // Report final profit
37    cout << m->getInventoryValue() << " cents in the inventory\n";
38    // Clean up and exit
39    delete sim; delete l; delete m;
40    return 0;
41 }
```

Now we can repeat the experiments shown in Table 3.2, but using the single trajectory $x_1 \bullet x_2$. The outcome is shown below, and, of course, it matches the earlier simulation that was done by hand. Note that the output at time t follows the prompt for input at that time, and the state at time t precedes the prompt.

```
0 > qqqqnd
output @ t = 0, nothing
You have 115 cents @ t = 1
1 > w
output @ t = 1, Coffee!
You have 15 cents @ t = 2
2 > c
output @ t = 2, nothing
```

```
You have 15 cents @ t = 3
3 > w
output @ t = 3, nickel
output @ t = 3, dime
You have 0 cents @ t = 4
4 > qqqddd
output @ t = 4, nothing
You have 105 cents @ t = 5
5 > c
output @ t = 5, Coffee!
You have 5 cents @ t = 6
6 > w
output @ t = 6, nickel
You have 0 cents @ t = 7
7 > quit
600 cents in the inventory
```

3.2 NETWORK MODELS

A network model has two parts. First is the set of components that constitute the network, and these can be atomic or network models. The second part describes how the network model and its components are connected. The output of the network's components can be connected to the input of other components and the output of the network itself, and the input of the network can be connected to the input of its components.

Network models, just like atomic models, have a set X of inputs and a set Y of outputs, and the network acts on an input trajectory to produce an output trajectory. The transformation of input into output is accomplished by the model's components. Their collective state defines the state of the network. A state transition function is, in a similar fashion, defined for the network model by the state transition functions of its components; likewise the output function of the network.

The network is aware only of the input and output of its components, and therefore cannot distinguish between two models that, given the same input trajectory, produce identical output trajectories. The internal workings of its components are invisible. Consequently, every network model can be reduced to an atomic model that exactly mimics its observable behavior. This property of the network is called *closure under coupling*.[2]

In principle, we could perform this reduction and then use the software from Section 3.1.5 to conduct our simulations. In practice, this is infeasible. Nonetheless, closure under coupling has one immediate consequence for our simulation software; the reduction procedure yields an algorithm for simulating network models.

---

[2]Some people prefer the term *closure under composition* (see, e.g., Lynch *et al.* [80].)

3.2.1 The Parts of a Network Model

To define the resultant of a network, we need a precise description of its parts. The network itself is denoted by N. It has a set X of input and a set Y of output. The set D contains the components of the network (but not the network itself). For each model $d \in D \cup \{N\}$, there is a set of components that affect d. Note that the set $D \cup \{N\}$ contains all the components of the network *and* the network itself. The set of influencers of a model d is denoted I_d. The family of sets of influencers is called $\bar{I}$.

For each model d' in the set I_d of influencers of d there is a coupling function $z_{d',d}$. The coupling function has one of three forms: (1) if d' is the network (i.e., $d' = N$ and $d \in D$), then $z_{N,d}$ converts input from the network to input for d; (2) if d' and d are components (i.e., $d', d \in D$), then $z_{d',d}$ converts output from d' to input for d; or (3) if d is the network (i.e., $d' \in D$ and $d = N$), then $z_{d',N}$ converts output from d' to output from the network. The set containing all of the network's coupling functions is called Z.[3]

For clarity, the parts of a component d are denoted by the subscript d; that is, X_d is the set of inputs to d and Y_d is the set of outputs from d. Similarly, X_N is the set of inputs to the network and Y_N is the set of outputs from the network. With this convention, the parts of the network model are summarized by

$$X_N = \text{input set}$$

$$Y_N = \text{output set}$$

$$D_N = \text{set of components}$$

$$\bar{I}_N = \{I_d \mid d \in D \cup \{N\}\} \text{ the family of sets of influencers}$$

$$Z_N = \{z_{d',d} \mid d' \in I_d \text{ and } d \in D \cup \{N\}\} \text{ the set of coupling functions where}$$

$$z_{N,d} : X_N^b \to X_d^b$$

$$z_{d',N} : Y_{d'}^b \to Y_N^b$$

$$z_{d',d} : Y_{d'}^b \to X_d^b$$

Figure 3.4 illustrates this collection of objects and their roles in the network model. By allowing networks to contain other networks as components, we can create a hierarchy (or tree) of models that decompose a complex system into successively smaller parts. At the leaves of the hierarchy are atomic models. Network models fill the intermediary positions. Because every network has a resultant, it is possible to collapse any subhierarchy into an atomic model, and this change will be unnoticed by models elsewhere in the tree (unless, of course, the model is a part of the hierarchy

---

[3]This method for describing a network is very general but also very cumbersome. It is avoided (or, rather, stated in pictures) by using block diagrams, neighborhood diagrams, computational stencils, and other visual techniques that show how components are connected. These techniques, however, are unsuited for giving a precise definition of the network's dynamic behavior.

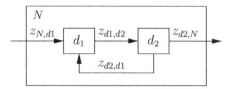

FIGURE 3.4 A network with two components. The algebraic definition of this network has $D = \{d_1, d_2\}$, $\bar{I} = \{I_{d_1}, I_{d_2}, I_N\}$, $I_{d_1} = \{N, d_2\}$, $I_{d_2} = \{d_1\}$, $I_N = \{d_2\}$, and $Z = \{z_{N,d_1}, z_{d_1,d_2}, z_{d_2,d_1}, z_{d_2,N}\}$.

that was collapsed). This property requires, however, that components communicate only with their siblings and their parent. This is enforced by requiring that (1) each instance of a component be part of at most one instance of a network and (2) if a model is in the set D_N of a network N, then the influencers of that model must also be in D_N or be N itself.

3.2.2 The Resultant of a Network Model

The atomic model that mimics a network is called its *resultant*. This atomic model has a set S_r of states, a set X_r of inputs, a set Y_r of outputs, a state transition function δ_r, and an output function λ_r. The subscript r distinguishes the parts of the resultant from the parts of the components in the network and the parts of the network itself.

The set of states of the resultant is constructed recursively with the function *STATE*. This function accepts a model d, which can be atomic or network, and returns its set of states. If the model is atomic then *STATE* acts in the obvious way, simply returning S_d. If the model is a network then *STATE* gives the cross product of the sets of states of its atomic and network components, specifically

$$STATE(d) = \begin{cases} S_d & \text{if } d \text{ is an atomic model} \\ \times_{d' \in D_d} STATE(d') & \text{if } d \text{ is a network model} \end{cases} \tag{3.15}$$

The set of states of the resultant of a network N is

$$S_r = STATE(N) \tag{3.16}$$

and the resultant and network have the same input–output sets:

$$X_r = X_N \tag{3.17}$$

$$Y_r = Y_N \tag{3.18}$$

As is the set of states, the output function is defined by a recursive descent into the network. The output generated by a state $s_r \in S_r$ is

$$\lambda_r(s_r) = \cup_{d \in I_N} z_{d,N}(\lambda_d(s_d)) \tag{3.19}$$

The function λ_d is evaluated directly if d is an atomic model. If d is a network model, then λ_d is found by applying Equation 3.19 to it, that is, by finding the output of its resultant. The result of λ_r is the collective output, possibly modified by the coupling functions, of the components that influence the network (i.e., that are in I_N).

The state transition function of the resultant is defined in a similar way. To determine the next value of an element s_d in the resultant state s_r, it is necessary to find the input to the model d and then apply its state transition function. From its siblings, d receives the input

$$x_d^b = \cup_{d' \in I_d - \{N\}} z_{d',d}(\lambda_{d'}(s_{d'})) \tag{3.20}$$

where $\lambda_{d'}$ is computed directly if d' is an atomic model or by Equation 3.19 if it is a network model, that is, by using the output function of its resultant. The bag x_d^b does not contain input applied to the network to which d belongs. The next state of the resultant is

$$\delta_r(s_r, x^b) = \delta_r((s_{d_1}, s_{d_2}, \ldots, s_{d_k}), x^b) = (s'_{d_1}, s'_{d_2}, \ldots, s'_{d_k}) \tag{3.21}$$

where
$$s'_{d_j} = \begin{cases} \delta_{d_j}(s_{d_j}, x_{d_j}^b) & \text{if } N \notin I_{d_j} \\ \delta_{d_j}(s_{d_j}, x_{d_j}^b \cup z_{N,d_j}(x^b)) & \text{if } N \in I_{d_j} \end{cases}$$

The second case in Equation 3.21 handles input to the network that is destined for the component. If d_j is an atomic model, then δ_{d_j} is calculated directly. Otherwise, Equation 3.21 is used, namely, the state transition function of the resultant of d_j.

This set of definitions and Algorithm 3.2 for simulating an atomic model are a complete description of a simulation engine. Nonetheless, the simulation software will be organized somewhat differently. The relatively simple definition given here tells us *what* a correct implementation of the simulator must do, not *how* it must do it. Every simulator for discrete-time systems is in this sense identical—two simulators that are given the same model must produce the same result regardless of how they are constructed.

3.2.3   An Example of a Network Model and Its Resultant

To illustrate this mathematical construction, consider a machine that computes the logical function

$$y(n + 1) = y(n) \oplus ((x_1(n) \oplus x_2(n)) \tag{3.22}$$

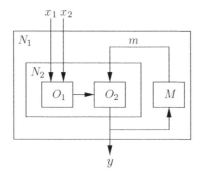

FIGURE 3.5 A logical function constructed from two types of atomic models.

where $\oplus$ is exclusive–or (i.e., binary addition). The machine has two inputs: x_1 and x_2. It has a single output y and remembers its previous output for use in computing its next output. The machine is constructed with two types of atomic components— one computes the exclusive–or function and the other has a memory to store y. The model's organization is illustrated in Figure 3.5.

The component that calculates exclusive–or is denoted O for exclusive–OR. It has two inputs and a single output. The input bag always contains 2 bits: b_1 and b_2. The output bag contains a single bit. The O machine has two possible states corresponding to the two possible results of its logical operation. The input, output, and state sets are

$$X_O = Y_O = S_O = \{0, 1\}$$

The output function and state transition functions are

$$\lambda_O(s_O) = \{s_O\}$$
$$\delta_O(s_O, \{b_1, b_2\}) = b_1 \oplus b_2$$

The memory component, denoted M for *memory*, has a single input, single output, and 2^2 possible states. It is defined by

$$X_M = Y_M = \{0, 1\}$$
$$S_M = \{0, 1\} \times \{0, 1\}$$
$$\delta_M((q_1, q_2), \{x\}) = (q_2, x)$$
$$\lambda_M((q_1, q_2)) = \{q_1\}$$

Both models have state transition functions that are only partially defined. Recall that the state transition function takes a state in S and a bag in the set X^b to a new state in S. To obtain a fully defined state transition function, a new state must be unambiguously defined for every combination of state and bag of inputs. The bag $\{1\}$, however, is in X_O^b, but δ_O is not defined for it. Similarly, the bag $\{1, 0\}$ is in X_M^b, but δ_M is ambiguous about how this modifies the state of M. It is common to have state transition functions that are only partially defined. Make sure, however, that the simulation does not stray into these undefined areas.

The complete machine is built in two stages. The first stage, denoted N_1, contains the second stage, called N_2, and the memory machine M. The second stage contains the two O machines. It is apparent from the definition of the atomic components and the construction of the network that this machine requires three timesteps to finish one calculation of Equation 3.22. After changing the input, two transient values appear at the output before the third, final value emerges. This mimics the settling time of digital circuits, which require several clock cycles to complete an operation.

The definitions of N_1 and N_2 are clearly and unambiguously illustrated in Figure 3.5. Nonetheless, algebraic definitions are given below to demonstrate their use in a simulation. Note that the sets of influencers have double (bilevel) subscripts; the second part of the subscript indicates whether the set belongs in $\bar{I}_{N_1}$ or $\bar{I}_{N_2}$.

The network N_2 is defined by

$$X_{N_2} = \{x_1, x_2, m\} \times \{0, 1\}$$

$$Y_{N_2} = \{0, 1\}$$

$$D_{N_2} = \{O_1, O_2\}$$

$$\bar{I}_{N_2} = \{I_{O_1, N_2}, I_{O_2, N_2}, I_{N_2, N_2}\}$$

where

$$I_{O_1, N_2} = \{N_2\}$$

$$I_{O_2, N_2} = \{N_2, O_1\}$$

$$I_{N_2, N_2} = \{O_2\}$$

$$Z_{N_2} = \{z_{O_1, O_2}, z_{N_2, O_1}, z_{O_2, N_2}, z_{N_2, O_2}\}$$

where

$$z_{O_1, O_2}(\{b\}) = \{b\}$$

$$z_{N_2, O_1}(\{\ldots, (x_1, b_1), (x_2, b_2), \ldots\}) = \{b_1, b_2\}$$

$$z_{O_2, N_2}(\{b\}) = \{b\}$$

$$z_{N_2, O_2}(\{\ldots, (m, b), \ldots\}) = \{b\}$$

Note that the set of input contains labels for the bits; the labels correspond to the name of the edge in Figure 3.5 on which the bit appears. Also note that the coupling functions for N_2 are only partially defined. For example, it is not clear how N_2 handles two m labeled bits in its input bag. Again, the simulation must avoid these undefined cases.

The network N_1 is defined by

$$X_{N_1} = \{x_1, x_2\} \times \{0, 1\}$$

$$Y_{N_1} = \{0, 1\}$$

$$D_{N_1} = \{N_2, M\}$$

$$\bar{I}_{N_1} = \{I_{N_2,N_1}, I_{M,N_1}, I_{N_1,N_1}\}$$

where

$$I_{N_1,N_1} = \{N_2\}$$

$$I_{N_2,N_1} = \{N_1, M\}$$

$$I_{M,N_1} = \{N_2\}$$

$$Z_{N_1} = \{z_{N_1,N_2}, z_{M,N_2}, z_{N_2,N_1}, z_{N_2,M}\}$$

where

$$z_{N_1,N_2}(\{(x_1, b_1), (x_2, b_2)\}) = \{(x_1, b_1), (x_2, b_2)\}$$

$$z_{M,N_2}(\{b\}) = \{(m, b)\}$$

$$z_{N_2,N_1}(\{b\}) = \{b\}$$

$$z_{N_2,M}(\{b\}) = \{b\}$$

Input to this network is also a pair of bits. Again, the labels correspond to the edges in Figure 3.5 on which the bits appear.

Now we can use Algorithm 3.2 and Equations 3.15–3.21 to simulate, by hand, a single timestep for this system. One timestep will be onerous enough to not bear repeating; a computer does these calculations more quickly and more reliably. The initial state of O_1 and O_2 is zero. The initial state of M is $(0, 0)$. Input to the machine is held constant at $\{(x_1, 1), (x_2, 0)\}$. The first step of Algorithm 3.2 computes the output of N_1; this is done with Equation 3.19. Expanding the recursive steps depth first and from left to right gives

$$\lambda_{N_1}(s_{N_1}) = \bigcup_{d \in I_{N_1,N_1}} z_{d,N_1}(\lambda_d(s_d))$$

$$= z_{N_2,N_1}(\lambda_{N_2}(s_{N_2}))$$

$$= z_{N_2,N_1}(\bigcup_{d \in I_{N_2,N_2}} z_{d,N_2}(\lambda_d(s_d)))$$

$$= z_{N_2,N_1}(z_{O_2,N_2}(\lambda_{O_2}(s_{O_2})))$$

$$= z_{N_2,N_1}(z_{O_2,N_2}(\{0\}))$$

$$= z_{N_2,N_1}(\{0\})$$

$$= \{0\}$$

Algorithm 3.2 next uses Equation 3.21 to compute a new state for N_1. We have taken a shortcut by reusing part of the calculation above; the output of N_2 is needed, which we already know. The next state of N_1 is given by

$$\delta_{N_1}(s_{N_1}, \{(x_1, 1), (x_2, 0)\}) =$$

$$(\delta_M(s_M, x_M^b), \delta_{N_2}(s_{N_2}, x_{N_2}^b \cup z_{N_1,N_2}(\{(x_1, 1), (x_2, 0)\}))) \qquad (3.23)$$

The first half of the state of the resultant, the state of the memory component M, is

$$\begin{aligned}
\delta_M(s_M, x_M^b) &= \delta_M(s_M, \cup_{d \in I_{M,N_1} - \{N_1\}} z_{d,M}(\lambda_d(s_d))) \\
&= \delta_M(s_M, z_{N_2,M}(\lambda_{N_2}(s_{N_2}))) \\
&= \delta_M(s_M, z_{N_2,M}(\{0\})) \\
&= \delta_M(s_M, \{0\}) \\
&= (0, 0) \qquad (3.24)
\end{aligned}$$

The second half of the state of the resultant, the state of the network N_2, is

$$\begin{aligned}
\delta_{N_2}&(s_{N_2}, x_{N_2}^b \cup z_{N_1,N_2}(\{(x_1, 1), (x_2, 0)\})) \\
&= \delta_{N_2}(s_{N_2}, (\cup_{d \in I_{N_2,N_1} - \{N_1\}} z_{d,N_2}(\lambda_d(s_d))) \cup z_{N_1,N_2}(\{(x_1, 1), (x_2, 0)\})) \\
&= \delta_{N_2}(s_{N_2}, z_{M,N_2}(\lambda_M(s_M)) \cup z_{N_1,N_2}(\{(x_1, 1), (x_2, 0)\})) \\
&= \delta_{N_2}(s_{N_2}, \{(m, 0)\} \cup z_{N_1,N_2}(\{(x_1, 1), (x_2, 0)\})) \\
&= \delta_{N_2}(s_{N_2}, \{(m, 0)\} \cup \{(x_1, 1), (x_2, 0)\}) \\
&= \delta_{N_2}(s_{N_2}, \{(m, 0), (x_1, 1), (x_2, 0)\}) \\
&= (\delta_{O_1}(s_{O_1}, x_{O_1}^b \cup z_{N_2,O_1}(\{(m, 0), (x_1, 1), (x_2, 0)\})), \qquad (3.25) \\
&\qquad \delta_{O_2}(s_{O_2}, x_{O_2}^b \cup z_{N_2,O_2}(\{(m, 0), (x_1, 1), (x_2, 0)\})))
\end{aligned}$$

The first part of this pair, the next state of O_1, is

$$\begin{aligned}
\delta_{O_1}&(s_{O_1}, x_{O_1}^b \cup z_{N_2,O_1}(\{(m, 0), (x_1, 1), (x_2, 0)\})) \\
&= \delta_{O_1}(s_{O_1}, (\cup_{d \in I_{O_1,N_2} - \{N_2\}} z_{d,O_1}(\lambda_d(s_d))) \cup z_{N_2,O_1}(\{(m, 0), (x_1, 1), (x_2, 0)\})) \\
&= \delta_{O_1}(s_{O_1}, z_{N_2,O_1}(\{(m, 0), (x_1, 1), (x_2, 0)\})) \\
&= \delta_{O_1}(s_{O_1}, \{1, 0\}) \\
&= 1 \qquad (3.26)
\end{aligned}$$

The second part, the next state of O_2, is

$$\delta_{O_2}(s_{O_2}, x^b_{O_2} \cup z_{N_2,O_2}(\{(m,0),(x_1,1),(x_2,0)\}))$$

$$= \delta_{O_2}(s_{O_2}, (\cup_{d \in I_{O_2,N_2} - \{N_2\}} z_{d,O_2}(\lambda_d(s_d))) \cup z_{N_2,O_2}(\{(m,0),(x_1,1),(x_2,0)\}))$$

$$= \delta_{O_2}(s_{O_2}, z_{O_1,O_2}(\lambda_{O_1}(s_{O_1})) \cup z_{N_2,O_2}(\{(m,0),(x_1,1),(x_2,0)\}))$$

$$= \delta_{O_2}(s_{O_2}, \{0\} \cup z_{N_2,O_2}(\{(m,0),(x_1,1),(x_2,0)\}))$$

$$= \delta_{O_2}(s_{O_2}, \{0\} \cup \{0\})$$

$$= \delta_{O_2}(s_{O_2}, \{0,0\})$$

$$= 0 \qquad (3.27)$$

Substituting Equations 3.27 and 3.26 into Equation 3.25 gives

$$\delta_{N_2}(s_{N_2}, x^b_{N_2} \cup z_{N_1,N_2}(\{(x_1,1),(x_2,0)\})) = (1,0) \qquad (3.28)$$

Putting Equations 3.28 and 3.24 into Equation 3.23 gives the final solution:

$$\delta_{N_1}(s_{N_1}, \{(x_1,1),(x_2,0)\})$$

$$= (\delta_M(s_M, x^b_M), \delta_{N_2}(s_{N_2}, x^b_{N_2} \cup z_{N_1,N_2}(\{(x_1,1),(x_2,0)\})))$$

$$= ((0,0),(1,0)) \qquad (3.29)$$

This calculation is tedious but simple. Having computed the state and output of the network N_1, we find that the first iteration of Algorithm 3.2 is complete and, with enough patience, we can calculate the next iteration in the same way.

3.2.4   Simulating the Resultant

Closure under coupling can transform the simulator for a single atomic model into a simulator for network models. To do this, the simulation engine from Section 3.1.5 needs four new classes: the *Network*, the *Resultant*, the *Event*, and the *Set*. The revised class diagram is shown in Figure 3.6. The *Set* class is exactly what its name indicates. It could be implemented with a simple alias for the STL *set* class, or in some other way conceived specifically for the simulator. The essential features of the *Set* are that elements can be added to and removed from it, that it contains at most one copy of each element, and that we can iterate through its contents.

The *Resultant* encapsulates a *Network* object to make it appear as an *Atomic* object. The *Resultant*'s output function does two things; it puts output from its *Network*'s components that are in I_N into the *Bag* of output from the *Resultant*, and it caches inputs to the other components for use in computing the state transition function. Recall that the output function is always calculated before the state transition

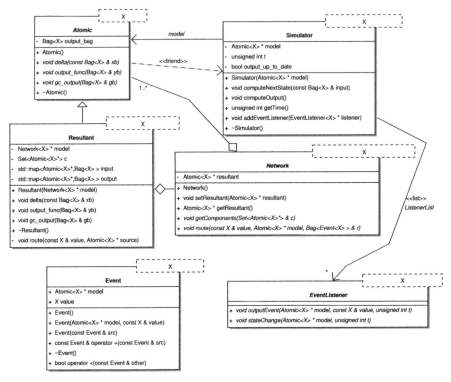

FIGURE 3.6 Class diagram of a top–down simulator for network models.

function, and so these cached values will be available when they are needed. The state transition function calculates new states for the network's components.

The *Network* class, which is always contained in a *Resultant*, has two abstract methods. The *getComponents* method fills the *Set* provided to it with pointers to the components, *Resultant* and *Atomic*, of the network. The *route* method computes the bags of input for each component, but unlike the hand calculation in Section 3.2.3, which obtains the input for a model by looking backward to the source, the *route* method begins at the source and moves its output forward to the destinations. This avoids the slow recalculation, evident in the hand simulation of Section 3.2.3, of output functions that generate input for several components.

The arguments to the *route* method are the source of the event; the event itself, which can be an input or an output; and a *Bag* into which *Event* objects are placed that describe the event's destination. Each *Event* object points to a model connected to the event's source and contains the event after its transformation by the appropriate z function. Recipients of the event are from the set E_d of models that are influenced by the source d; this set is defined by

$$E_d = \{d' \mid d \in I_{d'}\} \tag{3.30}$$

Inversely, the set I_d of influencers of d can be defined by swapping I and E to obtain

$$I_d = \{d' \mid d \in E_{d'}\}$$

Each *Event* in the *Bag* of receivers contains the contribution of the source d to the bags of input for the models in E_d and, if the network is in E_d, its bag of output. To be precise, the *route* method is given a source d and constructs the bag

$$R_d = \{(d', z_{d,d'}(\lambda_d(s_d))) \mid d' \in E_d\} \tag{3.31}$$

where each pair in R_d is an *Event* object. Input in R_d for the model d' is stored in the input *map* of the *Resultant* for later use while calculating the state transition function.

The *Resultant* is the only new class with a substantial implementation. To simulate a *Network* model, it is passed to the constructor of the *Resultant*, and then the *Resultant* is passed to the *Simulator*. If a *Network A* is contained inside of a *Network B*, then a *Resultant* containing A is placed in the bag of components of B. Routing of input and output is done by referencing *Resultants*. The code that implements the *Resultant* is listed below. The rest of the simulation engine is defined in the included dtss_network.h file.

_____ ***Implementation of the Resultant Class*** _____

```
1   #ifndef _dtss_resultant_h
2   #define _dtss_resultant_h
3   #include "dtss_network.h"
4
5   namespace adtss
6   {
7
8   template <typename X> class Resultant: public Atomic<X>
9   {
10      public:
11         Resultant(Network<X>* model);
12         void delta(const Bag<X>& xb);
13         void output_func(Bag<X>& yb);
14         void gc_output(Bag<X>&);
15         ~Resultant() { delete model; }
16      private:
17         Network<X>* model;
18         Set<Atomic<X>*> c;
19         std::map<Atomic<X>*,Bag<X> > input, output;
20         void route(const X& value, Atomic<X>* source);
21   };
22
23   template <typename X>
24   Resultant<X>::Resultant(Network<X>* model):
25      Atomic<X>(),model(model)
```

```
26   {
27       model->setResultant(this);
28       model->getComponents(c);
29   }
30
31   template <typename X>
32   void Resultant<X>::delta(const Bag<X>& xb)
33   {
34       // Send the input to the proper components
35       for (typename Bag<X>::const_iterator iter = xb.begin();
36               iter != xb.end(); iter++)
37           route(*iter,this);
38       // Compute the next state of each component
39       for (typename Set<Atomic<X>*>::iterator iter = c.begin();
40               iter != c.end(); iter++)
41           (*iter)->delta(input[*iter]);
42   }
43
44   template <typename X>
45   void Resultant<X>::output_func(Bag<X>& yb)
46   {
47       // Compute the output of each component and
48       // send those outputs to their destinations
49       for (typename Set<Atomic<X>*>::iterator iter = c.begin();
50               iter != c.end(); iter++) {
51           // Compute the model's output
52           Bag<X>& y = output[*iter];
53           (*iter)->output_func(y);
54           // Route the output to its destinations
55           for (typename Bag<X>::iterator y_iter = y.begin();
56                   y_iter != y.end(); y_iter++)
57               route(*y_iter,*iter);
58       }
59       // Copy the network output to yb
60       Bag<X>& y = output[this];
61       for (typename Bag<X>::iterator iter = y.begin();
62               iter != y.end(); iter++)
63           yb.insert(*iter);
64   }
65
66   template <typename X>
67   void Resultant<X>::gc_output(Bag<X>&)
68   {
69       // Let the components clean up their output
70       for (typename Set<Atomic<X>*>::iterator iter = c.begin();
71               iter != c.end(); iter++) {
72           (*iter)->gc_output(output[*iter]);
73           // Clear the output bag for the component
74           output[*iter].clear();
```

```
75      // Clear the input bag for the component
76      input[*iter].clear();
77   }
78   // Clear the input and output bag for the resultant
79   input[this].clear();
80   output[this].clear();
81 }
82
83 template <typename X>
84 void Resultant<X>::route(const X& value, Atomic<X>* source)
85 {
86    Bag<Event<X> > r;
87    model->route(value,source,r);
88    for (typename Bag<Event<X> >::const_iterator iter = r.begin();
89         iter != r.end(); iter++) {
90       // If this is an output from the network
91       if ((*iter).model == this) output[this].insert((*iter).value);
92       // otherwise it goes to an internal component
93       else input[(*iter).model].insert((*iter).value);
94    }
95 }
96
97 } // end of namespace
98
99 #endif
```

On careful examination, the *Network* and *Resultant* are seen to have a small defect. The *route* methods act on the input to and output from the model one element at a time. It is therefore very difficult to implement coupling functions that operate on several elements at simultaneously. For instance, a model with output set $\{0, 1\}$ can produce bags that contain arbitrary collections of zeros and ones. A coupling function $z_1(\{b_1, b_2, \ldots, b_n\}) = \{b_1 \vee b_2 \vee \cdots \vee b_n\}$ is difficult to implement with the proposed software, but $z_2(\{b_1, b_2, \ldots, b_n\}) = \{\neg b_1, \neg b_2, \ldots, \neg b_n\}$ is easily accomplished.

The justification for this restriction is a practical one; when the simulation engine is extended to include discrete-event systems, transient events will make functions such as z_1 very difficult to use. Consequently, functions such as z_2 predominate. If a function such as z_1 is needed, a separate atomic model is defined that collects the required inputs, undergoes an instantaneous state transition to compute the function, and produces the result as an output. This topic will be revisited in Chapter 4.

The logical function described in Section 3.2.3 will demonstrate how the simulator is used. Observe that the coupling functions are similar to z_2 above. The decision to use a single template parameter to set the type of object used for input and output requires selecting an object type that is suitable for every model. In this instance, we use a port_value_t structure that contains a bit field, which is needed by every model; and a port field, which is needed by the networks. The atomic models simply ignore the port field. The less-than operator is required because the *Bag* class is, in fact, just a *multiset* from the C++ Standard Template Library.

The implementations of the exclusive–or and memory models follow directly from their definitions. Note that the *delta* methods of both classes check that the input bag contains the proper number of elements. This runtime test is helpful for debugging and, even when inactive (i.e., when compiling with NDEBUG defined), is a reminder that the model accepts a restricted range of input. The implementations of the exclusive–or and memory models are listed below.

_____ ***Exclusive–Or and Memory Models*** _____

```
1   #ifndef _xor_memory_models_h_
2   #define _xor_memory_models_h_
3   #include "adtss.h"
4   #include <cassert>
5
6   // Structure used for input from and output to the models
7   struct port_value_t
8   {
9      char port; // Port on which the I/O appears
10     bool bit; // Bit appearing at the port
11     bool operator<(const port_value_t& other) const { // For the STL
12        return bit < other.bit;
13     }
14  };
15
16  // Definition of the exclusive-or model
17  class Xor: public adtss::Atomic<port_value_t>
18  {
19     public:
20        Xor():adtss::Atomic<port_value_t>(),s(false){} // State is 0
21        // State transition function
22        void delta(const adtss::Bag<port_value_t>& xb)
23        {
24           // Make sure the input bag is acceptable
25           assert(xb.size() == 2);
26           // Process the two input events
27           adtss::Bag<port_value_t>::iterator iter = xb.begin();
28           bool x1 = (*iter).bit, x2 = (*(++iter)).bit;
29           s = (x1 && !x2) || (x2 && !x1);
30        }
31        // Output function
32        void output_func(adtss::Bag<port_value_t>& yb)
33        {
34           port_value_t y;
35           y.bit = s;
36           yb.insert(y);
37        }
```

```
38        // Garbage collection method does not do anything
39        void gc_output(adtss::Bag<port_value_t>&){}
40     private:
41        bool s;
42   };
43
44   // Definition of the memory machine
45   class Memory: public adtss::Atomic<port_value_t>
46   {
47      public:
48         Memory():adtss::Atomic<port_value_t>()
49         {
50            s[0] = s[1] = false;
51         }
52         // State transition function
53         void delta(const adtss::Bag<port_value_t>& xb)
54         {
55            // Make sure the input bag is acceptable
56            assert(xb.size() == 1);
57            // Process the input
58            s[0] = s[1];
59            s[1] = (*(xb.begin())).bit;
60         }
61         // Output function
62         void output_func(adtss::Bag<port_value_t>& yb)
63         {
64            port_value_t output;
65            output.bit = s[0];
66            yb.insert(output);
67         }
68         // Garbage collection method does not do anything
69         void gc_output(adtss::Bag<port_value_t>&){}
70      private:
71         bool s[2];
72   };
73
74   #endif
```

The code for N_1 and N_2 is listed next. N_1 contains the *Resultant* that contains the network N_2, not N_2 itself: N_1 puts this *Resultant* into its set of components and uses it to route events. Classwide (i.e., static) constants that implement the models' input ports are another feature of the classes that implement the networks. If the ports are constant, there is no risk that they will be accidentally overwritten and cause obscure, difficult-to-find errors. By making them classwide variables (i.e., static) we can ensure that the memory used by the simulation is reduced. This is a small advantage, and the model must be large before it yields any real benefits.

Nonetheless, every instance of the class should have the same set of input and output variables, and so defining them as class wide constants is a reasonable thing to do.

_____ *N1 Model* _____

```
1   #ifndef _n1_h_
2   #define _n1_h_
3   #include "adtss.h"
4   #include "n2.h"
5   #include "xor_memory_models.h"
6
7   class N1: public adtss::Network<port_value_t>
8   {
9      public:
10         static const int x1, x2; // Labels for input ports
11         // Create the network; components set their own initial state
12         N1():adtss::Network<port_value_t>(),
13            n2(new N2()),m(){}
14         // Get the set of components in this network
15         void getComponents(adtss::Set<adtss::Atomic<port_value_t>*>& c)
16         {
17            c.insert(&n2);
18            c.insert(&m);
19         }
20         // Route input and output within the network
21         void route(const port_value_t& value,
22               adtss::Atomic<port_value_t>* src,
23               adtss::Bag<adtss::Event<port_value_t> >& r)
24         {
25            adtss::Event<port_value_t> e;
26            e.value = value;
27            // Input to the network
28            if (src == getResultant()) {
29               e.model = &n2;
30               r.insert(e);
31            }
32            // Output from N2
33            else if (src == &n2) {
34               // Output from the network
35               e.model = getResultant();
36               r.insert(e);
37               // Input to M
38               e.model = &m;
39               r.insert(e);
40            }
41            // Output from M
42            else if (src == &m) {
```

```
43              // Input to N2
44              e.model = &n2;
45              e.value.port = N2::m;
46              r.insert(e);
47            }
48          }
49      private:
50          adtss::Resultant<port_value_t> n2;
51          Memory m;
52  };
53
54  #endif
```

_____ ***N2 Model*** _____

```
1   #ifndef _n2_h_
2   #define _n2_h_
3   #include "adtss.h"
4   #include "xor_memory_models.h"
5
6   class N2: public adtss::Network<port_value_t>
7   {
8       public:
9
10          static const int m, x1, x2; // Labels for the input ports
11
12          N2():adtss::Network<port_value_t>(),
13              xor1(),xor2(){}
14
15          void getComponents(adtss::Set<adtss::Atomic<port_value_t>*>& c)
16          {
17              c.insert(&xor1);
18              c.insert(&xor2);
19          }
20
21          void route(const port_value_t& value,
22              adtss::Atomic<port_value_t>* src,
23              adtss::Bag<adtss::Event<port_value_t> >& r)
24          {
25              adtss::Event<port_value_t> e;
26              e.value = value;
27              // Input to the network
28              if (src == getResultant()) {
29                  // Input to the m port
30                  if (value.port == m) e.model = &xor2;
31                  // Input to one of the bit ports
32                  else e.model = &xor1;
33                  r.insert(e);
34              }
```

```
35      // Output from O1
36      else if (src == &xor1) {
37          // Input to O2
38          e.model = &xor2;
39          r.insert(e);
40      }
41      // Output from O2
42      else if (src == &xor2) {
43          // Output from the network
44          e.model = getResultant();
45          r.insert(e);
46      }
47      }
48  private:
49      Xor xor1, xor2;
50  };
51
52  #endif
```

_____ ***N1 and N2 Port Definitions*** _____

```
1   #include "n1.h"
2   #include "n2.h"
3   // Ports have unique numbers within the scope of their class
4   const int N2::m = 0;
5   const int N2::x1 = 1;
6   const int N2::x2 = 2;
7   const int N1::x1 = N2::x1;
8   const int N1::x2 = N2::x2;
9
```

The main function for the simulator, which is listed below, reads a pair of input bits from standard input, applies these inputs for a complete machine cycle (three clock cycles), and prints the output of the machine at each clock cycle.

_____ ***Main Function for the Logical Machine Simulator*** _____

```
1   #include "adtss.h"
2   #include "n1.h"
3   #include <iostream>
4   using namespace std;
5
6   class MachineListener: public adtss::EventListener<port_value_t>
7   {
8   public:
9       void outputEvent(adtss::Atomic<port_value_t>* model,
10              const port_value_t& x, unsigned int t)
```

```
11      {
12          cout << x.bit << " ";
13      }
14      void stateChange(adtss::Atomic<port_value_t>*,unsigned int){}
15  };
16
17  int main()
18  {
19      // Create the model
20      adtss::Resultant<port_value_t>* m =
21          new adtss::Resultant<port_value_t>(new N1());
22      // Setup the simulator and a listener for reporting outputs
23      MachineListener* l = new MachineListener();
24      adtss::Simulator<port_value_t>* sim =
25          new adtss::Simulator<port_value_t>(m);
26      sim->addEventListener(l);
27      // Counters for the clock and machine cycle
28      int clck = 0, machine_cycle = 0;
29      // Run the simulation
30      while (true) {
31          // Get the input from stdin
32          adtss::Bag<port_value_t> input;
33          port_value_t x1, x2;
34          x1.port = N1::x1;
35          x2.port = N1::x2;
36          cin >> x1.bit >> x2.bit;
37          // Quit if the input has ended
38          if (cin.eof()) break;
39          input.insert(x1);
40          input.insert(x2);
41          // Print the time and input
42          cout << "xx M" << machine_cycle << " C" << clck <<
43              "\t" << x1.bit << " " << x2.bit << "\t";
44          // Print the time and output at the next machine cycle
45          cout << "yy M" << ++machine_cycle <<
46              " C" << clck << "-" << clck+2 << "\t";
47          // Advance the simulation by one machine cycle
48          for (int t = 0; t < 3; t++) {
49              clck++;
50              sim->computeNextState(input);
51          }
52          cout << endl;
53      }
54      // Clean up and exit
55      delete sim; delete l; delete m;
56      return 0;
57  }
```

Now we have a complete simulator for the logical function defined by Equation 3.22. For reference, it is rewritten here:

$$y(n + 1) = y(n) \oplus ((x_1(n) \oplus x_2(n))$$

The time n in this function counts machine cycles. Three timesteps of the model are needed to complete one machine cycle. Consequently, logical input–logical output is read at every third clock cycle.

The memory possessed by this model gives it an interesting transient behavior. If the inputs x_1 and x_2 are maintained such that $x_1 \oplus x_2$ is 1, then the output will oscillate between 1 and 0. If the input changes to $x_1 \oplus x_2 = 0$, then the output will stick to its previous value. The oscillating behavior can be resumed by setting $x_1 \oplus x_2$ back to 1.

We can compute the output trajectory by hand using the definition of y as a function of x_1 and x_2. Recall that $y(0) = 0$. If we apply $x_1[0, 3) = 111$ and $x_2[0, 3) = 000$, the output is

$$y(1) = y(0) \oplus (x_1(0) \oplus x_2(0)) = 0 \oplus (1 \oplus 0) = 1$$
$$y(2) = y(1) \oplus (x_1(1) \oplus x_2(1)) = 1 \oplus (1 \oplus 0) = 0$$
$$y(3) = y(2) \oplus (x_1(2) \oplus x_2(2)) = 0 \oplus (1 \oplus 0) = 1$$

The simulator, of course, agrees with this calculation. Feeding the input

```
1 0
1 0
1 0
```

into the simulator produces the output

```
xx M0 C0      1 0     yy M1 C0-2      0 0 1
xx M1 C3      1 0     yy M2 C3-5      1 1 0
xx M2 C6      1 0     yy M3 C6-8      0 0 1
```

where the columns preceded by xx are the inputs at each machine cycle and the columns preceded by yy are the output produced at and between machine cycles. Because each machine cycle requires three timesteps, there are two transient outputs for every machine output: the last column of the simulator's report is y.

If the machine is subsequently fed $x_1[3, 5) = 00$ and $x_2[3, 5) = 00$, then

$$y(4) = y(3) \oplus (x_1(3) \oplus x_2(3)) = 1 \oplus (0 \oplus 0) = 1$$
$$y(5) = y(4) \oplus (x_1(4) \oplus x_2(4)) = 1 \oplus (0 \oplus 0) = 1$$

and the output will remain 1 while the input is constant. The simulator, of course, agrees with this calculation as well: feeding it

```
1 0
1 0
1 0
0 0
0 0
```

produces the output

```
xx M0 C0        1 0    yy M1 C0-2      0 0 1
xx M1 C3        1 0    yy M2 C3-5      1 1 0
xx M2 C6        1 0    yy M3 C6-8      0 0 1
xx M3 C9        0 0    yy M4 C9-11     1 1 1
xx M4 C12       0 0    yy M5 C12-14    1 1 1
```

where the last column of the simulator's output is y.

If the machine is next fed $x_1[5, 10) = 11100$ and $x_2[5, 10) = 00000$, the output will swing from 1 to 0 to 1 and back to 0, where it remains. Putting

```
1 0
1 0
1 0
0 0
0 0
1 0
1 0
1 0
0 0
0 0
```

into the simulator gives the result

```
xx M0 C0        1 0    yy M1 C0-2       0 0 1
xx M1 C3        1 0    yy M2 C3-5       1 1 0
xx M2 C6        1 0    yy M3 C6-8       0 0 1
xx M3 C9        0 0    yy M4 C9-11      1 1 1
xx M4 C12       0 0    yy M5 C12-14     1 1 1
xx M5 C15       1 0    yy M6 C15-17     1 1 0
xx M6 C18       1 0    yy M7 C18-20     0 0 1
xx M7 C21       1 0    yy M8 C21-23     1 1 0
xx M8 C24       0 0    yy M9 C24-26     0 0 0
xx M9 C27       0 0    yy M10 C27-29    0 0 0
```

just as expected.

Correct operation of this system depends critically on the proper timing of changes in the input. The input values are permitted to change at every third tick of the clock and must be held constant otherwise. The simulation code enforces this in its main loop. The behavior of the model is much more difficult to anticipate if this restriction is removed. To demonstrate this, the author has changed the main function of the simulation program to apply a new input value at every tick of the clock, rather than holding the input constant between machine cycles. The code is listed below.

_____ ***Main Program to Apply Input Immediately*** _____

```
1   #include "adtss.h"
2   #include "n1.h"
3   #include <iostream>
4   using namespace std;
5
6   class MachineListener: public adtss::EventListener<port_value_t>
7   {
8      public:
9         void outputEvent(adtss::Atomic<port_value_t>* model,
10                const port_value_t& x, unsigned int t)
11        {
12           // Print the time and output at the next machine cycle
13           cout << "yy C " << t << "\t" << x.bit << endl;
14        }
15        void stateChange(adtss::Atomic<port_value_t>*,unsigned int){}
16  };
17
18  int main()
19  {
20     // Create the model
21     adtss::Resultant<port_value_t>* m =
22        new adtss::Resultant<port_value_t>(new N1());
23     // Setup the simulator and output listener
24     MachineListener* l = new MachineListener();
25     adtss::Simulator<port_value_t>* sim =
26        new adtss::Simulator<port_value_t>(m);
27     sim->addEventListener(l);
28     // Run the simulation
29     while (true) {
30        // Get the input from stdin
31        adtss::Bag<port_value_t> input;
32        port_value_t x1, x2;
33        x1.port = N1::x1;
34        x2.port = N1::x2;
35        cin >> x1.bit >> x2.bit;
36        // Quit if the input has ended
37        if (cin.eof()) break;
38        input.insert(x1);
```

```
39      input.insert(x2);
40      // Print the time and input
41      cout << "xx C" << sim->getTime() << "\t" <<
42          x1.bit << " " << x2.bit << "\t";
43      // Advance the simulation
44      sim->computeNextState(input);
45    }
46    // Clean up and exit
47    delete sim; delete l; delete m;
48    return 0;
49  }
```

Now we must define input trajectories in terms of clock, rather than machine, cycles. When written in terms of ticks of the clock, the previous input $x_1[0, 10) = 1110011100$ becomes

$$x'_1[0, 30) = 111\ 111\ 111\ 000\ 000\ 111\ 111\ 111\ 000\ 000$$

and the input $x_2[0, 10)$ becomes

$$x'_2[0, 30) = 000\ 000\ 000\ 000\ 000\ 000\ 000\ 000\ 000\ 000$$

If we feed these trajectories into the new simulator, the output is

xx	C0	1 0	yy	C	0	0
xx	C1	1 0	yy	C	1	0
xx	C2	1 0	yy	C	2	1
xx	C3	1 0	yy	C	3	1
xx	C4	1 0	yy	C	4	1
xx	C5	1 0	yy	C	5	0
xx	C6	1 0	yy	C	6	0
xx	C7	1 0	yy	C	7	0
xx	C8	1 0	yy	C	8	1
xx	C9	0 0	yy	C	9	1
xx	C10	0 0	yy	C	10	1
xx	C11	0 0	yy	C	11	1
xx	C12	0 0	yy	C	12	1
xx	C13	0 0	yy	C	13	1
xx	C14	0 0	yy	C	14	1
xx	C15	1 0	yy	C	15	1
xx	C16	1 0	yy	C	16	1
xx	C17	1 0	yy	C	17	0
xx	C18	1 0	yy	C	18	0
xx	C19	1 0	yy	C	19	0
xx	C20	1 0	yy	C	20	1
xx	C21	1 0	yy	C	21	1

```
xx C22   1 0      yy C 22 1
xx C23   1 0      yy C 23 0
xx C24   0 0      yy C 24 0
xx C25   0 0      yy C 25 0
xx C26   0 0      yy C 26 0
xx C27   0 0      yy C 27 0
xx C28   0 0      yy C 28 0
xx C29   0 0      yy C 29 0
```

This y (i.e., the value at every third line) and the y from the previous simulation are the same. Now, let us modify x_2' so that its value changes in the middle of every machine cycle. This could simulate the improper operation of some component in the system, noise in the circuit, or some other undesirable condition. Keeping $x'[0, 30)$ the same, we change $x_2'[0, 30)$ into

$$x_2'[0, 30) = 010\ 010\ 010\ 010\ 010\ 010\ 010\ 010\ 010\ 010$$

and feeding this into the simulation produces

```
xx C0    1 0      yy C 0   0
xx C1    1 1      yy C 1   0
xx C2    1 0      yy C 2   1
xx C3    1 1      yy C 3   0
xx C4    1 0      yy C 4   1
xx C5    1 1      yy C 5   1
xx C6    1 0      yy C 6   1
xx C7    1 1      yy C 7   1
xx C8    1 0      yy C 8   0
xx C9    0 1      yy C 9   1
xx C10   0 0      yy C 10 0
xx C11   0 1      yy C 11 1
xx C12   0 0      yy C 12 1
xx C13   0 1      yy C 13 1
xx C14   0 0      yy C 14 1
xx C15   1 1      yy C 15 0
xx C16   1 0      yy C 16 1
xx C17   1 1      yy C 17 1
xx C18   1 0      yy C 18 1
xx C19   1 1      yy C 19 1
xx C20   1 0      yy C 20 0
xx C21   1 1      yy C 21 1
xx C22   1 0      yy C 22 0
xx C23   1 1      yy C 23 0
xx C24   0 0      yy C 24 0
xx C25   0 1      yy C 25 0
xx C26   0 0      yy C 26 0
xx C27   0 1      yy C 27 1
```

```
xx C28  0 0     yy C 28 0
xx C29  0 1     yy C 29 1
```

Looking at every third line, the corresponding output of the logical machine is $y[0, 10) = 1101110001$, which is clearly not what is expected from Equation 3.22 and the inputs x_1 and x_2 if they are obtained by looking at every third value in x_1' and x_2'. Timing matters, a fact amply demonstrated by our simulation.

The simulation engine built in this section simulates network models from the top, starting with the uppermost network, to the bottom, stopping at the atomic models. After a series of improvements, this top–down simulator would evolve into an implementation of Zeigler's abstract simulators [152, 157]. Top–down architectures, based on the abstract simulators, are widely used and are discussed and refined in a large body of literature (see, e.g., Refs. 26, 51, and 144). This architecture is particularly well suited to component-based simulations (see, e.g., Refs. 23, 24, 64, 127, and 148) and, more recently, Web-based simulations (see, e.g., Refs. 81 and 88).

3.3   A SIMULATOR FOR DISCRETE-TIME SYSTEMS

A simple and effective simulator can be built by focusing on the atomic models and relegating the network models to telling the simulator how atomic models are connected. The simulator devised in this section works from the bottom up. Network models are intermediate steps through which events pass as they travel between the atomic components; every operation begins and ends with an atomic model.

The basis for this approach has two parts:

1. The state transition function of the resultant of a network is defined by the state transition functions of the atomic components at the leaves of the tree rooted in that network. We can, therefore, skip the construction of resultants for the intermediate networks and work directly with the atomic models at the leaves.

2. The sets of influencees can be used to compute the set of atomic components, which may be anywhere in the hierarchy of models, that are influenced by any particular atomic component. The calculation starts with an atomic model, ends with a set of atomic models, and is done recursively by employing the sets of influencees and coupling functions of each network encountered along the way.

The set A_N of atomic models that are beneath a network model N is found by descending recursively into the network and adding to A_N all of the atomic models that are found. The set A_N is defined by

$$A_N = \{d \in D_N \mid d \text{ is atomic}\} \cup_{\{N' \in D_N \mid N' \text{ is a network}\}} A_{N'} \qquad (3.32)$$

If N is the network to be simulated, then A_N is the set of atomic models that the simulator operates on. Assuming that the input x_d^b that should be applied to each model $d \in A_N$ is known, we can compute the state transition function for the network with a simple for loop:

for $d \in A_N$ **do**
$\quad s_d \leftarrow \delta_d(s_d, x_d^b)$
end

The difficult step is to find x_d^b. This problem has three parts: (1) taking the output of $d \in A_N$ to the appropriate bags of input for the other models in A_N; (2) taking input to the network N to the appropriate bags of input for the atomic models in A_N; and (3) taking the output of d to the appropriate bags of output for the network models that are part of the tree rooted at N, a step that is required solely for the benefit of an *EventListener* that may need it.

Consider part 1 first: how, given an output from an atomic model d, to find the set of atomic models that d influences and to insert the corresponding values into the bags of input for those models. We start with the models that have the same parent as d. The parent is denoted $PARENT(d)$. The atomic components of $PARENT(d)$ that d influences directly are in E_d (see Equation 3.30), and to the bag of input for each atomic model d' in E_d is added the value $z_{d,d'}(\lambda_d(s_d))$. This takes care of the atomic siblings of d. The other $d' \in E_d$ are networks belonging to $PARENT(d)$ or d' is $PARENT(d)$ itself.

If d' is a network belonging to $PARENT(d)$, then we proceed as follows. First we find the components of d' that d' influences; these models are in $D_{d'}$. Then, to the bag of input for each such atomic component d'', we add the value $z_{d,d'}(z_{d',d''}(\lambda_d(s_d)))$. For the network components we simply repeat this procedure: finding the components in d'' that d'' influences, updating the bags of input for the atomic models, and again repeating this procedure for the network models.

Otherwise d' is $PARENT(d)$ (i.e., the network itself). In this case, the preceding paragraph is applied to $PARENT(d')$ [unless, of course, $PARENT(d)$ is the root of the tree of models, in which case the output has left the system and we are done]. In other words, we find the set of components of $PARENT(d')$ that d' influences and proceed as follows. To the bag of input for each such atomic component d'' we add the value $z_{d,d'}(z_{d',d''}(\lambda_d(s_d)))$. For the network components we repeat the procedure described in this paragraph or in the preceding paragraph as appropriate.

Algorithm 3.6 succinctly describes this recursive procedure. It begins with a model in A_N and adds a value to the bag of input of every model in A_N that can be reached from it. The route procedure is called with the atomic model d that produced the output, the *parent* of the model d, and the output $y^b = \lambda_d(s_d)$. Associated with every atomic model $d' \in A_N$ (including, of course, d) is a bag $x_{d'}^b$ of input that is filled as the calculation proceeds. The coupling functions and sets of influencees used by the procedure belong to the network referred to by the *parent* argument.

```
1  procedure route(parent,d,yᵇ)
2  foreach d′ ∈ E_d do
3      d′ is an atomic component of parent
4      if d′ is atomic then
5          x^b_{d′} ← x^b_{d′} ∪ z_{d,d′}(yᵇ)
6      d′ is a network component of parent
7      else if d′ ≠ parent then
8          route(d′,d′,z_{d,d′}(yᵇ))
9      Else if this is an output from parent
10     else if d′ = parent and PARENT(d′) exists then
11         route(PARENT(d′),d′,z_{d,d′}(yᵇ))
12     end
13 end
```

Algorithm 3.6   Procedure to route input and output within a network model. The set E_d of influencees and coupling functions $z_{d,d′}$ belong to the network *parent*.

The other two parts of the routing problem—putting input into a network model and observing output from a network model—are conveniently solved by Algorithm 3.6. An input x^b is injected into a network N by calling route with N for the first and second arguments (i.e., $parent = d = N$) and x^b for the third argument. A network model produces an output whenever the third condition is true (i.e., the "output from *parent*" condition), and *EventListeners* registered with the *Simulator* are notified when this occurs.

Algorithm 3.7 describes the complete simulation procedure. It applies an input trajectory $x < t_0, t_n >$ to a network N with a set of atomic components A_N. For each component $d \in A_N$ there is a bag x^b_d of input and its state s_d. Notifications for *EventListeners* have been omitted even though they will appear in the implementation.

```
1  for t_k ∈< t_0, t_n > do
2      Clear the bags of input
3      foreach d ∈ A_N do
4          x^b_d ← ∅
5      end
6      Route the input to N
7      route(N,N,x(t_k))
8      Compute and route output from the components
9      foreach d ∈ A_N do
10         route(PARENT(d),d,λ_d(s_d))
11     end
12     Change the state of the components
13     foreach d ∈ A_N do
14         s_d ← δ_d(s_d, x^b_d)
15     end
16 end
```

Algorithm 3.7   Bottom–up simulation algorithm for a discrete-time model.

The classes that implement the bottom–up simulator are nearly the same as those used by the top–down simulator. The *Resultant*, which isn't necessary, is eliminated. One new class, the *Dtss* class, is added, and the *Atomic* and *Network* classes are modified to inherit from it. The *Dtss* class holds two pieces of information: the parent of the model and the type of the model. The parent field of the *Dtss* class is used to implement the *PARENT* function. The type information is used by the route procedure and to initialize the simulation engine[4]. The *Network* and *Atomic* classes are otherwise unchanged.

The *Event* class does not require any modification, but we have an opportunity to usefully expand the capability of the *EventListener* class. The simulator, now aware of every event as it moves through the couplings of the network, can inform the listener of every output of every atomic and network model. Likewise, the listener can be informed of changes to the state of every atomic model. This significantly expands the ability of an *EventListener* to observe, report, record, and visualize the operation of a large model. The *outputEvent* method of the new *EventListener* accepts an *Event* that carries the model, network or atomic, that produced the output and the output itself.

There is a similar opportunity to expand the capability of the *Simulator* class by allowing its clients to inject input directly into any component of a multicomponent model. This is an essential capability for building interactive simulations and for integrating the simulator into multisimulator federations. The *computeNextState* method of the new *Simulator* accepts a *Bag* of *Event* objects. Each *Event* in the *Bag* holds a model and an input for that model. If the model is atomic, then the input is put into its bag of inputs. If the target is a network, then Algorithm 3.6 is used to deliver the input to the proper set of atomic models.

The revised class diagram is shown in Figure 3.7, from which the implementations of the *Dtss*, *Network*, *Atomic*, *Event*, and *EventListener* classes are easily inferred. The *Event* class has two fields and methods for setting and accessing them. The *EventListener* is a pure virtual class and has no implementation, just a definition. The *Dtss* class contains its parent, methods for setting and getting the parent, and the virtual *typeIsNetwork* and *typeIsAtomic* methods; these are implemented by the *Network* and *Atomic* classes. The *Network* class returns itself when *typeIsNetwork* is called and NULL when *typeIsAtomic* is called. The *Atomic* class does the opposite.

The *Simulator* class is the only one with a substantial implementation. It implements Algorithm 3.7 with the small modifications discussed above to permit a client of the simulator to inject input into any component and to notify listeners when a component produces output or changes state. Algorithm 3.6 is used to move events through the model. The source code for the *Simulator* is listed below.

---

[4]This extra type information isn't really necessary; we could have used the C++ RunTime Type Identification (RTTI) system instead. The author prefers not to use the RTTI system, in part, for reasons of performance and, in part, for reasons of aesthetics. The RTTI system imposes a small performance penalty relative to the use of an explicitly stored field. In addition to this performance penalty, using the RTTI system tends to produce messy and verbose code for casting objects. The author avoids both of these problems by building type information into the *Dtss* base class. The primary benefit of using the RTTI system is that it prevents the type identification errors that inevitable occur as the number of classes grows. In this particular case, the list of types is small and fixed, and so maintenance of this solution is not a concern.

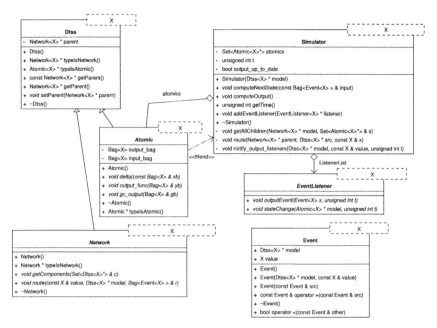

FIGURE 3.7   Class diagram of the bottom–up simulation engine for discrete-time systems.

General Simulator for a Discrete-Time Model

```
1   #ifndef _dtss_simulator_h_
2   #define _dtss_simulator_h_
3   #include "dtss_models.h"
4   #include <iostream>
5
6   namespace adtss
7   {
8
9   template <typename X> class Simulator {
10     public:
11       // Create a simulator for the supplied model
12       Simulator(Dtss<X>* model);
13       // Compute the next state of the model and invoke callbacks
14       void computeNextState(const Bag<Event<X> >& input);
15       // Compute the model's output and make outputEvent callbacks
16       void computeOutput();
17       // Get the simulation time.
18       unsigned int getTime() { return t; }
19       // Add an event listener
20       void addEventListener(EventListener<X>* listener) {
21           listeners.push_back(listener);
22       }
23     private:
24       Set<Atomic<X>*> atomics; // The complete set of atomic models
25       unsigned int t; // Simulation clock
```

```
26      bool output_up_to_date; // Is the model output up to date?
27      // List of event listeners
28      typedef std::list<EventListener<X>*> ListenerList;
29      ListenerList listeners;
30      // Get all of the children belonging to a network
31      void getAllChildren(Network<X>* model, Set<Atomic<X>*>& s);
32      // Move an input or output value to its destination
33      void route(Network<X>* parent, Dtss<X>* src, const X& x);
34      // Tell all EventListeners about an output
35      void notify_output_listeners(Dtss<X>* model,
36          const X& value, unsigned int t);
37  };
38
39  template <typename X>
40  Simulator<X>::Simulator(Dtss<X>* model):
41     t(0),output_up_to_date(false)
42  {
43     // If this is an atomic model then it is the only
44     // atomic model to simulate
45     if (model->typeIsAtomic() != NULL)
46        atomics.insert(model->typeIsAtomic());
47     // Otherwise get all of the atomic models by recursion
48     else getAllChildren(model->typeIsNetwork(),atomics);
49  }
50
51  template <typename X>
52  void Simulator<X>::computeNextState(const Bag<Event<X> >& input)
53  {
54     // Compute the output at time t
55     computeOutput();
56     // Deliver the injected input
57     for (typename Bag<Event<X> >::iterator iter = input.begin();
58           iter != input.end(); iter++) {
59        if ((*iter).model->typeIsAtomic()) {
60           (*iter).model->typeIsAtomic()->input_bag.insert((*iter).value);
61        }
62        else {
63           route((*iter).model->typeIsNetwork(),(*iter).model,(*iter).value);
64        }
65     }
66     // Advance the simulation clock
67     t++;
68     // Update the state of every atomic component
69     for (typename Set<Atomic<X>*>:: iterator aiter = atomics.begin();
70           aiter != atomics.end(); aiter++) {
71        // Compute the new state of the model
72        (*aiter)->delta((*aiter)->input_bag);
73        // Notify listeners that the state has changed
74        for (typename ListenerList::iterator liter = listeners.begin();
```

```
75              liter != listeners.end(); liter++) {
76          (*liter)->stateChange(*aiter,t);
77        }
78      }
79      // Cleanup
80      for (typename Set<Atomic<X>*>:: iterator iter = atomics.begin();
81            iter != atomics.end(); iter++) {
82        (*iter)->gc_output((*iter)->output_bag);
83        (*iter)->output_bag.clear();
84        (*iter)->input_bag.clear();
85      }
86      output_up_to_date = false;
87  }
88
89  template <typename X>
90  void Simulator<X>::computeOutput()
91  {
92      // Return if the output function has been evaluated
93      if (output_up_to_date) return;
94      // Compute the output
95      output_up_to_date = true;
96      for (typename Set<Atomic<X>*>::iterator aiter = atomics.begin();
97            aiter != atomics.end(); aiter++) {
98        // Get the output from the model
99        (*aiter)->output_func((*aiter)->output_bag);
100       // Move the output to its destination
101       Bag<X>& y = (*aiter)->output_bag;
102       for (typename Bag<X>::iterator yiter = y.begin();
103             yiter != y.end(); yiter++) {
104         route((*aiter)->getParent(),*aiter,*yiter);
105       }
106     }
107 }
108
109 template <typename X>
110 void Simulator<X>::getAllChildren(Network<X>* model, Set<Atomic<X>*>& s)
111 {
112     // Get the components of the network
113     Set<Dtss<X>*> c;
114     model->getComponents(c);
115     // Add the atomic components of the network to s and
116     // recursively add the atomic components of the sub-networks
117     for (typename Set<Dtss<X>*>::iterator citer = c.begin();
118           citer != c.end(); citer++) {
119       if ((*citer)->typeIsAtomic()) s.insert((*citer)->typeIsAtomic());
120       else getAllChildren((*citer)->typeIsNetwork(),s);
121     }
122 }
123
```

```
124   template <typename X>
125   void Simulator<X>::route(Network<X>* parent, Dtss<X>* src, const X& x)
126   {
127      // Notify event listeners of the output. Recall that parent = src only
128      // if x is an input to a network. In all other cases, it is an output
129      // from a model.
130      if (parent != src) // Make sure it is an output and not an input
131         notify_output_listeners(src,x,t);
132      // If the parent is null (e.g., if we are simulating a
133      // single atomic model) then there is nothing to do
134      if (parent == NULL) return;
135      // Get the set of models that are influenced by x
136      Bag<Event<X> > r;
137      parent->route(x,src,r);
138      // Route the input to each element in r
139      for (typename Bag<Event<X> >::iterator iter = r.begin();
140            iter != r.end(); iter++) {
141         // If the destination is an atomic model
142         if ((*iter).model->typeIsAtomic() != NULL) {
143            (*iter).model->typeIsAtomic()->input_bag.insert((*iter).value);
144         }
145         // If the destination is a network component of the parent
146         else if (parent != (*iter).model) {
147            route((*iter).model->typeIsNetwork(),
148                  (*iter).model,(*iter).value);
149         }
150         // If the destination is the parent
151         else { // if (*iter).model == parent
152            route(parent->getParent(),parent,(*iter).value);
153         }
154      }
155   }
156
157   template <typename X>
158   void Simulator<X>::notify_output_listeners(Dtss<X>* model,
159         const X& value, unsigned int t)
160   {
161      Event<X> event(model,value);
162      for (typename ListenerList::iterator iter = listeners.begin();
163            iter != listeners.end(); iter++)
164         (*iter)->outputEvent(event,t);
165   }
166
167   } // end of namespace
168
169   #endif
```

The logical function described in Section 3.2.3, which was first implemented in Section 3.2.4, will demonstrate how this bottom–up simulator is used. The *Xor* and *Memory* classes remain just as they are. The *N1* and *N2* classes change in two ways: (1) the constructor is modified to set the parent of the network's components, and (2) the pointers to the *Resultant*s are replaced by pointers to the *Network*s themselves. The revised *N1* and *N2* classes are listed below.

_____ ***Revised N1 Model*** _____

```
1   #ifndef _n1_h_
2   #define _n1_h_
3   #include "adtss.h"
4   #include "n2.h"
5   #include "xor_memory_models.h"
6
7   class N1: public adtss::Network<port_value_t>
8   {
9     public:
10        static const int x1, x2;
11
12        N1():adtss::Network<port_value_t>(),
13            n2(),m()
14        {
15            n2.setParent(this);
16            m.setParent(this);
17        }
18
19        void getComponents(adtss::Set<adtss::Dtss<port_value_t>*>& c)
20        {
21            c.insert(&n2);
22            c.insert(&m);
23        }
24
25        void route(const port_value_t& value, adtss::Dtss<port_value_t>* src,
26            adtss::Bag<adtss::Event<port_value_t> >& r)
27        {
28            adtss::Event<port_value_t> e;
29            e.value = value;
30            // Input to the network
31            if (src == this) {
32                e.model = &n2;
33                r.insert(e);
34            }
35            // Output from N2
36            else if (src == &n2) {
37                // Output from the network
38                e.model = this;
39                r.insert(e);
40                // Input to M
```

```
41          e.model = &m;
42          r.insert(e);
43        }
44        // Output from M
45        else if (src == &m) {
46          // Input to N2
47          e.model = &n2;
48          e.value.port = N2::m;
49          r.insert(e);
50        }
51      }
52    private:
53      N2 n2;
54      Memory m;
55  };
56
57  #endif
```

_____ ***Revised N2 Model*** _____

```
1   #ifndef _n2_h_
2   #define _n2_h_
3   #include "adtss.h"
4   #include "xor_memory_models.h"
5
6   class N2: public adtss::Network<port_value_t>
7   {
8     public:
9       static const int m, x1, x2;
10
11      N2():adtss::Network<port_value_t>(),
12          xor1(),xor2()
13      {
14          xor1.setParent(this);
15          xor2.setParent(this);
16      }
17
18      void getComponents(adtss::Set<adtss::Dtss<port_value_t>*>& c)
19      {
20          c.insert(&xor1);
21          c.insert(&xor2);
22      }
23
24      void route(const port_value_t& value, adtss::Dtss<port_value_t>* src,
25          adtss::Bag<adtss::Event<port_value_t> >& r)
26      {
27          adtss::Event<port_value_t> e;
28          e.value = value;
29          // Input to the network
```

```
30          if (src == this) {
31              // Input to the m port
32              if (value.port == m) e.model = &xor2;
33              // Input to one of the bit ports
34              else e.model = &xor1;
35              r.insert(e);
36          }
37          // Output from O1
38          else if (src == &xor1) {
39              // Input to O2
40              e.model = &xor2;
41              r.insert(e);
42          }
43          // Output from O2
44          else if (src == &xor2) {
45              // Output from the network
46              e.model = this;
47              r.insert(e);
48          }
49      }
50   private:
51      Xor xor1, xor2;
52  };
53
54  #endif
```

The main function is modified to accommodate the new *Simulator* and *EventListener* interfaces. The *EventListener*, because it now receives notification of output by every component, must filter the unwanted events. For this simulation, the *MachineEventListener* filters incoming events by examining their source and reporting output only from *N1*. Input to the simulation must also be put into an *Event* that carries both the input value and the model that is its target. This change is made in the while loop that extracts data from the console and advances the simulation clock.

The modified code is listed below. Given identical inputs, the bottom up simulation of the logical machine produces the same state and output trajectories as the top–down simulation. To demonstrate this fact, the simulation described in Section 3.2.4, preceding the code heading "Main program to Apply Input Immediately," is repeated here. Feeding the input

1 0
1 0
1 0
0 0
0 0
1 0
1 0

```
1 0
0 0
0 0
```

into the simulator gives the result

```
xx M0 C0        1 0     yy M1  C0-2     0 0 1
xx M1 C3        1 0     yy M2  C3-5     1 1 0
xx M2 C6        1 0     yy M3  C6-8     0 0 1
xx M3 C9        0 0     yy M4  C9-11    1 1 1
xx M4 C12       0 0     yy M5  C12-14   1 1 1
xx M5 C15       1 0     yy M6  C15-17   1 1 0
xx M6 C18       1 0     yy M7  C18-20   0 0 1
xx M7 C21       1 0     yy M8  C21-23   1 1 0
xx M8 C24       0 0     yy M9  C24-26   0 0 0
xx M9 C27       0 0     yy M10 C27-29   0 0 0
```

just as before.

_____ *Modified Main Function* _____

```cpp
#include "adtss.h"
#include "n1.h"
#include <iostream>
using namespace std;

class MachineListener: public adtss::EventListener<port_value_t>
{
   public:
       MachineListener(adtss::Dtss<port_value_t>* top):top(top){}
       void outputEvent(adtss::Event<port_value_t> x, unsigned int t)
       {
           if (x.model == top) cout << x.value.bit << " ";
       }
       void stateChange(adtss::Atomic<port_value_t>*,unsigned int){}
   private:
       adtss::Dtss<port_value_t>* top;
};

int main()
{
   // Create the model
   N1* m = new N1();
   // Setup the simulator and output listener
   MachineListener* l = new MachineListener(m);
   adtss::Simulator<port_value_t>* sim =
      new adtss::Simulator<port_value_t>(m);
   sim->addEventListener(l);
```

```
28    // Counters for the clock and machine cycle
29    int clck = 0, machine_cycle = 0;
30    // Run the simulation
31    while (true) {
32       // Get the input from stdin
33       adtss::Bag<adtss::Event<port_value_t> > input;
34       port_value_t x1, x2;
35       x1.port = N1::x1;
36       x2.port = N1::x2;
37       cin >> x1.bit >> x2.bit;
38       // Quit if the input has ended
39       if (cin.eof()) break;
40       input.insert(adtss::Event<port_value_t>(m,x1));
41       input.insert(adtss::Event<port_value_t>(m,x2));
42       // Print the time and input
43       cout << "xx M" << machine_cycle << " C" << clck <<
44          "\t" << x1.bit << " " << x2.bit << "\t";
45       // Print the time and output at the next machine cycle
46       cout << "yy M" << ++machine_cycle <<
47          " C" << clck << "-" << clck+2 << "\t";
48       // Advance the simulation by one machine cycle
49       for (int t = 0; t < 3; t++) {
50          clck++;
51          sim->computeNextState(input);
52       }
53       cout << endl;
54    }
55    // Clean up and exit
56    delete sim; delete l; delete m;
57    return 0;
58 }
```

3.4 MEALY/MOORE-TYPE SYSTEMS

The output of a Moore-type system is a function of its state; a Moore output function has the form

$$\lambda : S \to Y$$

These systems are already familiar to us. The output of a Mealy-type system is a function of its state and current input; a Mealy output function has the form

$$\lambda : S \times X \to Y$$

By discarding the input that is supplied to the output function, we can build a Mealy-type system to mimic any Moore-type system. In this sense, the Mealy-type system

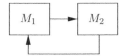

FIGURE 3.8 Two Mealy-type systems arranged in a feedback configuration.

is a more general construct. Why, then, did we not build our simulation engine for Mealy-type systems?

Trouble comes when we build a network of Mealy-type components. Suppose that we have two Mealy-type machines M_1 and M_2 arranged in the feedback configuration shown in Figure 3.8. These particular Mealy machines are a pair of identical finite-state automata with the state transition and output function shown in Figure 3.9. The circles show states, and the arcs show the response of the system to an input. The letter before the slash is the input that causes the state transition and the letter after the slash is the corresponding output.

We cannot know the output of M_1 without knowing the output of M_2, which supplies M_1 with input. We cannot know the output of M_2 without knowing the output of M_1, but this requires the output of M_2. This problem can be resolved only if there exists a consistent and unique choice of outputs for M_1 and M_2.

Suppose that M_1 begins in state p and M_2 begins in state q. The output from M_1 can be a or b. If it is a, then the input to M_1 is b and, therefore, so is the output from M_2. This, unfortunately, requires the input to M_2 to be b, and so the output from M_1 must be b, not a. We have arrived at a contradiction: the output from M_1 cannot be a.

Suppose instead that the output from M_1 is b. Then the input to it must be a. Therefore, the output from M_2 must also be a, but this requires its input to be a and so the output from M_1 must be a, not b. Again a contradiction: the output from M_1 cannot be b. Clearly, the machine cannot start in the state (p, q), and (q, p) is likewise untenable.

The state (p, p) gives us a small reprieve. If the output of M_1 is a and the output of M_2 is b, then the machine moves into the state (p, q), but then it gets stuck. The state (q, q) is a little more attractive. The complete system can move to the state (p, p) if both machines produce an output of a and then get stuck, or it can move (or, rather, stay) in the state (q, q) if both machines produce an output of b.

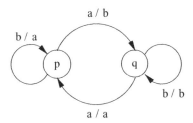

FIGURE 3.9 State transition and output function for the Mealy systems M_1 and M_2.

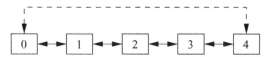

FIGURE 3.10 An arrangement of five cells in a one-dimensional cellular automaton. The dashed-connection is present when the cells form a ring, and absent when they form a line.

This particular problem is a symptom of more fundamental ills. A network of discrete models that has cycles without delays is, in general, ill-defined. The arrangement shown in Figure 3.9 is not a system because we cannot define a resultant for the network. In some special cases this problem might be avoided; our example, for instance, could be simplified by eliminating the state p and the arcs attached to it. With this simplification it is well behaved but not very interesting.

This problem will appear again in connection with discrete-event systems that react instantaneously to input. Prohibiting instantaneous events, and thereby eliminating cycles without delays, severely hobbles the modeler and is therefore impractical. A satisfactory solution is, perhaps surprisingly, found in the Moore-type discrete-time systems that we studied in this chapter.

3.5 CELLULAR AUTOMATA

The well-known "Game of Life," which was popularized in a *Scientific American* article in 1970 [48], is an instance of a class of systems called *cellular automata*. A cellular automaton comprises a set of discrete-time systems—the cells in the automaton—that are arranged in a grid. Each cell interacts with its immediate neighbors. In a one-dimensional cellular automaton, the cells are arrayed in a line and interact with their neighbors to the left and right; this is illustrated in Figure 3.10. To visualize the collective state of the cellular automaton, a color is assigned to each state of its cells, and these are drawn side by side. The trajectory of the automaton is depicted by arranging its subsequent states in order, one above the other. This creates a mosaic that can reveal surprising patterns in the collective behavior of the otherwise simple cells.

Cellular automata are easy to model and simulate as discrete-time networks. For illustration purposes, we will consider one-dimensional cellular automata with cells that have two states: white and black, abbreviated w and b. A cell is implemented with the *Cell* class, which is derived from the *Atomic* class of the simulation engine. The *Cell* has a state and a location within the cellular automaton. Its *delta* method accepts a structure that contains the state and location of the neighboring cells. Input from the left and right neighbors and the *Cell*'s current state are passed to a virtual method called *cell_rule*. This method examines its three arguments and returns the next state of the cell. To implement any particular cell, all that is needed is to implement the *cell_rule* method. The *output_func* method of the *Cell* simply returns its current state. The source code for the *Cell* class is listed below.

_____ *The Cell Class* _____

```
1   #ifndef Cell_h_
2   #define Cell_h_
3   #include "adtss.h"
4
5   typedef enum { BLACK, WHITE } state_t;
6   // Structure used for input to and output from a cell
7   struct IO_Type
8   {
9       state_t state; // The cell's discrete state
10      int src; // Location of the cell that produced the event
11      bool operator<(const IO_Type& other) const  // Needed by the STL
12      {
13          return src < other.src;
14      }
15  };
16
17  class Cell: public adtss::Atomic<IO_Type>
18  {
19      public:
20          // Constructor puts the cell into its initial state
21          Cell(state_t s0, int location):
22              adtss::Atomic<IO_Type>(),
23              s(s0),location(location) {}
24          // State transition function
25          void delta(const adtss::Bag<IO_Type>& xb)
26          {
27              // Edges are WHITE
28              state_t left = WHITE, right = WHITE;
29              for (adtss::Bag<IO_Type>::iterator iter = xb.begin();
30                      iter != xb.end(); iter++) {
31                  if ((*iter).src == location-1) left = (*iter).state;
32                  else right = (*iter).state;
33              }
34              s = cell_rule(left,right,s);
35          }
36          // Output function
37          void output_func(adtss::Bag<IO_Type>& yb)
38          {
39              IO_Type output;
40              output.state = s;
41              output.src = location;
42              yb.insert(output);
43          }
44          // The gc_output method is not needed
45          void gc_output(adtss::Bag<IO_Type>&){}
46          // Get the location of the cell
47          int getLocation() const { return location; }
```

```
48    // Get the discrete state of the cell
49    state_t getState() const { return s; }
50  protected:
51    // This is the rule for computing the cell's next state
52    virtual state_t cell_rule(state_t left, state_t right, state_t s) = 0;
53  private:
54    state_t s;
55    const int location;
56 };
57
58 #endif
```

The *CellularAutomaton* class, which is derived from the *Network* class of the simulation engine, contains an array of *Cell* objects. Output from a cell is sent to its two neighbors: output from the cell at position i goes to the cells at positions $i + 1$ (right) and $i - 1$ (left). Output from the two cells at the ends of the array can be discarded or sent to the cell at the opposite end. The array is initially empty, and cells are explicitly assigned to their locations with the *placeCell* method. The source code for the *CellularAutomaton* class is listed below.

The CellularAutomaton Class

```
1  #ifndef CellularAutomaton_h
2  #define CellularAutomaton_h
3  #include "Cell.h"
4
5  class CellularAutomaton: public adtss::Network<IO_Type>
6  {
7    public:
8      // Create an automaton with space for size cells
9      CellularAutomaton(int size, bool ring):
10         adtss::Network<IO_Type>(),
11         size(size),ring(ring)
12      {
13         cell = new Cell*[size];
14         for (int i = 0; i < size; i++) cell[i] = NULL;
15      }
16      void getComponents(adtss::Set<adtss::Dtss<IO_Type>*>& c)
17      {
18         for (int i = 0; i < size; i++) c.insert(cell[i]);
19      }
20      void route(const IO_Type& value, adtss::Dtss<IO_Type>* model,
21            adtss::Bag<adtss::Event<IO_Type> >& r)
22      {
23         adtss::Event<IO_Type> x;
24         x.value = value;
25         // Get the positions of the cells to the left and right
26         int left = value.src - 1, right = value.src + 1;
```

```
27        // Wrap the left end of the automaton to form a ring
28        if (left < 0 && ring) {
29            x.value.src = size;
30            x.model = cell[size-1];
31            r.insert(x);
32        }
33        // or just send the event to the left
34        else if (left >= 0) {
35            x.value.src = value.src;
36            x.model = cell[left];
37            r.insert(x);
38        }
39        // Wrap the right end of the automaton to form a ring
40        if (right == size && ring) {
41            x.value.src = -1;
42            x.model = cell[0];
43            r.insert(x);
44        }
45        // or just send the event to the right
46        else if (right < size) {
47            x.value.src = value.src;
48            x.model = cell[right];
49            r.insert(x);
50        }
51    }
52    // The destructor destroys the Cells too
53    ~CellularAutomaton()
54    {
55        for (int i = 0; i < size; i++)
56            delete cell[i];
57        delete [] cell;
58    }
59    // The placed cell is adopted by the CellularAutomaton
60    void placeCell(Cell* new_cell)
61    {
62        new_cell->setParent(this);
63        if (cell[new_cell->getLocation()] != NULL)
64            delete cell[new_cell->getLocation()];
65        cell[new_cell->getLocation()] = new_cell;
66    }
67 private:
68    int size;
69    bool ring;
70    Cell** cell;
71 };
72
73 #endif
```

TABLE 3.3 Bits Describes a
Cell's State Transition Function

Left, State, Right	Bit
bbb	7
bbw	6
bwb	5
bww	4
wbb	3
wbw	2
wwb	1
www	0

We could create each cell type, one at a time, by deriving new classes from the *Cell* class. Every cell maps three binary values—left input, state, and right input—to one binary value—the next state. The state transition function is completely defined by 2^3 cases: one for each combination of input and state. If each cell type is coded as a new class, then 2^8 classes are needed.

A more compact solution is to create one class called *BinaryCell* with a constructor that accepts a byte encoding the desired behavior. The encoding of the rules in the 8 bits is shown in Table 3.3. With this encoding, the rule is implemented by shifting the bits right: 4 bits for a left neighbor that is black, 2 bits for a state that is black, 1 bit for a right neighbor that is black, and 0 bits for a state and neighbors that are white. After shifting, the next state of the model is given by the least significant bit. The implementation of this class is shown below.

_____ ***The BinaryCell Class*** _____

```
1   #ifndef BinaryCell_h_
2   #define BinaryCell_h_
3   #include "Cell.h"
4
5   class BinaryCell: public Cell
6   {
7       public:
8           BinaryCell(state_t s0, int location, unsigned char rule):
9               Cell(s0,location),rule(rule) {}
10      protected:
11          state_t cell_rule(state_t left, state_t right, state_t s)
12          {
13              // Calculate the number of bit shifts
14              unsigned char shift = 0;
15              if (left == BLACK) shift += 4;
16              if (s == BLACK) shift += 2;
```

```
17        if (right == BLACK) shift += 1;
18        // Extract the outcome
19        if ((rule >> shift) & 0x01) return BLACK;
20        else return WHITE;
21      }
22   private:
23      const unsigned char rule;
24  };
25
26  #endif
```

The simulation program takes four arguments from the command line: the number of cells to use, the number of generations to simulate, a byte encoding the transition function, and a flag indicating whether the cells form a ring or a line. If a line is selected, then the color of the nonspace beyond the line's edge is white. An *EventListener* is used to update the display when a cell changes state and to save the final image in a file. The cellular automaton is created with a single black cell at its center and the other cells white. The main simulation program is listed below.

_____ *Main Simulation Program* _____

```
1  #include "CellularAutomaton.h"
2  #include "Display.h"
3  #include "BinaryCell.h"
4  using namespace std;
5  using namespace adtss;
6
7  // The event listener displays the state of the cells when it changes
8  class CellListener: public EventListener<IO_Type>
9  {
10   public:
11      // Create display for the simulation
12      CellListener(int num_cells, int num_generations):
13         display(Display::initializeDisplay(num_cells,num_generations)){}
14      // Draw the state of a cell to the off-screen buffer
15      void showState(const Cell* cell, int gen)
16      {
17         // Draw a white cell (red = green = blue = 255)
18         if (cell->getState() == WHITE)
19            display.setColor(cell->getLocation(),gen,255,255,255);
20         // or draw a black cell (red = green = blue = 0)
21         else display.setColor(cell->getLocation(),gen,0,0,0);
22      }
23      // Update the screen
24      void update() { display.redraw(); }
25      // The listener ingores output events
26      void outputEvent(Event<IO_Type>, unsigned int){}
27      // Update the appearance of the cell when its state changes
```

```
28        void stateChange(Atomic<IO_Type>* model, unsigned int t)
29        {
30            Cell* cell = dynamic_cast<Cell*>(model);
31            showState(cell,t);
32        }
33        // Save the image to a file
34        void saveImage() { display.toBmp("image.bmp"); }
35    private:
36        Display& display; // Reference to the display
37 };
38
39 int main(int argc, char** argv)
40 {
41    // Get the number of generations to run the simulation
42    if (argc != 5) {
43        cout << "Requires # cells, # generations, rule #, and ring | line"
44            << endl;
45        return 0;
46    }
47    // Get the model parameters from the command line
48    int num_cells = atoi(argv[1]);
49    int num_gens = atoi(argv[2]);
50    unsigned char rule = atoi(argv[3]);
51    bool ring = (strcmp(argv[4],"ring") == 0);
52    // Create the display
53    CellListener* listener = new CellListener(num_cells,num_gens);
54    // Create the cellular automaton
55    CellularAutomaton* automaton = new CellularAutomaton(num_cells,ring);
56    // Create the cells with a black one at the center and all others white
57    for (int i = 0; i < num_cells; i++) {
58        // Create and initialize the cell
59        state_t s0 = WHITE;
60        if (i == num_cells/2) s0 = BLACK;
61        Cell* cell = new BinaryCell(s0,i,rule);
62        // Display it
63        listener->showState(cell,0);
64        // Add it to the automata
65        automaton->placeCell(cell);
66    }
67    // Run the simulation
68    Bag<Event<IO_Type> > empty_input; // This is a closed system
69    Simulator<IO_Type>* sim = new Simulator<IO_Type>(automaton);
70    sim->addEventListener(listener);
71    for (int i = 0; i < num_gens; i++) {
72        // Display the output
73        listener->update();
74        // Compute the next state
75        sim->computeNextState(empty_input);
76    }
```

```
77      // Save the final image to a file
78      listener->saveImage();
79      // Clean up and exit
80      delete sim; delete listener; delete automaton;
81      return 0;
82  }
```

Wolfram [147] has cataloged all of the one-dimensional cellular automata. Our *BinaryCell* class uses Wolfram's encoding of the transition rule, but produces images with time beginning at the bottom rather than at the top as is done in Wolfram's catalog. Figure 3.11 shows Wolfram's rule 188, which produces diagonal stripes. Figure 3.12 is one of the more vibrant cellular automata that appears in the catalog. The two images in Figure 3.12 appear almost identical, but small differences appear after generation 30, when the cells at the edge first turn black. In both figures, the image on the left is produced by the cellular automaton when wrapped into a ring and the image on the right is produced when the ends are left dangling. The cellular automata in both cases have 60 cells and are simulated for 60 generations.

3.6 SUMMARY

This chapter introduced the fundamental concept of a dynamic system, a modeling framework derived from that concept, and a software architecture that satisfies the requirements established in Chapter 1. With very little embellishment, this foundation will support more complicated, but more useful, models of discrete-event and hybrid systems. A solid grasp of the basic concepts, as they are manifest in this relatively tame setting, is therefore crucial to what follows.

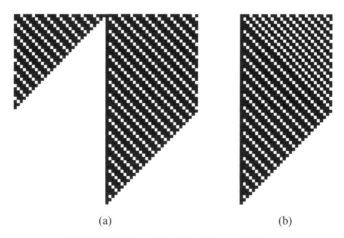

(a) (b)

FIGURE 3.11 Rule 188: (a) ring; (b) line.

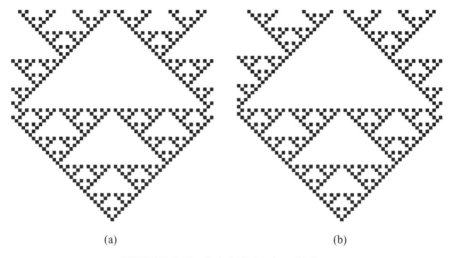

(a)   (b)

FIGURE 3.12   Rule 210: (a) ring; (b) line.

The discrete-event systems presented in Chapter 4 can both reproduce all of the examples in this chapter and offer an elegant alternative to the vending machine's awkward *wait* input, which was described in Section 3.1.3. Equipped with a good understanding of these discrete-time systems, we find that their reproduction as discrete-event systems is a helpful study aide (a task therefore left to the reader). The cellular automata, too, are reborn as discrete event systems and their scope expanded to permit stepping out of synch, which is an important feature of many agent-based models. Discrete-event systems are also an indispensable stepping stone to simulating hybrid systems, the topic of Chapter 5.

CHAPTER 4

DISCRETE-EVENT SYSTEMS

Discrete-event systems are a generalization of discrete-time systems that allow time to be continuous. The trajectories of a discrete-event system are functions from the time base $\mathbb{R} \times \mathbb{N}$ to its sets of input, output, and state. These trajectories change value only a finite number of times in any finite interval. This is the defining characteristic of a discrete-event system; the events that cause these discrete changes give the class of systems its name.

The expanded time base raises two issues that are responsible for the relatively complicated (with respect to discrete-time systems) description of discrete-event systems and their simulators. The first is that events may occur at any instant. Consequently, the model must include machinery to describe the subset of $\mathbb{R} \times \mathbb{N}$ where its events occur. The second is that time advances in a plane. Only the real part of this plane reflects physical time; the discrete part is an artifact of modeling change with instantaneous events (Maler and Manna offer an insightful discussion [82, 83]). The structure imposed on time to permit an orderly evolution of the system, although not complicated, is unlike the additive group typical of discrete time (i.e., with time base $\mathbb{N}$) and differential (i.e., with time base $\mathbb{R}$) systems.

Apart from these issues and their consequences, the basic approach to defining a state transition function and the general organization of the simulation software are unchanged. As with discrete-time systems, an iterative simulation procedure for simulating atomic models is derived from a state transition function, set of primitive segments, and the semigroup property. Likewise, a procedure is defined for reducing networks to their resultants, and this is embodied in a bottom–up simulation engine

Building Software for Simulation: Theory and Algorithms, with Applications in C++, By James J. Nutaro
Copyright © 2011 John Wiley & Sons, Inc.

comprising familiar pieces: the *Network* and *Atomic* classes for building models and the *Simulator* and *EventListener* classes for executing simulations.

4.1 ATOMIC MODELS

An atomic model of a discrete-event system has a set X of input, a set Y of output, a set S of states, and set Q of *total* states that are a subset of $S \times \mathbb{R}$. The total state $(s, e) \in Q$ has two pieces of information: the state s of the system and the real time e for which it has occupied that state. The occupation time is needed to completely define the system's behavior; unlike a discrete-time system, where input arrives at regular intervals and each state is occupied at exactly one point in time, a discrete-event system can linger in a state indefinitely and the response to input is influenced by the time spent dwelling there.

4.1.1 Time and Trajectories

The structure of time used here has been widely adopted, appearing (albeit implicitly or with different notation) in Matveev and Savkin's study of hybrid systems [84], Rönngren and Liljenstam's proposal for ordering events in parallel discrete-event simulations [122], in the abstract simulator described by Chow et al. [25] for parallel DEVS models, and as part of the Ptolemy II simulation environment [75]. Two elements (t_1, c_1) and (t_2, c_2) of the time base are equal if both components are equal; thus, equality is defined by

$$(t_1, c_1) = (t_2, c_2) \iff t_1 = t_2 \wedge c_1 = c_2 \tag{4.1}$$

Time is ordered first by its real part and then by its discrete part; the relation $<$ is defined by

$$(t_1, c_1) < (t_2, c_2) \iff (t_1 = t_2 \wedge c_1 < c_2) \vee t_1 < t_2 \tag{4.2}$$

The operator ϕ gives the real part of a pair (t, c):

$$\phi((t, c)) = t \tag{4.3}$$

The advance operator $\rhd$ takes the place of addition in the definition of a discrete-event system. This operator advances its first argument by an amount equal to its second argument according to the following rule:

$$(t, c) \rhd (h, k) = \begin{cases} (t + h, 0) & \text{if } h \neq 0 \\ (t, c + k) & \text{if } h = 0 \end{cases} \tag{4.4}$$

The $\triangleright$ operator, unlike addition for the real and natural numbers, is not commutative or associative. Observe that

$$(1, 1) \triangleright (0, 1) = (1, 2)$$

but

$$(0, 1) \triangleright (1, 1) = (1, 0)$$

and so $a \triangleright b \neq b \triangleright a$; the first and second arguments cannot be interchanged. Also observe that

$$((1, 0) \triangleright (1, 1)) \triangleright (0, 1) = (2, 1)$$

but

$$(1, 0) \triangleright ((1, 1) \triangleright (0, 1)) = (2, 0)$$

and so $(a \triangleright b) \triangleright c \neq a \triangleright (b \triangleright c)$; changing the order in which $\triangleright$ is applied changes the outcome of the calculation.

The trajectories of a discrete-event system are functions from $\mathbb{R} \times \mathbb{N}$ to the set X (an input trajectory), Y (an output trajectory), and Q (a state trajectory). The operator ℓ gives the real length of a trajectory, specifically

$$\ell(z < (t_1, c_1), (t_2, c_2) >) = \phi((t_2, c_2)) - \phi((t_1, c_1)) = t_2 - t_1 \tag{4.5}$$

Recall that the trajectories of a discrete-event system change only a finite number of times in any interval of finite length. The input and output trajectories satisfy one additional property—they are equal to the nonevent Φ at all except a finite number of points in any finite interval. Trajectories that satisfy this second property are called *event trajectories*, and legitimate discrete-event systems provided an event trajectory at their input produce an event trajectory at their output.[1]

Figure 4.1 illustrates an event trajectory. Real time flows from left to right. At each real instant of time there can be a finite number of discrete transitions. Discrete time at each point of real time flows from bottom to top. The value of each event is written at its location in the time plane.

The rules introduced in Section 3.1.1 for concatenating trajectories are unchanged, but the convenience of "translate and concatenate," the $\bullet$ operator, is lost because without addition trajectories are not easily translated. The $\cdot$ operator is still applicable, and it will play the same role in defining the state transition function of a discrete-event system that it played for discrete-time systems.

---

[1]A system that, given an event trajectory at its input, does not produce an event trajectory at its output is called *illegitimate* or, more recently, *Zeno*. The term illegitimate is due to Zeigler (see, e.g., Ref. 152); Zeno is a modern term, inspired by Zeno's paradox of Achilles and the Tortoise, for the same concept (see, e.g., Ref. 160).

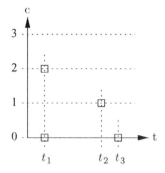

FIGURE 4.1 An event trajectory with an events at $(t_1, 0)$, $(t_1, 2)$, $(t_2, 1)$, and $(t_3, 0)$.

4.1.2 The State Transition Function

Discrete-event systems can act autonomously, changing state and producing output without any provocation from their environment. A system may also act on input, either responding immediately or after a delay. The time advance function is used for both of these purposes; it schedules output from the model and autonomous changes in its state.

The time advance function has the form

$$ta : S \rightarrow R_0^\infty$$

where R_0^∞ is the set of nonnegative real numbers with infinity:

$$R_0^\infty = \{x \mid x \in \mathbb{R} \wedge x \geq 0\} \cup \{\infty\}$$

The duration of a state s is the value assigned to it by the time advance function. On entering s, the system remains in that state until $ta(s)$ elapses or some intervening input drives the system into a new state. The set Q of *total* states is defined in terms of the time advance function by

$$Q = \{(s, e) \mid s \in S \wedge 0 \leq e \leq ta(s)\} \tag{4.6}$$

Three things are need to compute the state transition function of a discrete-event system: a total state, a time advance function, and an input trajectory. With these factors the state transition function constructs a state trajectory that is piecewise constant. The state of the discrete-event system changes when events appear in the input trajectory and when autonomous changes are indicated by the time advance function.

Recall that to define the state transition function of a discrete-time system, the input trajectory was decomposed into pieces of unit length and fed, one at a time, into the system. In a similar manner, an event trajectory is decomposed into primitive segments that either (1) have exactly one event, which starts the trajectory, or (2) contain no events. Specifically, a trajectory $x[t_\alpha, t_\beta)$ with events at times $t_1, \ldots, t_n$ is broken into the pieces $x_\alpha, x_1, \ldots, x_n$ such that the initial segment x_α is defined over the interval $[t_\alpha, t_1)$, the intermediate x_k, with $1 \leq k < n$, which are defined over $[t_k, t_{k+1})$, and the terminal segment x_n is defined over $[t_n, t_\beta)$. The segments x_1, $x_2, \ldots, x_n$ are equal to Φ everywhere except at their beginnings. The exception is x_α, which contains only Φ if $t_\alpha < t_1$ or has an empty domain with $\ell(x_\alpha) = 0$ otherwise. If x has no events or contains only a single event at its beginning, then it is already primitive.

The function δ takes an initial total state and a primitive segment $x[t_0, t_f)$ and returns the total state at the end of that segment. This is the discrete-event analog of the single-step transition function of a discrete-time system, but δ is complicated by the ability of the discrete-event system to take autonomous action. To traverse x, several small steps may be required by the time advance function and, consequently, δ is defined recursively. The recursion has five cases: input at the start of the trajectory, input and autonomous action that occur simultaneously, intermediate autonomous action, nonaction while advancing to intermediate events, and termination at the end of the trajectory.

Definitive action by the system is required in the first three cases, and for each a function is defined to describe the system's response. The effect of autonomous action is given by the internal transition function; it has the form

$$\delta_{\text{int}} : S \rightarrow S$$

and takes the system from its state at the time of the autonomous event to a subsequent state. The effect of an input is given by the external transition function. It gives the next state as a function of the total state (s, e) at the time of the input and the input itself; it has the form

$$\delta_{\text{ext}} : Q \times X \rightarrow S$$

where Q is the total set of states defined by Equation 4.6. It is possible for an autonomous action and an input to occur at the same time, and this case is the province of the confluent transition function. This is really a special case of the external transition function where $e = ta(s)$; it has the form

$$\delta_{\text{con}} : S \times X \rightarrow S$$

From an initial state $(s, e) \in Q$, δ gives the response of the system to a primitive trajectory $x[t_0, t_f)$ as

$$\delta((s, e), x[t_0, t_f)) = \tag{4.7}$$

1. Input event at the beginning: $\delta((\delta_{ext}(s, e, x(t_0)), 0), x[t_0 \triangleright (0, 1), t_f))$ if $x(t_0) \neq \Phi \wedge e < ta(s)$

2. Input event at the beginning with a simultaneous autonomous action: $\delta((\delta_{con}(s, x(t_0)), 0), x[t_0 \triangleright (0, 1), t_f))$ if $x(t_0) \neq \Phi \wedge e = ta(s)$

3. Intermediate autonomous action: $\delta((\delta_{int}(s), 0), x[t_0 \triangleright (0, 1), t_f))$ if $x(t_0) = \Phi \wedge e = ta(s)$

4. Nonaction: $\delta((s, ta(s)), x[t_0 \triangleright (ta(s) - e, 0), t_f))$ if $x(t_0) = \Phi \wedge e < ta(s) \wedge ta(s) - e \leq \ell(x)$

5. Terminal event: $(s, e + \ell(x))$ if 1–4 do not apply

The first two cases process the event at the start of the trajectory if such an event exists. Because x is a primitive trajectory, t_0 is the only possible location of an input. The third case executes autonomous events that are scheduled by the time advance function. The fourth case moves the system through real intervals of inaction that precede an internal event. In each of these cases, recursive calls to δ preserve the primitiveness of x; it comprises only Φ following the advance of t_0. The fifth case terminates the calculation if the real length of x is too short to accommodate the next autonomous action or if x is empty, in which case $x(t_0)$ is undefined and conditions 1–4 do not hold.

The total state transition function Δ gives the response of the system to an arbitrary event trajectory x. If x is a primitive trajectory, then

$$\Delta((s, e), x) = \delta((s, e), x) \tag{4.8}$$

If x is not a primitive trajectory, then it is decomposed into its primitive segments so that

$$x = x_\alpha \cdot x_1 \cdot \cdots \cdot x_n$$

and Δ is defined recursively by

$$\Delta((s, e), x_\alpha \cdot x_1 \cdot \cdots \cdot x_n) = \Delta(\delta((s, e), x_\alpha), x_1 \cdot \cdots \cdot x_n) \tag{4.9}$$

The total state transition function processes the trajectory one primitive segment at a time, and the calculation finishes when the last such trajectory is processed.

4.1.3 The Output Function

Output from a discrete-event system is due to its autonomous actions. The system can produce output in the absence of input, and it can produce output in response to input when the input induces an autonomous event. Just as with discrete-time systems, there is a delay between the introduction of an input and the production of an output, and this delay exists for the same reason—the discrete-event system is a Moore-type system. The delay imposed by the Moore formulation of the discrete-event system is $(0, 1)$, and this minimal delay occurs when the model has a time advance of zero. Longer delays occur if the time advance is positive.

The *total* output function Λ of the discrete event system has the form

$$\Lambda : Q \to Y \cup \{\Phi\}$$

and it takes the *total* state of the system to a value in its *total* set of output. The output function λ, like the internal, external, and confluent functions, defines the behavior of the system in terms of the set S of states; it has the form

$$\lambda : S \to Y$$

The total output function Λ is defined in terms of λ by

$$\Lambda((s, e)) = \begin{cases} \lambda(s) & \text{if } e = ta(s) \\ \Phi & \text{otherwise} \end{cases} \tag{4.10}$$

The elapsed time e is equal to the time advance when case 2, a confluent event, or case 3, an internal event, in Equation 4.7 occur, and so these two cases coincide with the production of an output.

4.1.4 Legitimate Systems

For a system to be legitimate, its time advance function must ensure that in any interval of real finite length the system takes only a finite number of actions. Conversely, to traverse an infinite sequence of states must require an infinite amount of real time. Specifically, every series of states $s_1, s_2, \ldots$ that can be produced by the system must be such that

$$\lim_{n \to \infty} \sum_{k=1}^{n} ta(s_k) \to \infty$$

Zeigler [157] gives two conditions that are sufficient to ensure that this is true:

1. The set S of states is finite and every cycle that can be produced by the state transition function includes a state s such that $ta(s) > 0$.
2. There exists a lower bound $b > 0$ such that for all $s \in S$, $ta(s) > b$.

The first condition is necessary and sufficient. Any system with a finite number of states must, in the absence of an external influence, settle into one particular state that has an infinite time advance or endlessly tour a set of states that require some positive time to traverse. The second condition is only sufficient. If the time advance is strictly positive, then time will always progress. It is possible, however, to have some subset of states that have a time advance of zero but always lead to a state with a positive time advance. In this case, the second condition is violated even though the system is legitimate.

Ames [4] distinguishes two types of illegitimate behavior. A chattering Zeno system gets stuck when it enters an endless sequence of states that have a zero time advance; a system with $ta(s) = 0$ for all $s \in S$ is one example. A genuinely[2] Zeno system has an infinite series of states that, although each has a positive time advance, violates the legitimacy criteria. For example, a system that traverses a series of states $s_1, s_2, \ldots$, where $ta(s_k) = 1/k$, is genuinely Zeno; the elements in this series of time advances are positive but the series converges to zero and its sum converges to a finite number. (The sum of the time advances converges to 2 and the system, begun in state s_1 at time t, gets stuck just prior to $t + 2$.)

Every reasonable model of a real system is legitimate. Illegitimate systems are usually due to errors made while building the model, and often these errors are discovered when a simulation program fails to stop. The examples given above are extreme, but illegitimate models can occur quite easily in practice, and care must be taken to avoid them.

4.1.5 An Example of an Atomic Model

A simple system that has a single input, single output, and single state variable will demonstrate the state transition and output functions. The model accepts a real-valued, nonnegative input that it multiplies by the elapsed time. The product is produced when a time equal to it has expired. If an input arrives while an output is pending, the new input replaces the stored value. An input that coincides with an output is treated as having an elapsed time equal to the time advance. On producing an output, the stored value is set to ∞. The functions that define this system are

$$\delta_{\text{int}}(q) = \infty$$

$$\delta_{\text{ext}}(q, e, x) = xe$$

$$\delta_{\text{con}}(q, x) = xq$$

$$ta(q) = \lambda(q) = q$$

We will feed this system four primitive trajectories and calculate, using Equations 4.7 and 4.10, the state and output resulting from each. The trajectories are

$$x_1[(0, 0), (1, 0)), \text{ with } x_1(t) = \begin{cases} 1 & \text{if } t = (0, 0) \\ \Phi & \text{otherwise} \end{cases}$$

$$x_2[(1, 0), (1, 1)), \text{ with } x_2(t) = \begin{cases} 0 & \text{if } t = (1, 0) \\ \Phi & \text{otherwise} \end{cases}$$

$$x_3[(1, 1), (2, 0)), \text{ with } x_3(t) = \Phi$$

---

[2] A chattering Zeno system is no less illegitimate than a genuinely Zeno system, and so this name is an odd choice.

and

$$x_4[(2, 0), (2, 2)), \text{ with } x_4(t) = \begin{cases} 2 & \text{if } t = (2, 0) \\ \Phi & \text{otherwise} \end{cases}$$

The system starts with $q = \infty$ and has been in that state for one unit of time. Using Equation 4.7 to compute its response to x_1, we have

$$\delta((\infty, 1), x_1[(0, 0), (1, 0))) = \delta((1, 0), x_1[(0, 1), (1, 0))) \qquad \text{(Case 1)}$$
$$= \delta((1, 1), x_1[(1, 0), (1, 0))) \qquad \text{(Case 4)}$$
$$= (1, 1) \qquad \text{(Case 5)}$$

With the system in total state $(1, 1)$, applying x_2 gives

$$\delta((1, 1), x_2[(1, 0), (1, 1))) = \delta((0, 0), x_2[(1, 1), (1, 1))) \qquad \text{(Case 2)}$$
$$= (0, 0) \qquad \text{(Case 5)}$$

With the system in total state $(0, 0)$, we apply x_3 and get

$$\delta((0, 0), x_3[(1, 1), (2, 0))) = \delta((\infty, 0), x_3[(1, 2), (2, 0))) \qquad \text{(Case 3)}$$
$$= (\infty, 1) \qquad \text{(Case 5)}$$

and the system returns to where it began. Finally, injecting x_4 gives

$$\delta((\infty, 1), x_4[(2, 0), (2, 2))) = \delta((2, 0), x_4[(2, 1), (2, 2)) \qquad \text{(Case 1)}$$
$$= (2, 0) \qquad \text{(Case 5)}$$

and the final, total state is $(2, 0)$.

The output trajectory $y[(0, 0), (2, 2))$ produced by this simulation is

$$y(t) = \begin{cases} 1 & \text{if } t = (1, 0) \\ 0 & \text{if } t = (1, 1) \\ \Phi & \text{otherwise} \end{cases}$$

and the state trajectory $q[(0, 0), (2, 2))$ is

$$q(t) = \begin{cases} \infty & \text{if } t = (0, 0) \\ 1 & \text{if } t \in [(0, 1), (1, 1)) \\ 0 & \text{if } t = (1, 1) \\ \infty & \text{if } t \in [(1, 2), (2, 0)) \\ 2 & \text{if } t \in [(2, 1), (2, 2)) \end{cases}$$

Next we construct the composite trajectory $x = x_1 \cdot x_2 \cdot x_3 \cdot x_4$. Its canonical decomposition into primitive parts is

$$x = x_\alpha[(0, 0), (0, 0)) \cdot x_1 \cdot (x_2 \cdot x_3) \cdot x_4$$

where x_α is an empty trajectory, x_1 and x_4 are as already defined, and the third primitive segment is $x_2 \cdot x_3$. Beginning again in the total state $(\infty, 1)$ and using Equation 4.9 to apply x gives

$$\begin{aligned} \Delta((\infty, 1), x_\alpha \cdot x_1 \cdot (x_2 \cdot x_3) \cdot x_4) &= \Delta(\delta((\infty, 1), x_\alpha), x_1 \cdot (x_2 \cdot x_3) \cdot x_4) \\ &= \Delta((\infty, 1), x_1 \cdot (x_2 \cdot x_3) \cdot x_4) \quad &\text{(Case 5)} \\ &= \Delta(\delta((\infty, 1), x_1), (x_2 \cdot x_3) \cdot x_4) \\ &= \Delta((1, 1), (x_2 \cdot x_3) \cdot x_4) \quad &\text{(Previous calculation)} \\ &= \Delta(\delta((1, 1), (x_2 \cdot x_3)), x_4) \end{aligned}$$

To calculate the response of the system to $(x_2 \cdot x_3)$, we use the fact that

$$\delta((1, 1), (x_2 \cdot x_3)) = \Delta((1, 1), x_2 \cdot x_3) = \Delta(\Delta((1, 1), x_2), x_3)$$

and proceeding from the inside to the outside, obtain

$$\begin{aligned} \Delta(\Delta((1, 1), x_2), x_3) &= \Delta(\delta((1, 1), x_2), x_3) \\ &= \Delta((0, 0), x_3) \quad &\text{(Previous calculation)} \\ &= \delta((0, 0), x_3) \\ &= (\infty, 1) \quad &\text{(Previous calculation)} \end{aligned}$$

as expected. Finally, applying x_4, we obtain

$$\Delta((\infty, 1), x_4) = \delta((\infty, 1), x_4) = (2, 0) \quad \text{(Previous calculation)}$$

just as before.

TABLE 4.1 Table-Driven Simulation of a Discrete-Event System

t	s	$ta(s)$	y	x	Type
$(0, 0)$	∞	∞	—	1	init,in,1
$(0, 1)$	1	1	—		ext
$(1, 0)$	—	—	1	0	in,out
$(1, 1)$	0	0	0		con,out
$(1, 2)$	∞	∞	—		int
$(2, 0)$	—	—	—	2	in
$(2, 1)$	2	2	—		ext
$(2, 2)$	—	—	—	—	final,0

Discrete-event simulation by hand is greatly facilitated with a table similar to the one used for discrete-time simulation (recall Tables 3.1 and 3.2). The table has six columns: the time t, state s, time advance $ta(s)$, output y, input x, and the type of event occurring at t. The start and end of the trajectory and its intermediate events can be listed in a separate table and marked off as they are used.

The first row is filled in with the initial time, state and related values, and the appropriate input; its event type is "init," and the initial elapsed time is recorded with it. Subsequent rows are filled by first determining the event type, which can be "in," "out," "int," "ext," "con," or some combination of these, and then filling in the columns according to the event type. An "out" event does not change the state of the system, but may have a value in the y column; similarly, an "in" event puts a value in the x column. The new state due to all other events is calculated using the state, input, and elapsed time from the previous row; the elapsed time in a given row is the difference between $\phi(t)$ in that row and the previous row. Note that output appears in every row where the elapsed time is equal to the time advance. The type "final" is assigned to the last row and it records the ending value of e. Table 4.1 shows a simulation of the abovementioned model using this method. The procedure is quickest if nonevents in the x and y columns and unchanged values in the s and $ta(s)$ columns are omitted from the table.

4.1.6 The Interrupt Handler in the Robotic Tank

The model of the tank's interrupt handler is a more complicated example of an atomic model. The event graph in Figure 2.6 illustrates its operation. The state space representation of this model must adhere to the two conventions that we established for it in Section 2.2.4; input changes the state variables immediately and without altering the time to the next interrupt, and output occurs immediately after the *End interrupt* event finishes its work.

The interrupt handler that is actually used in the tank simulator is slightly more complicated that the one shown in Figure 2.6. For reasons of computational efficiency, it restricts output events to instances where the voltage at the motors actually changes, whereas the event graph in Figure 2.6 indicates output after every *End interrupt* event.

When the interrupt handler was implemented in this way, the simulation was unable to keep up with time in the real world and could not be used interactively. The reason for this is that the interrupt handler provides input to the model of the tank's physics, and calculating a state change for that model takes a (relatively) long time. When the output of the interrupt handler is restricted to just those instances where the voltage actually changes, the simulation avoids unnecessary, time-consuming updates of the physics model and is therefore able to to be used interactively.

With this change, the code is simpler (but the event graph messier) if the model uses the output voltages e_l and e_r as state variables in place of the switch positions s_l and s_r. To determine when a new output value must be produced, two new state variables are needed to remember the voltages at the last output. These variables are termed e_l' and e_r'.

The operation of the interrupt indicator also requires a small modification with respect to its description in Section 2.2.4. An extra phase is needed to produce output after the *End interrupt* event occurs. The interrupt handler now has three distinct phases, corresponding to the two types of events and the production of an output. These phases are EXEC, WAIT, and OUTPUT. In the EXEC phase the model has executed the *Start interrupt* event and is waiting for the *End interrupt* event. In the WAIT phase the model has produced its output (if one was required) and is waiting for the *Start interrupt* event. In the discrete instant of time between the EXEC and WAIT phases is the transitory OUTPUT phase, and it changes the voltage signal.

The period between interrupts is most conveniently expressed in terms of the desired signal frequency, rather than in terms of the number of machine cycles that separate interrupts. There are (see beginning of Section 2.2.4) about eight calls to the interrupt handler in each period of the voltage signal. Therefore, a voltage signal with frequency f_e requires an interrupt period t_e given by

$$t_e = \frac{1}{8f_e} \tag{4.11}$$

With these changes, the complete set of state variables are the voltages e_l and e_r at the motors; the last voltages e_l' and e_r' supplied as output, the counter c, the left motor ON time o_l and right motor ON time o_r, the directions r_l and r_r of the left and right motors, the phase i (which was the Boolean interrupt indicator), and the time σ remaining until the next event. The range of the voltage variables is the set $\{0, -7.2, 7.2\}$. The range of the counter and the motor ON times is the set of natural numbers in the interval $[0, 255]$. The direction indicators r_l and r_r are true if the motor runs in reverse and false otherwise. The phase i has the range $\{$ EXEC, WAIT, OUTPUT$\}$. The time σ remaining to the next event has the range $[0, \max\{t_e, 432 \times 10^{-6}\}]$. The state of the model can be written, although somewhat awkwardly, as the tuple $(e_l, e_r, e_l', e_r', c, o_l, o_r, r_l, r_r, i, \sigma)$, and the set of states is the cross product of the ranges of the state variables.

For brevity

$$q = (e_l, e_r, e_l', e_r', c, o_l, o_r, r_l, r_r, i, \sigma)$$

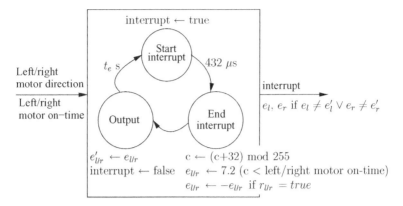

FIGURE 4.2 Corrected event graph for the tank's interrupt handler.

is used to indicate the state of the system. Input to the model has the form (o'_l, r'_l, o'_r, r'_r), which carries the desired values for the ON times and directional switches of the motors. Output from the model are bags that contain the interrupt indicator and, possibly, the pair of voltages (e_l, e_r).

In spite of its large set of states, the behavior of the model is quite simple. Figure 4.2 shows the modified event graph, which includes the new state variables and phase.[3] The *Output* and *Start interrupt* events produce output. As before, input is applied immediately but has no effect on the time of the next event.

The time advance function is the simplest part of the interrupt handler's definition. It returns the time remaining until the next event and is defined by

$$ta(q) = \sigma$$

The output function generates events at the start and end of an interrupt. An interrupt begins when the time advance expires and the model is in its WAIT phase. At this time, an *interrupt* signal is produced for the packet processor. An interrupt ends when the time advance expires and the model is in its OUTPUT phase. Another *interrupt* signal is produced at this time, along with new voltage values for the motors. Specifically, we obtain

$$\lambda(q) = \begin{cases} \{interrupt\} & \text{if } i = \text{WAIT} \\ \{interrupt\} & \text{if } i = \text{OUTPUT} \wedge (e_l = e'_l \wedge e_r = e'_r) \\ \{interrupt, (e_l, e_r)\} & \text{if } i = \text{OUTPUT} \wedge (e_l \neq e'_l \vee e_r \neq e'_r) \\ \Phi & \text{otherwise} \end{cases}$$

---

[3]False predicates have a numerical value of zero and true predicates a value of one. So, for example, the voltage e_l is 7.2 if $c <$ left motor ON time and 0 if it is not.

```
1  if i = WAIT then
2      i ← EXEC
3      σ ← 432 × 10⁻⁶
4  else if i = EXEC then
5      c ← c + 32 mod 255
6      e_l ← 7.2(c < o_l)
7      e_r ← 7.2(c < o_r)
8      if r_l = true then  e_l ← −e_l
9      if r_r = true then  e_r ← −e_r
10     i ← OUTPUT
11     σ ← 0
12 else if i = OUTPUT then
13     e'_l ← e_l
14     e'_r ← e_r
15     i ← WAIT
16     σ ← t_e
17 end
```

Algorithm 4.1   The internal transition function of the interrupt handler.

The transition functions are only slightly more complicated. The internal transition function implements the logic for the *Start interrupt*, *End interrupt*, and *Output* events that appear in the event graph. The effect of an *Output* event is to set the values of e'_l and e'_r to e_l and e_r and to schedule a *Start interrupt* event. To schedule the event, the model is placed into its WAIT phase and σ is set to the interrupt period. The effect of a *Start interrupt* event is to schedule an *End interrupt* event. It is scheduled by putting the model into its EXEC phase and setting σ to the time needed to execute the interrupt. The effect of an *End interrupt* event is to increment the counter, set the voltage values, and schedule an immediate *Output* event. The internal transition function is calculated using Algorithm 4.1.

The external transition function is simpler. On receiving an input, it decrements σ and changes the ON time and direction of each motor. The response of the system to an input (o'_l, r'_l, o'_r, r'_r) is

$$\delta_{\text{ext}}(q, e, (o'_l, r'_l, o'_r, r'_r)) = (e_l, e_r, e'_l, e'_r, c, o'_l, o'_r, r'_l, r'_r, i, \sigma - e)$$

The confluent transition function applies the internal and then the external transition functions. In effect, this prioritizes autonomous action over input. The confluent transition function is defined by

$$\delta_{\text{con}}(q, (o'_l, r'_l, o'_r, r'_r)) = \delta_{ext}(\delta_{int}(q), 0, (o'_l, r'_l, o'_r, r'_r))$$

In spite of its simple dynamics, the size of the model's state space makes simulation by hand impractical. Therefore, a demonstration must wait until the necessary simulation software is built.

4.1.7 Systems with Bags for Input and Output

Just as with discrete-time systems, discrete-event systems in practice are built to accept bags of objects as input and produce bags of objects as output. This does not require any substantial changes to the basic definition of a discrete-event system, but the details differ in small ways. The sets X^b and Y^b are bags of elements from X and Y, and the output function λ and the transition functions δ_{ext} and δ_{con} have the forms

$$\lambda : S \to Y^b$$

$$\delta_{\text{ext}} : Q \times X^b \to S$$

$$\delta_{\text{con}} : S \times X^b \to S$$

These are used from this point forward.

4.1.8 A Simulator for Atomic Models

A simulation engine that has great practical utility can be constructed as a special case of Equation 4.7. This simulation engine will let us do four things with the model: (1) ask for the time at which its next autonomous action will occur, (2) ask for the output that it will produce at that time, (3) compute the autonomous action at that time, and (4) inject input into the model at any time in the interval spanning the last change of state and the next autonomous event.

The first two tasks are simple. If the the last event—internal, external, or confluent—put the system into a state s at time t_L, then the next autonomous action will occur at time $t_L \rhd (ta(s), 0)$. This is the amount of time that t is advanced by case 4 of Equation 4.7 when $e = 0$, that is, immediately preceding a change of state by cases 1–3. The output at that time is $\lambda(s)$.

For the last two tasks, the simulator accepts only two types of trajectories: an empty trajectory terminating at the next autonomous action or a trajectory that ends in a single input at some time $t \in [tL, tL \rhd (ta(s), 0)]$. The input trajectory x therefore spans the interval $[tL, t] = [tL, t \rhd (0, 1))$. If x has no events, then it is already a primitive trajectory; otherwise it is decomposed into $x_a[tL, t) \cdot x_1[t, t \rhd (0, 1))$. The model can respond to x in one of three ways:

1. $\delta_{\text{ext}}(s, \phi(t) - \phi(t_L), x)$ if $t < t_L \rhd (ta(s), 0)$
2. $\delta_{\text{int}}(s)$ if $x(t) = \Phi$ and $t = t_L \rhd (ta(s), 0)$
3. $\delta_{\text{con}}(s, x)$ if $x(t) \neq \Phi$ and $t = t_L \rhd (ta(s), 0)$

Cases 2 and 3 produce an output event at time $t_L \rhd (ta(s), 0)$.

In practice, the most important trajectories satisfy the above constraints; other types of trajectories end in stretches of inaction that are of little interest because s does not change. By restricting the allowable trajectories, the simulator cannot be started with an elapsed time other than zero. Nor can it be given a trajectory spanning, for example, $[t_L, t_L \triangleright (ta(s)/2, 0))$ that contains only nonevents, but nothing of interest occurs in this interval or anywhere that the elapsed time is not $ta(s)$ unless, of course, an input becomes available. So the usefulness of the simulator is not diminished by these restrictions.

Their chief advantage is an improvement in the computational speed of the simulator, and the importance of this improvement grows with the size of the model. For a single atomic model, these restrictions are clearly unnecessary and a simple, direct iterative algorithm derived from Equation 4.7 is more versatile. For large network models there is a noticeable benefit because we can take advantage of very efficient algorithms for event scheduling. Even greater benefits are derived when moving those simulations onto a parallel computer where the above mentioned restrictions are essential for obtaining good performance. For the moment, however, we will focus on the simple case of a single atomic model.

The simulator for an atomic, discrete-event model is similar to, almost a copy of, the simulator for an atomic, discrete-time model (see Section 3.1.5). The simulator for a discrete-event model has four classes: the *Bag* class, the *Atomic* class, the *EventListener* class, and the *Simulator* class. To avoid clashes with other libraries that might be used in a simulation program, these four classes are put into the *adevs* (*a d*iscrete-*e*vent system *s*imulator) namespace. The three main classes—*Atomic*, *Simulator*, and *EventListener*—and their relationships are shown in Figure 4.3.

The *Bag* is an alias to the *multiset* class from the C++ Standard Template Library. The *EventListener* class is identical to the one used in the discrete-time simulator.

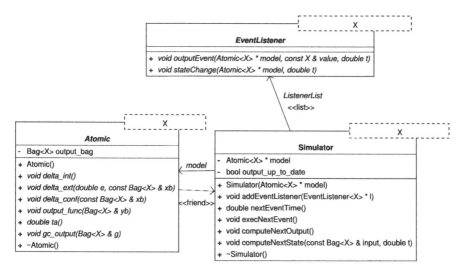

FIGURE 4.3 Class diagram of the simulation software for atomic, discrete event models.

It has two virtual methods that the *Simulator* invokes to notify the listener that an output was produced or that a state transition has taken place.

The *Atomic* class has six virtual methods. It retains the *gc_output* method that the *Simulator* uses to tell the model to delete objects it produced as output. It also retains the *output_func* method that implements the model's output function. The *delta* function of the discrete time simulator is replaced by three methods, one for each primitive transition function of the discrete event model. The *delta_int* method implements the internal transition function, the *delta_ext* method implements the external transition function, and the *delta_conf* method implements the confluent transition function. Finally, the method *ta* is added to implement the model's time advance function.

The *Simulator* retains the *addEventListener* and *computeOutput* methods of the discrete-time simulator, but where it has three methods for interacting with the simulation, the discrete-event simulator has four. Two of these methods are for obtaining information. The *nextEventTime* method returns the time of the next autonomous action. The *computeOutput* method invokes the *outputEvent* method of registered *EventListeners* to inform them of the model's output at the next event time.

The other two are for advancing the simulation clock. The *execNextEvent* method computes the output and next state of the model at the next event time, invoking the *outputEvent* and *stateChange* methods of all registered *EventListeners* as it proceeds. This method accepts no input; it executes the model's internal transition function. Input is applied with the *computeNextState* method. It accepts a *Bag* of input and the time at which to apply it, which must be less than or equal to the *nextEventTime*. At that time, an external or confluent event, as appropriate, is executed and the method notifies any *EventListeners* of the action by calling their *stateChange* and, for a confluent event, *outputEvent* methods.

Virtual methods, to be implemented by the programmer, constitute most of the simulation engine. The only class with a substantial implementation is the *Simulator*, and its implementation is shown below. Not in this implementation is the time pair (t, c). The real time t appears explicitly, but c is incremented implicitly each time *computeNextState* is called with the same argument for time. Nothing is gained by making the c explicit, except possibly to allow users of the *Simulator* to record the complete timestamp for each event. If this information is needed, it can be recovered with a counter that is set to zero each time the real part of the simulation clock advances and is incremented after calls to *computeNextState* that do not advance the clock.[4]

_____ ***Implementation of the Simulator Class*** _____

```
1   #ifndef _adevs_simulator_h_
2   #define _adevs_simulator_h_
3   #include "adevs_atomic.h"
4   #include <cfloat>
```

---

[4]The pair (t, c) appears again in Appendix B, where it is needed to build a simulator for multicore and multiprocessor computers.

```
5   #include <cassert>
6
7   namespace adevs
8   {
9
10  template <typename X> class Simulator {
11     public:
12        Simulator(Atomic<X>* model):
13           model(model),tN(model->ta()),tL(0.0),
14           output_up_to_date(false){}
15        void addEventListener(EventListener<X>* l)
16        {
17           listeners.push_back(l);
18        }
19        double nextEventTime() { return tN; }
20        void computeNextState(const Bag<X>& input, double t);
21        // Execute the autonomous event at time nextEventTime()
22        void execNextEvent()
23        {
24           Bag<X> empty;
25           computeNextState(empty,nextEventTime());
26        }
27        void computeNextOutput();
28     private:
29        Atomic<X>* model; // The model to simulate
30        double tN, tL; // Time of the next and previous event
31        bool output_up_to_date; // Is the output up to date?
32        // List of event listeners
33        typedef std::list<EventListener<X>*> ListenerList;
34        ListenerList listeners;
35  };
36
37  template <typename X>
38  void Simulator<X>::computeNextState(const Bag<X>& input, double t)
39  {
40     // If this is an external event
41     if (t < tN && !input.empty()) model->delta_ext(t-tL,input);
42     // If this coincides with an autonomous action
43     else if (t == tN) {
44        computeNextOutput();
45        if (!input.empty()) model->delta_conf(input);
46        else model->delta_int();
47     }
48     // Find the next event time
49     double ta = model->ta();
50     if (ta < DBL_MAX) tN = t + ta;
51     else tN = DBL_MAX;
52     // Set the simulation clock and notify listeners of the change in state
53     tL = t;
```

```
54    for (typename ListenerList::iterator iter = listeners.begin();
55        iter != listeners.end(); iter++) {
56      (*iter)->stateChange(model,t);
57    }
58    // Cleanup
59    model->gc_output(model->output_bag);
60    model->output_bag.clear();
61    output_up_to_date = false;
62  }
63
64  template <typename X>
65  void Simulator<X>::computeNextOutput()
66  {
67    // Return if the output function has been evaluated
68    if (output_up_to_date) return;
69    // Compute the output
70    output_up_to_date = true;
71    model->output_func(model->output_bag);
72    // Notify registered listeners of the output events
73    for (typename Bag<X>::iterator yiter = model->output_bag.begin();
74        yiter != model->output_bag.end(); yiter++) {
75      for (typename ListenerList::iterator iter = listeners.begin();
76          iter != listeners.end(); iter++) {
77        (*iter)->outputEvent(model,*yiter,tN);
78      }
79    }
80  }
81
82  } // end of namespace
83
84  #endif
```

4.1.9   Simulating the Interrupt Handler

An implementation of the interrupt handler developed in Section 4.1.6 demonstrates how the simulation software is used. The class *InterruptHandler* is derived from *Atomic*; its virtual methods are implemented to realize the model's transition functions, time advance function, and output function. Input and output to this model (and throughout the implementation of the tank; see Appendix A, Section A.2.2) are instances of the class *SimEvent*, which has two attributes: a union containing one of five types of specific events and a flag showing which of these types is actually present.

The interrupt handler reacts to events with the type *SimMotorOnTime* and produces events with the type *SimInterrupt* and *SimMotorVoltage*. The *SimMotorOnTime* event carries information about the ON times for the motors and the direction in which they should turn. The *SimInterrupt* event has no information other than its type, and the *SimMotorVoltage* event has the voltages at the left and right motors. Output produced by the model is not allocated dynamically, and so it does not need to be freed by the garbage collection method. The implementation of the *InterruptHandler* is listed below.

_____ ***Header File for the InterruptHandler*** _____

```
1   #ifndef INTERRUPT_HANDLER_H_
2   #define INTERRUPT_HANDLER_H_
3   #include "adevs.h"
4   #include "SimEvents.h"
5
6   // This is the model of the computer's interrupt handler.
7   class InterruptHandler: public adevs::Atomic<SimEvent>
8   {
9      public:
10        // Phases of the interrupt handler
11        typedef enum { OUTPUT, EXEC, WAIT } Phase;
12        // Create an interrupt handler that executes with the
13        // specified frequency.
14        InterruptHandler(double freq);
15        // State transition functions
16        void delta_int();
17        void delta_ext(double e, const adevs::Bag<SimEvent>& xb);
18        void delta_conf(const adevs::Bag<SimEvent>& xb);
19        // Output function
20        void output_func(adevs::Bag<SimEvent>& yb);
21        // Time advance function
22        double ta();
23        void gc_output(adevs::Bag<SimEvent>&){}
24        // Methods for getting the values of the state variables
25        unsigned int getCounter() const { return counter; }
26        unsigned int getLeftOnTime() const { return left_on_time; }
27        unsigned int getRightOnTime() const { return right_on_time; }
28        bool getLeftReverse() const { return reverse_left; }
29        bool getRightReverse() const { return reverse_right; }
30        double getLastLeftOutput() const { return last_left_v; }
31        double getLastRightOutput() const { return last_right_v; }
32        double getLeftOutput() const { return left_v; }
33        double getRightOutput() const { return right_v; }
34        Phase getPhase() const { return phase; }
35        double getInterruptPeriod() const { return interrupt_period; }
36     private:
37        const double interrupt_period; // Clock period
38        // Magnitude of the voltage at the motor when turned on
39        const double motor_voltage;
40        const double exec_time; // Execution time of the interrupt
41        double ttg; // Time to the next internal event
42        unsigned char counter, left_on_time,
43                  right_on_time; // On/off counters
```

```
44      bool reverse_left, reverse_right; // Motor direction
45      double last_left_v, last_right_v; // Previous output voltages
46      double left_v, right_v; // Next output voltages
47      Phase phase; // The current phase of the model
48  };
49
50  #endif
```

_____ *Implementation of the InterruptHandler* _____

```
1   #include "InterruptHandler.h"
2   #include <iostream>
3   using namespace std;
4   using namespace adevs;
5
6   InterruptHandler::InterruptHandler(double freq):
7      Atomic<SimEvent>(),
8      interrupt_period(1.0/(8.0*freq)), // Initialize the model
9      motor_voltage(7.2),
10     exec_time(0.432E-6),
11     ttg(interrupt_period),
12     counter(0),
13     left_on_time(0),
14     right_on_time(0),
15     reverse_left(false),
16     reverse_right(false),
17     last_left_v(0.0),
18     last_right_v(0.0),
19     left_v(0.0),
20     right_v(0.0),
21     phase(WAIT)
22  {
23  }
24
25  void InterruptHandler::delta_int()
26  {
27     // Start an interrupt
28     if (phase == WAIT)
29     {
30        phase = EXEC;
31        ttg = exec_time;
32     }
33     // End an interrupt and send the output
34     else if (phase == EXEC)
35     {
36        // Increment the counter
37        counter += 32;
38        // Compute the next output voltage
39        left_v = motor_voltage*(counter < left_on_time);
```

```
40      if (reverse_left) left_v = -left_v;
41      right_v = motor_voltage*(counter < right_on_time);
42      if (reverse_right) right_v = -right_v;
43      // Send the voltage and interrupt signal
44      phase = OUTPUT;
45      ttg = 0.0;
46   }
47   // Wait for the next interrupt
48   else if (phase == OUTPUT)
49   {
50      // Remember the last output voltages
51      last_left_v = left_v;
52      last_right_v = right_v;
53      // Wait for the next interrupt
54      phase = WAIT;
55      ttg = interrupt_period;
56   }
57 }
58
59 void InterruptHandler::delta_ext(double e, const Bag<SimEvent>& xb)
60 {
61    // Decrement the time to go
62    ttg -= e;
63    // Look for input
64    for (Bag<SimEvent>::iterator iter = xb.begin();
65         iter != xb.end(); iter++)
66    {
67       assert((*iter).getType() == SIM_MOTOR_ON_TIME);
68       left_on_time = (*iter).simMotorOnTime().left;
69       right_on_time = (*iter).simMotorOnTime().right;
70       reverse_left = (*iter).simMotorOnTime().reverse_left;
71       reverse_right = (*iter).simMotorOnTime().reverse_right;
72    }
73 }
74
75 void InterruptHandler::delta_conf(const Bag<SimEvent>& xb)
76 {
77    delta_int();
78    delta_ext(0.0,xb);
79 }
80
81 void InterruptHandler::output_func(Bag<SimEvent>& yb)
82 {
83    // If this is the end of an interrupt
84    if (phase == OUTPUT)
85    {
86       // If the voltage changed, then send the new values
87       if (last_left_v != left_v || last_right_v != right_v)
88       {
```

```
89      SimMotorVoltage volts;
90      volts.el = left_v;
91      volts.er = right_v;
92      yb.insert(SimEvent(volts));
93    }
94    // Send the interrupt indicator
95    yb.insert(SimEvent(SIM_INTERRUPT));
96    }
97    // If this is the start of an interrupt
98    else if (phase == WAIT) yb.insert(SimEvent(SIM_INTERRUPT));
99  }
100
101 double InterruptHandler::ta() { return ttg; }
```

An input trajectory is provided to the simulation program via standard input, and it computes the resulting state and output trajectory. The simulation ends with the last input. The frequency of the voltage signal that the interrupt handler produces is set on the command line. The implementation of this simulator is listed below. It is another example of a model being reused in a new context: the *InterruptHandler*, originally constructed as part of the interactive tank simulator, has been extracted from that simulator and is being reused in this new simulation program.

_____ ***Simulation of the InterruptHandler*** _____

```
1  #include "adevs.h"
2  #include "InterruptHandler.h"
3  #include <iostream>
4  using namespace std;
5  using namespace adevs;
6
7  // Listener for recording the state and output of the interrupt handler
8  class InterruptListener: public EventListener<SimEvent>
9  {
10   public:
11     InterruptListener(){}
12     void outputEvent(Atomic<SimEvent>* model,
13         const SimEvent& value, double t)
14     {
15        cout << "Output, t = " << t << ", ";
16        if (value.getType() == SIM_INTERRUPT)
17           cout << "interrupt" << endl;
18        else if (value.getType() == SIM_MOTOR_VOLTAGE)
19           cout << "el = " << value.simMotorVoltage().el <<
20              ", er = " << value.simMotorVoltage().er << endl;
21     }
22     void stateChange(Atomic<SimEvent>* model, double t)
23     {
24        InterruptHandler* ih = dynamic_cast<InterruptHandler*>(model);
```

```
25          cout << "State, t = " << t;
26          cout << ", el = " << ih->getLeftOutput();
27          cout << ", er = " << ih->getRightOutput();
28          cout << ", e'l = " << ih->getLastLeftOutput();
29          cout << ", e'r = " << ih->getLastRightOutput();
30          cout << ",\n\tc = " << ih->getCounter();
31          cout << ",ol = " << ih->getLeftOnTime();
32          cout << ",or = " << ih->getRightOnTime();
33          cout << ",rl = " << ih->getLeftReverse();
34          cout << ",rr = " << ih->getRightReverse();
35          cout << ",i = ";
36          if (ih->getPhase() == InterruptHandler::WAIT)
37              cout << "WAIT" << endl;
38          else if (ih->getPhase() == InterruptHandler::EXEC)
39              cout << "EXEC" << endl;
40          else if (ih->getPhase() == InterruptHandler::OUTPUT)
41              cout << "OUTPUT" << endl;
42      }
43  };
44
45  int main(int argc, char** argv)
46  {
47      // Make sure that a frequency was given
48      if (argc != 2) {
49          cout << "Must provide a signal frequency" << endl;
50          return 0;
51      }
52      // Set the output precision to make the small time advances apparent
53      cout.precision(12);
54      // Create the model, event listener, and simulator
55      InterruptHandler* ih = new InterruptHandler(atof(argv[1]));
56      InterruptListener* l = new InterruptListener();
57      Simulator<SimEvent>* sim = new Simulator<SimEvent>(ih);
58      sim->addEventListener(l);
59      // Print the initial state of the model
60      l->stateChange(ih,0.0);
61      // Run the simulation
62      while (true) {
63          // Bag for injecting the input
64          Bag<SimEvent> input;
65          // The value to inject
66          SimMotorOnTime motor_setting;
67          // Time to inject the input
68          double t; int c;
69          // Read the time and input values
70          unsigned int o_l, o_r;
71          cin >> t >> c >> o_l >> motor_setting.reverse_left
72              >> o_r >> motor_setting.reverse_right;
73          motor_setting.left = (unsigned char)o_l;
```

```
74       motor_setting.right = (unsigned char)o_r;
75       // If this is the end of the input, then quit
76       if (cin.eof()) break;
77       // Simulate until time t and then inject the input
78       while (sim->nextEventTime() < t) {
79          cout << endl;
80          sim->execNextEvent();
81       }
82       // Simulate the transient events
83       for (int i = 0; i < c && sim->nextEventTime() == t; i++) {
84          cout << endl;
85          sim->execNextEvent();
86       }
87       // Inject the input
88       input.insert(SimEvent(motor_setting));
89       cout << endl;
90       sim->computeNextState(input,t);
91    }
92    // Clean up
93    delete sim; delete l; delete ih;
94    return 0;
95 }
```

For this example, the interrupt handler operates at 2000 Hz, and so its period t_e is precisely 6.25×10^{-5} s (Equation 4.11). The input trajectory $x[(0, 0), (t_e, 0)]$ has an event $x((t_e/2, 0)) = (255, 0, 255, 1)$, which sets the left motor to full ahead and right to full reverse, and an event $x((t_e, 0)) = (0, 0, 0, 0)$, which changes the motor settings to full stop before the computer has a chance to act on the previous command. The input file exp1 that describes this trajectory contains two lines:

```
3.125E-5 0 255 0 255 1
6.25E-5 0 0 0 0 0
```

Running the simulation produces

```
$ ./a.out 2000 < exp1
State, t = 0, el = 0, er = 0, e'l = 0, e'r = 0,
       c = 0,ol = 0,or = 0,rl = 0,rr = 0,i = WAIT

State, t = 3.125e-05, el = 0, er = 0, e'l = 0, e'r = 0,
       c = 0,ol = 255,or = 255,rl = 0,rr = 1,i = WAIT

Output, t = 6.25e-05, interrupt
State, t = 6.25e-05, el = 0, er = 0, e'l = 0, e'r = 0,
       c = 0,ol = 0,or = 0,rl = 0,rr = 0,i = EXEC
$
```

The simulator prints the initial state at time $(0, 0)$. The input trajectory sets the counters for the left and right motors at time $(t_e/2, 0)$. At time $(t_e, 0)$ the interrupt handler is activated and produces its {*interrupt*} output; simultaneously, the second input is applied, forestalling the activation of the motors.

The importance of minimizing the number of voltage events created by the interrupt handler is convincingly demonstrated by running the motors at half-power. The input file

```
0 0 127 0 127 1
1 0 0 0 0 0
```

spins the tank in a place for one second. The interrupt handler generates 35,753 outputs; 3972 of these are *SimMotorVoltage* events. The problem with producing a voltage event at every simulated interrupt is immediately apparent, the naive scheme produces 10 times more input events for the *TankPhysics* model, whose state transitions are time-consuming to compute. This extra work slows the simulator to a pace that is unacceptable for interactive use. Restricting *SimMotorVoltage* events to just those that represent a real change in voltage is an essential optimization.

4.2   NETWORK MODELS

Networks of discrete-time models and networks of discrete event models are constructed in the same way. The network has a set of component models, connections between those models, and connections between the input and output of the network and the input and output of its components. Discrete-event networks are closed under coupling, and the procedure for reducing a network to its atomic equivalent defines the simulation procedure for multicomponent systems. These aspects will all be familiar from the study of discrete-time systems undertaken in Chapter 3.

Because the atomic components of a discrete-event model each operate at their own pace, the resultant of a discrete-event network is more complicated than its discrete-time counterpart. The new complications are due almost entirely to the time advance function. Discounting these particulars, the material in this section will be familiar from Chapter 3. Input and output events are routed recursively through the model. Also familiar are the basic steps of the algorithm: calculating outputs, transforming outputs into inputs, and then computing new states. The interface to the simulator also remains essentially unchanged.

4.2.1   The Parts of a Network Model

The structure and composition of a discrete-event network are defined in exactly the same way as with a discrete-time network. Summarizing Section 3.2.1, a network model is defined by

X_N = set of input to network

Y_N = set of output from network

D = set of components

$\bar{I} = \{I_d \mid d \in D \cup \{N\}\}$family of sets of influencers

$Z = \{z_{d',d} \mid d' \in I_d \text{ and } d \in D \cup \{N\}\}$set of coupling functions where

$$z_{N,d} : X_N^b \rightarrow X_d^b$$

$$z_{d',N} : Y_{d'}^b \rightarrow Y_N^b$$

$$z_{d',d} : Y_{d'}^b \rightarrow X_d^b$$

Also recall that the sets I_d of influencers define sets E_d of influencees (see Section 3.2.4), by

$$E_d = \{d' \mid d \in I_{d'}\}$$

and that this set is used in the construction of the simulator.

4.2.2 The Resultant of a Network Model

The resultant of a network of discrete event models is an atomic model whose set of states, transition functions, and output function are defined by its interconnected components. To simplify notation that would otherwise be very messy, the construction undertaken here assumes that all of the network's components are atomic models (this is the same approach taken by Zeigler [157]). Section 3.2.2 describes the recursive descent into the network that completes the reduction procedure.

The sets of input and output of the resultant are the sets X_N and Y_N of the network. The set S_r of states of the resultant is the cross product of the sets of total states of its components so that

$$S_r = \times_{d \in D} Q_d \tag{4.12}$$

and the time advance function ta_r of the resultant is

$$ta_r(s_r) = \min_{d \in D} ta_d(s_d) - e_d \tag{4.13}$$

which gives the least time remaining until the next autonomous action in the network.

The imminent components are those that will next undergo an autonomous event; they constitute the set

$$IMM = \{d \mid ta_d(s_d) - e_d = ta_r(s_r)\} \tag{4.14}$$

The subset $IMM \cap I_N$, which are attached to output of the network, contribute their output events to the network's output; its output function is

$$\lambda_r(s_r) = \cup_{d \in IMM \cap I_N} z_{d,N}(\lambda_d(s_d)) \tag{4.15}$$

The transition functions of the resultant are more complicated. Before a new state is computed for a component, the inputs to it must be known. These are found in almost exactly the same way as in a discrete time network, but only the imminent models produce output. The set of components $IMM \cap (I_d - \{N\})$ provide input to d at an internal or confluent transition of the resultant, and the input provided by these is

$$x_d^b = \cup_{d' \in IMM \cap (I_d - \{N\})} z_{d',d}(\lambda_{d'}(s_{d'})) \tag{4.16}$$

This bag of values does not include contributions from input to the network, but it does include all of the input to a component that originates with its siblings.

At an internal transition of the resultant, there is no input to the network. Therefore, Equation 4.16 is sufficient for calculating inputs to the components, and the internal transition function is defined by

$$\delta_{\text{int},r}(s_r) = ((s_1', e_1'), (s_2', e_2'), \ldots, (s_n', e_n')) \tag{4.17}$$

where

$$(s_j', e_j') = \begin{cases} (s_j, e_j + ta(s_r)) & \text{if } x_j^b = \emptyset \land j \notin IMM \\ (\delta_{\text{int},j}(s_j), 0) & \text{if } x_j^b = \emptyset \land j \in IMM \\ (\delta_{\text{ext},j}(s_j, e_j + ta(s_r), x_j^b), 0) & \text{if } x_j^b \neq \emptyset \land j \notin IMM \\ (\delta_{\text{con},j}(s_j, x_j^b), 0) & \text{if } x_j^b \neq \emptyset \land j \in IMM \end{cases}$$

The internal transition function alters the state of the resultant by altering the states of its components, and for each component there are four possible outcomes. In the first case, no event occurs at the component and only its elapsed time is advanced. The other three cases change the state of the component according to its disposition: an internal event if it is imminent, an external event if it receives input, and a confluent event if both of these conditions apply.

At an external transition of the resultant there are no imminent models and only the input x_r^b to the resultant can induce a change of state in its components. The external transition function of the resultant moves its input to the appropriate sets of components and changes their states with their external transition functions. All of the other components sit idly, merely having their elapsed time advanced. The external transition function is defined by

$$\delta_{\text{ext},r}(s_r, e, x_r^b) = ((s_1', e_1'), (s_2', e_2'), \ldots, (s_n', e_n')) \tag{4.18}$$

where

$$(s_j', e_j') = \begin{cases} (s_j, e_j + e) & \text{if } N \notin I_j \vee z_{N,j}(x_r^b) = \emptyset \\ (\delta_{\text{ext},j}(s_j, e_j + e, z_{N,j}(x_r^b)), 0) & \text{otherwise} \end{cases}$$

The first case applies to a component that receives no input from the network, and the second case applies to all other components.

The confluent transition function is nearly identical to the internal transition function, but includes a special provision for components that are influenced by the network. For this purpose, the set of functions $\zeta_j(x^b)$ are defined, one for each component, to give its collective input received from its siblings and the network. For each $j \in D$, ζ_j accepts a bag of input x^b to the network and gives the bag of input to j as

$$\zeta_j(x^b) = \begin{cases} x_j^b & \text{if } N \notin I_j \\ x_j^b \cup z_{N,j}(x^b) & \text{if } N \in I_j \end{cases} \tag{4.19}$$

The x_j^b in this equation is defined by Equation 4.16. The definition of the confluent transition function is

$$\delta_{\text{con},r}(s_r, x_r^b) = ((s_1', e_1'), (s_2', e_2'), \ldots, (s_n', e_n')) \tag{4.20}$$

where

$$(s_j', e_j') = \begin{cases} (s_j, e_j + ta(s_r)) & \text{if } \zeta_j(x_r^b) = \emptyset \wedge j \notin IMM \\ (\delta_{\text{int},j}(s_j), 0) & \text{if } \zeta_j(x_r^b) = \emptyset \wedge j \in IMM \\ (\delta_{\text{ext},j}(s_j, e_j + ta(s_r), \zeta_j(x_r^b)), 0) & \text{if } \zeta_j(x_r^b) \neq \emptyset \wedge j \notin IMM \\ (\delta_{\text{con},j}(s_j, \zeta_j(x_r^b)), 0) & \text{if } \zeta_j(x_r^b) \neq \emptyset \wedge j \in IMM \end{cases}$$

This is identical to Equation 4.17 except that the bag of input to each component contains contributions from the network.

4.2.3   An Example of a Network Model and Its Resultant

This example consists of two machines for working metal. A press flattens small, metal balls into disks. It has a bin to hold balls that are waiting to be pressed. A drill

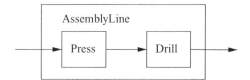

FIGURE 4.4 A press and drill.

puts a hole in the center of each disk, and it also has a bin to hold disks waiting to be drilled. The press flattens a ball in one second, but the drill needs two seconds to do its job. These machines are connected as shown in Figure 4.4. The algebraic description of this network is easily deduced from the diagram (see Section 3.2.1).

Input to and output from the network and its components are natural numbers that describe a quantity of parts: balls and disks with and without holes. Using the subscript m to denote a machine model and t_m the machining time, we can express the set of states of a machine as

$$S_m = \mathbb{N} \times R_0^\infty$$

where $(p, \sigma) \in S_m$ describes the number p of parts for the machine to process and the time σ remaining to process the first of those parts. The time advance is

$$ta_m((p, \sigma)) = \begin{cases} \sigma & \text{if } p > 0 \\ \infty & \text{otherwise} \end{cases}$$

and when this time expires, the internal transition function

$$\delta_{int,m}((p, \sigma)) = (p - 1, t_m)$$

removes the part from the machine and the output function

$$\lambda_m((p, \sigma)) = 1$$

makes the part available to the next machine in the assembly line.

On receiving a number q of parts, the external transition function

$$\delta_{ext,m}((p, \sigma), e, q) = \begin{cases} (p + q, \sigma - e) & \text{if } p > 0 \\ (p + q, t_m) & \text{if } p = 0 \end{cases}$$

places the parts into the bin and begins operating on one of them if the bin was empty. When new parts arrive and a part is completed simultaneously, the confluent transition function

$$\delta_{\text{con},m}((p, \sigma), q) = (p + q - 1, t_m)$$

ejects the completed part, stores the incoming parts, and begins operating on a new part.

The model of the assembly line has two copies of the machine model; the model of the press is denoted by the subscript p and the drill, by d. The subscript r is used for the resultant of the network, and its state is

$$s_r = (((p_p, \sigma_p), e_p), ((p_d, \sigma_d), e_d))$$

The drill and press begin without parts in their bins. Their initial states are $(0, 2)$ and $(0, 1)$, respectively. The initial state of the resultant is $(((0, 1), 0), ((0, 2), 0))$, and its elapsed time e_r is zero. For this experiment, the input to the assembly line is

$$x[(0, 0), (3, 0)) = \begin{cases} 1 & \text{if } t = (0, 0) \\ 2 & \text{if } t = (1, 1) \\ \Phi & \text{otherwise} \end{cases}$$

The primitive decomposition of this trajectory has three parts: the empty trajectory $x_\alpha[(0, 0), (0, 0))$, the first input trajectory $x_1[(0, 0), (1, 1))$ with $x_1((0, 0)) = 1$, and the second input trajectory and $x_2[(1, 1), (3, 0))$ with $x_2((1, 1)) = 2$.

Case 5 of Equation 4.7 processes x_α without altering the state or elapsed time, and x_1 is processed next. Case 1 of Equation 4.7 changes the state of the system to

$$\delta_{ext,r}((((0, 1), 0), ((0, 2), 0)), 0, 1) = ((\delta_{ext,m}((0, 1), 0, 1), 0), ((0, 2), 0))$$

$$= (((1, 1), 0), ((0, 2), 0))$$

and time advances to $(0, 1)$. The time advance of the assembly line is now

$$ta_r(((1, 1), 0), ((0, 2), 0)) = \min\{1, \infty\} = 1$$

Case 4 of Equation 4.7 sets the elapsed time e of the resultant to 1 and advances the trajectory to time $(1, 0)$. The elapsed time is equal to the time advance, but the output of the assembly line is

$$\lambda_r(((1, 1), 0), ((0, 2), 0)) = \Phi$$

because the drill does not produce an output. Case 3 of Equation 4.7 now moves the system into the state

$$\delta_{int,r}(((1, 1), 0), ((0, 2), 0)) = ((\delta_{int,m}((1, 1)), 0), (\delta_{ext,m}((0, 2), 1, 1), 0))$$
$$= (((0, 1), 0), ((1, 2), 0))$$

at time $(1, 1)$ and sets $e_r = 0$. Case 5 finishes x_1.

The trajectory x_2 is applied next. The time advance of the assembly line is now

$$ta_r(((0, 1), 0), ((1, 2), 0)) = \min\{\infty, 2\} = 2$$

and so the input at time $(1, 1)$ triggers an external transition, putting the system into the state

$$\delta_{ext,r}((((0, 1), 0), ((1, 2), 0)), 0, 2) = ((\delta_{ext,m}((0, 1), 0, 2), 0), ((1, 2), 0))$$
$$= (((2, 1), 0), ((1, 2), 0))$$

at time $(1, 2)$ and setting $e_r = 0$. The time advance is now

$$ta_r(((2, 1), 0), ((1, 2), 0)) = \min\{1, 2\} = 1$$

Case 4 advances the time to $(2, 0)$ and sets $e = 1$. The output of the resultant at this time is

$$\lambda_r(((2, 1), 0), ((1, 2), 0)) = \Phi$$

because the drill needs another unit of time before it produces an output. Case 3 is applied at $(2, 0)$, and the next state is

$$\delta_{int,r}(((2, 1), 0), ((1, 2), 0)) = ((\delta_{int,m}((2, 1)), 0), \delta_{ext,m}((1, 2), 1, 1), 0))$$
$$= (((1, 1), 0), ((2, 1), 0))$$

at time $(2, 1)$ and $e_r = 0$. The time advance is now

$$ta_r(((1, 1), 0), ((2, 1), 0)) = \min\{1, 1\} = 1$$

and case 4 advances the time to $(3, 0)$ and sets $e_r = 1$. Now the drill produces its first part, and the output of the resultant is

$$\lambda_r(((1, 1), 0), ((2, 1), 0)) = 1$$

Case 5 ends the simulation.

This recursion amply demonstrates the definition of a network, but a table-driven procedure is more practical when hand calculations are necessary. The table contains

TABLE 4.2   Table-Driven Simulation of a Network of Discrete-Event Systems

	Press					Drill				
t	s	$ta(s)$	y	x	type	s	$ta(s)$	y	x	type
(0, 0)	(0, 1)	∞	—	1	in,init,0	(0, 2)	∞	—	—	init,0
(0, 1)	(1, 1)	1	—	—	ext	—	—	—	—	—
(1, 0)	—	—	1	—	out	—	—	—	1	in
(1, 1)	(0, 1)	∞	—	2	int,in	(1, 2)	2	—	—	ext
(1, 2)	(2, 1)	1	—	—	ext	—	—	—	—	—
(2, 0)	—	—	1	—	out	—	—	—	1	in
(2, 1)	(1, 1)	1	—	—	int	(2, 1)	1	—	—	ext
(3, 0)	—	—	1	—	out,final,1	—	—	1	1	in,out,final,1

a column for time and five columns for each component. As before, proceed row by row calculating input, output, and state transition events as required. In this case, however, the x column of each component will contain contributions from the y columns of its influencers. For this purpose, it is helpful to keep the coupling diagram near at hand. A repetition of the preceding simulation using a table-driven approach is shown in Table 4.2.

4.2.4   Simulating the Resultant

Just as was done in Section 3.2.4 for discrete-time systems, closure under coupling can be used to transform the simulator described in Section 4.1.8 for a single atomic model into a simulator for network models. For this purpose, four new classes are added to Figure 4.3: the *Network*, the *Resultant*, the *Event*, and the *Set*. The revised class diagram is shown in Figure 4.5.

The *Set*, *Event*, and *Network* classes are the same ones used in the discrete time simulator; they are described in Section 3.2.4. The *Event* class holds input to or output from a model, and it carries these events through the *Network*. The *Set* has four essential features; elements can be added to and removed from it, it contains at most one copy of each element, and we can iterate through its elements. The *Network* class has two abstract methods, one for routing input and output events through the network and another for getting its set of components. The *Network* also has a pointer to its *Resultant*.

The *Resultant* is an atomic model that encapsulates the *Network* and computes the state transition, output, and time advance functions defined for it in Section 4.2.2. As with the discrete-time simulator, the calculation of input for the components proceeds forward using the set E_d of influencees, rather than backward using the set I_d of influencers. The *Resultant* is otherwise an unadorned implementation of the time advance function (Equation 4.13), output function (Equation 4.15), and external (Equation 4.18), internal (Equation 4.17), and confluent (Equation 4.20) transition functions of the network.

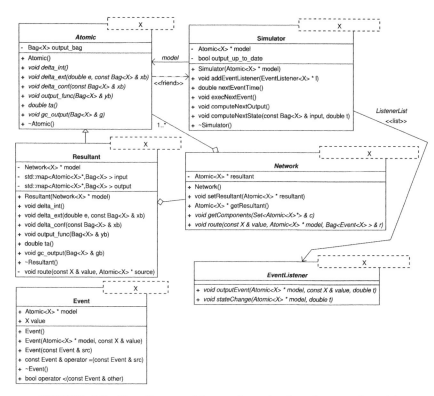

FIGURE 4.5 Class diagram of the top–down simulator for network models.

The implementation of the *Resultant* is listed below. The similarity of this *Resultant* with the discrete-time resultant extends even to the reuse of code; the *route* method is the same one listed in Section 3.2.4.

_____ ***Implementation of the Resultant*** _____

```
1   #ifndef _adevs_resultant_h
2   #define _adevs_resultant_h
3   #include "adevs_network.h"
4   #include <vector>
5
6   namespace adevs
7   {
8
9   template <typename X> class Resultant: public Atomic<X>
10  {
11      public:
12          Resultant(Network<X>* model);
13          void delta_int();
14          void delta_ext(double e, const Bag<X>& xb);
15          void delta_conf(const Bag<X>& xb);
```

```
16        void output_func(Bag<X>& yb);
17        double ta();
18        void gc_output(Bag<X>& gb);
19        ~Resultant() { delete model; }
20     private:
21        Network<X>* model;
22        // Structure for the state and elapsed time of the components
23        struct total_state_t
24        {
25           double e; Atomic<X>* m;
26           // The STL set needs the less than operator
27           bool operator<(const total_state_t& b) const { return m < b.m; }
28        };
29        std::vector<total_state_t> c;
30        std::map<Atomic<X>*,Bag<X> > input, output;
31        void route(const X& value, Atomic<X>* source);
32     };
33
34  template <typename X>
35  Resultant<X>::Resultant(Network<X>* model):
36     Atomic<X>(),model(model)
37  {
38     model->setResultant(this);
39     // Get the atomic components
40     Set<Atomic<X>*> ctmp; model->getComponents(ctmp);
41     // Set the elapsed time to zero and save the total state
42     typename Set<Atomic<X>*>::iterator iter = ctmp.begin();
43     for (; iter != ctmp.end(); iter++) {
44        total_state_t s;
45        s.e = 0.0; s.m = *iter;
46        c.push_back(s);
47     }
48  }
49
50  template <typename X>
51  void Resultant<X>::delta_int()
52  {
53     // Save the time advance because it will change as the state is updated
54     double time_adv = ta();
55     // Input for each component was computed in the output_func method and
56     // so only the new states are computed here.
57     for (typename std::vector<total_state_t>::iterator iter = c.begin();
58           iter != c.end(); iter++) {
59        // Get the bag of input for the model
60        Bag<X>& xb = input[(*iter).m];
61        // Is this model in IMM?
62        if ((*iter).m->ta()-(*iter).e <= time_adv) {
63           // Internal event if no input
64           if (xb.empty()) (*iter).m->delta_int();
```

```
65        // Confluent event otherwise
66        else (*iter).m->delta_conf(xb);
67        // Reset the elapsed time
68        (*iter).e = 0.0;
69      }
70      // otherwise, does it have input?
71      else if (!xb.empty()) {
72        (*iter).m->delta_ext((*iter).e + time_adv,xb);
73        (*iter).e = 0.0;
74      }
75      // just update the elapsed time otherwise
76      else (*iter).e += time_adv;
77    }
78  }
79
80  template <typename X>
81  void Resultant<X>::delta_ext(double e, const Bag<X>& xb)
82  {
83    // Send the input to the proper components
84    for (typename Bag<X>::const_iterator iter = xb.begin();
85         iter != xb.end(); iter++)
86      route(*iter,this);
87    // Compute next state of each component
88    for (typename std::vector<total_state_t>::iterator iter = c.begin();
89         iter != c.end(); iter++) {
90      // Get the bag of input for the model
91      Bag<X>& xb = input[(*iter).m];
92      // Update the elapsed time
93      (*iter).e += e;
94      // If it has input, apply the external transition function
95      if (!xb.empty()) {
96        (*iter).m->delta_ext((*iter).e,xb);
97        (*iter).e = 0.0;
98      }
99    }
100 }
101
102 template <typename X>
103 void Resultant<X>::delta_conf(const Bag<X>& xb)
104 {
105   // Send the input to the proper components
106   for (typename Bag<X>::const_iterator iter = xb.begin();
107        iter != xb.end(); iter++)
108     route(*iter,this);
109   // The confluent transition is the same as the internal transition
110   // when the network inputs have been routed to their destinations
111   delta_int();
112 }
113
```

```
114   template <typename X>
115   void Resultant<X>::output_func(Bag<X>& yb)
116   {
117       // Compute the output of each component and
118       // send those outputs to their destinations
119       for (typename std::vector<total_state_t>::iterator iter = c.begin();
120           iter != c.end(); iter++) {
121           // If this model is in the set IMM
122           if ((*iter).m->ta()-(*iter).e <= ta()) {
123               Bag<X>& y = output[(*iter).m];
124               (*iter).m->output_func(y);
125               for (typename Bag<X>::iterator y_iter = y.begin();
126                   y_iter != y.end(); y_iter++)
127                   route(*y_iter,(*iter).m);
128           }
129       }
130       // Copy the network output to yb
131       Bag<X>& y = output[this];
132       for (typename Bag<X>::iterator iter = y.begin();
133           iter != y.end(); iter++)
134           yb.insert(*iter);
135   }
136
137   template <typename X>
138   double Resultant<X>::ta()
139   {
140       double min_to_go = DBL_MAX;
141       for (typename std::vector<total_state_t>::iterator iter = c.begin();
142           iter != c.end(); iter++)
143           min_to_go = std::min((*iter).m->ta()-(*iter).e,min_to_go);
144       return min_to_go;
145   }
146
147   template <typename X>
148   void Resultant<X>::gc_output(Bag<X>& gb)
149   {
150       // Let the components clean up their output
151       for (typename std::vector<total_state_t>::iterator iter = c.begin();
152           iter != c.end(); iter++) {
153           (*iter).m->gc_output(output[(*iter).m]);
154           // Clear the output bag for the component
155           output[(*iter).m].clear();
156           // Clear the input bag for the component
157           input[(*iter).m].clear();
158       }
159       // Clear the input and output bag for the resultant
160       input[this].clear();
161       output[this].clear();
162   }
```

```
163
164   template <typename X>
165   void Resultant<X>::route(const X& value, Atomic<X>* source)
166   {
167       Bag<Event<X> > r;
168       model->route(value,source,r);
169       for (typename Bag<Event<X> >::const_iterator iter = r.begin();
170            iter != r.end(); iter++) {
171           // If this is an output from the network
172           if ((*iter).model == this) output[this].insert((*iter).value);
173           // otherwise it goes to an internal component
174           else input[(*iter).model].insert((*iter).value);
175       }
176   }
177
178   } // end of namespace
179
180   #endif
```

The press and drill will demonstrate how the simulation engine is used. The implementation of the machine model is listed below. This code mirrors the definitions given in Section 4.2.3. The constructor accepts the processing time t_m that distinguishes the drill and press, and it sets the initial state to $p = 0$ and $\sigma = t_m$. Also observe that the *delta_conf* method takes advantage of the fact that

$$\delta_{\mathrm{con},m}(s, q) = \delta_{\mathrm{ext},m}(\delta_{\mathrm{int},m}(s), 0, q)$$

The implementation of the assembly line, which is a reflection of Figure 4.4, is also listed below.

_____ ***Implementation of the Machine Model*** _____

```
1    #ifndef _Machine_h_
2    #define _Machine_h_
3    #include "adevs.h"
4
5    class Machine: public adevs::Atomic<int>
6    {
7        public:
8            Machine(double tm):
9                adevs::Atomic<int>(),
10               tm(tm),p(0),sigma(tm){}
11           void delta_int() { p--; sigma = tm; }
12           void delta_ext(double e, const adevs::Bag<int>& xb)
13           {
14               if (p > 0) sigma -= e;
15               else sigma = tm;
```

```
16        for (adevs::Bag<int>::iterator iter = xb.begin();
17              iter != xb.end(); iter++)
18          p += (*iter);
19      }
20      void delta_conf(const adevs::Bag<int>& xb)
21      {
22          delta_int();
23          delta_ext(0.0,xb);
24      }
25      void output_func(adevs::Bag<int>& yb) { yb.insert(1); }
26      double ta()
27      {
28          if (p > 0) return sigma;
29          else return DBL_MAX;
30      }
31      void gc_output(adevs::Bag<int>&){}
32      double getSigma() const { return sigma; }
33      int getParts() const { return p; }
34   private:
35      const double tm; // Machining time
36      int p; // Number of parts in the bin
37      double sigma; // Time to the next output
38  };
39
40  #endif
```

_____ ***Implementation of the Assembly-Line Model*** _____

```
1   #ifndef _AssemblyLine_h_
2   #define _AssemblyLine_h_
3   #include "Machine.h"
4
5   class AssemblyLine: public adevs::Network<int>
6   {
7      public:
8        AssemblyLine():
9          adevs::Network<int>(),
10         // Create the components
11         press(1.0),drill(2.0){}
12
13       void getComponents(adevs::Set<adevs::Atomic<int>*>& c)
14       {
15           c.insert(&press);
16           c.insert(&drill);
17       }
18       void route(const int& value, adevs::Atomic<int>* model,
19             adevs::Bag<adevs::Event<int> >& r)
20       {
21           adevs::Event<int> x;
```

```
22          x.value = value;
23          // External input to the network goes to the press
24          if (model == getResultant()) x.model = &press;
25          // Output from the drill leaves the assembly line
26          else if (model == &drill) x.model = getResultant();
27          // Output from the press goes to the drill
28          else if (model == &press) x.model = &drill;
29          r.insert(x);
30        }
31        Machine* getPress() { return &press; }
32        Machine* getDrill() { return &drill; }
33      private:
34        Machine press, drill;
35    };
36
37    #endif
```

The main function reads an input trajectory from standard input and injects it into the simulator. When the input ends, the program finishes executing the model's autonomous events, terminating when the time of next event is at infinity. An *EventListener* records the output and state of the assembly line as the simulation progresses. The main simulation loop and the listener are listed below.

_____ ***Main Simulation Loop for the Assembly-Line Model*** _____

```
1   #include "AssemblyLine.h"
2   #include <iostream>
3   using namespace std;
4   using namespace adevs;
5
6   // Listener for recording the state and output of the assembly line.
7   class AssemblyLineListener: public EventListener<int>
8   {
9     public:
10        AssemblyLineListener(AssemblyLine* assembly_line):
11          assembly_line(assembly_line){}
12        void outputEvent(Atomic<int>* model, const int& value, double t)
13        {
14          // Output from the AssembyLine
15          cout << "Output, t = " << t << ", y = " << value << endl;
16        }
17        void stateChange(Atomic<int>* model, double t)
18        {
19          // Print the state of the assembly line's components
20          cout << "State, t = " << t;
21          cout << ", press = (" << assembly_line->getPress()->getParts()
22              << "," << assembly_line->getPress()->getSigma() << "), ";
```

```
23          cout << "drill = (" << assembly_line->getDrill()->getParts()
24              << "," << assembly_line->getDrill()->getSigma() << ")"
25              << endl;
26      }
27   private:
28      AssemblyLine* assembly_line;
29 };
30
31 int main()
32 {
33    // Create the model, event listener, and simulator
34    AssemblyLine* assembly_line = new AssemblyLine();
35    Resultant<int>* r = new Resultant<int>(assembly_line);
36    AssemblyLineListener* l = new AssemblyLineListener(assembly_line);
37    Simulator<int>* sim = new Simulator<int>(r);
38    sim->addEventListener(l);
39    // Print the initial state of the model
40    l->stateChange(r,0.0);
41    // Run the simulation
42    while (true) {
43       // Bag for injecting the input
44       Bag<int> input;
45       // The value to inject
46       int blanks;
47       // Time to inject the input
48       double t; int c;
49       // Read the time and input values
50       cin >> t >> c >> blanks;
51       // If this is the end of the input, then quit
52       if (cin.eof()) break;
53       // Simulate until time t and then inject the input
54       while (sim->nextEventTime() < t) {
55          cout << endl;
56          sim->execNextEvent();
57       }
58       // Simulate the transient events
59       for (int i = 0; i < c && sim->nextEventTime() == t; i++) {
60          cout << endl;
61          sim->execNextEvent();
62       }
63       // Inject the input
64       input.insert(blanks);
65       cout << endl;
66       sim->computeNextState(input,t);
67    }
68    // Run until the simulation completes
69    while (sim->nextEventTime() < DBL_MAX) {
70       cout << endl;
71       sim->execNextEvent();
```

```
72      }
73      // Clean up
74      delete sim; delete l; delete r;
75      return 0;
76   }
```

Giving the input file

```
0 0 1
2 1 2
```

to the simulator repeats the calculations done by hand in Section 4.2.3. The manual simulation produced the response of the assembly line up to time $(3, 0)$. The computer simulation agrees with the manual simulation to that point, and goes beyond it to produce the final part at time $(7, 0)$ and terminate at $(7, 1)$. The output of this simulation is shown below. When reading the output, recall that the integer part of the clock advances implicitly when an output is produced or the state is changed: the first line shows time $(0, 0)$, the second $(0, 1)$, the third $(1, 1)$, the fourth $(2, 2)$ following the input at $(2, 1)$, and so on.

```
$ ./a.out < input
State, t = 0, press = (0,1), drill = (0,2)

State, t = 0, press = (1,1), drill = (0,2)

State, t = 1, press = (0,1), drill = (1,2)

State, t = 2, press = (2,1), drill = (1,2)

Output, t = 3, y = 1
State, t = 3, press = (1,1), drill = (1,2)

State, t = 4, press = (0,1), drill = (2,1)

Output, t = 5, y = 1
State, t = 5, press = (0,1), drill = (1,2)

Output, t = 7, y = 1
State, t = 7, press = (0,1), drill = (0,2)
$
```

A comparison of the outcomes produced by the file input_a with contents

```
0 0 1
3 0 1
```

and file input_b with contents

```
0 0 1
3 1 1
```

shows the importance of distinguishing between distinct events that occur at the same real time t. Putting input_a into the simulator produces

```
$ ./a.out < input_a
State, t = 0, press = (0,1), drill = (0,2)

State, t = 0, press = (1,1), drill = (0,2)

State, t = 1, press = (0,1), drill = (1,2)

Output, t = 3, y = 1
State, t = 3, press = (1,1), drill = (0,2)

State, t = 4, press = (0,1), drill = (1,2)

Output, t = 6, y = 1
State, t = 6, press = (0,1), drill = (0,2)
$
```

in which the state of the press at time $(3, 1)$ is $(1, 1)$ and the state of the drill is $(0, 2)$. Putting input_b into the simulator produces

```
$ ./a.out < input_b
State, t = 0, press = (0,1), drill = (0,2)

State, t = 0, press = (1,1), drill = (0,2)

State, t = 1, press = (0,1), drill = (1,2)

Output, t = 3, y = 1
State, t = 3, press = (0,1), drill = (0,2)

State, t = 3, press = (1,1), drill = (0,2)

State, t = 4, press = (0,1), drill = (1,2)

Output, t = 6, y = 1
State, t = 6, press = (0,1), drill = (0,2)
$
```

in which the state of the press at time $(3, 1)$ is $(0, 1)$ and the state of the drill is $(0, 2)$. Not until time $(3, 2)$ does the input drive the press into state $(1, 1)$. The trajectories in files input_a and input_b produce quantitatively different results.

4.3 A SIMULATOR FOR DISCRETE-EVENT SYSTEMS

A bottom–up simulator for discrete-event systems could be built just as the simulator for discrete-time systems was in Section 3.3. The algorithm would be nearly identical, with changes only to accommodate the definitions of the state transition function and output function of the discrete-event system. These changes would closely resemble the differences between the *Resultant* classes of the discrete-time and discrete-event simulators.

At any particular moment in time, most of the components in a large discrete-event system do not produce output or change state. If we are interested in just those moments when an event actually occurs, then a simple implementation, built in the mold of the discrete-time simulator, is wasteful of computational resources. There are three specific burdens that can be shed with a little effort.

The first burden is in the calculation of the network's state transition and output functions. The internal, external, and confluent transition functions of the *Resultant* iterate through every atomic model in the network and either compute a new state for it or update its elapsed time. It is likely that only a handful of those components will actually change state, and if we can deal with just those models, then the cost of incrementing the elapsed times of the others can be avoided. When a model has many components, this savings is substantial.

The second burden is in the calculation of the network's time advance function. This requires finding the minimum value in a set, and the naive implementation used in the *Resultant* iterates over every member of the set to find that minimum. If, however, the models are kept sorted in the order of their next event times, then the imminent models can be identified quickly when the output and state transition functions need to be evaluated.

The third burden is the memory required for the input and output bags used by the routing algorithm. These bags are required only if a model is producing output or receiving input, and these actions are relatively infrequent. In principle, only a small number of bags need be allocated for the small number of models that are active in each iteration. Doing this can save a substantial amount of memory when a very large number of components are being simulated. Moreover, the bags will generally hold only a small number of objects, and those do not need to be kept in any particular order. Two optimizations will take advantage of these facts to reduce the effort, in time and space, expended by the simulation engine to manage input and output events.

By accounting for these issues, an efficient simulation engine is substantially more complicated than the top–down simulator demonstrated in Section 4.2.4. Bear in mind, however, that the efficient simulator is nothing more nor less than a simulator for the class of systems described above. Construction will begin with the major data structures: the event schedule and the bag. Having these, the remainder is straightforward, and much of it is borrowed from the simulator for discrete time systems. Algorithm 3.6 is used to transform events from input to output and vice versa, and the interface to the simulator will closely resemble that for discrete-time systems except where, as illustrated in Section 4.2.4, modifications are required to suit the irregular advance of time.

4.3.1 The Event Schedule

The purpose of the event schedule is to keep the set of atomic models sorted in order of the times of their next autonomous actions. A large number of data structures are available for this purpose (see, e.g., Refs. 15, 41, 42, 54, and 121, but note that there is a vast literature on this subject), but the binary heap (hereafter, simply "the heap") is particularly appropriate for two reasons:

1. The number of entries in the heap is at most the number of atomic models in the simulator, and in practice the size of the heap is often much smaller. An explicit heap, which is implemented inside an array, takes advantage of this property to fit itself into a small, contiguous region of memory.
2. The most common operation required by the simulator is rescheduling an atomic model. It is relatively inexpensive to move an object to a new position inside a heap, and this efficient rescheduling function can be implemented easily.

An explicit heap stores its N items in the first $N + 1$ elements of an array. The array can, therefore, be small to start and grow as needed; moreover, the contents of the array do not need to be reorganized when this is done. Adding more space incurs the cost of expanding the current block of memory allocated for the heap or, if this block is too small, of finding a new block and copying the heap's elements to it. If the size of the heap is doubled at each instance, resizing will occur infrequently over the course of a long simulation run. The heap is guaranteed to stop growing when its size is greater than or equal to the number of atomic models in the simulation, and it may cease to grow long before that point is reached.

The heap organizes its atomic models into a binary tree. The position assigned to a model is chosen such that the time of its next event is less than or equal to the time of next event of its children (or child). This is illustrated in Figure 4.6.

The first node, the smallest element in the heap, has the first position in the array. Its two children occupy positions 2 and 3. The children of position 2 have positions 4 and 5; the children of position 3 have positions 6 and 7. The rule is that the model

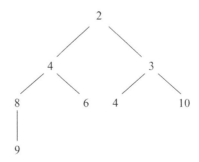

FIGURE 4.6 A collection of elements sorted and stored in a binary tree.

−1	2	4	3	8	6	4	10	9

FIGURE 4.7   The binary tree of Figure 4.6 stored in an array.

at position k in the heap has its left child at position $2k$ and right child, at position $2k + 1$. The zeroth position in the array is a sentinel value, and its purpose will become clear in a moment. The models occupy positions from one on. This is illustrated in Figure 4.7.

The heap supports four operations: finding the item or items with the smallest priority, inserting a new item into the heap, removing an item from the heap, and moving an item within the heap. The last two operations require that a model can be found quickly inside of the array. For this purpose, the variable q_index is added to the *Atomic* class. The value of q_index is zero if the model is not in the heap and has the model's array index otherwise.

The *Schedule* class is a heap designed specifically for the simulator. Its implementation is listed below. The *Schedule* has a single template parameter that must match the type of object used for input and output by the atomic models that it contains. A detailed description of the *Schedule*'s operation follows its listing.

_____ ***Implementation of the Schedule Class*** _____

```
1   #ifndef __adevs_schedule_h_
2   #define __adevs_schedule_h_
3   #include "adevs_models.h"
4   #include <cfloat>
5   #include <cstdlib>
6
7   namespace adevs
8   {
9
10  template <class X> class Schedule
11  {
12      public:
13          // Creates a scheduler with the default or specified initial capacity.
14          Schedule(unsigned int capacity = 100):
15          capacity(capacity),size(0),heap(new heap_element[capacity])
16          {
17              heap[0].priority = -1.0; // This is a sentinel value
18          }
19          // Get the model at the front of the queue.
20          Atomic<X>* getMinimum() const { return heap[1].item; }
21          // Get the time of the next event.
22          double minPriority() const { return heap[1].priority; }
23          // Get the imminent models and set their active flags to true.
24          void getImminent(Bag<Atomic<X>*>& imm) const { getImminent(imm,1); }
25          // Remove the model at the front of the queue.
```

```
26      void removeMinimum();
27      // Remove the imminent models from the queue.
28      void removeImminent();
29      // Add, remove, or move a model as required by its priority.
30      void schedule(Atomic<X>* model, double priority);
31      // Returns true if the queue is empty, and false otherwise.
32      bool empty() const { return size == 0; }
33      // Get the number of elements in the heap.
34      unsigned int getSize() const { return size; }
35      // Destructor.
36      ~Schedule() { delete [] heap; }
37   private:
38      // Definition of an element in the heap.
39      struct heap_element
40      {
41         Atomic<X>* item;
42         double priority;
43         // Constructor initializes the item and priority
44         heap_element():item(NULL),priority(DBL_MAX){}
45      };
46      unsigned int capacity, size;
47      heap_element* heap;
48      // Double the schedule capacity
49      void enlarge();
50      // Move the item at index down and return its new position
51      unsigned int percolate_down(unsigned int index, double priority);
52      // Move the item at index up and return its new position
53      unsigned int percolate_up(unsigned int index, double priority);
54      // Construct the imminent set recursively
55      void getImminent(Bag<Atomic<X>*>& imm, unsigned int root) const;
56   };
57
58   template <class X>
59   void Schedule<X>::getImminent(Bag<Atomic<X>*>& imm, unsigned int root) const
60   {
61      // Stop at the bottom or where the next priority is not the minimum
62      if (root > size || heap[1].priority < heap[root].priority) return;
63      heap[root].item->active = true; // Put the model into the imminent set
64      imm.insert(heap[root].item);
65      getImminent(imm,root*2); // Look for imminents in the left subtree
66      getImminent(imm,root*2+1); // Look in the right subtree
67   }
68
69   template <class X>
70   void Schedule<X>::removeMinimum()
71   {
72      if (size == 0) return; // Don't do anything if the heap is empty
73      size--; // Otherwise reduce the size of the schedule
74      // Set index to 0 to show that this model is not in the schedule
```

```
75      heap[1].item->q_index = 0;
76      // If the schedule is empty, give the last element the priority DBL_MAX
77      if (size == 0)
78      {
79         heap[1].priority = DBL_MAX;
80         heap[1].item = NULL;
81      }
82      // Otherwise fill the hole left by the deleted model
83      else
84      {
85         unsigned int i = percolate_down(1,heap[size+1].priority);
86         heap[i] = heap[size+1];
87         heap[i].item->q_index = i;
88         heap[size+1].item = NULL;
89      }
90   }
91
92   template <class X>
93   void Schedule<X>::removeImminent()
94   {
95      if (size == 0) return;
96      double tN = minPriority();
97      while (minPriority() <= tN) removeMinimum();
98   }
99
100  template <class X>
101  void Schedule<X>::schedule(Atomic<X>* model, double priority)
102  {
103     if (model->q_index != 0) // If the model is in the schedule
104     {
105        // Remove the model if the next event time is infinite
106        if (priority >= DBL_MAX)
107        {
108           // Move the item to the top of the heap
109           double min_priority = minPriority();
110           model->q_index = percolate_up(model->q_index,min_priority);
111           heap[model->q_index].priority = min_priority;
112           heap[model->q_index].item = model;
113           // Remove it and return
114           removeMinimum();
115           return;
116        }
117        // Decrease the time to next event
118        else if (priority < heap[model->q_index].priority)
119           model->q_index = percolate_up(model->q_index,priority);
120        // Increase the time to next event
121        else if (heap[model->q_index].priority < priority)
122           model->q_index = percolate_down(model->q_index,priority);
123        // Don't do anything if the priority is unchanged
```

```
124      else return;
125      heap[model->q_index].priority = priority;
126      heap[model->q_index].item = model;
127    }
128    // If it is not in the schedule and the next event time is
129    // not at infinity, then add it to the schedule
130    else if (priority < DBL_MAX)
131    {
132      // Enlarge the heap to hold the new model
133      size++;
134      if (size == capacity) enlarge();
135      // Find a slot and put the item into it
136      model->q_index = percolate_up(size,priority);
137      heap[model->q_index].priority = priority;
138      heap[model->q_index].item = model;
139    }
140    // Otherwise, the model is not enqueued and has no next event
141  }
142
143  template <class X>
144  unsigned int Schedule<X>::percolate_down(unsigned int index, double priority)
145  {
146    unsigned int child;
147    for (; index*2 <= size; index = child)
148    {
149      child = index*2;
150      if (child != size && heap[child+1].priority < heap[child].priority)
151        child++;
152      if (heap[child].priority < priority)
153      {
154        heap[index] = heap[child];
155        heap[index].item->q_index = index;
156      }
157      else break;
158    }
159    return index;
160  }
161
162  template <class X>
163  unsigned int Schedule<X>::percolate_up(unsigned int index, double priority)
164  {
165    // Position 0 has priority -1 and this method is always called
166    // with priority >= 0 and index > 0.
167    while (priority <= heap[index/2].priority)
168    {
169      heap[index] = heap[index/2];
170      heap[index].item->q_index = index;
171      index /= 2;
172    }
```

```
173      return index;
174    }
175
176    template <class X>
177    void Schedule<X>::enlarge()
178    {
179      heap_element* rheap = new heap_element[capacity*2];
180      for (unsigned int i = 0; i < capacity; i++)
181        rheap[i] = heap[i];
182      capacity *= 2;
183      delete [] heap;
184      heap = rheap;
185    }
186
187    } // end of namespace
188
189    #endif
```

There are three methods for getting the elements that have the next event times. The first two, *getMinimum* and *minPriority* return the item or priority, respectively, stored at the first position in the array. To support the third method, *getImminent*, the variable active is added to the *Atomic* class. This variable is used by the simulator to quickly determine whether a model is in the set of imminents. The *getImminent* method recursively descends into the heap to find the models whose time of next event is equal to the *minPriority*, sets the active flag for those models, and puts them into the *Bag* of imminent models. The descent along any branch of the tree stops when a model is found that has a time of next event larger than the minimum.

Using a *Bag* and active flag, rather than a *Set*, to store the imminent models is an optimization that saves the cost of otherwise expensive membership tests. The *Schedule* avoids these tests because each imminent model appears exactly once in the heap. The active flag is used by the simulator to rapidly test for membership in the imminent set. This is important because membership in the imminent set is a central part of the simulation algorithm and an expensive membership test seriously degrades the simulator's performance.

There are three public methods for inserting, removing, and moving items: *schedule*, *removeImminent*, and *removeMinimum*. To do their job, these methods rely on a pair of private methods that are the workhorses of the data structure: *percolate_up* and *percolate_down*. These methods accept a position to adjust and its new priority and rearrange the heap to create an opening where the new priority belongs. The location of the hole is returned and then the model can be inserted into it.

The *percolate_up* method reduces a model's time of next event by moving it toward the top of the heap. This method compares the next event time of the model to be adjusted with the next event time of its parent and, if the model to be adjusted has a next event time that is less than or equal to the parent's, parent and child change places. This is repeated until the comparison fails, and thus we have found the proper

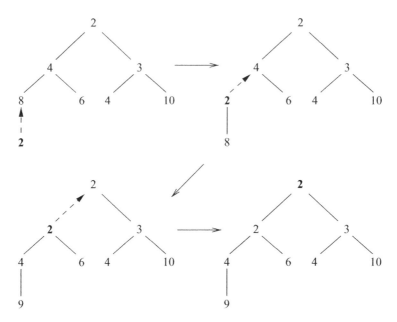

FIGURE 4.8   Moving a model up with *percolate_up*; the boldfaced **2** is being adjusted.

position of the model. A next event time of −1 is given to the sentinel at position zero to avoid a special test for the top of the heap. The operation of the *percolate_up* method is illustrated in Figure 4.8.

The *percolate_down* method increases a model's time of next event by moving it toward the bottom of the heap. This method compares the next event time of the position to be adjusted with the next event time of its children and, if the least of these event times is smaller than the parent's, then the parent and that child change places. This is repeated until the comparison fails or the bottom of the heap is reached, and thus we have the model's proper position. The operation of the *percolate_down* method is illustrated in Figure 4.9.

The *removeMinimum* method removes the first element in the heap by replacing it with the last element in the heap and then percolating that element down to its proper position. The last (now first) element sinks into the heap and settles at the location where its time of next event is smaller than that of its children and greater than or equal to that of its parent. The old minimum, the element that was removed, has its q_index set to zero to indicate that it is no longer in the schedule. The new minimum is the smaller of the children of the removed minimum or it is NULL (with an infinite priority) if the heap is empty.

To remove all of the imminent models, the *removeImminent* method repeatedly removes the minimum element until either the heap is empty or the next event time of the smallest element is larger than the next event time of the imminent models.

The *schedule* method can insert a model into the heap, remove a model from the heap, and adjust the position of a model in the heap. It takes one of four actions when

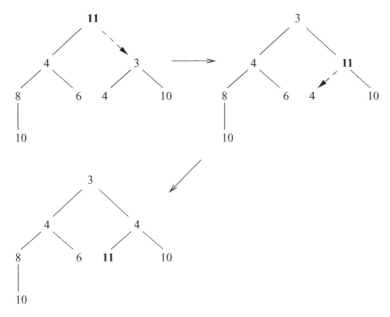

FIGURE 4.9 Moving a model down with *percolate_down*; the boldfaced **11** is being adjusted.

given a model and the time of its next event. If the model is already in the heap, then (1) it is removed if the time of next event is at infinity or (2) its position is adjusted to match its next event time; if the model is not in the heap, then (3) it is inserted if its next event time is not at infinity–otherwise, (4) the model is not in the heap and has its next event at infinity, and so the schedule does nothing with it.

Inserting a model into and moving it within the schedule are done with the *enlarge*, *percolate_up*, and *percolate_down* methods. A model is inserted in two steps: (1), the size of the heap is increased by 1 and additional memory is allocated if required, and (2) the model is placed in the last position of the heap and percolated up until it occupies its proper place. To adjust the position of a model that is already in the schedule, it is percolated up if the time of next event is reduced; percolated down, if the time of next event is increased; or left in place if the time of next event is unchanged.

Removing a model from the heap requires two steps: (1) it is percolated up to the first position (i.e., the minimum position) and (2) then it is removed with a call to *removeMinimum*. Careful attention must be paid to how the *percolate_up* method is implemented. It is tempting, but incorrect, to stop moving a model up when its time of next event is *less than* its parent's. If there are several models with the same priority, then this saves a few swaps and compares. However, *this could leave the model that we want to delete at a position below the root of the tree*. Therefore the test for upward motion must be *less than or equal to* when comparing child to parent. The *percolate_up* algorithm presented in many (perhaps all) data structure books

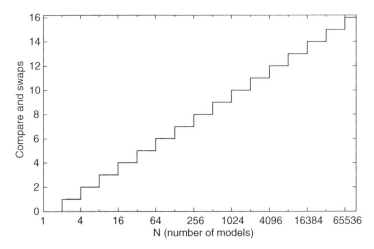

FIGURE 4.10   Maximum number of compare and swaps required by *percolate_up* and *percolate_down* as a function of the number of models in the heap. The x axis has a logarithmic scale; the heap's ability to manage a large number of models is readily apparent.

use $<$ and so it is important to keep in mind this peculiar requirement of our event schedule (see, e.g., Weiss' *Data Structures and Algorithm Analysis in C* [145]).[5]

The time required to place a model in or remove a model from the heap is determined chiefly by the *percolate_up* and *percolate_down* methods. The number of iterations of the `for` loops of these methods is, at most, equal to the height of the heap. If it holds N atomic models, then the height is at most $\lfloor \log_2 N \rfloor$. This is deduced by first observing that the number of nodes in a heap of height h is between 2^h and $2^{h+1} - 1$ (a heap with a single element has a height of zero), that is, that $N \in [2^h, 2^{h+1} - 1]$. For a given N, the smallest integer value of h that satisfies this expression is $\lfloor \log_2 N \rfloor$, and hence the bound on the execution time.

To insert or move a model within the heap requires one call to *percolate_up* or *percolate_down*, and so the cost of an insertion or adjustment is bounded by $\lfloor \log_2 N \rfloor$. To remove a model requires one call to *percolate_up* and a second call to *percolate_down*, and so it is twice as expensive as an insertion or adjustment. Nonetheless, the heap's operations in general have an execution time proportional to $\lfloor \log_2 N \rfloor$, which is plotted Figure 4.10.

The only exception to this rule is the *enlarge* method. Its time is spent chiefly in allocating a new array, copying the old array to the new, and then deallocating the old. The memory allocation is itself quite slow, and compounding this are the memory assignments required to transfer the array contents. Fortunately, the heap is very rarely enlarged. In a long-running simulation, *enlarge* is called early to grow the heap to some size that is generally smaller than N, and calls later in the run are

---

[5]Another solution is to use -1, or some other time of next event that is invalid, to remove a model from the heap. This requires that the sentinel value be less than -1, or whatever other value is used for removal.

exceedingly rare. Therefore, the *enlarge* method is not a significant contributor to the running time of most simulations.

4.3.2   The Bag

Small, unordered collections of objects are used throughout the simulation engine, which does three things with them: iterate through the elements, insert an element, and remove an element. A lightweight class, built specifically for this role, improves the performance of the simulation engine by reducing the execution time of these common operations. This lightweight class is the *Bag*, which stores its elements in an array. The array grows to hold the largest number of elements put into the bag, but does not shrink as elements are removed. As the bag is reused over its lifetime, its size, much like the size of the heap, stabilizes and so the aggregate cost of resizing is small for a long-running simulation.

Elements are inserted into the bag by placing them at the back of the array. If the array is too small, then its size doubles before the element is inserted. An element is removed by moving the last item in the bag to the position of the removed item. To remove every element from the array, it suffices to set its size to 0. In this way, elements are always stored contiguously and can be easily traversed.

The complete listing of the bag class is shown below. It implements a part of the STL *multiple associative container* interface, but it does not satisfy the time constraints for some of those methods. The most commonly used methods—*insert*, *remove*, and *clear*—require a simple assignment and, possibly, increment operation. The *iterator* is likewise simple, a thin veneer over the underlying array. Only two methods do not execute in constant time: (1) if the *insert* method needs to enlarge the array, then it must iterate through the entire collection to assign the elements of the old array to the new array; and (2) if the *erase* method needs to locate a specific element in the array, then it must search element by element to find it.

_____ ***Implementation of the Bag Class*** _____

```
1  #ifndef _adevs_bag_h
2  #define _adevs_bag_h
3  #include <cstdlib>
4
5  namespace adevs
6  {
7
8  // The Bag is (almost) a model of a STL Multiple Associative Container.
9  // The STL methods that are implemented conform to the standard except
10  // in regards to their computational complexity.
11  template <class T> class Bag
12  {
13      public:
14          // A bidirectional iterator for the Bag
15          class iterator
```

```
16      {
17          public:
18              iterator(unsigned int start = 0, T* b = NULL):
19              i(start),b(b){}
20              iterator(const iterator& src):
21              i(src.i),b(src.b){}
22              const iterator& operator=(const iterator& src)
23              {
24                  i = src.i;
25                  b = src.b;
26                  return *this;
27              }
28              bool operator==(const iterator& src) const {
29                  return i==src.i;
30              }
31              bool operator!=(const iterator& src) const {
32                  return i!=src.i;
33              }
34              T& operator*() { return b[i]; }
35              const T& operator*() const { return b[i]; }
36              iterator& operator++() { i++; return *this; }
37              iterator& operator--() { i--; return *this; }
38              iterator& operator++(int) { ++i; return *this; }
39              iterator& operator--(int) { --i; return *this; }
40          private:
41              friend class Bag<T>;
42              unsigned int i;
43              T* b;
44      };
45      typedef iterator const_iterator;
46      // Create an empty bag with an initial capacity
47      Bag(unsigned int cap = 8):
48      cap_(cap),size_(0),b(new T[cap]){}
49      // Copy constructor uses the = operator of T
50      Bag(const Bag<T>& src):cap_(src.cap_),size_(src.size_)
51      {
52          b = new T[src.cap_];
53          for (unsigned int i = 0; i < size_; i++)
54              b[i] = src.b[i];
55      }
56      // Assignment opeator uses the = operator of T
57      const Bag<T>& operator=(const Bag<T>& src)
58      {
59          cap_ = src.cap_;
60          size_ = src.size_;
61          delete [] b;
62          b = new T[src.cap_];
63          for (unsigned int i = 0; i < size_; i++)
64              b[i] = src.b[i];
```

```
65          return *this;
66       }
67       // Count the instances of a stored in the bag
68       unsigned count(const T& a) const
69       {
70          unsigned result = 0;
71          for (unsigned i = 0; i < size_; i++)
72             if (b[i] == a) result++;
73          return result;
74       }
75       // Get the number of elements in the bag
76       unsigned size() const { return size_; }
77       // Same as size()==0
78       bool empty() const { return size_ == 0; }
79       // Get an iterator pointing to the first element in the bag
80       iterator begin() const { return iterator(0,b); }
81       // Get an interator starting just after the last element
82       iterator end() const { return iterator(size_,b); }
83       // Erase the first instance of k
84       void erase(const T& k)
85       {
86          iterator p = find(k);
87          if (p != end()) erase(p);
88       }
89       // Erase the element pointed to by p
90       void erase(iterator p)
91       {
92          size_--;
93          b[p.i] = b[size_];
94       }
95       // Remove all of the elements from the bag
96       void clear() { size_ = 0; }
97       // Find the first instance of k, or end() if no instance is found.
98       // Uses == for comparing T.
99       iterator find(const T& k) const
100      {
101         for (unsigned i = 0; i < size_; i++)
102            if (b[i] == k) return iterator(i,b);
103         return end();
104      }
105      // Put t into the bag
106      void insert(const T& t)
107      {
108         if (cap_ == size_) enlarge(2*cap_);
109         b[size_] = t;
110         size_++;
111      }
112      ~Bag() { delete [] b; }
113   private:
```

```
114      unsigned cap_, size_;
115      T* b;
116      // Adds the specified capacity to the bag.
117      void enlarge(unsigned adjustment)
118      {
119         cap_ = cap_ + adjustment;
120         T* rb = new T[cap_];
121         for (unsigned i = 0; i < size_; i++)
122            rb[i] = b[i];
123         delete [] b;
124         b = rb;
125      }
126   };
127
128 } // end of namespace
129
130 #endif
```

Only a handful of bags are actually needed at any moment, and it is wasteful to create separate bags for each atomic model and to create and destroy bags while routing an event. The simulator can reduce its use of memory by having a cache of bags that are reused as needed.

This cache is implemented by the *ObjectPool* class, which stores a collection of reusable objects. It has two methods plus a constructor and a destructor. The constructor creates an initial pool of objects. The *make_obj* method gets an object from the pool and returns it or, if the pool is empty, creates a new object. The *destroy_obj* method puts the supplied object into the pool. It is the responsibility of the caller to ensure that the object is restored to its initial state before being returned for reuse. The destructor deletes the pool. The code for the *ObjectPool* is listed below.

_____ *Implementation of the ObjectPool Class* _____

```
1  #ifndef __adevs_object_pool_h_
2  #define __adevs_object_pool_h_
3  #include "adevs_bag.h"
4
5  namespace adevs
6  {
7
8  template <class T> class object_pool
9  {
10    public:
11       // Construct a pool with a specific initial population
12       object_pool(unsigned int pop = 0):pool()
13       {
14          for (unsigned int i = 0; i < pop; i++)
15             pool.insert(new T());
```

```
16        }
17        // Create an object
18        T* make_obj()
19        {
20            T* obj;
21            if (pool.empty()) obj = new T;
22            else
23            {
24                obj = *((pool.end())--);
25                pool.erase(pool.end()--);
26            }
27            return obj;
28        }
29        // Return an object to the pool
30        void destroy_obj(T* obj) { pool.insert(obj); }
31        // Delete all objects in the pool
32        ~object_pool()
33        {
34            typename Bag<T*>::iterator iter = pool.begin();
35            for (; iter != pool.end(); iter++) delete *iter;
36        }
37    private:
38        Bag<T*> pool;
39 };
40
41 } // end of namespace
42
43 #endif
```

4.3.3 The Simulation Engine

What the previous simulation engine did with an atomic model, this simulation engine does with a network model: (1) obtain the time of its next autonomous action, (2) get the output of the network and its components at that time, (3) compute its next internal event, and (4) inject an input in the interval spanning the last change of state and the next autonomous action. The simulator accepts the same types of trajectories as before, applying them to the resultant of the network to compute its next state.

The classes that constitute the simulation engine are shown in Figure 4.11. These are very similar to the classes that constitute the discrete-time simulator in Section 3.3. Time, of course, is changed from an integer in the discrete-time simulator to a double in the discrete-event simulator; the integer part of the simulation clock is implicit. The *Dtss* class is changed to the *Devs* class, which stands for *discrete-event system*, and the namespace is likewise changed to *adevs*, which stands for *a discrete-event simulator*. The *Atomic* class requires a new interface that is by now familiar. The most significant changes are in the *Simulator* class, for which the interface must change in small ways and the implementation change greatly.

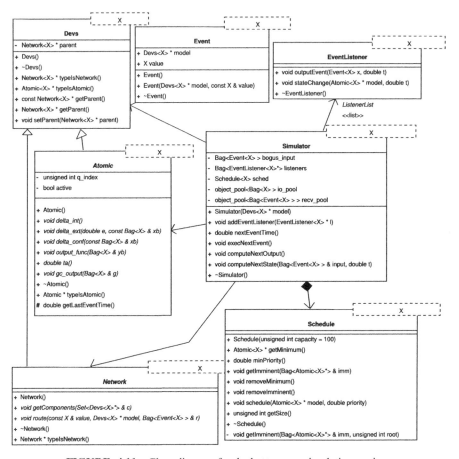

FIGURE 4.11 Class diagram for the bottom–up simulation engine.

The *Simulator* uses a *Schedule* to keep its components sorted in the order of their next autonomous events. The imminent set is stored in the *Bag* called *imm*, and the set of models that have been activated by input are in the *Bag* called *activated*. The active flag of the *Atomic* model is used to test for membership in these bags. Each *Atomic* object is assigned as needed a *Bag* from the object pools to store its input and output, and every *Atomic* model maintains its own time of last event that is initially zero.

The constructor for the *Simulator* descends depth first into the network, finding atomic models that have a finite-time advance and inserting them into the schedule. The private *schedule* method is used to do this. It sets the time of the model's last event and computes its next event time as the last event time plus the time advance. The check for an infinite time advance helps to avoid a problem that might arise from adding the largest representable double with some other number. If, for example, the result is *not a number* (nan) or *infinity* (inf), then the *Schedule* is likely to break. The

GNU C++ compiler (or, at least, version 4.2.3) gives DBL_MAX when a positive double is added to it, but there is no guarantee that another compiler will give the same result. The extra test is therefore a necessary precaution. Once the next event time is known, the model is assigned to its proper position in the event schedule.

The time of the *Network*'s next autonomous action is equal to the next event time of its imminent components, and these are the *Atomic* models at the top of the event schedule. Therefore, the *nextEventTime* method simply returns the smallest event time in the *Schedule*.

The *computeNextOutput* method *assumes* that there will be no input between that last event and the next autonomous event, and proceeds to calculate the imminent set and the inputs for models that are influenced by the imminent components. The method first tests whether the imminent set is empty; if it is not, then the necessary calculations have already been done and the method returns. Otherwise, the imminent models are obtained directly from the *Schedule*, which puts them into the *imm* bag and sets their active flags to true. The output of the imminent models is computed and routed, using Algorithm 3.6, to the models that should receive it. The recipients that are not already in the *imm* or *activated* bags are inserted into the *activated* bag and their active flag is set to true. The *route* method invokes the *outputEvent* method of *EventListeners* that are registered with the *Simulator*.

The *computeNextState* method applies to the network the two types of allowed trajectories. If the bag of input is empty and *t* is equal to the time of the next event, then this is an empty trajectory ending at the next autonomous action. In this case, the *computeNextOutput* method is called to ensure that the imminent and activated bags are up-to-date and new states for those models are computed. Otherwise, it is necessary to undo the speculative calculation of the imminent and activated bags and then route the injected input to the appropriate components. Once this is done, new states are computed for the activated models. Finally, the imminent (if any) and activated models are rescheduled, the output from the imminent models is deleted, and the bags used for input and output calculations are returned to the pool.

The *Simulator* takes advantage of the *ObjectPool* class to minimize the number of *Bags* that are created for handling input and output and for routing events. The *route* method uses a *Bag* from the object pool instead of creating a new one and then destroying it. The *inject_input* and *clean_up* methods complement one another to assign a bag for input to an atomic model when it is needed and to retract that bag when the model has finished using it. The *clean_up* method likewise complements the *computeNextOutput* method by giving the *Atomic* models a chance to delete their output objects and then retracting the bag that was assigned to that model for storing its output.

The code for the *Simulator* is listed below. Its implementation requires only 275 lines of code (as counted with the UNIX command `wc -l`). The supporting classes (*Schedule, Bag, ObjectPool, Atomic, Network*, etc.) bring the total lines of code for the discrete event simulation engine to 942. About a third of that, 362 lines, is for the *Bag, ObjectPool*, and *Schedule*, which are optimizations. The core of the simulation engine is quite simple.

_____ *Implementation of the Simulator Class* _____

```
1   #ifndef __adevs_simple_simulator_h_
2   #define __adevs_simple_simulator_h_
3   #include "adevs_models.h"
4   #include "adevs_event_listener.h"
5   #include "adevs_sched.h"
6   #include "adevs_bag.h"
7   #include "adevs_set.h"
8   #include "object_pool.h"
9   #include <cassert>
10  #include <cstdlib>
11  #include <iostream>
12  #include <vector>
13
14  namespace adevs
15  {
16
17  // This class implements the bottom up simulation procedure
18  template <class X> class Simulator
19  {
20      public:
21          // Create a simulator for the model
22          Simulator(Devs<X>* model);
23          // Add an event listener
24          void addEventListener(EventListener<X>* l) { listeners.insert(l); }
25          // Get the time of the next event
26          double nextEventTime() { return sched.minPriority(); }
27          // Execute the simulation cycle at nextEventTime()
28          void execNextEvent()
29          {
30              computeNextOutput();
31              computeNextState(bogus_input,sched.minPriority());
32          }
33          // Compute the output values of the imminent models.  This will
34          // notify the EventListener of output events.
35          void computeNextOutput();
36          // Apply the input at time t and then compute the next state. This
37          // will produce output too if t == nextEventTime().
38          void computeNextState(Bag<Event<X> >& input, double t);
39          // Deletes the simulator, but leaves the model intact.
40          ~Simulator();
41      private:
42
43          Bag<Event<X> > bogus_input; // Empty bag for execNextEvent()
44          Bag<EventListener<X>*> listeners; // Registered event listeners
45          Schedule<X> sched; // The event schedule
46          // Set of imminent models and models activated by input
47          Bag<Atomic<X>*> imm, activated;
```

```
48        // Pools of preallocated, commonly used objects
49        object_pool<Bag<X> > io_pool;
50        object_pool<Bag<Event<X> > > recv_pool;
51        // Schedule an atomic model for t + ta()
52        void schedule(Atomic<X>* model, double t);
53        // Route an event from a source having the specified parent
54        void route(Network<X>* parent, Devs<X>* src, X& x);
55        // Add an event to the input bag for an atomic model. If the model's
56        // active flag is false, then this method adds the model to the
57        // activated bag and sets its active flag to true.
58        void inject_event(Atomic<X>* model, X& value);
59        // Set the model's active flag to false, delete the contents of
60        // its output bag, and return the input and output bags to the pool
61        void clean_up(Atomic<X>* model);
62        // Notify listeners of an output event.
63        void notify_output_listeners(Devs<X>* model,
64              const X& value, double t);
65        // Notify listeners of a change in state
66        void notify_state_listeners(Atomic<X>* model, double t);
67        // Put the atomic leaves of the network into the set s
68        void getAllChildren(Network<X>* model, Set<Atomic<X>*>& s);
69   };
70
71   template <class X>
72   Simulator<X>::Simulator(Devs<X>* model)
73   {
74      // Put an atomic model into the schedule
75      if (model->typeIsAtomic() != NULL)
76         schedule(model->typeIsAtomic(),0.0);
77      // Otherwise find the set of atomic components and put those into
78      // the schedule
79      else {
80         Set<Atomic<X>*> A;
81         getAllChildren(model->typeIsNetwork(),A);
82         for (typename Set<Atomic<X>*>::iterator iter = A.begin();
83            iter != A.end(); iter++)
84            schedule(*iter,0.0);
85      }
86   }
87
88   template <class X>
89   void Simulator<X>::schedule(Atomic<X>* model, double t)
90   {
91      model->tL = t; // Set the time of the last event
92      double dt = model->ta(); // Compute the time advance
93      // Schedule the model for activity at its time of next event
94      if (dt == DBL_MAX) sched.schedule(model,DBL_MAX);
95      else sched.schedule(model,t+dt);
96   }
```

```
97
98   template <class X>
99   void Simulator<X>::getAllChildren(Network<X>* model, Set<Atomic<X>*>& s)
100  {
101      Set<Devs<X>*> tmp;
102      model->getComponents(tmp); // Get the set of components
103      // Put the atomic components into s and call getAllChildren for
104      // the network components
105      typename Set<Devs<X>*>::iterator iter;
106      for (iter = tmp.begin(); iter != tmp.end(); iter++) {
107          if ((*iter)->typeIsNetwork() != NULL)
108              getAllChildren((*iter)->typeIsNetwork(),s);
109          else
110              s.insert((*iter)->typeIsAtomic());
111      }
112  }
113
114  template <class X>
115  void Simulator<X>::computeNextOutput()
116  {
117      // If the imminent set is up to date, then just return
118      if (imm.empty() == false) return;
119      // Get the imminent models from the schedule. This sets the active flags.
120      sched.getImminent(imm);
121      // Compute output functions and route the events. The bags of output
122      // are held for garbage collection at a later time.
123      for (typename Bag<Atomic<X>*>::iterator imm_iter = imm.begin();
124           imm_iter != imm.end(); imm_iter++) {
125          Atomic<X>* model = *imm_iter;
126          // Don't recalculate the model's output if we already have it
127          if (model->y == NULL) {
128              model->y = io_pool.make_obj();
129              model->output_func(*(model->y));
130              // Route each event in y
131              for (typename Bag<X>::iterator y_iter = model->y->begin();
132                   y_iter != model->y->end(); y_iter++)
133                  route(model->getParent(),model,*y_iter);
134          }
135      }
136  }
137
138  template <class X>
139  void Simulator<X>::computeNextState(Bag<Event<X> >& input, double t)
140  {
141      // If t is less than the next event time, make sure that
142      // computeNextOutput() has not been called
143      if (t < sched.minPriority() && !imm.empty())
144          throw exception("input can not precede output");
145      // If the output function needs to be computed, then do it
```

```
146      else if (t == sched.minPriority() && imm.empty())
147          computeNextOutput();
148      // Route the injected inputs
149      for (typename Bag<Event<X> >::iterator iter = input.begin();
150          iter != input.end(); iter++) {
151          Atomic<X>* amodel = (*iter).model->typeIsAtomic();
152          if (amodel != NULL) inject_event(amodel,(*iter).value);
153          else route((*iter).model->typeIsNetwork(),(*iter).model,
154              (*iter).value);
155      }
156      // Compute the states of atomic models.
157      for (typename Bag<Atomic<X>*>::iterator iter = imm.begin();
158          iter != imm.end(); iter++) {
159          // Compute the new state
160          if ((*iter)->x == NULL) (*iter)->delta_int();
161          else (*iter)->delta_conf(*((*iter)->x));
162          // Notify listeners of the change in state
163          notify_state_listeners(*iter,t);
164          // Adjust the position of the model in the schedule
165          schedule(*iter,t);
166      }
167      for (typename Bag<Atomic<X>*>::iterator iter = activated.begin();
168          iter != activated.end(); iter++) {
169          // Compute the new state
170          (*iter)->delta_ext(t-(*iter)->tL,*((*iter)->x));
171          // Notify listeners of the change in state
172          notify_state_listeners(*iter,t);
173          // Adjust the position of the model in the schedule
174          schedule(*iter,t);
175      }
176      // Cleanup after the models that changed state in this iteration
177      for (typename Bag<Atomic<X>*>::iterator iter = imm.begin();
178          iter != imm.end(); iter++)
179          clean_up(*iter);
180      for (typename Bag<Atomic<X>*>::iterator iter = activated.begin();
181          iter != activated.end(); iter++)
182          clean_up(*iter);
183      // Empty the bags
184      imm.clear();
185      activated.clear();
186  }
187
188  template <class X>
189  void Simulator<X>::clean_up(Atomic<X>* model)
190  {
191      model->active = false;
192      if (model->x != NULL) {
193          model->x->clear();
194          io_pool.destroy_obj(model->x);
```

```
195      }
196      if (model->y != NULL) {
197         model->gc_output(*(model->y));
198         model->y->clear();
199         io_pool.destroy_obj(model->y);
200      }
201      model->x = model->y = NULL;
202   }
203
204   template <class X>
205   void Simulator<X>::inject_event(Atomic<X>* model, X& value)
206   {
207      if (model->active == false) activated.insert(model);
208      if (model->x == NULL) model->x = io_pool.make_obj();
209      model->active = true;
210      model->x->insert(value);
211   }
212
213   template <class X>
214   void Simulator<X>::route(Network<X>* parent, Devs<X>* src, X& x)
215   {
216      // Notify event listeners if this is an output event
217      if (parent != src) notify_output_listeners(src,x,sched.minPriority());
218      // No one to do the routing, so return
219      if (parent == NULL) return;
220      // Compute the set of receivers for this value
221      Bag<Event<X> >* recvs = recv_pool.make_obj();
222      parent->route(x,src,*recvs);
223      // Deliver the event to each of its targets
224      Atomic<X>* amodel = NULL;
225      typename Bag<Event<X> >::iterator recv_iter = recvs->begin();
226      for (; recv_iter != recvs->end(); recv_iter++) {
227         // if the destination is an atomic model, then add the event to the
228         // I/O bag for that model and put the model in the list of
229         // activated models
230         amodel = (*recv_iter).model->typeIsAtomic();
231         if (amodel != NULL) inject_event(amodel,(*recv_iter).value);
232         // if this is an external output from the parent model
233         else if ((*recv_iter).model == parent)
234            route(parent->getParent(),parent,(*recv_iter).value);
235         // otherwise it is an input to a coupled model
236         else route((*recv_iter).model->typeIsNetwork(),(*recv_iter).model,
237               (*recv_iter).value);
238      }
239      recvs->clear();
240      recv_pool.destroy_obj(recvs);
241   }
242
243   template <class X>
```

```
244   void Simulator<X>::notify_output_listeners(Devs<X>* model,
245         const X& value, double t)
246   {
247     Event<X> event(model,value);
248     typename Bag<EventListener<X>*>::iterator iter;
249     for (iter = listeners.begin(); iter != listeners.end(); iter++)
250         (*iter)->outputEvent(event,t);
251   }
252
253   template <class X>
254   void Simulator<X>::notify_state_listeners(Atomic<X>* model, double t)
255   {
256     typename Bag<EventListener<X>*>::iterator iter;
257     for (iter = listeners.begin(); iter != listeners.end(); iter++)
258         (*iter)->stateChange(model,t);
259   }
260
261   template <class X>
262   Simulator<X>::~Simulator()
263   {
264     // Clean up the models with stale IO
265     typename Bag<Atomic<X>*>::iterator imm_iter;
266     for (imm_iter = imm.begin(); imm_iter != imm.end(); imm_iter++)
267         clean_up(*imm_iter);
268     for (imm_iter = activated.begin(); imm_iter != activated.end();
269           imm_iter++)
270         clean_up(*imm_iter);
271   }
272
273   } // End of namespace
274
275   #endif
```

To illustrate the use of this simulation engine, consider again the assembly line modeled in Section 4.2.4. The *Machine* class does not require any change to be used with the new simulation engine. The *AssemblyLine*, because it will no longer be contained in a *Resultant*, can in its *route* method send and receive events directly to and from itself. It must also change the signature of its *getComponents* and *route* methods to accept a *Devs* object rather than an *Atomic* object and, finally, the drill and press must have their parent field set to the *AssemblyLine* so that the routing algorithm will work. The new implementation is listed below.

Implementation of the AssemblyLine for the New Simulation Engine

```
1   #ifndef _AssemblyLine_h_
2   #define _AssemblyLine_h_
3   #include "Machine.h"
```

```
4
5    class AssemblyLine: public adevs::Network<int>
6    {
7       public:
8          AssemblyLine():
9             adevs::Network<int>(),
10            press(1.0),drill(2.0) // Create the component models
11         {
12            // Remember to set their parent, otherwise the Simulator will
13            // not be able to route their output events
14            press.setParent(this);
15            drill.setParent(this);
16         }
17         void getComponents(adevs::Set<adevs::Devs<int>*>& c)
18         {
19            c.insert(&press);
20            c.insert(&drill);
21         }
22         void route(const int& value, adevs::Devs<int>* model,
23               adevs::Bag<adevs::Event<int> >& r)
24         {
25            adevs::Event<int> x;
26            x.value = value;
27            // External input to the network goes to the press
28            if (model == this) x.model = &press;
29            // Output from the drill leaves the assembly line
30            else if (model == &drill) x.model = this;
31            // Output from the press goes to the drill
32            else if (model == &press) x.model = &drill;
33            r.insert(x);
34         }
35         Machine* getPress() { return &press; }
36         Machine* getDrill() { return &drill; }
37      private:
38         Machine press, drill;
39   };
40
41   #endif
```

The main simulation program must also change to accommodate the new interfaces. The *AssemblyLineListener* filters events to extract just output from the network and to print the state of the drill and press separately; the *AssemblyLine* no longer appears in the *stateChange* callback. This will change the program's output slightly because the state of a *Machine* is printed only when it is altered, rather than at every simulation event. The final change is where input is injected into the simulation; this must now be put into an *Event* that is directed to the *AssemblyLine*. The new implementation is listed below.

_____ ***The Main Function for the New Assembly-Line Simulation*** _____

```
1    #include "AssemblyLine_bottom_up.h"
2    #include <iostream>
3    using namespace std;
4    using namespace adevs;
5
6    // Listener for recording the state and output of the assembly line.
7    class AssemblyLineListener: public EventListener<int>
8    {
9        public:
10           AssemblyLineListener(AssemblyLine* assembly_line):
11               assembly_line(assembly_line){}
12           void outputEvent(Event<int> y, double t)
13           {
14               // Output from the AssembyLine
15               if (y.model == assembly_line)
16                   cout << "Output, t = " << t << ", y = " << y.value << endl;
17           }
18           void stateChange(Atomic<int>* model, double t)
19           {
20               // Get the model of the machine
21               Machine* m = dynamic_cast<Machine*>(model);
22               // Print the state of the machine
23               cout << "State, t = " << t;
24               if (model == assembly_line->getPress()) cout << ", press = (";
25               else cout << ", drill = (";
26               cout << m->getParts() << "," << m->getSigma() << ")" << endl;
27           }
28       private:
29           AssemblyLine* assembly_line;
30   };
31
32   int main()
33   {
34       // Create the model, event listener, and simulator
35       AssemblyLine* assembly_line = new AssemblyLine();
36       AssemblyLineListener* l = new AssemblyLineListener(assembly_line);
37       Simulator<int>* sim = new Simulator<int>(assembly_line);
38       sim->addEventListener(l);
39       // Print the initial state of the model
40       l->stateChange(assembly_line->getDrill(),0.0);
41       l->stateChange(assembly_line->getPress(),0.0);
42       // Run the simulation
43       while (true) {
44           // Bag for injecting the input
45           Bag<Event<int> > input;
46           // The value to inject
47           int blanks;
```

```
48    // Time to inject the input
49    double t; int c;
50    // Read the time and input values
51    cin >> t >> c >> blanks;
52    // If this is the end of the input, then quit
53    if (cin.eof()) break;
54    // Simulate until time t and then inject the input
55    while (sim->nextEventTime() < t) {
56        cout << endl;
57        sim->execNextEvent();
58    }
59    // Simulate the transient events
60    for (int i = 0; i < c && sim->nextEventTime() == t; i++) {
61        cout << endl;
62        sim->execNextEvent();
63    }
64    // Inject the input
65    Event<int> input_event(assembly_line,blanks);
66    input.insert(input_event);
67    cout << endl;
68    sim->computeNextState(input,t);
69    }
70    // Run until the simulation completes
71    while (sim->nextEventTime() < DBL_MAX) {
72        cout << endl;
73        sim->execNextEvent();
74    }
75    // Clean up
76    delete sim; delete l; delete assembly_line;
77    return 0;
78 }
```

To repeat the previous calculations, this simulator is fed the input lines

```
0 0 1
2 1 2
```

and its output, which is shown below, agrees with, but is more verbose than, its top–down counterpart. When reading the output, recall that the integer part of the clock advances implicitly when the state is changed. Blocks of printed output associated with each discrete moment are separated by a blank line: the first block occurs at time $(0, 0)$, the second block at $(0, 1)$, the third block at $(1, 1)$, the fourth at $(2, 2)$ following the input at $(2, 1)$, and so on.

```
$ ./a.out < input
State, t = 0, drill = (0,2)
State, t = 0, press = (0,1)
```

```
State, t = 0, press = (1,1)

State, t = 1, press = (0,1)
State, t = 1, drill = (1,2)

State, t = 2, press = (2,1)

Output, t = 3, y = 1
State, t = 3, press = (1,1)
State, t = 3, drill = (1,2)

State, t = 4, press = (0,1)
State, t = 4, drill = (2,1)

Output, t = 5, y = 1
State, t = 5, drill = (1,2)

Output, t = 7, y = 1
State, t = 7, drill = (0,2)
$
```

Similarly, feeding this simulation with the file input_a containing

```
0 0 1
3 0 1
```

produces

```
$ ./a.out < input_a
State, t = 0, drill = (0,2)
State, t = 0, press = (0,1)

State, t = 0, press = (1,1)

State, t = 1, press = (0,1)
State, t = 1, drill = (1,2)

Output, t = 3, y = 1
State, t = 3, drill = (0,2)
State, t = 3, press = (1,1)

State, t = 4, press = (0,1)
State, t = 4, drill = (1,2)

Output, t = 6, y = 1
State, t = 6, drill = (0,2)
$
```

and file `input_b` with contents

```
0 0 1
3 1 1
```

gives the output

```
1$ ./a.out < input_b
State, t = 0, drill = (0,2)
State, t = 0, press = (0,1)

State, t = 0, press = (1,1)

State, t = 1, press = (0,1)
State, t = 1, drill = (1,2)

Output, t = 3, y = 1
State, t = 3, drill = (0,2)

State, t = 3, press = (1,1)

State, t = 4, press = (0,1)
State, t = 4, drill = (1,2)

Output, t = 6, y = 1
State, t = 6, drill = (0,2)
$
```

both agreeing with the top–down simulation in Section 4.2.4.

4.4 THE COMPUTER IN THE TANK

Equipped with a complete simulation engine for discrete-event systems, we can complete the work started in Section 4.1.8 by building the rest of the model of the tank's computer. The *PacketProcessing* model, whose phase graph is shown in Figure 2.7, has three state variables: the time σ remaining until the next internal event, the phase, and the queue of packets that are waiting to be processed. The packets are stored in a first-in/first-out queue, which is implemented with a list. There are two phases, interrupted and operating, and a single Boolean value keeps track of which phase the model is in. The time to the next internal event is a positive number implemented by a double.

The *PacketProcessing* model has two types of input: interrupts from the interrupt handler and packets from the radio. These arrive as two types of *SimEvent* objects. *SimInterrupt* events come from the interrupt handler. *SimPacket* events, which contain the duty cycles and directions for the left and right motors, come from the radio.

The model produces *SimMotorOnTime* events that contain the left and right motor ON times and directions. The header file for the *PacketProcessing* model is listed below.

_____ ***Header File for the PacketProcessing Model*** _____

```
1   #ifndef PACKET_PROCESSING_H_
2   #define PACKET_PROCESSING_H_
3   #include "adevs.h"
4   #include "SimEvents.h"
5   #include <list>
6   // This is the model of the computer's packet processing code.
7   // Input events must have the type SIM_PACKET or SIM_INTERRUPT.
8   // Output events have the type SIM_MOTOR_ON_TIME.
9   class PacketProcessing: public adevs::Atomic<SimEvent>
10  {
11     public:
12        PacketProcessing();
13        // State transition functions
14        void delta_int();
15        void delta_ext(double e, const adevs::Bag<SimEvent>& xb);
16        void delta_conf(const adevs::Bag<SimEvent>& xb);
17        // Output function
18        void output_func(adevs::Bag<SimEvent>& yb);
19        // Time advance function
20        double ta();
21        void gc_output(adevs::Bag<SimEvent>&){}
22     private:
23        // Computer time needed to process one packet
24        const double processing_time;
25        // Time to process the next packet
26        double sigma;
27        // Are we interrupted?
28        bool interrupt;
29        // FIFO queue holding packets that need processing
30        std::list<SimPacket> q;
31  };
32
33  #endif
```

The definitions of the internal, external, and confluent transition functions; output function; and time advance function can be inferred from the phase graph in Figure 2.7. The dotted arc S4 defines the internal transition function. The arcs S0 through S3 define the external transition function, which is briefly summarized by a three-step process: (1) if the model is not interrupted, then decrement the time remaining to process the current packet; (2) put new packets into the back of the queue and switch the mode if an interrupt indicator is received; and (3) if the model was idle and a packet is now available, then begin to process it. The operation of the external transition function can be inferred without ambiguity because the events S0 through S3 produce the same result regardless of the order in which they are applied.

The confluent transition function must resolve the situation where S4, S0, S3, or all of these are eligible to be active at the same time. The phase graph does not supply a rule for this situation, and so we must create one to complete the state space description of the model. Any ordering of the external events S3 and S0 will produce the same result, and so the question is where S4 should sit in the sequence. The intention of the phase graph is that S4 occur while the model is in the OPERATE phase. Because an interrupt can move the model out of this phase, it seems reasonable to apply S4 prior to engaging any of the external events. This implies that the confluent transition function is calculated by first applying the internal transition function and then the external transition function.

The output function and time advance function are less complicated. The model will produce output only when it is in the OPERATE phase, and the output is a *SimMotorOnTime* event that carries the ON times and directions contained in the packet at the front of the queue. If the model is operating, then the time until the next internal event is σ. If the model is interrupted, then the next internal event is at infinity. The implementation of the *PacketProcessing* model is listed below.

_____ ***Implementation of the PacketProcessing Model*** _____

```
 1  #include "PacketProcessing.h"
 2  #include <cmath>
 3  using namespace std;
 4  using namespace adevs;
 5
 6  PacketProcessing::PacketProcessing():
 7      Atomic<SimEvent>(),
 8      processing_time(0.0016),
 9      sigma(DBL_MAX),
10      interrupt(false)
11  {
12  }
13
14  void PacketProcessing::delta_int()
15  {
16      q.pop_front();
17      if (q.empty()) sigma = DBL_MAX;
18      else sigma = processing_time;
19  }
20
21  void PacketProcessing::delta_ext(double e, const Bag<SimEvent>& xb)
22  {
23      // If we are not interrupted and are processing a packet, then
24      // reduce the time remaining to finish with that packet
```

```
25    if (!interrupt && !q.empty()) sigma -= e;
26    // Process input events
27    for (Bag<SimEvent>::const_iterator iter = xb.begin();
28         iter != xb.end(); iter++)
29    {
30        if ((*iter).getType() == SIM_PACKET)
31            q.push_back((*iter).simPacket());
32        else if ((*iter).getType() == SIM_INTERRUPT)
33            interrupt = !interrupt;
34    }
35    // If we are idle and there are more packets, then start
36    // processing the next one
37    if (sigma == DBL_MAX && !q.empty()) sigma = processing_time;
38 }
39
40 void PacketProcessing::delta_conf(const Bag<SimEvent>& xb)
41 {
42    delta_int();
43    delta_ext(0.0,xb);
44 }
45
46 void PacketProcessing::output_func(Bag<SimEvent>& yb)
47 {
48    // Set the motor on times from the data in the completed packet
49    assert(!q.empty());
50    assert(!interrupt);
51    SimMotorOnTime on_time;
52    on_time.left = fabs(q.front().left_power)*255.0;
53    on_time.right = fabs(q.front().right_power)*255.0;
54    on_time.reverse_left = q.front().left_power < 0.0;
55    on_time.reverse_right = q.front().right_power < 0.0;
56    yb.insert(SimEvent(on_time));
57 }
58
59 double PacketProcessing::ta()
60 {
61    if (interrupt) return DBL_MAX; // No work while interrupted
62    else return sigma; // Otherwise continue processing the packet
63 }
```

To build the model of the computer, the *PacketProcessing* and *InterruptHandler* models are connected as shown in Figure 2.8. Packets delivered to the computer are routed to the *PacketProcessing* model; motor settings from the *PacketProcessing* model are sent to the *InterruptHandler*; voltage signals from the *InterruptHandler* become output from the computer, and interrupts go to the *PacketProcessing* model. The *Computer* class that implements this model is listed below.

_____ *Header File for the Computer Model* _____

```
1   #ifndef Computer_h_
2   #define Computer_h_
3   #include "PacketProcessing.h"
4   #include "InterruptHandler.h"
5
6   // This is a model of the computer. It contains an InterruptHandler
7   // and a PacketProcessing model.
8   class Computer:
9      public adevs::Network<SimEvent>
10  {
11     public:
12        // Create a computer whose interrupt handler has the
13        // specified frequency.
14        Computer(double freq);
15        // Get the components of the computer
16        void getComponents(adevs::Set<adevs::Devs<SimEvent>* > &c);
17        // Route events within the computer
18        void route(const SimEvent& value, adevs::Devs<SimEvent>* model,
19              adevs::Bag<adevs::Event<SimEvent> > &r);
20     private:
21        PacketProcessing p;
22        InterruptHandler i;
23  };
24
25  #endif
```

_____ *Source File for the Computer Model* _____

```
1   #include "Computer.h"
2   #include <cassert>
3   using namespace adevs;
4
5   Computer::Computer(double freq):
6      Network<SimEvent>(),
7      p(),
8      i(freq)
9   {
10     p.setParent(this);
11     i.setParent(this);
12  }
13
14  void Computer::getComponents(Set<Devs<SimEvent>* > &c)
15  {
16     c.insert(&i);
17     c.insert(&p);
18  }
19
20  void Computer::route(const SimEvent& value, Devs<SimEvent>* model,
```

```
21      Bag<Event<SimEvent> > &r)
22  {
23      // Packets and interrupts go to the packet processing model
24      if (value.getType() == SIM_PACKET || value.getType() == SIM_INTERRUPT)
25          r.insert(Event<SimEvent>(&p,value));
26      // Motor on times go to the interrupt handler
27      else if (value.getType() == SIM_MOTOR_ON_TIME)
28          r.insert(Event<SimEvent>(&i,value));
29      // Motor voltages are external outputs
30      else if (value.getType() == SIM_MOTOR_VOLTAGE)
31          r.insert(Event<SimEvent>(this,value));
32      // Any other type is an error
33      else assert(false);
34  }
```

To exercise the model, we can write a simulation program that sets the duty ratio and direction for the motors by sending a packet to the computer and then recording the voltage signals that it produces. The familiar form of the simulator's main function is listed below. It injects a single packet at the start of the simulation and runs for a handful of periods of the voltage signal; Figure 4.12 plots the voltages at the left and right motors. Both signals have a positive amplitude, but the left motor is on more often than the right, and the response of the tank is an arcing, clockwise turn.

_____ *Source File for the Computer Simulator* _____

```
1   #include "Computer.h"
2   #include "SimEvents.h"
3   #include <fstream>
4   using namespace std;
5   using namespace adevs;
6
7   class ComputerListener: public EventListener<SimEvent>
8   {
9       public:
10          ComputerListener(const Computer* computer):
11              EventListener<SimEvent>(),computer(computer),
12              vout("voltage.dat")
13          {
14              vout << 0 << " " << 0 << " " << 0 << endl; // Print volts @ t=0
15          }
16          void outputEvent(Event<SimEvent> y, double t)
17          {
18              if (y.model == computer) {
19                  SimMotorVoltage event = y.value.simMotorVoltage();
20                  vout << t << " " << event.el << " " << event.er << endl;
21              }
22          }
23          void stateChange(Atomic<SimEvent>*,double){}
```

```
24      private:
25          const Computer* computer;
26          ofstream vout;
27      };
28
29      int main(int argc, char** argv)
30      {
31          // Get the parameters for the experiment from the command line
32          if (argc != 4) {
33              cout << "freq left_throttle right_throttle" << endl;
34              return 0;
35          }
36          // Get the frequency of the voltage signal from the first argument
37          double freq = atof(argv[1]);
38          // Create a command from the driver that contains the duty ratios and
39          // directions.
40          SimPacket sim_command;
41          sim_command.left_power = atof(argv[2]);
42          sim_command.right_power = atof(argv[3]);
43          // Create computer, simulator, and event listener.
44          Computer* computer = new Computer(freq);
45          Simulator<SimEvent>* sim = new Simulator<SimEvent>(computer);
46          ComputerListener* l = new ComputerListener(computer);
47          // Add an event listener to plot the voltage signals
48          sim->addEventListener(l);
49          // Inject the driver command into the simulation at time 0
50          Bag<Event<SimEvent> > input;
51          SimEvent cmd(sim_command);
52          Event<SimEvent> event(computer,cmd);
53          input.insert(event);
54          sim->computeNextState(input,0.0);
55          // Run the simulation
56          while (sim->nextEventTime() <= 0.004)
57              sim->execNextEvent();
58          // Clean up and exit
59          delete sim; delete computer; delete l;
60          return 0;
61      }
```

4.5 CELLULAR AUTOMATA REVISITED

This chapter began with a statement that discrete-event simulations are a generalization of discrete-time systems. The cellular automata constructed in Section 3.5 will demonstrate this fact. Let $T(l, c, r)$ be the cell's transition rule, which maps its present state c and states of its left l and right r neighbors into a new state. Consider

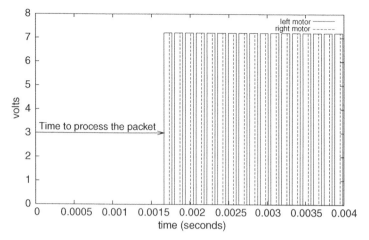

FIGURE 4.12 Output of the computer in response to a packet that sets a 50% duty ratio for the right motor and 75% for the left motor. The frequency of the computer's clock is 7.4 kHz.

the discrete-event system

$$S = \{0, 1\}$$

$$X = Y = S \times \mathbb{N}$$

$$\delta_{\text{int}}(s) = s$$

$$\delta_{\text{ext}}(s, e, \{(b_l, k - 1), (b_r, k + 1)\}) = T(b_l, s, b_r)$$

$$\delta_{\text{con}}(s, x^b) = \delta_{\text{ext}}(s, 0, x^b)$$

$$\lambda(s) = (s, k)$$

$$ta(s) = 1$$

which models a cell at location k. For the moment, assume that each cell begins with its elapsed time equal to 1. If N of these cells are connected to identical neighbors, differing only in k, to form a ring, then the output trajectories have nonevents except at $t = (m, 0)$, where $m \in \mathbb{N}$. Likewise, the input trajectories are Φ except at $t = (m, 0)$, where their values are $\{(b_r, k + 1), (b_l, k - 1)\}$ for $k \in [1, N - 1]$; for the cell at $k = 1$, the input values arrive from N and 2; similarly for the cell at $k = N$. The state trajectories change value in the discrete instant following an input, that is, from state s at $t = (m, 0)$ to state $T(b_l, s, b_r)$ at $(m, 1)$.

The discrete-time cell is quite similar in form. It has identical sets of states, inputs, and outputs; an identical output function; and the state transition function is

$$\delta(s, \{(b_l, k - 1), (b_r, k + 1)\}) = T(b_l, s, b_r) \tag{4.21}$$

This is precisely what was rendered in code in Section 3.5.

It is intuitively obvious that the discrete-event cell mimics its discrete-time counterpart; we now proceed to establish this in a formal way. The function $\bar{g}$ maps a discrete-time trajectory $x_d[m, m + 1)$ to an event trajectory $x_e[(m, 0), (m + 1, 0))$ by assigning $x_d(m)$ to $x_e((m, 0))$ and $x_e(t) = \Phi$ for all $t \in [(m, 1), (m + 1, 0))$. The function $\bar{h}$ takes the total state $(s, 1)$ of the discrete-event system to the state s of the discrete-time system. Letting δ_d and δ_e be the single step-state transition functions for the discrete-time and discrete-event models (i.e., as in Equations 3.8, and 4.7), respectively, and λ (from above) and Λ (Equation 4.10) be the output functions of the discrete time and discrete event systems, respectively, two facts are readily verified:

1. $\bar{h}(\delta_e((s, 1), \bar{g}(x_d))) = \delta_d(\bar{h}((s, 1)), x_d)$
2. $\Lambda((s, 1)) = \lambda(\bar{h}((s, 1)))$

This establishes a homomorphic mapping of the discrete-event system to the discrete-time system (this is an I/O system homomorphism [157]). Informally, the discrete-event system begun in total state $(s, 1)$ has all the capabilities of the discrete-time system started in state s. Moreover, because the structure of the discrete-time and discrete-event networks are identical, the discrete-event cellular automaton is a componentwise reproduction of the discrete-time automaton. A discrete-event automaton, however, can do much more than its discrete-time counterpart. The elapsed time need not be uniform across the space of cells, and if some variety is allowed, this produces asynchronous cellular automata, which are a subject of considerable interest in biology and the social sciences (see, e.g., Refs. 13, 28, 55, 129, and 134).

To illustrate, consider trajectories produced by a ring composed of the asynchronous cell listed below. The cells are left-looking (oriented toward the left); the transition rule is $T(b_l, s, b_r) = b_l$. Moreover, each cell is allowed a separate time advance and so they must record the previous output of the left neighbor to have it available when a state transition occurs. Each cell begins, as required by our simulation software, with an elapsed time of zero. The initial state of the cells alternates between 0, colored black, and 1, colored white. Note that in the figures the cells are arranged from top to bottom and time moves from left to right; this is not the visual arrangement used in Section 3.5.

────────────────────────── ***Left-Looking Event Cell*** ──────────────────────────

```cpp
#ifndef LookLeft_h_
#define LookLeft_h_
#include "adevs.h"

#define BLACK 0
#define WHITE 1

// A left looking event automaton. The CellEvent structure
// contains an integer that is the cell's position and
// another integer that has its state.
class LookLeft: public adevs::Atomic<adevs::CellEvent<int> >
```

```
12    {
13        public:
14            // Constructor puts the cell into its initial state of
15            // black if the location is even and white otherwise
16            LookLeft(int width, int location, double P):
17                adevs::Atomic<adevs::CellEvent<int> >(),
18                location(location),width(width),P(P)
19            {
20                s = l = WHITE;
21                // We have a state 0
22                if (location % 2 == 0) s = BLACK;
23                else l = BLACK; // or our neighbor does
24                c = 0.0;
25            }
26            void delta_int() { c = 0.0; s = l; }
27            void delta_ext(double e, const adevs::Bag<adevs::CellEvent<int> >& xb)
28            {
29                c += e;
30                l = (*(xb.begin())).value;
31            }
32            void delta_conf(const adevs::Bag<adevs::CellEvent<int> >& xb)
33            {
34                delta_int();
35                delta_ext(0.0,xb);
36            }
37            double ta() { return P-c; }
38            // Output function
39            void output_func(adevs::Bag<adevs::CellEvent<int> >& yb)
40            {
41                adevs::CellEvent<int> y;
42                y.x = (location+1)%width;
43                y.value = l;
44                yb.insert(y);
45            }
46            // The gc method is not needed
47            void gc_output(adevs::Bag<adevs::CellEvent<int> >&){}
48            // Get the location of the cell
49            int getLocation() const { return location; }
50            // Get the state of the cell
51            int getState() const { return s; }
52        private:
53            int s, l; // Own and left neighbor's discrete state
54            double c; // Time spent in own, current discrete state
55            const int location, width; // Our postion in the space and its size
56            const double P; // Time interval between changes of s
57    };
58
59    #endif
```

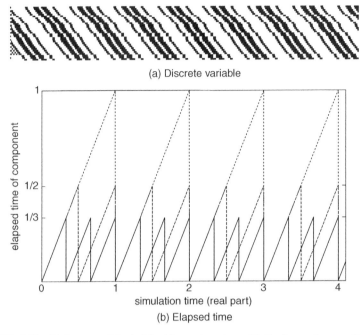

(a) Discrete variable

(b) Elapsed time

FIGURE 4.13   Trajectory of the left looking automaton with the time advance of each cell selected at random from $\frac{1}{2}$, $\frac{1}{3}$, and 1: (a) discrete variable; (b) elapsed time.

Figure 4.13 shows 125 units of time for this model with the time advance of each cell selected at random from $\frac{1}{2}$, $\frac{1}{3}$, and 1. The trajectory initially appears to be irregular, but at the sixth set of bands settles into a recognizable pattern. The elapsed time for each component is periodic as well. Indeed, the individual components return simultaneously to zero every unit of real time. Moreover, the number of discrete states is finite and must also repeat. It follows that the *total* state trajectory of the resultant of this network is periodic: the observed repetitions in the discrete state persist indefinitely.

If, however, the time advance is fixed at 1 then a discrete time system emerges once again. The initial chaos (but ultimate order) produce by an irregular time advance vanishes, replaced by a simple arrangement that translates colors to the left at each step. Figure 4.14 shows 125 steps of this arrangement. The periodicity of this cellular automaton is immediately apparent, and the close connection between discrete-event and discrete-time systems is vividly revealed.

4.6   SUMMARY

Just as discrete-time systems are derived by application of the semigroup property to sequences, this chapter has derived discrete-event systems by its application to event

FIGURE 4.14   Trajectory of the synchronous, left-looking automaton.

trajectories. Indeed, the latter systems subsume the former in the strictest sense. This imparts the practical advantage of a simulation framework that deals simultaneously with both. The common heritage of these classes of systems is also reflected in the common aspects of their simulation software. In particular, the intuitive approach to simultaneity inherent in a discrete-time worldview finds a natural home here.

The use of state space models as fundamental building blocks also lends itself to the incorporation of continuous systems in our discrete-event models (or vice versa). Indeed, numerical methods for solving differential equations *are* discrete-event systems. There is no conceptual divide to be crossed; the simulation problem is entirely one of implementation. This problem has been tackled successfully in several contexts (the literature here is vast, but see, e.g., Refs. 11, 30, 34, 66, 67, 77, and 110), and from our present vantage point, the common element of these methods are readily seized on and exploited. Significantly, the approach taken in Chapter 5 does require any modification of our concept of a discrete-event system. Continuous simulation is handled in its entirety, and with surprising ease, in the context of a discrete-event worldview.

CHAPTER 5

HYBRID SYSTEMS

Hybrid systems comprise continuous and discrete-event subsystems that interact. The continuous parts, unlike the discrete-event parts, cannot be simulated in their original form. Instead, continuous models are approximated with discrete-event models amenable to computer simulation. Any number of approximating systems can be used, each answering in a different way three fundamental questions:

1. In any finite interval of time, the continuous system traverses an infinity of states, but estimates can be computed for only a finite number of them (i.e., the discrete system must be legitimate); which points are picked?
2. To calculate these points requires knowledge of the trajectory between them; what is assumed?
3. The system interacts with its environment; how are inputs and outputs, continuous and discrete, handled?

For the moment, consider only questions 1 and 2 in relation to a single, ordinary differential equation

$$\dot{x} = f(x)$$

This continuous model can be approximated by (1) discretizing time into points separated by intervals of duration h and (2) assuming that x follows a line in those

Building Software for Simulation: Theory and Algorithms, with Applications in C++, By James J. Nutaro
Copyright © 2011 John Wiley & Sons, Inc.

intervals. This yields the discrete-time system

$$x(t_0 + (n + 1)h) = x(t_0 + nh) + hf(x(t_0 + nh))$$

which estimates x at times $t_0 + kh$ for $k = 0, 1, 2, \ldots$. Indeed, this is Euler's method for the numerical solution of an ordinary differential equation.

Another approach is to discretize x into points separated by intervals of length q, thus yielding a set of discrete states $x_0 + kq$ for $k = \ldots, -2, -1, 0, 1, 2, \ldots$. The goal now is to determine when x takes on these discrete values. By again assuming that x is a line between calculated points, the discrete-event system

$$ta(k) = \begin{cases} q/|f(x_0 + kq)| & \text{if } f(x_0 + kq) \neq 0 \\ \infty & \text{otherwise} \end{cases}$$

$$\delta_{\text{int}}(k) = k + f(x_0 + kq)/|f(x_0 + kq)|$$

$$\lambda(k) = x_0 + \delta_{\text{int}}(k)q$$

generates an output trajectory which approximates the continuous x. This is a first-order quantized state system (see, e.g., Refs. 70, 100, and 158).

To be concrete, consider a rock dropped from a bridge. Its downward velocity v is described by the ordinary differential equation

$$\dot{v} = g - \frac{D}{m}v \tag{5.1}$$

where m is the rock's mass, g is acceleration due to gravity, and D is the coefficient of aerodynamic drag. It is not necessary to simulate this system; the rock's speed can be written down once and for all if the rock's initial velocity v_0 is known. With this information, we have

$$v(t) = \frac{g}{D/m}\left(1 - \exp\left(-\frac{D}{m}t\right)\right) + v_0 \exp\left(-\frac{D}{m}t\right) \tag{5.2}$$

and that this is the solution to Equation 5.1 can be verified by taking its derivative with respect to time.

Applying Euler's method, we select an interval of duration h and approximate this continuous model with the discrete system

$$v_{k+1} = v_k + h\left(g - \frac{D}{m}v_k\right)$$

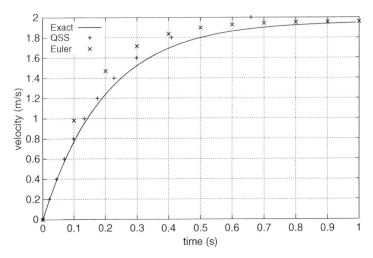

FIGURE 5.1   The Euler method and quantized state method applied to the model of a falling rock with $g = 9.8$ m/s^2, $m = 1$ kg, $D = 5$, and $v_0 = 0$ m/s. The discrete models use $h = 0.1$ and $q = 0.2$ respectively.

where v_k is the speed of the rock at time kh. A quantized state approximation using q yields the discrete-event model

$$ta(k) = \begin{cases} q/|g - (D/m)(v_0 + kq)| & \text{if } g - (D/m)(v_0 + kq) \neq 0 \\ \infty & \text{otherwise} \end{cases}$$

$$\delta_{\text{int}}(k) = k + (g - (D/m)(v_0 + kq))/|g - (D/m)(v_0 + kq)|$$

$$\lambda(k) = v_0 + \delta_{\text{int}}(k)q$$

Figure 5.1 compares the exact trajectory and the event trajectories produced by these approximations.

Euler's method and its kin, which discretize time, are the mainstays of numerical analysis and will be the focus of this chapter. Quantized state methods are nonetheless attractive for many applications (see, e.g., Refs. 70, 93, 94, 103, and 138) and can be incorporated with ease into the framework developed here; this intriguing topic is discussed in several textbooks (see, e.g., those by Zeigler et al. [157] and Cellier and Kofman [20]).[1]

---

[1]Notation in this chapter differs from the previous parts of the book and may be confusing. The set Q stands for a set of discrete states rather than set of total states; q is a member of Q or, in the code, a continuous state variable. So, too, x is a continuous state variable or, in the code, a discrete input. Usage of any symbol is consistent within a section, but beware of changes between sections. This unfortunate situation is a compromise between conflicting uses of x, q, and Q in the literature on discrete-event and hybrid systems.

5.1 AN ELEMENTARY HYBRID SYSTEM

Consider a system with a state that evolves continuously but an input that is discrete; the lopsided square wave that drives the tank's motors is one example. The input signal u takes values $u_0, u_1, \ldots, u_n$ at times $t_0, t_1, \ldots, t_n$. The equation that describes this system is

$$\dot{x} = f(x, u) \tag{5.3}$$

Begun in state $x_0 = x(t_0)$ and fed the input trajectory $u[t_0, t)$, with $t > t_n$, the state trajectory of the system is the solution to Equation 5.3:

$$x(t) = x_0 + \sum_{j=0}^{n-1} \int_{t_j}^{t_{j+1}} f(x(\tau), u_j) \, d\tau + \int_{t_n}^{t} f(x(\tau), u_n) \, d\tau \tag{5.4}$$

Euler's method is adapted to approximate this system in the following way. A fixed stepsize h is used to compute $x(t)$ through intervals in which u is constant. Changes in u are inputs to the discrete-event system. The external transition function responds to them by using the elapsed time for the integration step and then storing the new value of u. This ensures that the endpoints of the integrals are handled precisely. This method is realized by the (output-free) discrete-event model

$$X = \mathbb{R}$$
$$S = \mathbb{R} \times \mathbb{R}$$
$$\delta_{\text{int}}((x, u)) = (x + hf(x, u), u)$$
$$\delta_{\text{ext}}((x, u), e, u') = (x + ef(x, u), u')$$
$$\delta_{\text{con}}((x, u), u') = (x + hf(x, u), u')$$
$$ta((x, u)) = h$$

which has a state trajectory that approximates the continuous x.

A simplified model of an unloaded electric motor will illustrate the method. The current i through the motor is related to the voltage v at its terminals by

$$\dot{i} = (v - iR)/L \tag{5.5}$$

where R is the resistance of the motor windings and L is their inductance. To have a simple calculation, take $L = R = 1$ so that Euler's method, applied to Equation 5.5, gives

$$i(t + h) = i(t) + h(v(t) - i(t)) = (1 - h)i(t) + hv(t) \tag{5.6}$$

where i and v are known at time t. Observe that $h < 2$ is necessary for the calculated i to remain bounded, and $h << 2$ is needed to compute something similar to the

TABLE 5.1 Simulation of Equation 5.5 Using Euler's Method[a]

t	i, u	v	Event
$(0, 0)$	$0, 0$	—	init,0
$(0.5, 1)$	$0, 0$	—	int
$(0.75, 0)$	—	1	in
$(0.75, 1)$	$0, 1$	—	ext
$(1.25, 1)$	$0.5, 1$	—	int
$(1.5, 0)$	—	0	in
$(1.5, 1)$	$0.625, 0$	—	ext
$(2, 1)$	$0.3125, 0$	—	int
$(2.25, 0)$	—	1	in
$(2.25, 1)$	$0.234375, 1$		ext,final,0

[a]Where $h = 0.5$, v is a square wave with period 0.75 and amplitude 1, $v((0, 0)) = 0$, and $i = u = 0$ initially. Output events have been omitted.

correct continuous trajectory. Arbitrarily choosing $h = 0.5$ and v to be a square wave with period 0.75 and amplitude of 1, the discrete-event model calculates i at times $0.5, 0.75, 1.25, 1.5, 2, 2.25, \ldots$. These discrete instants capture precisely the moments when v changes and approximate i in the intervening spans. Table 5.1 shows the state and input trajectory for this simulation.

5.2 NETWORKS OF CONTINUOUS SYSTEMS

The network structure used for discrete systems is also applicable to continuous systems (see, e.g., Refs. 149 and 157), but it is most valuable as a modeling aide and rarely used in simulations. Because continuous systems are concerned with the real or, more generally, complex numbers, algebraic operations can reduce every network to a set of ordinary differential equations, or if not, then this indicates a special difficulty with the model. If a hard case is not ill-defined, then it is a differential algebraic model; Cellier and Kofman [20] give a good introduction to simulation algorithms for these systems. The formulation in Section 5.1 can be applied to any network that is reducible to a set of ordinary differential equations.

A continuous input u_c is incorporated into the state space of the model as follows. If u_c is a function of x alone, replace $f(x, u_c(x))$ with $z(x) = f(x, u_c(x))$ and solve the differential equation $\dot{x} = z(x)$. If u_c is a function of t as well, then add a new state variable τ that satisfies $\dot{\tau} = 1$, define a new function $z(x, \tau) = f(x, u_c(x, \tau))$, and solve the pair of differential equations

$$\dot{x} = z(x, \tau)$$

$$\dot{\tau} = 1$$

which is an input free system. Armed with this trick, continuous inputs do not require special handling by the simulation program.

5.3 HYBRID MODELS AS DISCRETE-EVENT SYSTEMS

A model of a sampled data system must provide output at fixed intervals, regardless of how the continuous equations are solved; similarly, a model of a threshold sensor must provide output at the moment of a threshold crossing, regardless of the timestep used for integration. Simulation methods for a hybrid system must therefore coordinate discrete-events and the timestep of the numerical integration scheme.

A continuous model in its state space form can be approximated by an atomic, discrete-event model that encapsulates methods for event detection and numerical integration. If the continuous model is connected to discrete components, then interactions with those occur by discrete-events: discrete sensor readings, square waves, and so forth. This arrangement of a hybrid model, which splits continuous and discrete-event elements, is illustrated in Figure 5.2.

The hybrid model has a vector $x \in \mathbb{R}^m$ of continuous state variables and a set Q of discrete states that describe switch settings, operating modes, and so forth. The differential equation that governs the model's continuous evolution depends, in general, on the discrete state q and so has the form

$$\dot{x} = f(x, q) \tag{5.7}$$

The occurrence of autonomous events in this system is conditional on both q and x. Just as in a pure discrete-event system, the real time that will elapse prior to the next internal event is a function of the present state. The hybrid analog of the time advance function has the form

$$G : (\mathbb{R}^m \times Q) \to R_0^\infty$$

and events happen when $G((x, q)) = 0$.

Referring again to Figure 5.2, the continuous variables are exposed only through the event trajectory that is produced as output. If the last event was at time t_k and the value of x at that time is x_k, then the value of x at the next event, some time h later, is

$$x_{k+1} = x_k + \int_{t_k}^{t_k+h} f(x(t), q) \, dt \tag{5.8}$$

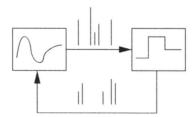

FIGURE 5.2   Separation of a model into discrete-event and continuous components which interact by discrete-events.

If the next event is autonomous, then $h = G((x_k, q))$ in the formulation given above. Otherwise, the system was interrupted by an external event and $h \leq G((x_k, q))$. Regardless, the value of x at the event can be obtained with any suitable numerical method and Equation 5.8 therefore poses no special difficulty.

The effect of the event is a separate matter: x and q can change discontinuously in response to discrete input, the occurrence of an internal event, or both. Just as with a discrete-event system, three transition functions account for the three possible cases:

$$\hat{\delta}_{\text{int}} : (\mathbb{R}^m \times Q) \to (\mathbb{R}^m \times Q)$$

$$\hat{\delta}_{\text{ext}} : (\mathbb{R}^m \times Q) \times R_0^\infty \times X^b \to (\mathbb{R}^m \times Q)$$

$$\hat{\delta}_{\text{con}} : (\mathbb{R}^m \times Q) \times X^b \to (\mathbb{R}^m \times Q)$$

define the response of the system to internal, external, and confluent events respectively. Similarly, the output function

$$\hat{\lambda} : (\mathbb{R}^m \times Q) \to Y^b$$

generates discrete output when an autonomous event occurs. These "hatted" functions are an abbreviated description of the discrete-event system

$$\delta_{\text{int}}((x_k, q)) = \hat{\delta}_{\text{int}}((x_{k+1}, q))$$

$$\delta_{\text{ext}}((x_k, q), e, x^b) = \hat{\delta}_{\text{ext}}((x_{k+1}, q), e, x^b)$$

$$\delta_{\text{con}}((x_k, q), x^b) = \hat{\delta}_{\text{con}}((x_{k+1}, q), x^b) \tag{5.9}$$

$$ta((x_k, q)) = G((x_k, q))$$

$$\lambda((x_k, q)) = \hat{\lambda}((x_{k+1}, q))$$

where x_{k+1} is calculated by Equation 5.8 with $h = ta((x_k, q))$ for internal and confluent events and in the output function, and with $h = e$ for external events.

A simple model will illustrate the essential concepts. Consider the system shown in Figure 5.3, which has a single continuous variable constrained by surfaces at 0 and 1. It follows a line from 1 to 0, bounces off that surface, returns to 1, bounces again, and this repeats forever. This system has a single discrete variable d, with the range $\{1, -1\}$, that gives the continuous variable x its direction. The system can be interrupted at any time by an input $u \in \{1, -1\}$, which immediately changes the value of d. The model produces an output each time it encounters a constraining surface.

Beginning with $x \in [0, 1]$, the continuous trajectory between events is described by

$$\dot{x} = d \tag{5.10}$$

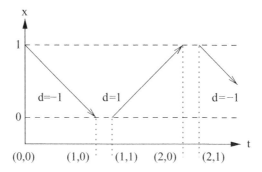

FIGURE 5.3   State trajectory of the bouncing hybrid system.

the time remaining to the next internal event is

$$G((x, d)) = \begin{cases} x & \text{if } d = -1 \\ 1 - x & \text{if } d = 1 \end{cases} \tag{5.11}$$

and the system's response to discrete-events is

$$\hat{\delta}_{int}((x, d)) = (x, -d)$$

$$\hat{\delta}_{ext}((x, d), e, u) = (x, u)$$

$$\hat{\delta}_{con}((x, d), u) = (x, u)$$

$$\hat{\lambda}((x, d)) = x$$

It is trivial to solve Equation 5.8 for this system; doing so and then substituting the preceding equations into Equation 5.9 gives the discrete-event model[2]

$$\delta_{int}((x, d)) = \hat{\delta}_{int}((x_{k+1}, d)) = ((d + 1)/(2d), -d)$$

$$\delta_{ext}((x, d), e, u) = \hat{\delta}_{ext}((x_{k+1}, d), e, u) = (x + ed, u)$$

$$\delta_{con}((x, d), u) = \hat{\delta}_{con}((x_{k+1}, d), u) = ((d + 1)/(2d), u)$$

$$ta((x, d)) = G((x, d)) = \begin{cases} x & \text{if } d = -1 \\ 1 - x & \text{if } d = 1 \end{cases}$$

$$\lambda((x, d)) = \hat{\lambda}((x_{k+1}, d)) = (d + 1)/(2d)$$

---

[2]The equation $(d + 1)/(2d)$ is zero when $d = -1$ and x is descending. It is one when $d = 1$ and x is climbing.

The output of this model when begun in state $(0, 1)$ and fed, for instance, the input trajectory $u[(0, 0), (\infty, 0))$ with

$$u(t) = \begin{cases} 1 & \text{if } t = (1.5, 0) \\ \Phi & \text{otherwise} \end{cases}$$

is $y[(0, 0), (\infty, 0))$ with

$$y(t) = \begin{cases} 1 & \text{if } t = (1, 0) \text{ or } t = (2m, 0), \, m \in \mathbb{N} \\ 0 & \text{if } t = (2m + 1, 0), \, m \in \mathbb{N} - \{0\} \\ \Phi & \text{otherwise} \end{cases}$$

which can be confirmed by a table-driven simulation or logical argument (both are excellent exercises).

The continuous trajectory, of course, is calculated only at discrete points. If a more detailed sampling of x is required, then G must be reformulated to invoke calculations at smaller intervals. This is accomplished by (1) introducing an upper limit for G equal to the largest sampling period $h_{\max}$ and (2) adding checks to $\hat{\lambda}$ and $\hat{\delta}_{\text{int}}$ for satisfaction of the conditions $x = 1$ and $x = 0$. The reformulated equations are

$$G((x, d)) = \begin{cases} \min\{h_{\max}, x\} & \text{if } d = -1 \\ \min\{h_{\max}, 1 - x\} & \text{if } d = 1 \end{cases}$$

$$\hat{\delta}_{\text{int}}((x, d)) = \begin{cases} (x, -d) & \text{if } x = 1 \vee x = 0 \\ (x, d) & \text{otherwise} \end{cases}$$

$$\hat{\delta}_{\text{ext}}((x, d), e, u) = (x, u)$$

$$\hat{\delta}_{\text{con}}((x, d), u) = \hat{\delta}_{\text{ext}}(\hat{\delta}_{\text{int}}((x, d)), 0, u)$$

$$\hat{\lambda}((x, d)) = \begin{cases} x & \text{if } x = 1 \vee x = 0 \\ \Phi & \text{otherwise} \end{cases}$$

That the output is unchanged is easily verified. The state trajectory, however, is sampled more often: in the absence of input, with a frequency $1/h_{\max}$.

5.4 NUMERICAL SIMULATION OF HYBRID SYSTEMS

The formulation above assumes that G can be calculated without future knowledge of x. Lacking a direct expression for the location of events in time, they must be defined instead by locations in the model's state space. This is reminiscent of the activity-scanning approach to discrete-event simulation (see, e.g., Ref. 157), but the event condition depends simultaneously on continuous and discrete variables. Specifically, autonomous events are described by a set of threshold functions

$$g_1(x(t_k + h), q) = 0$$
$$g_2(x(t_k + h), q) = 0$$
$$\vdots$$
$$g_p(x(t_k + h), q) = 0$$

and $G(x(t_k), q)$ is defined implicitly as the smallest, nonnegative h that satisfies at least one of these equalities or ∞ if no such h exists.

To illustrate this construction, consider the time advance of the bouncing system described in the previous section. Equation 5.11 is defined implicitly by the surface

$$g((x(t_k + h), d)) = x(t_k + h) - (d + 1)/2 = 0$$

and, because we know that $x(t_k + h) = x_k + hd$, this equation can be solved directly to obtain G.

Two methods are required for simulation of the hybrid system: a numerical integration method for advancing the continuous solution and a root-finding method to locate events between integration steps. These topics are covered by most introductory textbooks on numerical analysis (see, e.g., Refs. 71, 114, and 151) and in the specific context of hybrid simulation by a growing body of literature (see, e.g., Refs. 20 and 36). Almost any method is suitable, but those that readily accommodate changes in the step size and discrete adjustments of the state variables are most desirable because discrete-events will frequently occasion the need for both.

To demonstrate how a simulator is constructed, two particular methods are considered here. Corrected Euler with error control is used for numerical integration. This method is part of the Runge–Kutta family. Given a step size h and present value x_k at time t_k, the next value at time $t_k + h$ is computed with the two-stage rule

$$k_1 = hf(x_k)$$
$$k_2 = hf(x_k + k_1/2)$$
$$x_{k+1} = x_k + k_2$$

The magnitude of the error ϵ incurred by a step is approximately

$$\epsilon \approx |k_2 - k_1|$$

If after a step the error is too large, the step size is reduced and the integration retried. Conversely, if the error is very small, then the step size is increased to speed up the simulation. Having obtained the estimate ϵ using the step size h, the adjusted step size h_{tol} that satisfies an error tolerance ϵ_{tol} is estimated by

$$h_{\text{tol}} \approx \frac{h\epsilon_{\text{tol}}}{\epsilon}$$

For our purposes, the step size will begin at some maximum value $h_{\max}$ after each event and then be reduced if necessary; in this case the new trial step is $0.8 \min\{h_{\text{tol}}, h\}$.

Having selected a step size h that satisfies the error criteria and then tentatively advancing the trajectory, we now look to see if an event threshold lies between the old state x_k and the new, tentative state x_{k+1}. A simple, but often effective, method is to interpolate each g_j in the interval $[t_k, t_k + h]$ and look for a root of the interpolating function. The two endpoints for the interpolation are

$$g_{j,k} = g_j(x_k, q)$$
$$g_{j,k+1} = g_j(x_{k+1}, q)$$

There are three possibilities for this pair of points:

1. If $g_{j,k} \approx 0$ or $g_{j,k+1} \approx 0$, then an event has been found and an internal transition occurs at time t_k or $t_k + h$, respectively.
2. If both have the same sign, so that $g_{j,k}g_{j,k+1} > 0$, then g_j does not cross zero and there is no event in the interval.
3. If the points have opposite signs, so that $g_{j,k}g_{j,k+1} < 0$, then there is an event in the interval.

In possibilities 1 and 2, the time of the next autonomous event is known: it occurs now or at the next integration step.

In possibility 3, the existence of an intermediate event is known, but its time of occurrence must still be found. A procedure for doing so is illustrated in Figure 5.4. To start, we take $t_k = 0$, which is possible because the system is time-invariant, and approximate the function $g_j(t)$ in the interval $[0, h]$ with the line

$$g_j(t) \approx \frac{g_{j,k}(h - t) + g_{j,k+1}t}{h}$$

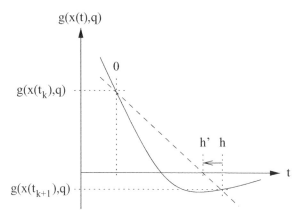

FIGURE 5.4   Using linear interpolation to locate an event in time.

Setting this equal to zero and solving for t gives the location of the event in time at

$$t \approx \frac{h g_{j,k}}{g_{j,k} - g_{j,k+1}}$$

Now the integration step is reduced to this estimate of the event time and a new x_{k+1} is calculated. If this state satisfies condition 1 or 2 in the preceding paragraph, then the search ends; the event is found or the interval has shrunk so as not to include it. Otherwise, these steps are repeated.

To implement this procedure, the discrete-event model has, in addition to its the discrete state q, two copies of the continuous state: the present value x and tentative next value x'. For each g_k, there is a Boolean variable e_k that is true if $g_k(x, q) \approx 0$ or $g_k(x', q) \approx 0$ and false otherwise. The variable h keeps the time separating x and x'. The model first looks ahead by a single integration step to calculate x'. Next, it looks for events at the ends of the interval $[0, h]$ and for events within it that might have been missed. There are four cases. The simplest is where the g_k neither are zero at the ends of the interval nor change sign. In this case, there are no events and, barring external input, the state h units of time later is x'.

The other three cases involve discrete-events. If at the left end of the interval any of the g_k are within ϵ_{tol} of zero, then the e_k are set accordingly and an internal event occurs immediately. Conversely, if this is true at the right end of the interval and none of the g_k have otherwise changed sign, then an event occurs at h, with state x', and the e_k are again set accordingly. Otherwise, an event occurs inside the interval and must be located with greater precision—a new h is estimated, a new x' calculated, and the process repeated. Algorithm 5.1 shows this procedure in detail, using the corrected Euler and linear interpolation methods described above.

With Algorithm 5.1, the discrete-event model that simulates a hybrid system can be written compactly as follows. Let $s = ((x, q), x', \bar{e}, h)$ be the state of the model where $\bar{e}$ is the vector of event flags $e_1, \ldots, e_p$. The error tolerance ϵ_{tol} and maximum

Input: $x, q, h_{max}, \epsilon_{tol}$
Output: $x', h, e_1, \ldots, e_p$

1 Tentatively advance x to satisfy the error criteria
2 $h \leftarrow h_{\max}$
3 **repeat**
4      $k_1 \leftarrow hf(x, q), k_2 \leftarrow hf(x + \frac{1}{2}k_1, q)$
5      $x' \leftarrow x + k_2, \epsilon \leftarrow |k_2 - k_1|$
6   **if** $\epsilon_{tol} \leq \epsilon$ **then** $h \leftarrow 0.8 \min\{h, h\epsilon_{tol}/\epsilon\}$
7 **until** $\epsilon \leq \epsilon_{tol}$
8 Look for events in $[0, h]$
9 **foreach** $k \in [1, p]$ **do** $g_k \leftarrow g_k(x, q), e_k \leftarrow |g_k| \leq \epsilon_{tol}$
10 Found an event at the start of the interval
11 **if** $(\exists e_k)(e_k = true)$ **then** $h \leftarrow 0, x' \leftarrow x$, return
12 **repeat**
13   **foreach** $k \in [1, p]$ **do**
14         $g_k' \leftarrow g_k(x', q), e_k \leftarrow |g_k'| \leq \epsilon_{tol}$
15   **if** $g_k' g_k < 0$ **then** $h \leftarrow \min\{h, hg_k/(g_k - g_k')\}$
16   **end**
17     $k_1 \leftarrow hf(x, q), k_2 \leftarrow hf(x + \frac{1}{2}k_1, q)$
18     $x' \leftarrow x + k_2$
19 **until** $(\forall k)(0 < g_k g_k' \vee e_k)$

Algorithm 5.1   Locate the internal event and tentatively advance x to it.

integration step $h_{\max}$ are fixed parameters. Let F be a function that applies Algorithm 5.1 to the state; $F(s)$ is equal to s except for x', $\bar{e}$, and h which the algorithm computes. Define also the function $I((x, q), \tau) = (x', q)$, where x' is x advanced by the step size τ. The discrete-event model is

$$\delta_{\mathrm{int}}(((x, q), x', \bar{e}, h)) = \begin{cases} F((\hat{\delta}_{\mathrm{int}}((x', q)), x', \bar{e}, h)) & \text{if } (\exists e_k)(e_k = true) \\ F(((x', q), x', \bar{e}, h)) & \text{otherwise} \end{cases}$$

$$\delta_{\mathrm{ext}}(((x, q), x', \bar{e}, h), e, u^b) = F((\hat{\delta}_{\mathrm{ext}}(I((x, q), e), e, u^b), x', \bar{e}, h))$$

$$\delta_{\mathrm{con}}(((x, q), x', \bar{e}, h), u^b) = F((\hat{\delta}_{\mathrm{con}}((x', q), u^b), x', \bar{e}, h)) \tag{5.12}$$

$$ta(s) = h$$

$$\lambda(s) = \begin{cases} \hat{\lambda}((x', q)) & \text{if } (\exists e_k)(e_k = true) \\ \Phi & \text{otherwise} \end{cases}$$

To summarize, at each event the continuous variable x is advanced to the present time. If there is an input or if an event threshold is reached, then the discrete transition function of the hybrid system is applied and, in the latter case, an output is also produced. The time advance at each event is the smaller of the integration step size and the time to the next internal event of the hybrid system.

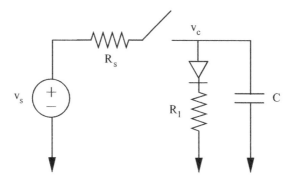

FIGURE 5.5   A model of a circuit with two discrete elements.

The electric circuit shown in Figure 5.5 will illustrate the simulation procedure, and the outcome of the simulation is listed in Table 5.2. This circuit has a load that operates when the voltage v_c is greater than the diode's threshold voltage. A capacitor stores energy to drive the load for short periods of time when the main power is disconnected. This capacitor charges rapidly when the load is disconnected, and it trickle-charges while the load is operating. The model has two discrete variables; $s \in \{0, 1\}$ for the switch with $s = 0$ open (not conducting) and $s = 1$ closed (conducting) and likewise for the diode; its state is indicated by d. The switch is an input to the system, and the diode state is determined by the capacitor voltage.

The voltage v_c is the model's only continuous state variable. It evolves in each mode as follows:

$$\dot{v}_c = \begin{cases} 0 & \text{if } s = 0, d = 0 \\ -\dfrac{v_c}{CR_l} & \text{if } s = 0, d = 1 \\ \dfrac{v_s - v_c}{CR_s} & \text{if } s = 1, d = 0 \\ \dfrac{1}{C}\left(\dfrac{v_s - v_c}{R_s} - \dfrac{v_c}{R_l}\right) & \text{if } s = 1, d = 1 \end{cases} \tag{5.13}$$

The diode conducts when v_c exceeds the threshold voltage v_{op} and stops conducting when the voltage drops below v_{cl}, where $v_{op} > v_{cl}$. A single function defines both cases:

$$g(v_c, d) = \begin{cases} v_c - v_{op} & \text{if } d = 0 \\ v_c - v_{cl} & \text{if } d = 1 \end{cases}$$

Significantly, the diode does not open and close at the same voltage level. If this were the case, then the model would be illegitimate, switching endlessly between its two states when v_c reached a threshold value. The model's output is the state of the diode.

TABLE 5.2 Discrete-Events in the Circuit Simulation[a]

t	v_c	(s, d)	$\bar{e}$	h	x'	u	y	Event
(0, 0)	0	(1, 0)	False	0.2	0.18	Φ	Φ	init,0
(0.2, 1)	0.18	(1, 0)	False	0.2	0.3276	Φ	Φ	int
(0.4, 1)	0.3276	(1, 0)	False	0.2	0.448632	Φ	Φ	int
(0.6, 1)	0.448632	(1, 0)	True	0.1035162642	0.5027534314	Φ	Φ	int
(0.7035162642, 0)	0.448632	(1, 0)	True	0.1035162642	0.5027534314	Φ	1	out
(0.7035162642, 1)	0.5027534314	(1, 1)	False	0.2	0.5018723334	Φ	Φ	int
(0.9035162642, 1)	0.5018723334	(1, 1)	False	0.2	0.5012731867	Φ	Φ	int
(1, 0)	0.5018723334	(1, 1)	False	0.2	0.5012731867	1	Φ	in
(1, 1)	0.5015458935	(0, 1)	False	0.2	0.4112676327	Φ	Φ	ext
(1.2, 1)	0.4112676327	(0, 1)	False	0.2	0.3372394588	Φ	Φ	int
(1.4, 1)	0.3372394588	(0, 1)	False	0.2	0.2765363562	Φ	Φ	int
(1.6, 1)	0.2765363562	(0, 1)	True	0.1013635251	0.2499263016	Φ	Φ	int
(1.7013635251, 0)	0.2765363562	(0, 1)	True	0.1013635251	0.2499263016	Φ	0	out
(1.7013635251, 1)	0.2499263016	(0, 0)	False	0.2	0.2499263016	Φ	Φ	int
(1.9013635251, 1)	0.2499263016	(0, 0)	False	0.2	0.2499263016	Φ	Φ	int,final,0

[a]The location of internal events in time can be calculated directly or with Algorithm 5.1. Output events for which $y = \Phi$ have been omitted.

The discrete transition functions for this circuit are

$$\hat{\delta}_{int}((v_c, s, d)) = (v_c, s, \neg d)$$

$$\hat{\delta}_{ext}((v_c, s, d), e, u) = (v_c, u, d)$$

$$\hat{\delta}_{con}((v_c, s, d), u) = \hat{\delta}_{ext}(\hat{\delta}_{int}((v_c, s, d)), 0, u)$$

$$\hat{\lambda}((v_c, s, d)) = \neg d$$

To keep the numbers simple, use $R_l = R_s = 1, C = 1, v_s = 1, v_{cl} = \frac{1}{4}$, and $v_{op} = \frac{1}{2}$ and begin with $d = 0, s = 1$, and $v_c = 0$. The discrete-event model uses $h_{max} = 0.2$ and $\epsilon = 0.05$. The capacitor begins to charge, and until the diode closes, the discrete equations (i.e., corrected Euler equations) that simulate v_c are

$$v_{c,k+1} = v_{c,k}(1 - h + h^2/2) + h - h^2/2$$

the error at each step is

$$\epsilon = |(1 - v_{c,k})h^2/2|$$

and the interpolating function for g, solved for time, is

$$t = \frac{(v_{c,k} - 0.5)h}{v_{c,k} - v_{c,k+1}}$$

causing the discrete-event model to undergoe the first three internal events listed in Table 5.2.

The diode closes at the fourth event when the real time is approximately 0.7. Because this internal event coincides with an event surface, $\hat{\lambda}$ and $\hat{\delta}_{int}$ determine the output and next state of the model. In its new mode, v_c is simulated with the difference equation

$$v_{c,k+1} = v_{c,k} + h(h - 1)(2v_{c,k} - 1)$$

the error at each step is

$$\epsilon = |(1 - 2v_{c,k})h^2|$$

the interpolated g solved for time is

$$t = \frac{(v_{c,k} - 0.25)h}{v_{c,k} - v_{c,k+1}}$$

and the discrete-event model evolves in this way until the switch is opened. If the simulation closed the diode at exactly $v_c = 0.5$, then both the actual system and its approximation would remain at that value. Instead, the simulated voltage overshoots the mark and descends slowly back to the correct solution.

At $t = (1, 0)$ the switch is opened. This external event advances v by the elapsed time and invokes the $\hat{\delta}_{\text{ext}}$ function of the hybrid system to change its state. In this new configuration, the discrete-event system simulates v_c by

$$v_{c,k+1} = (1 - h + h^2/2)v_{c,k}$$

the error at each step is

$$\epsilon' = |h^2 v_{c,k}/2|$$

and the interpolation function for g, solved for time, is as before. The capacitor is drained to the cutoff point after another three events, and the diode opens at the real time of $t \approx 1.7$.

Now the switch and diode are open and the equations governing the simulation are

$$v_{c,k+1} = v_c$$
$$\epsilon = 0$$
$$t = \infty$$

and so time advances with $h = h_{\max} = 0.2$ but nothing actually changes until the switch is closed again.

Working through this example, it quickly becomes apparent that an explicit formula for G saves a great deal of time and effort. When G can be calculated directly from the system's state, and so the location of the next event in time is known explicitly, the resulting change is commonly called a *time event* and G a *time event function*. If the next event time must be inferred from event surfaces in the state space, then the resulting change is called a *state event* and the g_k are *state event functions*. State events require much more computational effort on the part of the simulator, and so result in slower-running simulations. Time events are therefore preferable when they can be constructed.

5.5   A SIMULATOR FOR HYBRID SYSTEMS

The *Hybrid* class extends the *Atomic* class of the discrete-event simulator from Chapter 4 to implement the approximating system constructed above. Algorithms for finding event surfaces in time and for solving the differential equation are encapsulated in two classes: the *event_locator* and the *ode_solver*. The differential function, state and time event functions, and discrete transition functions of the hybrid system

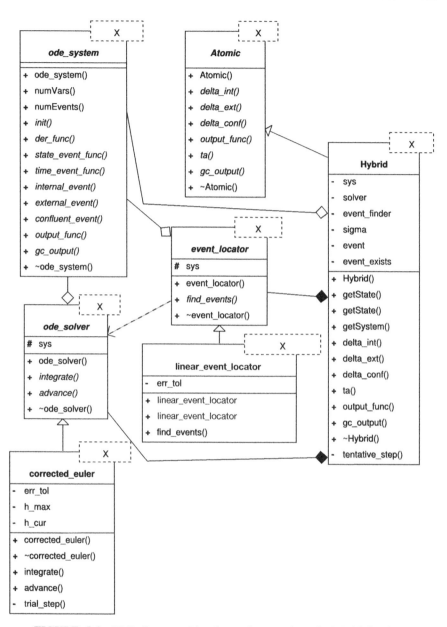

FIGURE 5.6   UML diagram of the classes that constitute the hybrid simulator.

are contained in a third class: the *ode_system*. The *Hybrid* class uses these three supporting classes to simulate a hybrid model. Figure 5.6 shows their relationships to each other and the simulation engine.

The *event_locator* uses the single method *find_events*, which looks for state events in a prescribed interval. Its arguments are the continuous state q of the hybrid model, the width h of the interval to search, the state q_{end} at the end of the interval, and an integration method for calculating states within the interval. The method returns true if an event is found and false otherwise. In the positive case, the time of the event is written to the supplied h, the elements of the array *events* are set to indicate which threshold function caused the event, and the state of the model at the event time is written to q_{end}. In the negative case, the elements of the *events* array are set to false but h and q_{end} retain the values supplied by the caller.

The *ode_solver* has two methods for advancing the continuous state variables. The *integrate* method takes the system from the state q at time t to the state q' at time $t + h$ where $h \leq h_{max}$. Integration methods with error control may use a value smaller than h_{max} to satisfy their tolerance for error. The method returns the step size that is actually used, and the final state q' is copied to q before returning. The *advance* method is identical to the *integrate* method except that it is guaranteed to advance the continuous trajectory to the end of the requested interval.

The hybrid model itself is implemented by extending the *ode_system* class. It has methods for computing the state event functions, the time event function, and the differential function. These are used by the *event_locator* and *ode_solver* classes. There are also four methods for implementing the discrete dynamics: *external_event*, *internal_event*, *confluent_event*, and *output_func*. These correspond to the hatted transition and output functions of the hybrid system. All of these methods accept an array q that holds the model's continuous state. This is maintained by the *Hybrid* class, which supplies it to the *ode_system* as needed. A model's discrete state, however, is captured by the member variables of its implementing class. Also observe that the discrete transition functions and output functions are supplied with an array of Boolean values; this array holds the e_k flags plus one extra in the last array position to indicate a time event. The *gc_output* method is used to reclaim objects created by the *output_func*.

Equation 5.12 is implemented by the *Hybrid* class. Its private *tentative_step* method implements the F function, which represents Algorithm 5.1 in the definition of the discrete-event model. The integration function I is realized with the *ode_solver*, which is also used by the *event_locator* to find state events (i.e., roots of the g_k) in the course of taking a tentative step. Time events are scheduled with the *ode_system*'s *time_event_func* method, which returns the time remaining to the nearest, explicitly known autonomous event. The time advance selected by the *tentative_step* method is the smallest timestep used by the *ode_solver*, the nearest state event found by the *event_locator*, and the next time event reported by the *ode_system*. The member variables of the *Hybrid* class are exactly the state variables of the discrete-event model, except for the extra Boolean variable *event_exists*, which saves a search through the e_ks by being true if any of them is true and false otherwise.

_____ ***The Hybrid Class*** _____

```
1  #ifndef _adevs_hybrid_h_
2  #define _adevs_hybrid_h_
3  #include <algorithm>
```

```cpp
#include "adevs_models.h"

namespace adevs
{

template <typename X> class ode_system
{
    public:
        // Make a system with N state variables and M state event functions
        ode_system(int N_vars, int M_event_funcs):
            N(N_vars),M(M_event_funcs){}
        // Get the number of state variables
        int numVars() const { return N; }
        // Get the number of state events
        int numEvents() const { return M; }
        // Copy the initial state of the model to q
        virtual void init(double* q) = 0;
        // Compute the derivative for state q and put it in dq
        virtual void der_func(const double* q, double* dq) = 0;
        // Compute the state event functions for state q and put them in z
        virtual void state_event_func(const double* q, double* z) = 0;
        // Compute the time event function using state q
        virtual double time_event_func(const double* q) = 0;
        // The internal transition function
        virtual void internal_event(double* q,
            const bool* state_event) = 0;
        // The external transition function
        virtual void external_event(double* q, double e,
            const Bag<X>& xb) = 0;
        // The confluent transition function
        virtual void confluent_event(double *q, const bool* state_event,
            const Bag<X>& xb) = 0;
        // The output function
        virtual void output_func(const double *q, const bool* state_event,
            Bag<X>& yb) = 0;
        // Garbage collection function
        virtual void gc_output(Bag<X>& gb) = 0;
        virtual ~ode_system(){}
    private:
        const int N, M;
};

template <typename X> class ode_solver
{
    public:
        ode_solver(ode_system<X>* sys):sys(sys){}
        // Take an integration step from state q of at most size h and
        // return the step size that was actually used. Copy the result of
        // the integration step to q.
```

```
53        virtual double integrate(double* q, double h_lim) = 0;
54        // Advance the system through exactly h units of time
55        virtual void advance(double* q, double h) = 0;
56        virtual ~ode_solver(){}
57    protected:
58        ode_system<X>* sys;
59  };
60
61  template <typename X> class event_locator
62  {
63    public:
64        event_locator(ode_system<X>* sys):sys(sys){}
65        // Find the first state event in the interval [0,h] starting from
66        // state qstart. The method returns true if an event is found,
67        // setting the events flags to true if the corresponding z entry in
68        // the state_event_func above triggered the event. The value of
69        // h is overwritten with the event time, and the state of the model
70        // at that time is copied to qend.
71        virtual bool find_events(bool* events, const double *qstart,
72                double* qend, ode_solver<X>* solver, double& h) = 0;
73        virtual ~event_locator(){}
74    protected:
75        ode_system<X>* sys;
76  };
77
78  template <typename X> class Hybrid: public Atomic<X>
79  {
80    public:
81        // Create and initialize a simulator for the system. All objects
82        // are adopted by the Hybrid object and are deleted when it is.
83        Hybrid(ode_system<X>* sys, ode_solver<X>* solver,
84                event_locator<X>* event_finder):
85            sys(sys),solver(solver),event_finder(event_finder)
86        {
87            q = new double[sys->numVars()];
88            q_trial = new double[sys->numVars()];
89            event = new bool[sys->numEvents()+1];
90            event_exists = false;
91            sys->init(q_trial); // Get the initial state of the model
92            for (int i = 0; i < sys->numVars(); i++) q[i] = q_trial[i];
93            tentative_step(); // Take the first tentative step
94        }
95        // Get the value of the kth state variable
96        double getState(int k) const { return q[k]; }
97        // Get the array of state variables
98        const double* getState() const { return q; }
99        // Get the system that this solver is operating on
100       ode_system<X>* getSystem() { return sys; }
101       void delta_int()
```

```
102        {
103            if (event_exists) // Execute the internal event
104                sys->internal_event(q_trial,event);
105            // Copy the new state vector to q
106            for (int i = 0; i < sys->numVars(); i++) q[i] = q_trial[i];
107            tentative_step(); // Take a tentative step
108        }
109        void delta_ext(double e, const Bag<X>& xb)
110        {
111            solver->advance(q,e); // Advance the state q by e
112            sys->external_event(q,e,xb); // Compute the external event
113            // Copy the new state to the trial solution
114            for (int i = 0; i < sys->numVars(); i++) q_trial[i] = q[i];
115            tentative_step(); // Take a tentative step
116        }
117        void delta_conf(const Bag<X>& xb)
118        {
119            if (event_exists) // Execute the confluent or external event
120                sys->confluent_event(q_trial,event,xb);
121            else sys->external_event(q_trial,ta(),xb);
122            // Copy the new state vector to q
123            for (int i = 0; i < sys->numVars(); i++) q[i] = q_trial[i];
124            tentative_step(); // Take a tentative step
125        }
126        double ta() { return sigma; }
127        void output_func(Bag<X>& yb)
128        {
129            if (event_exists) sys->output_func(q_trial,event,yb);
130        }
131        void gc_output(Bag<X>& gb) { sys->gc_output(gb); }
132        virtual ~Hybrid()
133        {
134            delete [] q; delete [] q_trial; delete [] event;
135            delete event_finder; delete solver; delete sys;
136        }
137    private:
138        ode_system<X>* sys; // The ODE system
139        ode_solver<X>* solver; // Integrator for the ode set
140        event_locator<X>* event_finder; // Event locator
141        double sigma; // Time to the next internal event
142        double *q, *q_trial; // Current and tentative states
143        bool* event; // Flags indicating the encountered event surfaces
144        bool event_exists; // True if there is at least one event
145        // Execute a tentative step and calculate the time advance function
146        void tentative_step()
147        {
148            // Check for a time event
149            double time_event = sys->time_event_func(q);
150            // Integrate up to that time at most
```

```
151        double step_size = solver->integrate(q_trial,time_event);
152        // Look for state events inside of the interval [0,step_size]
153        bool state_event_exists =
154            event_finder->find_events(event,q,q_trial,solver,step_size);
155        // Find the time advance and set the time event flag
156        sigma = std::min(step_size,time_event);
157        event[sys->numEvents()] = time_event <= sigma;
158        event_exists = event[sys->numEvents()] || state_event_exists;
159    }
160 };
161
162 } // end of namespace
163
164 #endif
```

The corrected Euler and linear interpolation methods from the previous section are easily adapted to the *ode_solver* and *event_locator* interfaces; the code is listed below. The *corrected_euler* class solves systems of equations. Its constructor accepts an error tolerance, which is applied individually to each differential equation, and a maximum step size, which should be selected to ensure stability. This integrator is modified slightly with respect to the earlier description; the object remembers the previous step size if it was chosen to control the integration error, thereby reducing the number of trial steps attempted when *integrate* is called. This can speed up the simulation substantially.

Likewise, the event locator is built for systems of equations. Its implementation is essentially as listed in Algorithm 5.1, but with two minor variations that improve its computational efficiency. First, the continuous variables are not needlessly integrated when $h = 0$; in this case, *qstart* is merely copied to *qend* before the method returns. The second adjustment, which is tricky, is to use an *event_in_interval* flag in place of the $\forall k$ that appears in the algorithm's last loop. On exiting the method's innermost for loop, this flag is true if, and only if, the nearest state event was found in $(0, h)$; if the event is at 0, then the method returns without looking further; if the event is at h, or not found at all, then *found_event* and the *events* flags are properly set but *qend* is not needlessly recomputed.

The Corrected Euler Integration Method

```
1 #ifndef _adevs_corrected_euler_h_
2 #define _adevs_corrected_euler_h_
3 #include <cmath>
4 #include "adevs_hybrid.h"
5
6 namespace adevs
7 {
8
9 template <typename X> class corrected_euler: public ode_solver<X>
```

```
10   {
11       public:
12           corrected_euler(ode_system<X>* sys, double err_tol, double h_max);
13           ~corrected_euler();
14           double integrate(double* q, double h_lim);
15           void advance(double* q, double h);
16       private:
17           double *dq, // derivative
18                  *qq, // trial solution
19                  *t,  // temporary variable for computing k2
20                  *k[2]; // k1 and k2
21           const double err_tol; // Error tolerance
22           const double h_max; // Maximum time step
23           double h_cur; // Previous timestep that satisfied error constraint
24           // Compute a step of size h, put it in qq, and return the error
25           double trial_step(double h);
26   };
27
28   template <typename X>
29   corrected_euler<X>::corrected_euler(ode_system<X>* sys, double err_tol,
30           double h_max):
31       ode_solver<X>(sys),err_tol(err_tol),h_max(h_max),h_cur(h_max)
32   {
33       for (int i = 0; i < 2; i++) k[i] = new double[sys->numVars()];
34       dq = new double[sys->numVars()];
35       qq = new double[sys->numVars()];
36       t = new double[sys->numVars()];
37   }
38
39   template <typename X>
40   corrected_euler<X>::~corrected_euler()
41   {
42       delete [] t; delete [] qq; delete [] dq;
43       for (int i = 0; i < 2; i++) delete [] k[i];
44   }
45
46   template <typename X>
47   void corrected_euler<X>::advance(double* q, double h)
48   {
49       double dt;
50       while ((dt = integrate(q,h)) < h) h -= dt;
51   }
52
53   template <typename X>
54   double corrected_euler<X>::integrate(double* q, double h_lim)
55   {
56       // Initial error estimate and step size
57       double err = DBL_MAX, h = std::min(h_cur*1.1,std::min(h_max,h_lim));
58       for (;;) {
```

```
59      // Copy q to the trial vector
60      for (int i = 0; i < this->sys->numVars(); i++) qq[i] = q[i];
61      // Make the trial step which will be stored in qq
62      err = trial_step(h);
63      // If the error is ok, then we have found the proper step size
64      if (err <= err_tol) { // Keep h if shrunk to control the error
65          if (h_lim >= h_cur) h_cur = h;
66          break;
67      }
68      // Otherwise shrink the step size and try again
69      else {
70          double h_guess = 0.8*err_tol*h/fabs(err);
71          if (h < h_guess) h *= 0.8;
72          else h = h_guess;
73      }
74  }
75  // Put the trial solution in q and return the selected step size
76  for (int i = 0; i < this->sys->numVars(); i++) q[i] = qq[i];
77  return h;
78 }
79
80 template <typename X>
81 double corrected_euler<X>::trial_step(double step)
82 {
83     int j;
84     // Compute k1
85     this->sys->der_func(qq,dq);
86     for (j = 0; j < this->sys->numVars(); j++) k[0][j] = step*dq[j];
87     // Compute k2
88     for (j = 0; j < this->sys->numVars(); j++) t[j] = qq[j] + 0.5*k[0][j];
89     this->sys->der_func(t,dq);
90     for (j = 0; j < this->sys->numVars(); j++) k[1][j] = step*dq[j];
91     // Compute next state and approximate error
92     double err = 0.0;
93     for (j = 0; j < this->sys->numVars(); j++) {
94         qq[j] += k[1][j]; // Next state
95         err = std::max(err,fabs(k[0][j]-k[1][j])); // Maximum error
96     }
97     return err; // Return the error
98 }
99
100 } // end of namespace
101 #endif
```

_____ *The Linear Interpolation Method for Locating State Events* _____

```
1  #ifndef _adevs_linear_event_locator_h_
2  #define _adevs_linear_event_locator_h_
3  #include "adevs_hybrid.h"
```

```
4    #include <cmath>
5
6    namespace adevs
7    {
8
9    template <typename X> class linear_event_locator: public event_locator<X>
10   {
11      public:
12         linear_event_locator(ode_system<X>* sys, double err_tol);
13         ~linear_event_locator();
14         bool find_events(bool* events, const double* qstart, double* qend,
15               ode_solver<X>* solver, double& h);
16      private:
17         double *z[2]; // State events at the start and end of [0,h]
18         const double err_tol; // Error tolerance
19   };
20
21   template <typename X>
22   linear_event_locator<X>::linear_event_locator(ode_system<X>* sys,
23         double err_tol):
24      event_locator<X>(sys),err_tol(err_tol)
25   {
26      z[0] = new double[sys->numEvents()];
27      z[1] = new double[sys->numEvents()];
28   }
29
30   template <typename X>
31   linear_event_locator<X>::~linear_event_locator()
32   {
33      delete [] z[0]; delete [] z[1];
34   }
35
36   template <typename X>
37   bool linear_event_locator<X>::find_events(bool* events,
38      const double* qstart, double* qend, ode_solver<X>* solver, double& h)
39   {
40      // Look for events at the start of the interval
41      this->sys->state_event_func(qstart,z[0]);
42      for (int i = 0; i < this->sys->numEvents(); i++) {
43         events[i] = fabs(z[0][i]) <= err_tol;
44         // If an event was found, the event time is zero
45         if (events[i]) h = 0.0;
46      }
47      // If an event was found at zero, put qstart in qend and return
48      if (h == 0.0) {
49         for (int i = 0; i < this->sys->numVars(); i++) qend[i] = qstart[i];
50         return true;
51      }
52      // Look for events inside of the interval [0,h]
```

```
53    for (;;) {
54        double tguess = h;
55        bool event_in_interval = false, found_event = false;
56        this->sys->state_event_func(qend,z[1]);
57        for (int i = 0; i < this->sys->numEvents(); i++) {
58            if ((events[i] = fabs(z[1][i]) <= err_tol)) found_event = true;
59            else if (z[0][i]*z[1][i] < 0.0) {
60                double tcandidate = z[0][i]*h/(z[0][i]-z[1][i]);
61                if (tcandidate < tguess) tguess = tcandidate;
62                event_in_interval = true;
63            }
64        }
65        // Calculate a new solution at tguess if an event was found
66        if (event_in_interval) {
67            h = tguess;
68            for (int i = 0; i < this->sys->numVars(); i++)
69                qend[i] = qstart[i];
70            solver->advance(qend,h);
71        }
72        // Stop when an event is located or is not detected in the interval
73        else return found_event;
74    }
75    // Will never reach this line
76    return false;
77 }
78
79 } // end of namespace
80
81 #endif
```

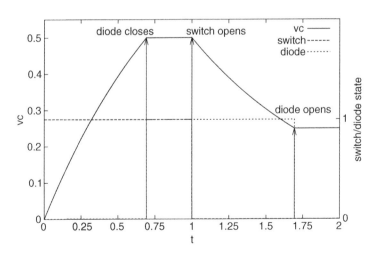

FIGURE 5.7 Simulation of the electric circuit.

A simulation of the electric circuit from Section 5.4 demonstrates how the *Hybrid* class is used. The complete simulation program is listed below. It prints the voltage and states of the switch and diode versus time, which are shown in Figure 5.7. This plot agrees very nicely with the data in Table 5.2.

_____ *Simulator for the Electric Circuit from Section 5.4* _____

```
1   #include "adevs.h"
2   #include <iostream>
3   using namespace std;
4   using namespace adevs;
5
6   class Circuit: public ode_system<bool>
7   {
8      public:
9         Circuit():
10           ode_system<bool>(1,1), // one state variable and event function
11           s(1),d(0), // diode and switch states
12           vs(1.0),C(1.0),Rs(1.0),Rl(1.0), // device parameters
13           vop(0.5),vcl(0.25){}
14        void init(double* q) { q[0] = 0.0; } // vc = 0
15        void der_func(const double* q, double *dq)
16        {
17           // ODE form of the differential equations
18           if (!s && !d) dq[0] = 0.0;
19           else if (!s && d) dq[0] = -q[0]/(C*Rl);
20           else if (s && !d) dq[0] = (vs-q[0])/(C*Rs);
21           else dq[0] = ((vs-q[0])/Rs-q[0]/Rl)/C;
22        }
23        void state_event_func(const double *q, double* z)
24        {
25           // This model uses the implicit form of the diode event
26           if (d==0) z[0] = q[0]-vop;
27           else z[0] = q[0]-vcl;
28        }
29        // As written here, this model does not have any time events
30        double time_event_func(const double* q) { return DBL_MAX; }
31        void internal_event(double* q, const bool* events)
32        {
33           assert(events[0]); // only one event type; make sure it fired
34           d = !d;
35        }
36        void external_event(double*,double,const Bag<bool>& xb)
37        {
38           s = *(xb.begin());
39        }
40        void confluent_event(double* q,const bool* events,
41              const Bag<bool>& xb)
```

```
42          {
43              internal_event(q,events);
44              external_event(q,0.0,xb);
45          }
46          void output_func(const double* q, const bool* events,
47                  Bag<bool>& yb)
48          {
49              assert(events[0]);
50              yb.insert(!d);
51          }
52          void gc_output(Bag<bool>&){}
53          bool getDiode() const { return d; }
54          bool getSwitch() const { return s; }
55      private:
56          bool s, d;
57          const double vs, C, Rs, Rl, vop, vcl;
58  };
59
60  class StateListener: public EventListener<bool>
61  {
62      public:
63          StateListener(Hybrid<bool>* c1, Circuit* c2):c1(c1),c2(c2){}
64          void stateChange(Atomic<bool>*,double t)
65          {
66              cout << t << " " << c1->getState(0) << " " <<
67                  c2->getSwitch() << " " << c2->getDiode() << endl;
68          }
69          void outputEvent(Event<bool>,double){}
70      private:
71          Hybrid<bool>* c1; Circuit* c2;
72  };
73
74  int main()
75  {
76      // Create the model
77      Circuit* circuit = new Circuit();
78      Hybrid<bool>* hybrid_model = new Hybrid<bool>(
79              circuit,new corrected_euler<bool>(circuit,1E-5,0.01),
80              new linear_event_locator<bool>(circuit,1E-5));
81      // Create the simulator
82      Simulator<bool>* sim = new Simulator<bool>(hybrid_model);
83      sim->addEventListener(new StateListener(hybrid_model,circuit));
84      // Simulate until the switch opens
85      while (sim->nextEventTime() <= 1.0) sim->execNextEvent();
86      // Open the switch
87      Bag<Event<bool> > xb; xb.insert(Event<bool>(hybrid_model,0));
88      sim->computeNextState(xb,1.0);
89      // Simulate for another three seconds
90      while (sim->nextEventTime() <= 4.0) sim->execNextEvent();
```

```
91      delete sim; delete hybrid_model;
92      return 0;
93  }
```

5.6 INTERACTIVE SIMULATION OF THE ROBOTIC TANK

In Chapter 4 the robot's computer was modeled, and now the gears, tracks, motors, and equations of motion can be connected to it. Section 2.2.3 gives the complete set of equations.

5.6.1 Correcting the Dynamics of a Turn

An ineffectual description of the event condition that initiates and ends a turn is obtained by rearranging Equation 2.19 to obtain the zero-crossing function

$$g = \frac{B}{2}|F_l - F_r| - S_l \tag{5.14}$$

When g is equal to zero, the discrete variable *turning* switches its binary value. Brief consideration reveals that this model is unable to begin or end a turn. After *turning* changes value, g is still zero, and so the model switches forever from turning to not turning and back, producing an illegitimate event trajectory.

This illegitimate behavior can be corrected with a hysteresis value ϵ to separate the torques that begin and end a turn. If ϵ is small, then the behavior of the model should very nearly approximate what was intended by Equation 5.14. This adjustment creates an event surface that moves when *turning* changes:

$$g = \begin{cases} \dfrac{B}{2}|F_l - F_r| - (S_l - \epsilon) & \text{if } turning = \text{true} \\[2mm] \dfrac{B}{2}|F_l - F_r| - S_l & \text{if } turning = \text{false} \end{cases} \tag{5.15}$$

This solves the illegitimacy problem, but a smooth g is also desirable so that linear interpolation gives a reasonable approximation. The absolute values are removed by creating two event surfaces, one for $F_l - F_r > 0$ and another for $F_l - F_r < 0$. The functions

$$g_r = \begin{cases} \dfrac{B}{2}(F_l - F_r) - (S_l - \epsilon) & \text{if } turning = \text{true} \\[2mm] \dfrac{B}{2}(F_l - F_r) - S_l & \text{if } turning = \text{false} \end{cases} \tag{5.16}$$

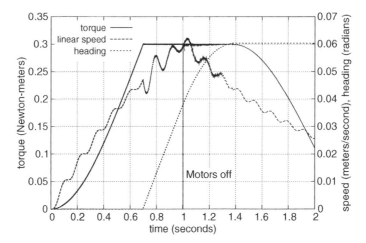

FIGURE 5.8 Tank shuddering through a turn with the duty ratio of the left motor at 75% and right motor at 50%.

initiate and end a clockwise (right-hand) turn and

$$
g_l = \begin{cases} \dfrac{B}{2}(F_r - F_l) - (S_l - \epsilon) & \text{if } turning = \text{true} \\[2mm] \dfrac{B}{2}(F_r - F_l) - S_l & \text{if } turning = \text{false} \end{cases} \tag{5.17}
$$

a counterclockwise (left-hand) turn. These are both continuous functions between discrete-events, and can be efficiently handled by the event detection algorithm described in Section 5.4.

Continuing the example in Section 4.4, we can now simulate the response of the entire tank to a sequence of commands from the driver. The first command sets the duty ratio for the right motor at 50% and for the left motor at 75% (Figure 5.12 shows the voltage signal produced by the computer). The tank responds by surging forward and making a shuddering turn to the right. Figure 5.8 shows the torque increasing until it breaks the tracks free and the tank begins the turn. Resistance from the laterally sliding tracks then draws power from the turn, reducing the torque and causing the tracks to stick again. This pattern rapidly repeats, keeping the torque near 0.3 as the tank staggers through its maneuver. One second later, a command from the driver sets the duty ratios to zero, and momentum carries the tank through the rest of a 3.5° turn.

Switching ω to zero instantaneously when the tracks stick has a curious effect on the model. It is apparent in Figure 5.8 when the torque peaks at 0.3, and is much more obvious in Figure 5.9, which shows a turn in place as the left and right motors work at 100% in opposite directions. At $t = 1$, when the motors are turned off, friction and electrical resistance slow the gears and deenergize the motor

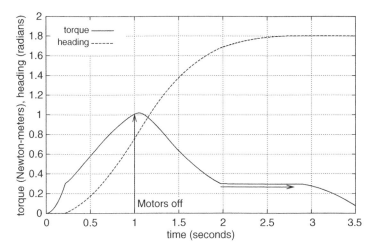

FIGURE 5.9 Tank spinning in place with the duty ratios at 100% for each motor, but working in opposite directions.

windings, thereby reducing the torque acting on the tank. In the instant before the tracks stick, viscous friction opposes the motors with a counterforce of about 0.02 N. After the tracks stick, this friction vanishes, and so does the counterforce. The motors and gears, their energy undiminished by the sudden transition, now apply torque sufficient to again overcome the sticking friction of the tracks, causing the tank to turn. High-speed switching between turning and not turning continues for 0.75 s until resistance in the motors, gearbox, and tracks removes enough energy to end the cycle.

Is this rapid switching an accurate portrayal of a real turn? Probably not. A more comprehensive analysis will likely to reveal a better model in this respect (see, e.g., Mosterman's and Biswas's discussion of this issue [90, 91]). The validity of the model, however, is undiminished by this curious phenomenon. The real tank and its model handle so sluggishly that the slight prolongation of a turn is unnotice-able to the driver; and the efficiency calculations that relate the frequency of the voltage and the consumption of power are calculated for straight-line motion. The issue must be revisited, however, if the model's scope of use is expanded at some later time.

5.6.2 A Simplified Model of the Motor

The corrected Euler integrator is adequate to construct the power–frequency plot shown in Figure 2.12 and for simulating single maneuvers like the ones above. However, the step size required for even a modest error tolerance of 10^{-2} ranges over five orders of magnitude, from 10^{-9} when the tank is accelerating to 10^{-4} as it trundles along at constant speed. The small step required for maneuvering makes this simulator impractical for interactive use.

This problem can be solved by using a more sophisticated numerical integration scheme or by devising a simpler model. The former is an advisable solution, and to implement it requires only that a new *ode_solver* be built and supplied to the *Hybrid* class. Suitable methods can be found in any textbook on numerical analysis.

Nonetheless, it is not uncommon for a model to have dynamics that cannot be simulated in detail, either for lack of information or for want of computing capabilities. The consequent simplifications often produce hybrid dynamics, a fact already observed in the tank where the fast, but continuous, switch of the transistors in the motor controller and the sudden slipping of the tracks are replaced by discrete transitions. The simplification pursued here will not have so dramatic an outcome, but it is still instructive to see how fast rates can be removed from a model to reduce its execution time while maintaining its validity.

To isolate the computational problem, we will focus solely on the circumstance where the duty ratios of both motors are at 100%; this requires no discrete-events because the motor switches are always closed and the tank moves in a straight line. The left and right treads are identical, and so four equations are sufficient to model the tank's motion:

$$\dot{v} = \frac{1}{m_t}\left(2F - B_r v\right) \tag{5.18}$$

$$\dot{i} = \frac{1}{L_m}(e - i R_m - \alpha\omega) \tag{5.19}$$

$$\dot{\omega} = \frac{1}{J_g}\left(\alpha i - \omega B_g - \frac{r}{g}F\right) \tag{5.20}$$

$$\dot{F} = \frac{1}{K_t}\left(\frac{r}{g}\omega - v\right) \tag{5.21}$$

The pair of identical forces F_r and F_l in Equations 2.19–2.31 have been replaced by a single force F, the equations that describe a turn have been eliminated, and the position of the tank is ignored. Retained are the speed of the tank and the dynamic behavior of the motors and gearbox (observe that ω in the equations above is *not* the rotational velocity of the tank, but the angular velocity of the gears); only three, rather than six, equations are needed for these because the pair acts indistinguishably.

Figure 5.10 shows the trajectories of the four state variables v, i, ω, and F. The voltage e is a constant 7.2 V. Figure 5.11 uses a logarithmic scale for time to show the initial inrush of current when the battery is connected to the motors. Using a per step error tolerance of 10^{-2}, the step size selection ranges from 10^{-9} at the start of the simulation to 10^{-4} after the initial transients have died off.

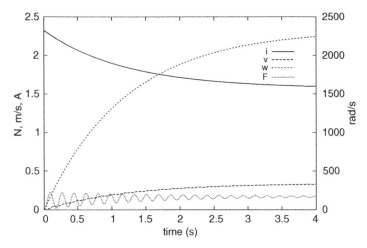

FIGURE 5.10   The tank accelerating under full throttle to its maximum speed.

The rapid, transient dynamic of the current is responsible for the small timesteps at the start of the simulation. This becomes apparent after looking at the ratios that determine the relative size of the derivatives $\dot{v}$, $\dot{\omega}$, $\dot{i}$, and $\dot{F}$. For the acceleration $\dot{v}$ the important ratios are

$$\frac{2}{m_t} = 2.5$$

$$\frac{B_r}{m_t} = 1.25$$

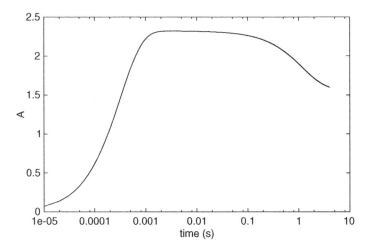

FIGURE 5.11   Initial inrush of current into the motors when the battery is connected at $t = 0$.

which indicate that the tank, chiefly because of its large mass, acts slowly relative to the rest of the system. The rate of change i of the motor current is governed by the ratios

$$\frac{R_m}{L_m} = 3100$$

$$\frac{\alpha}{L_m} = 1$$

where the larger ratio indicates that transients in the motor occur three orders of magnitude faster than the tank's acceleration. The ratios governing the acceleration $\dot{\omega}$ of the gears are

$$\frac{\alpha}{J_g} = 833.3$$

$$\frac{B_g}{J_g} = 0.5583$$

$$\frac{(r/g)}{J_g} = 61.27$$

and their contribution to the computational effort is about 3 times smaller than that of the motors, but on roughly the same order of magnitude. The ratios governing the propulsive force F of the tracks are

$$\frac{(r/g)}{K_t} = 0.07353$$

$$\frac{1}{K_t} = 1000$$

which is nearly the same as those for the gears. This analysis suggests that the computational costs are driven first by the model of the motor, then by the gears and tracks, and last by the acceleration of the tank's hull.

The system's eigenvalues reveal a more precise picture of how the different components constrain the step size (for details, see almost any textbook on linear algebra; e.g., Strang's *Linear Algebra and Its Applications* [136]). For each state variable there is one eigenvalue, and the largest determines the step size requirement; fast dynamics have large eigenvalues and require correspondingly small steps by the integrator. The smallest eigenvalue gives a sense of how constraining this really is. If the largest and smallest eigenvalues are close together, then the parts of the system operate at more or less the same rate and simplifications are unlikely to improve the execution time. Conversely, if the eigenvalues are far apart, then eliminating the most dynamic components can reduce the running time. The range of eigenvalues in the tank's model is broad, just as the ratio analysis above suggested; the smallest has a magnitude of 0.8 and the largest, 4000.

Now consider a simpler model that ignores the transient current. By assuming that i is an instantaneous function of ω, we can set $\dot{i} = 0$ and obtain the algebraic relationship

$$i = \frac{e - \alpha\omega}{R_m} \tag{5.22}$$

Substituting this into Equations 5.18–5.21 gives the three-variable model

$$\dot{v} = \frac{1}{m_t}\left(2F - B_r v\right) \tag{5.23}$$

$$\dot{\omega} = \frac{1}{J_g}\left(\frac{\alpha e - \alpha^2\omega}{R_m} - \omega B_g - \frac{r}{g}F\right) \tag{5.24}$$

$$\dot{F} = \frac{1}{K_t}\left(\frac{r}{g}\omega - v\right) \tag{5.25}$$

This eliminates the large ratio for $\dot{i}$ and changes the ratios governing the acceleration $\dot{\omega}$ of the gears to

$$\frac{\alpha^2/R_m + B_g}{J_g} = 0.827$$

$$\frac{(r/g)}{J_g} = 61.27$$

The magnitudes of the largest and smallest eigenvalues of this reduced model are 50 and 0.8, respectively. This is a considerable reduction in the maximum rate of the system and gives a correspondingly larger step size.

Figure 5.12 shows the trajectory of this simplified model. It is very similar to the plot that includes the motor because the inrush of current occurs so quickly that its long-term effects are negligible. The step sizes chosen by the integrator confirm the expected advantage; with an error tolerance of 10^{-2}, the timesteps during the initial transients are on the order of 10^{-5} and are 10^{-2} once the tank has gotten up to speed.

This reformulation of the model works well if the motors are at full power, but it is inadequate for operating at a smaller duty ratio. Figure 5.13 shows why; at a 50% duty ratio, the electric current in the more accurate model remains positive. This is because the motor controller switches fast enough for inductance to maintain the current when the batteries are disconnected. The reformulated model has no inductance, and the current actually reverses if the switches are opened while the tank is moving. This problem is corrected by using in Equation 5.22 the average voltage over an interrupt period rather than the instantaneous voltage. The correction requires a small change to the internal transition function of the *InterruptHandler*, which now computes e_l as

$$e_l = 7.2(\text{left motorontime}/255) \tag{5.26}$$

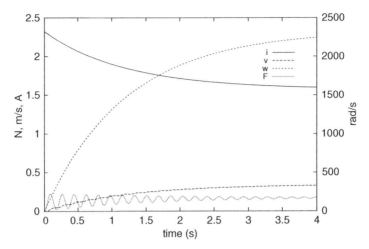

FIGURE 5.12 Simplified model of the tank accelerating under full throttle to its maximum speed.

and e_r in the same way. Figure 5.13 shows the effect of this alteration; the current in the simple model now agrees with the time-averaged current in the more detailed model.

5.6.3 Updating the Display

The driver's visual display of the tank needs to be updated at about 40 frames per second (FPS); each frame shows the tank's position and orientation and a trail of its previous positions. To do this, the state variables must be sampled and drawn every

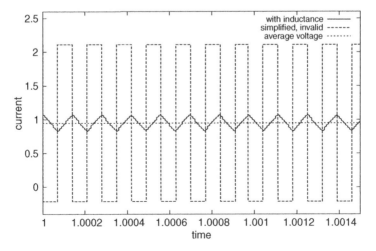

FIGURE 5.13 Comparison of the current for a 50% duty cycle in the original model, simplified model, and its correction.

25 ms. In Section 5.6.2 we saw that the simulator uses timesteps ranging from 10^{-5} to 10^{-2} s, calculating new states much more rapidly than required; indeed, faster than they can be rendered on the display.

Of the several possible solutions to this problem, ours is to have the model produce a SIM_TANK_POSITION event at regular intervals of 25 ms. The simulator, advanced in real time by the main loop of the simulation program, will therefore produce just the required outputs for the display. The display, in turn, is updated only when it receives an event that requires a new image.

This is accomplished by adding a time event to the model of the tank. A clock variable τ_c that satisfies $\dot{\tau}_c = -1$ is initialized with $\tau_c = 0.025$. The event surface at $\tau_c = 0$ is easily expressed as a time event that occurs after an interval τ_c. When the tank undergoes an internal event, it generates its position and orientation for the display and reinitializes τ_c to 25 ms.

5.6.4 Implementing the Tank Physics

The *TankPhysics* class is derived from the *Hybrid* class. It contains a *corrected_euler* object for simulating the model's continuous trajectory, a *linear_event_locator* object for detecting the start and end of a turn, and a *TankPhysicsEqns* object that implements the differential and discrete equations that govern the tank's motion. The code for the *TankPhysicsEqns* is listed below; it contains both the complete model, which was used for the efficiency experiments, and the simplified model, which is used for the interactive experiments. The selection is made with a Boolean flag passed to the constructor.

Coupling the *TankPhysics* to the *Computer* from section 4.4 completes the model of the tank. The code for the *Tank* class, whose components and couplings are illustrated in Figure 2.10, is also listed below. This model is accessed by the other major parts of the software, the *SimControl* and *Display*, via the *Simulator*'s interface for advancing time, injecting input, and listening for state and output events.

_____ *Header File for the TankPhysicsEqns* _____

```
1  #ifndef _TankPhysicsEqns_h_
2  #define _TankPhysicsEqns_h_
3  #include "adevs.h"
4  #include "adevs_hybrid.h"
5  #include "SimEvents.h"
6  #include <fstream>
7
8  class TankPhysicsEqns: public adevs::ode_system<SimEvent>
9  {
10     public:
11        // Create a tank at an intial position
12        TankPhysicsEqns(double x0, double y0, double theta0,
13              double cint, bool simple = false);
14        // Initialize the continuous state variables
15        void init(double* q);
16        // Differential functions
```

```
17      void der_func (const double *q, double *dq);
18      // State event function that detects turning movements
19      void state_event_func (const double *q, double *z);
20      // Sample x, y, and theta periodically
21      double time_event_func (const double *q);
22      // Expiration of the timer and collision events are internal
23      void internal_event(double* q, const bool* events);
24      // Change in the motor voltage is an external event
25      void external_event(double *q, double e,
26          const adevs::Bag<SimEvent> &xb);
27      // Confluent events
28      void confluent_event(double* q, const bool* events,
29          const adevs::Bag<SimEvent> &xb);
30      // Output position events for the display when the timer expires
31      void output_func(const double *q, const bool* events,
32          adevs::Bag<SimEvent> &yb);
33      // Garbage collection
34      void gc_output(adevs::Bag<SimEvent>&){}
35      // Get the resistance of the motor (left and right are the same)
36      double getMotorOhms() const { return Rm; }
37      // Is the tank turning?
38      bool isTurning() const { return turning; }
39      // Get the current in the motor
40      double getLeftCurrent(const double* q) const;
41      double getRightCurrent(const double* q) const;
42      // Index of the turning state events and timer time event
43      static const int TURNL, TURNR, TIMER_EXPIRE;
44      // Indices of the state variables
45      static const int WL, WR, FL, FR, IL, IR, X, Y, THETA, W, V, TIMER;
46      // Model parameters
47      const double mt, Jt, B, Br, Bs, Bl, Sl, Lm,
48          Rm, Jg, Bg, g, alpha, r, Kt;
49  private:
50      // Initial conditions
51      const double x0, y0, theta0;
52      // Hysteresis value for stopping turns
53      const double Hs;
54      // Communication interval for the numerical integration algorithm
55      const double cint;
56      // Motor voltages
57      double el, er;
58      // Is the tank turning?
59      bool turning;
60      // Use simplified dynamics?
61      const bool simple;
62  };
63
64  #endif
```

_____ ***Source File for the TankPhysicsEqns*** _____

```
1   #include "TankPhysics.h"
2   using namespace std;
3   using namespace adevs;
4
5   // Indices for the state event array
6   const int TankPhysicsEqns::TURNL=0, TankPhysicsEqns::TURNR=1,
7       TankPhysicsEqns::TIMER_EXPIRE=2;
8   // Indices for the state variable array
9   const int TankPhysicsEqns::WL=0, TankPhysicsEqns::FL=1,
10      TankPhysicsEqns::IL=11, TankPhysicsEqns::WR=3, TankPhysicsEqns::FR=4,
11      TankPhysicsEqns::IR=10, TankPhysicsEqns::X=6, TankPhysicsEqns::Y=7,
12      TankPhysicsEqns::THETA=8, TankPhysicsEqns::W=9, TankPhysicsEqns::V=5,
13      TankPhysicsEqns::TIMER=2;
14
15  TankPhysicsEqns::TankPhysicsEqns(double x0, double y0, double theta0,
16          double cint, bool simple):
17      // The simple model has two fewer state variables
18      ode_system<SimEvent>(12-simple*2,2),
19      // Set the model parameters and initial conditions
20      mt(0.8),Jt(5E-4),B(0.1),Br(1.0),Bs(14.0),Bl(0.7),Sl(0.3),
21      Lm(1E-3),Rm(3.1),Jg(1.2E-6),Bg(6.7E-7),g(204.0),alpha(1E-3),
22      r(0.015),Kt(0.001),x0(x0),y0(y0),theta0(theta0),
23      Hs(1E-3),cint(cint),el(0.0),er(0.0),turning(false),
24      simple(simple){}
25
26  void TankPhysicsEqns::init(double* q)
27  {
28      q[W] = q[V] = q[FR] = q[FL] = q[WR] = q[WL] = 0.0;
29      if (!simple) q[IL] = q[IR] = 0.0;
30      q[X] = x0;
31      q[Y] = y0;
32      q[THETA] = theta0;
33      q[TIMER] = cint;
34  }
35
36  void TankPhysicsEqns::der_func(const double *q, double *dq)
37  {
38      double il = getLeftCurrent(q), ir = getRightCurrent(q);
39      // Timer just counts down
40      dq[TIMER] = -1.0;
41      if (!simple) {
42          dq[IL] = (el-il*Rm-alpha*q[WL])/Lm;
43          dq[IR] = (er-ir*Rm-alpha*q[WR])/Lm;
44      }
45      dq[WL] = (alpha*il-q[WL]*Bg-(r/g)*q[FL])/Jg;
46      dq[WR] = (alpha*ir-q[WR]*Bg-(r/g)*q[FR])/Jg;
47
```

```
48      dq[FL] = ((r/g)*q[WL]-(q[V]+B*q[W]/2.0))/Kt;
49      dq[FR] = ((r/g)*q[WR]-(q[V]-B*q[W]/2.0))/Kt;
50      dq[X] = q[V]*sin(q[THETA]);
51      dq[Y] = q[V]*cos(q[THETA]);
52      assert(turning || q[W] == 0.0);
53      dq[THETA] = q[W];
54      // These equations change when the tank turns or does not turn
55      dq[V] = (q[FL]+q[FR]-(Br+Bs*(double)turning)*q[V])/mt;
56      dq[W] = (double)turning*(B*(q[FL]-q[FR])/2.0-Bl*q[W])/Jt;
57   }
58
59   void TankPhysicsEqns::state_event_func(const double *q, double *z)
60   {
61      double torque_l = B*(q[FL]-q[FR])/2.0;
62      double torque_r = -torque_l;
63      z[TURNL] = torque_l-(Sl-(double)turning*Hs);
64      z[TURNR] = torque_r-(Sl-(double)turning*Hs);
65   }
66
67   double TankPhysicsEqns::time_event_func(const double *q)
68   {
69      return std::max(0.0,q[TIMER]);
70   }
71
72   void TankPhysicsEqns::internal_event(double* q, const bool* events)
73   {
74      // Start or end a turn; this produces an output so reset the timer
75      if (events[TURNL] || events[TURNR]) {
76         q[TIMER] = cint;
77         q[W] = 0.0;
78         turning = !turning;
79      }
80      // Otherwise is was a timer event, so just reset the timer
81      else q[TIMER] = cint;
82   }
83
84   void TankPhysicsEqns::external_event(double *q, double e,
85         const Bag<SimEvent> &xb)
86   {
87      // Set the motor voltage
88      Bag<SimEvent>::iterator iter = xb.begin();
89      for (; iter != xb.end(); iter++) {
90         assert((*iter).getType() == SIM_MOTOR_VOLTAGE);
91         el = (*iter).simMotorVoltage().el;
92         er = (*iter).simMotorVoltage().er;
93      }
94   }
95
96   void TankPhysicsEqns::confluent_event(double *q, const bool* events,
```

```
97          const Bag<SimEvent> &xb)
98    {
99       internal_event(q,events);
100      external_event(q,0.0,xb);
101   }
102
103   void TankPhysicsEqns::output_func(const double *q, const bool* events,
104         Bag<SimEvent> &yb)
105   {
106      // Produce a position event
107      SimTankPosition pos;
108      pos.x = q[X]; pos.y = q[Y]; pos.theta = q[THETA];
109      yb.insert(SimEvent(pos));
110   }
111
112   double TankPhysicsEqns::getLeftCurrent(const double* q) const
113   {
114      if (simple) return (el-alpha*q[WL])/Rm;
115      else return q[IL];
116   }
117
118   double TankPhysicsEqns::getRightCurrent(const double* q) const
119   {
120      if (simple) return (er-alpha*q[WR])/Rm;
121      else return q[IR];
122   }
```

_____ ***Header File for the Tank Class*** _____

```
1    #ifndef Tank_h_
2    #define Tank_h_
3    #include "Computer.h"
4    #include "TankPhysics.h"
5
6    // This is the complete model of the tank with the TankPhysics and Computer
7    class Tank:
8       public adevs::Network<SimEvent>
9    {
10      public:
11         // Tank has an interrupt handler with the specified frequency,
12         // starts at the specified position, and generates events for
13         // the display at the given interval
14         Tank(double freq, double x0, double y0, double theta0, double cint);
15         // Get the components of the tank
16         void getComponents(adevs::Set<adevs::Devs<SimEvent>* > &c);
17         // Route events within the tank
18         void route(const SimEvent& value, adevs::Devs<SimEvent>* model,
19               adevs::Bag<adevs::Event<SimEvent> > &r);
20         // Get the physics model
```

```
21        const TankPhysics* getPhysics() const { return &physics; }
22        // Get the computer
23        const Computer* getComputer() const { return &computer; }
24    private:
25        Computer computer;
26        TankPhysics physics;
27    };
28
29    #endif
```

—————————— *Source File for the Tank Class* ——————————

```
1    #include "Tank.h"
2    #include <cassert>
3    #include <iostream>
4    using namespace std;
5    using namespace adevs;
6
7    Tank::Tank(double freq, double x0, double y0, double theta0, double cint):
8        Network<SimEvent>(),
9        computer(freq),
10       physics(new TankPhysicsEqns(x0,y0,theta0,cint,false))
11   {
12       computer.setParent(this);
13       physics.setParent(this);
14   }
15
16   void Tank::getComponents(Set<Devs<SimEvent>* > &c)
17   {
18       c.insert(&computer);
19       c.insert(&physics);
20   }
21
22   void Tank::route(const SimEvent& value, Devs<SimEvent>* model,
23       Bag<Event<SimEvent> > &r)
24   {
25       // Packets go to the computer
26       if (value.getType() == SIM_PACKET)
27           r.insert(Event<SimEvent>(&computer,value));
28       // Voltage events go to the tank physics model
29       else if (value.getType() == SIM_MOTOR_VOLTAGE)
30           r.insert(Event<SimEvent>(&physics,value));
31       // Position events are external output
32       else if (value.getType() == SIM_TANK_POSITION)
33           r.insert(Event<SimEvent>(this,value));
34       // Anything else is an error
35       else assert(false);
36   }
```

5.7 APPROXIMATING CONTINUOUS INTERACTION BETWEEN HYBRID MODELS

Most numerical integration methods are designed for models in state space form, and it is therefore desirable to put continuously interacting components into a single atomic unit. Other considerations in the design of the simulation software may nonetheless militate against this, and a method for approximating continuous interaction with discrete-events is therefore indispensable.

A widely used technique, described in its most general form by Giambiasi et al. [50], is to encode in an event a polynomial that approximates a continuous output. The recipient of the event uses the polynomial to approximate the original, continuous trajectory. The widespread use of this method testifies to its great utility: it is embedded in the dead-reckoning algorithms of the *IEEE Distributed Interactive Simulation* (DIS) standard [1] and has been widely used in event-based methods for numerical integration [70, 99, 142, 158].

Continuous trajectories are encoded in an event as follows. Given k samples $x_1, \ldots, x_k$ of the continuous function, and possibly some of its derivatives, at times $t_1, \ldots, t_k$, fit a polynomial to the data and send its coefficients in a discrete-event. The recipient keeps these coefficients and uses them to calculate approximate values of the continuous trajectory. In general, the more frequent the events and the greater the information embedded in the polynomial, the more accurate is the approximation.

Dead reckoning in the IEEE DIS standard probably represents the most familiar and most prominent use of polynomial events. Its purpose is to reduce the frequency of position updates for simulated objects in a distributed, interactive simulation. Each simulated object (aircraft, tank, ship, etc.) calculates, by any appropriate means, its time-varying position x and velocity v. It also maintains the last position x_o and velocity v_o that it broadcast on the simulation network and the time t_o when that information was sent. The recipients of this data approximate the object's position at time t with the line

$$\tilde{x} = x_o + (t - t_o)v_o \qquad (5.27)$$

The originator of the data calculates its estimated position whenever it recalculates its actual position, and new values for x_o, v_o, and t_o are sent if x and $\tilde{x}$ deviate by some predetermined quantity. Figure 5.14 illustrates this method.

Dead reckoning uses a truncated Taylor series to approximate the object's position, but any polynomial can be used in general; the specific choice will depend on the data that are available. For instance, Equation 5.27 could be expanded by using two velocity points v_o and v_o' at times t_o and some earlier time t_o' to more accurately approximate the actual velocity by

$$\tilde{v} = \frac{t - t_o'}{t_o - t_o'}v_o + \frac{t - t_o}{t_o' - t_o}v_o'$$

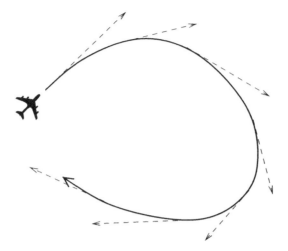

FIGURE 5.14 Illustration of dead reckoning in the *IEEE Standard for Distribute Interactive Simulation.* The solid line shows the aircraft's actual trajectory; the dashed lines, the approximate, piecewise polynomial trajectories communicated by the dead reckoning procedure.

and using x_o, v_o, and $\tilde{v}$ to estimate the position by

$$\tilde{x} = x_o + (t - t_o)\tilde{v}$$

which, by encoding more information, tends to give a better result.

Although this technique is very useful, it must be employed with some caution. When difficulties do occur, they are invariably due to the originator of the polynomial and its recipient not acting on the same signal. The originator, having accurate data for itself, will prefer these for its local calculations. Clearly, the recipient does not have this original data and must make do with the approximation. In a distributed simulation this effect is exacerbated by transmission delays in the communication network. The consequences for event detection are obvious, but nonetheless startling.

For instance, Figure 5.15 illustrates two aircraft flying a collision course and expected to crash into each other. Aircraft A is flying a straight line at constant speed. Aircraft B is turning, but its position is dead-reckoned by aircraft A using information received at the start of the turn. Aircraft B, with the more accurate view of its own path, will detect the midair collision. Aircraft A, unaware that B is turning, will not. The simulated outcome for A is in error and, much worse, A and B have inconsistent views of the world following the collision.

This use of polynomials can have an even more insidious effect on numerical integration methods by altering their stability properties. This problem occurs when

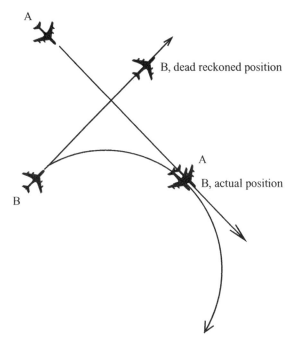

A

B, dead reckoned position

A

B, actual position

B

FIGURE 5.15 A collision that creates an inconsistent worldview because of error in a dead-reckoned position.

there is more than one state variable, which complicates the analysis somewhat; we will therefore consider a single illuminating case. Consider the stable, linear system

$$\dot{x} = -x + y$$

$$\dot{y} = x - 2y$$

and its simulation by the implicit Euler method, which uses the approximate system

$$x_{n+1} = x_n + h(-x_{n+1} + y_{n+1})$$

$$y_{n+1} = y_n + h(x_{n+1} - 2y_{n+1})$$

For a stable simulation, the matrix

$$\begin{bmatrix} 1+h & -h \\ -h & 1+2h \end{bmatrix}^{-1}$$

must have only eigenvalues with a magnitude of -1. This condition is equivalent to the roots of the polynomial

$$p(\lambda) = \lambda^2 - \left(\frac{2 + 3h}{1 + 3h + h^2} \right) \lambda + \frac{1}{1 + 3h + h^2}$$

being strictly -1. The roots are

$$\frac{2 + 3h \pm \sqrt{h(5h - 6)}}{2 + 6h + 2h^2}$$

and when $h = 0$, they equal 1. As $h \to \infty$ the h^2 in the denominator dominates, causing the roots to vanish. In fact, the magnitudes of the eigenvalues are less than 1 for all $h > 0$. This outcome is not entirely unexpected: the implicit Euler method is stable for any stable, linear system.

Now split this model into two discrete-time systems, as shown in Figure 5.16. The systems x and y are both simulated using the implicit Euler method with step size h, and they exchange state and derivative information at each step. The system x approximates y with the line $\tilde{y}(t)$ and y approximates x with the line $\tilde{x}(t)$. The simulation can be written as the pair of difference equations

$$x_{n+1} = x_n + h(-x_{n+1} + \tilde{y}(h))$$
$$y_{n+1} = y_n + h(\tilde{x}(h) - 2y_{n+1})$$
$$\tilde{x}(t) = x_n + t(-x_n + y_n)$$
$$\tilde{y}(t) = y_n + t(x_n - 2y_n)$$

This simulation is stable only if the matrix

$$\begin{bmatrix} (1 + h^2)/(1 + h) & h(1 - 2h)/(1 + h) \\ h(1 - h)/(1 + 2h) & (1 + h^2)/(1 + 2h) \end{bmatrix}$$

has only eigenvalues with magnitude ≤ 1. A sure sign of trouble are the diagonal entries that explode as h becomes large. Substituting $h = 2$, a stable selection when

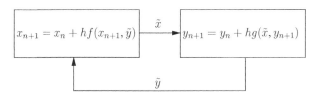

FIGURE 5.16   Separating the atomic model with state variables x and y into a network model with two parts.

implicit Euler is applied to the system as a whole, makes this simulation unstable, leaving it with the pair of eigenvalues 0.38 and 2.3. When the continuously interacting x and y are separated into two discrete modules, the unconditional stability of the implicit Euler scheme is lost.

In many instances, these problems can be mitigated by carefully considering them early in the design of a simulator. Inconsistency in distributed interactive simulations, and in virtual environments in general, have been studied extensively, and numerous techniques are available for alleviating problems caused by extrapolation and communication delays (see, e.g., Refs. 16, 44, 118, and 162). In the specific context of hybrid simulation, a judicious choice of integration scheme and careful control of the local step size will avert numerical problems (see, e.g., Refs. 69 and 155). In any case, an awareness of the potential difficulties posed by extrapolating polynomials is essential for avoiding unpleasant surprises when they are put to real use.

5.8   A FINAL COMMENT ON CELLULAR AUTOMATA

In Section 4.5, it was shown that asynchronous cellular automata subsume the familiar synchronous cellular automata. The asynchronous (cellular) automata are now shown to be a special case of a still more general class of systems: the differential automata, which are used as models of flexible manufacturing systems (see, e.g., Ref. 84). The transformation of asynchronous automata into differential automata is an example of how, by recognizing equivalences between seemingly disparate systems, the useful scope of the simulator is expanded. More generally, the type of transformation demonstrated here is a powerful enabler of multiformalism modeling. Automated transformation of verification-oriented models, grounded, for example, in hybrid input/output automata, one of the many flavors of Petri nets, labeled transition systems, or finite-state automata, into code for multidisciplinary simulation projects (see, e.g., Ref. 92) is an active area of research. AToM3 [33, 141], CD++ [143], the composability framework described by Sarjoughian and Mayer [85, 126], and the models of computation concept being explored by the Ptolemy and Kepler projects [53], among others, demonstrate the promising potential of this technique.

5.8.1   Differential Automata with Constant Derivatives

Differential automata are finite-state automata that have a set of differential equations associated with each discrete state. Discrete-events, which change the system's discrete state, occur when the automaton's continuous trajectory encounters an event surface. By changing the discrete state, the system selects a new set of differential equations to govern its motion away from the interrupting event surface.

In this particular example, the automaton's continuous variables follow a line between events. Its velocity depends on the discrete state q, of which there are only a finite number. The continuous state vector $\mathbf{x}$ satisfies

$$\dot{\mathbf{x}}(t) = v(q) \tag{5.28}$$

at each instance of real time t for which q is constant. When q changes at time (t, c), its subsequent value depends on $q((t, c))$ and $x((t, c))$; the new state at time $(t, c + 1)$ is[3]

$$q((t, c + 1)) = \Theta(\mathbf{x}((t, c)), q((t, c))) \tag{5.29}$$

The discrete change in the differential function takes effect at time $(t, c + 1)$, and $\mathbf{x}$ evolves from its value at the transition. Because $\mathbf{x}$ does not change discontinuously, the trajectory $\mathbf{x}(t)$, which satisfies Equation 5.28 and is a function from $\mathbb{R} \to \mathbb{R}^m$, is equal to $\mathbf{x}((t, c))$, a function from $\mathbb{R} \times \mathbb{N} \to \mathbb{R}^m$, for all $c \in \mathbb{N}$, and so the two technically distinct trajectories are interchangeable.

These systems can, of course, be modeled with a trivial hybrid system expressed in terms of differential functions, event surfaces, and discrete transitions. Specifically, it is the input/output-free system with $\dot{\mathbf{x}}$ as written above, $\hat{\delta}_{\text{int}}((\mathbf{x}, q)) = (\mathbf{x}, \Theta(\mathbf{x}, q))$, and G is the time remaining until Θ changes value.

5.8.2   Modeling Asynchronous Cellular Automata with Differential Automata

The discrete states of a cellular automaton can be numbered by treating its leftmost cell as the most significant bit in a binary number and its rightmost as the least significant. An automaton with n cells has 2^n discrete states. In addition to its binary state, each cell k has a clock τ_k that induces events in two ways: beginning from zero, τ_k grows until it reaches the cell's duration P_k; and beginning at P_k, τ_k shrinks until it reaches zero. The direction of the clock is the cell's third and final state variable.

The pair (b_k, d_k) is the discrete state of cell k, where $b_k \in \{0, 1\}$ is the binary state and $d_k \in \{1, -1\}$ is the direction of the clock; the set of discrete states is $Q = \{0, 1\} \times \{1, -1\}$. The clock τ_k begins, and remains, in the interval $[0, P_k]$. The differential automaton that models the cell is

$$\dot{\tau}_k = d_k \tag{5.30}$$

$$\Theta_k(\tau_k, (b_k, d_k)) = \begin{cases} (T(b_{k,l}, b_k, b_{k,r}), -d_k) & \text{if } (\tau_k = 0 \wedge d_k = -1) \\ & \vee (\tau_k = P_k \wedge d_k = 1) \\ (b_k, d_k) & \text{otherwise} \end{cases} \tag{5.31}$$

where T is as defined by Equation 4.21.

A cellular automaton with n cells is a differential automaton with the set of discrete states Q^n and the continuous state vector $\tau = [\tau_1 \ \tau_2 \ \cdots \ \tau_n]$. The dynamic equations

---

[3]The symbol Φ commonly denotes the discrete transition function of a differential automata, but this conflicts with our use of it for the nonevent, hence Θ.

for this model are

$$\dot{t} = [d_1 \, d_2 \, \cdots \, d_n] \tag{5.32}$$

$$\Theta(\tau, ((b_1, d_1), \ldots, (b_n, d_n))) = ((b_1', d_1'), \ldots, (b_n', d_n')) \tag{5.33}$$

where $(b_k', d_k') = \Theta_k(\tau_k, (b_k, d_k))$.

There are exactly two cellular automata with a single cell, and these give the simplest demonstration of the construction described above. The cell has a duration P. It is its own left and right neighbors, and so T is entirely defined by its action on the triples $(1, 1, 1)$ and $(0, 0, 0)$; for brevity T is written as a function of a single value. Two transition rules can be defined:

$$T_\alpha(b) = b \tag{5.34}$$

$$T_\beta(b) = \begin{cases} 1 & \text{if } b = 0 \\ 0 & \text{if } b = 1 \end{cases} \tag{5.35}$$

Both automata, the first with rule T_α and the second with rule T_β, have a pair of periodic trajectories. These are shown in Figure 5.17. The event surfaces are lines at $\tau = 0$ and $\tau = P$. Beginning with a direction $d = 1$, the clock moves up to P where a discrete-event occurs and causes the direction to change; it then moves to 0, where the direction changes again; and the cell bounces back and forth between these two constraining surfaces. Both automata need two bounces to return to their initial states and so have a period of length $2P$.

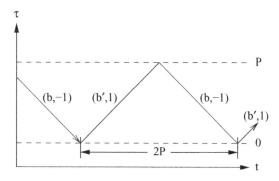

FIGURE 5.17 Event surfaces and periodic trajectories of two asynchronous automata, each with a single cell; in this drawing, $b' = T_\alpha(b)$ and $b = T_\alpha(b')$ for the first automaton, and similarly with respect to T_β for the second automaton.

5.8.3 A Homomorphism from Differential Automata to Asynchronous Cellular Automata

Every asynchronous cellular automaton is a homomorphic image of a differential automaton. We will consider here only the left-looking cellular automaton from Section 4.5 and assume that the set of states of the asynchronous automaton are those reachable from the initial conditions in the simulation code. It is a straightforward exercise to extend the argument to encompass all asynchronous cellular automata.

A state of the differential automaton is mapped to a state of the resultant of the asynchronous automaton in the following way. The discrete state b of a cell in the differential automaton is mapped to the state s of the corresponding cell in the asynchronous automaton. The b value of the left neighbor of the cell in the differential automaton is mapped to l of the cell in the asynchronous automaton. The parameter P is the same in both models.

Figure 5.18 depicts the relationships between the d_k and τ_k variables of the differential automaton and the e, e_k, and c_k of the asynchronous automaton. The elapsed time e of the asynchronous automaton's resultant is the time elapsed since the last transition of the differential automaton:

$$e = \min_{k \in [1.n]} \frac{(1 - d_k)P_k}{2} + d_k \tau_k \tag{5.36}$$

The elapsed time e_k of the kth component is the time passed since its last internal, external, or confluent event. Letting I_k be the set of indices of the neighboring cells (i.e., the set of influencers of k), e_k is

$$e_k = -e + \min_{j \in I_k \cup \{k\}} \frac{(1 - d_j)P_j}{2} + d_j \tau_j \tag{5.37}$$

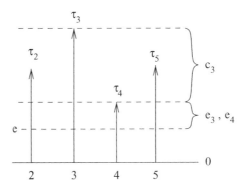

FIGURE 5.18 Relationships between the continuous components of cells 2 through 5 in the differential automaton and asynchronous automaton.

where e is the elapsed time from Equation 5.36. The consumed time c_k at cell k is the difference between the time passed by the same component in the differential automaton and the elapsed time in the asynchronous automaton

$$c_k = \frac{(1 - d_k)P_k}{2} + d_k \tau_k - e_k - e \tag{5.38}$$

where e and e_k are from Equations 5.36 and 5.37, respectively. This completes the rule for converting a state of the differential automaton to a state of an asynchronous automaton. Next, it is shown that this mapping is, in fact, a homomorphism.

First, we establish that the time to the next discrete transition of each model is equivalent. The differential automaton undergoes its next discrete change of state after a real interval

$$\min_{j \in [1,n]} \frac{(1 + d_j)P_j}{2} - d_j \tau_j \tag{5.39}$$

which is the smallest time at which a τ_j reaches its (upper or lower) limit. Recalling Equation 4.13, the time remaining for the resultant of the asynchronous automaton to change its discrete state is

$$\min_{j \in [1,n]} P_j - c_j - e_j - e \tag{5.40}$$

Substituting for c_j Equation 5.38 gives

$$P_j - c_j - e_j - e = P_j - \left(\frac{(1 - d_j)P_j}{2} + d_j \tau_j - e_j - e \right) - e_j - e$$

$$= P_j - \frac{(1 - d_j)P_j}{2} - d_j \tau_j$$

$$= \frac{(1 + d_j)P_j}{2} - d_j \tau_j \tag{5.41}$$

and substituting Equation 5.41 back into 5.40 yields Equation 5.39. Hence, the time advance of the differential automaton and its corresponding asynchronous automaton are equal.

Both systems are input-free and produce no output, so it is sufficient to consider just three cases for the state transition function: simulation through an interval shorter than the time advance of the resultant (i.e., case 5 of Equation 4.7), a simulation ending immediately prior to a discrete transition (i.e., case 4 of Equation 4.7), and a simulation ending at a discrete transition (i.e., case 3 of Equation 4.7). We examine each case in turn.

Case 4 follows directly from the preceding argument for equal time advances. Case 5 is similar. Over an interval of real length ϵ the τ_k of the differential automaton change by equal amounts, albeit possibly in opposite directions. Applying the mapping from differential to asynchronous automaton at the beginning of the interval and advancing e by ϵ gives a final value

$$e = \epsilon + \min_{k \in [1,n]} \frac{(1 - d_k)P_k}{2} + d_k \tau_k$$

Conversely, advancing the τ_k first and then applying the mapping gives

$$e = \min_{k \in [1,n]} \frac{(1 - d_k)P_k}{2} + d_k(\tau_k + d_k \epsilon) = \min_{k \in [1,n]} \frac{(1 - d_k)P_k}{2} + d_k \tau_k + d_k^2 \epsilon$$

and because $d_k^2 = 1$, this is exactly as desired. Observe also that neither the e_k nor c_k are altered; the advance of the minimal term in e_k is offset by the equal advance of e and also for c_k.

Case 3 likewise follows from the fact of equal time advances, from the definition of Θ for the differential automaton, and from the four conditions of the transition function of the asynchronous automaton: internal, external, and confluent and the instance of no event. It is immediately apparent that the discrete variables in each case behave as expected, and so now we consider the continuous variables in each scenario. It is helpful to recall Equation 4.17 and the fact that the elapsed time e is zero following each transition of the asynchronous automaton. Also observe that Equation 5.36 is zero at each transition of the differential automaton. The four conditions of the transition function of the asynchronous automaton are as follows:

Internal Event. Following the event, cell k of the asynchronous automaton has $e_k = c_k = 0$. Similarly, the τ_k of the cell in the differential automaton is P_k if d_k transitioned from 1 to -1; 0 if the opposite. In both of these cases, Equation 5.37 is zero, and so is Equation 5.38. Hence, the result is the same regardless of whether the mapping from differential automaton to asynchronous automaton is applied before or after the transition.

No Event. A nonevent at cell k advances e_k by the elapsed time e of the resultant; cell k changes in no other way. Now observe that, in the differential automaton, the cell and its neighbors' τ_ks are unchanged by the event, but the elapsed time e of the asynchronous automaton becomes zero. Therefore, Equation 5.37 ensures that e_k is advanced by e as required. For the same reason, Equation 5.38 ensures that c_k is unchanged. Hence, the result is the same regardless of whether the mapping from differential automaton to asynchronous automaton is applied before or after the transition.

External Event. Following an external event at cell k, its consumed time c_k is advanced by the value of $e_k - e$ immediately prior to the transition; e_k and e then become zero. Because a neighboring cell has undergone an internal event, Equation 5.36 is zero and, therefore, so is Equation 5.37. Equation 5.38 causes c_k to increase by $e_k - e$ when that quantity becomes zero following the

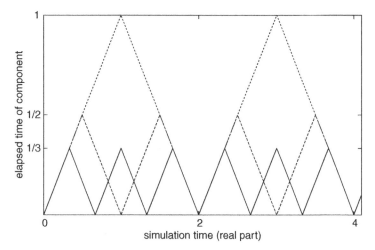

FIGURE 5.19   The clock variables of a differential automaton with component periods of 1, $\frac{1}{2}$, and $\frac{1}{3}$; its "smaller" asynchronous automaton is shown in Figure 4.13.

transition. Again, the result is the same regardless of whether the mapping from differential automaton to asynchronous automaton is applied before or after the transition.

Confluent Event. This is a composition of the cell's internal and external events. Therefore, this scenario is covered by the three cases listed above.

To conclude, the mapping described above is a homomorphism from the differential automaton described in Section 5.8.2 to the asynchronous automaton of Section 4.5. Observe also that the direction of the differential automaton cannot be recovered from the elapsed time of the asynchronous automaton, and so the mapping is not an isomorphism; the asynchronous automata really are "smaller." This is reflected in the longer period of the differential automaton, which is apparent in a comparison of Figures 5.19 and 4.13; the former shows the continuous phase space of the differential automaton corresponding to the left-looking asynchronous automaton illustrated in the latter. Indeed, the larger system has a period twice that of the smaller, a fact that might have been anticipated from the simple example shown in Figure 5.17.

One more comment can be made about the above construction. For a discrete-event simulation to calculate the differential automaton's trajectory, its direction must be added to the state variables of the left-looking asynchronous automaton. It is a simple matter to show that, with this change, the two systems are equivalent; the homomorphism shown above still applies (with, of course, an identity map for the d_ks in both systems), and a second morphism can be constructed in the other direction. The two systems are therefore isomorphic, each capable of simulating the other.

5.9 SUMMARY

This chapter completes the simulation framework by incorporating continuous dynamics. The approach taken here fits neatly into the discrete-event worldview, and at the same time permits the use of well-established algorithms for simulating hybrid systems. In principle, the atomic models described here could be generated automatically by a compiler for Modelica, ACSL, or any other language for continuous system simulation, and the resulting component incorporated into any kind of complex, discrete-event model. This idea is attractive for several reasons—very complicated continuous models could be built with relative ease, their simulators could be integrated directly with any modular framework for discrete-event simulation, and this could all be done with minimal coding.

In Section 5.8, it was shown that the asynchronous automata are homomorphic images of differential automata with constant derivatives. By adding state variables to the asynchronous automata, the relationship can be made to hold in the other direction; these particular differential automata are, in fact, discrete-event systems. Indeed, models expressed in a variety of forms (see, e.g., Refs. 80, 102, and 155) can be mapped to the constructs described here for simulation, and back again for other types of analysis. The greatest practical restriction on this application is the need for the continuous model to expose only a discrete-event interface.

Analytical frameworks for hybrid systems seldom impose this requirement; compare, for instance, the Hybrid I/O Automata [80], DEVS&DESS [157], and Ames' *Categorical Hybrid Systems* [5]. Closed under coupling, however, is a property intrinsic to most of these representational schemes, and the idea that any system expressed in their terms can be rearranged into a simulatable form is therefore intuitively appealing. Nonetheless, this has not been shown conclusively, nor are there established procedures for such a transformation where it is known to be achievable. The possibility, however, is intriguing; if computer languages for hybrid analysis (see, e.g., Refs. 17 and 161) could be compiled into the forms described above, these would become very practical, powerful tools for the engineering of computer- and communication-intensive systems.

CHAPTER 6

APPLICATIONS

The applications in this chapter highlight the main features of the simulation framework. The first application, which examines closed-loop control through a packet-switching network, shows how the software design promotes reuse of models across simulation frameworks. The second application is also concerned with control, it looks at using load to regulate frequency in an electrical power system. This example contains complicated state events and computationally demanding continuous dynamics and leaves open at least two interesting questions that a student might pursue.

6.1 CONTROL THROUGH A PACKET-SWITCHED NETWORK

Recent work in the design of networked control systems has focused extensively on communication networks that lose information. The simplest models use a Bernoulli process for packet losses and impose a fixed delay on packets that are successfully delivered. Control processes can be surprisingly robust to this type of error, and given the relative ease with which its consequences can be analyzed, it is tempting to select a control network whose behavior closely approximates this model (Hespanha et al. [57] give an overview of recent work in this area; see also the article by Feng-Li et al. [38]).

Conversely, interest in control over packet-switched networks is spurred by relatively inexpensive communication technology that exists for data-processing applications. This networking technology is designed to favor delay and variation in delay

---

Building Software for Simulation: Theory and Algorithms, with Applications in C++, By James J. Nutaro
Copyright © 2011 John Wiley & Sons, Inc.

over the loss of information. In an adequately provisioned network, lost packets are very rare. Even in a strained network, substantial delays and variations in delay will occur before lost packets become a problem.

Ethernet is one of the most common technologies for building local-area networks, and an Ethernet bus is capable of very high utilization rates with very little loss of information. This is accomplished by its media access control (MAC) mechanism, which works as follows (see, e.g., Ref. 137). Prior to and during a transmission, the network access device listens for a simultaneous transmission by other devices on the network. If a conflicting transmission occurs, then the signals are garbled, the data are lost, and each will try its transmission again. To avoid a second conflict, each network device waits for a time it selects at random before attempting to resend its message. If, after some number of attempts, the device has been unable to send its information, then the data are discarded and the upper layers of the network protocol are notified of the loss; otherwise it reports success.

If a UDP-like protocol is used at the upper layers of the protocol stack, then the lost message is simply discarded; no further effort is made to transmit it. Therefore, if the controller and plant set their number of retry attempts to zero, and if the background utilization of the network is constant, then the Ethernet network should be reasonably approximated by the Bernoulli packet loss model. Moreover, if the amount of control data on the network is negligible relative to other types of data, then the probability of losing a control packet is approximately the arrival rate of the other data divided by the maximum frame rate of the Ethernet.

By changing the retry count, a tradeoff can be made between the loss of control data and variation in its delay. A large retry count will prevent the loss of data, but could impose long delays relative to the plant and controller time constants; a small retry count has the opposite effect. It seems reasonable to assume that, for a particular plant, controller, and background utilization of the network, there is an optimal setting for the retry count; that is, there is an optimal tradeoff between the loss of data and its delay.

We will explore this question for a proportional–integral–derivative (PID) controller whose purpose is to keep a pendulum upright; the important features of this problem are illustrated in Figure 6.1 (see, e.g., Ref. 128 for a detailed discussion of the pendulum and its controller). The pendulum consists of an arm attached by a swivel joint to a wheeled cart. The cart is mounted on a track. A sensor provides the controller with angle measurements from the arm. A motor in the cart allows the controller to push it left and right on the track. By careful control of the force applied by the motor, the PID controller attempts to keep the arm upright (the position of the cart is not considered here).

6.1.1 Model of the Pendulum and Its PID Controller

The equation describing the motion of the inverted pendulum is

$$\begin{bmatrix} m_c + m_a & -Lm\cos(\theta)/2 \\ -Lm\cos(\theta)/2 & L^2 m_a/4 \end{bmatrix} \begin{bmatrix} \ddot{x} \\ \ddot{\theta} \end{bmatrix} = \begin{bmatrix} F - m_a L\dot{\theta}^2 \sin(\theta)/2 - D_c \dot{x} \\ m_a Lg\sin(\theta)/2 - D_a\dot{\theta} \end{bmatrix}$$

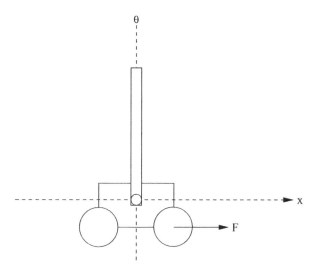

FIGURE 6.1 The inverted pendulum.

where the $m_a = 1$ kg is the mass of the arm; $m_c = 1$ kg is the mass of the cart; $D_a = D_c = 10^{-4}$ are the coefficients of friction for the arm's socket and cart's wheels, respectively; $g = 9.8$ m/s is acceleration due to gravity; and $L = 0.5$ m is the arm's length. The angle of the arm is sensed with a 10-bit analog-to-digital converter. This device provides 1024 measurement points, which are evenly distributed through its $360°$ of motion. The kth sensor threshold θ_k in radians is at

$$\theta_k = 2k\pi/1024 \tag{6.1}$$

If the last sensor reading was θ_k, then subsequent sensor readings are at θ_{k+1} and θ_{k-1}. The surfaces that describe these sensing events are

$$\theta - \theta_{k+1} = 0$$
$$\theta - \theta_{k-1} = 0$$

and the discrete variable k is included in the state space of the pendulum.

The sensor transmits a reading only when it detects a change in θ. This has the effect of coupling the sensor's data rate to the time derivatives of the pendulum. The data rate of the sensor is, therefore, quite small when the system is near equilibrium. Lost sensor readings, however, cannot be recovered by the controller (as, e.g., might be done by periodic sampling of the arm angle).

In response to a sensor reading, the manually tuned PID controller computes the motor force as

$$\epsilon_n = -\theta_n$$
$$h_n = t_n - t_{n-1}$$
$$F_n = 50\epsilon_n + 5(\epsilon_n - \epsilon_{n-1})h_n + (\epsilon_n - \epsilon_{n-1})/h_n$$

where θ_n is the nth sample received through the network, t_n is the time when the sample was received, and F_n is the control data that are sent immediately in response to a message from the arm angle sensor. Quantization and saturation effects for F are ignored, and control data are transmitted only in response to a new sensor reading. The code that implements both of these models is listed below. The model begins at equilibrium with $\theta = 0$, $x = 0$, and all derivatives equal to zero. The force F acting on the cart consists of the control force F_n and an initial nudge F_0 described by

$$F_0 = 10\exp(-20t) \tag{6.2}$$

so that $F = F_n + F_0$.

When the controller is connected directly to the cart and pendulum, the arm experiences an initial angular displacement of $7.5°$ and then settles into a swaying motion that covers a $3°$ arc. These lasting oscillations are due to the quantization of the arm angle; the controller lacks the information needed to completely damp the pendulum's motion. Figure 6.2 shows this response and the corresponding data provided to the controller by the arm angle sensor.

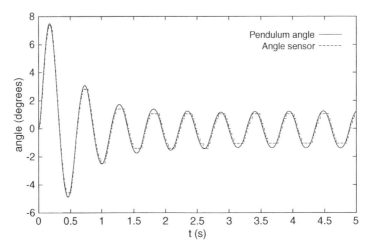

FIGURE 6.2 Response of the cart and pendulum to the PID controller using a quantized sensor.

––––––––––––––– *Header File for the CartModel Class* –––––––––––––––

```
1   #ifndef CART_MODEL_H
2   #define CART_MODEL_H
3   #include "adevs.h"
4
5   #define PI 3.1415926535897931
6   #define RAD_TO_DEG (180.0/PI)
7   // This is the dynamic model of the pendulum. The only input
8   // is the force applied by the cart's motor and the only output
9   // is the arm angle measurement.
10  class CartModel: public adevs::ode_system<double>
11  {
12    public:
13      CartModel();
14      // Arm angle in degrees; zero degrees is straight down
15      // and rotation is clockwise.
16      double angle(const double* q) const { return RAD_TO_DEG*q[theta]; }
17      void init(double* q);
18      void der_func(const double *q, double *dq);
19      void state_event_func(const double *q, double *z);
20      void internal_event(double* q, const bool* state_event);
21      void external_event(double* q, double e,
22            const adevs::Bag<double>& xb);
23      void confluent_event(double *q, const bool* state_event,
24            const adevs::Bag<double>& xb);
25      void output_func(const double *q, const bool* state_event,
26            adevs::Bag<double>& yb);
27      double time_event_func(const double*){ return DBL_MAX; }
28      void gc_output(adevs::Bag<double>&){}
29    private:
30      // State variable indices
31      const int x, theta, dx, dtheta, t;
32      // Model parameters
33      const double armMass, armFric, cartMass, cartFric,
34            armLen, g, mAngle;
35      int k; // Last output level for the quantized sensor
36      // Constraint matrix and vector for A [ddx ddtheta]^T = B
37      double A[4][4], B[2];
38      double F; // Motor force
39  };
40
41  #endif
```

––––––––––––––– *Source File for the CartModel Class* –––––––––––––––

```
1   #include "CartModel.h"
2   using namespace std;
3   using namespace adevs;
4
```

```
 5  CartModel::CartModel():
 6     ode_system<double>(5,2), // five cont. states, two event surfaces
 7     x(0), // position index
 8     theta(1), // arm angle index
 9     dx(2), // cart velocity index
10     dtheta(3), // arm angular velocity index
11     t(4), // time
12     armMass(1.0), // mass of the arm in kilograms
13     armFric(1E-4), // resistance to rotation
14     cartMass(1.0), // mass of the cart in kilograms
15     cartFric(1E-4), // resistance to lateral motion
16     armLen(0.5), // length of the arm in meters
17     g(9.8), // acc. due to gravity in meters/second^2
18     mAngle(2.0*PI/1024.0), // sensor thresholds
19     k(0)
20  {
21     k = 0; // Arm angle is initially zero
22     F = 0.0; // No initial control force
23     // Compute the entries of the constraint matrix that are fixed
24     A[0][0] = cartMass+armMass;
25     A[1][1] = armLen*armLen*armMass/4.0;
26  }
27
28  void CartModel::init(double* q)
29  {
30     q[x] = 0.0; // Start at the middle of the track
31     q[theta] = k*mAngle;
32     q[dx] = q[dtheta] = 0.0; // No motion
33     q[t] = 0.0;
34  }
35
36  void CartModel::der_func(const double* q, double* dq)
37  {
38     dq[t] = 1.0; // Time
39     dq[x] = q[dx]; // Velocities
40     dq[theta] = q[dtheta];
41     // Compute the constraint matrices
42     double Fnudge = 10.0*exp(-20.0*q[t]);
43     A[1][0] = A[0][1] = -armLen*armMass*cos(q[theta])/2.0;
44     B[0] = (F+Fnudge)
45        - armMass*armLen*q[dtheta]*q[dtheta]*sin(q[theta])/2.0
46        - cartFric*q[dx];
47     B[1] = armMass*armLen*g*sin(q[theta])/2.0 - armFric*q[dtheta];
48     // Compute determinant of the constraint matrix
49     double det = A[0][0]*A[1][1]-A[0][1]*A[1][0];
50     // Solve for the accelerations
51     dq[dx] = (A[1][1]*B[0]-A[0][1]*B[1])/det;
52     dq[dtheta] = (A[0][0]*B[1]-A[1][0]*B[0])/det;
53  }
```

```
54
55   void CartModel::state_event_func(const double* q, double* z)
56   {
57      z[0] = q[theta] - mAngle*(k-1);
58      z[1] = q[theta] - mAngle*(k+1);
59   }
60
61   void CartModel::internal_event(double *q, const bool *event_flags)
62   {
63      if (event_flags[0]) k--;
64      else k++;
65   }
66
67   void CartModel::external_event(double* q, double e, const Bag<double>& xb)
68   {
69      F = *(xb.begin());
70   }
71
72   void CartModel::confluent_event(double* q, const bool * event_flags,
73         const Bag<double>& xb)
74   {
75      internal_event(q,event_flags);
76      external_event(q,0.0,xb);
77   }
78
79   void CartModel::output_func(const double *q, const bool *event_flags,
80         Bag<double> &yb)
81   {
82      if (event_flags[0]) yb.insert((k-1)*mAngle);
83      else yb.insert((k+1)*mAngle);
84   }
```

_____ *The PIDControl Class* _____

```
1    #ifndef PIDCONTROL_H
2    #define PIDCONTROL_H
3    #include "adevs.h"
4
5    // This is a PID controller for the cart.
6    class PIDControl: public adevs::Atomic<double>
7    {
8       public:
9          PIDControl():adevs::Atomic<double>(),
10            err(0.0),err_int(0.0),
11            csignal(0.0),send_control(false){}
12         void delta_int() { send_control = false; }
13         void delta_ext(double e, const adevs::Bag<double>& xb)
14         {
15            // Error is the difference of the arm angle from zero
```

```
16      double new_err = -(*(xb.begin())); // New error value
17      err_int += new_err*e; // Integral of the error
18      double derr = (new_err-err)/e; // Derivative of the error
19      err = new_err; // Value of the error
20      csignal = 50.0*err+5.0*err_int+1.0*derr; // Control signal
21      send_control = true; // Send a new control value
22    }
23    void delta_conf(const adevs::Bag<double>& xb)
24    {
25      delta_int(); delta_ext(0.0,xb);
26    }
27    double ta() { if (send_control) return 0.0; return DBL_MAX; }
28    void output_func(adevs::Bag<double>& yb) { yb.insert(csignal); }
29    void gc_output(adevs::Bag<double>&){}
30  private:
31    double err, err_int, csignal;
32    bool send_control;
33 };
34
35 #endif
```

6.1.2 Integration with an Ethernet Simulator

Now the cart and its controller are separated by a 10-Mbps (megabits per second) Ethernet that is shared with several other computers. What these others do is unimportant, but they consume some fraction of the network's throughput. From the perspective of the cart and controller, additional network traffic degrades the performance of the communication channel by introducing delay, variation in delay, and, in some instances, lost data. When other users place very little data onto the network, their impact on the performance of the controller is negligible. As much as 40% of the network capacity can be consumed by other users before there is a noticeable change in the trajectory of the cart and pendulum, but greater use of the network degrades the controller's performance.

The simulator for this system has three parts: the controller and cart, the Ethernet, and the sources of background traffic. The first part is built with our simulation framework. A model of the network and traffic generators is available as part of the OMNeT++ (objective modular network testbed) simulation tool and its INeT extension (the software is available for download at http://www.omnetpp.org/). To build an integrated model, the simulator for the controller and cart are embedded in an OMNeT++ component, which in turn is connected to OMNeT++'s model of an Ethernet frame encapsulator and MAC device. The rest of the network is built using the graphical tools and NED language that are native to OMNeT++.

Figure 6.3 shows the classes that are directly involved in the integration of the cart and controller model with the OMNET++ simulator. The *CartPID* class encapsulates the *Simulator*, *PIDControl*, and *CartModel* classes within a single OMNET++ module. This module does three things: (1) it intercepts messages coming from the

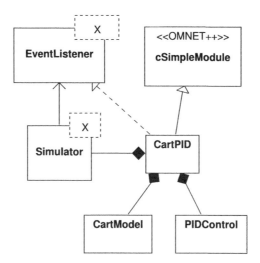

FIGURE 6.3 Classes involved directly in the integration of the cart and controller into an OMNeT++ model of an Ethernet network.

OMNET++ network and injects them into the cart–controller model via the *Simulator*'s *computeNextState* method, (2) it schedules self-events for the OMNET++ simulator in accordance with the time of next event obtained from the *Simulator*'s *nextEventTime* method, and (3) it intercepts output from the cart and controller and converts them into Ethernet frames that carry the sensor and control data. The code for the *CartPID* class is listed below. Most of its features are familiar from previous examples: use of the *EventListener* to intercept output events and changes of state and of the *Simulator* to control time and inject input.

Its only unusual aspect is the cancellation of self-events on the receipt of a message. This step is required because OMNeT++ places all of its events into a single future event list, from which they are removed only when the event time expires or the event is explicitly deleted. A change in the next event time of the cart and controller invalidates its scheduled next event, and so it must be removed from the future event list and the new, valid time inserted.

_____ ***Header File for the CartPID Class*** _____

```
1   #ifndef __CARTPID_H__
2   #define __CARTPID_H__
3   #include <omnetpp.h>
4   #include "CartModel.h"
5   #include "PIDControl.h"
6   #include "TrajRecorder.h"
7
8   class CartPID: public cSimpleModule, // From OMNET++
9       public adevs::EventListener<double>
```

```
10  {
11      public:
12          void outputEvent(adevs::Event<double> y, double t);
13          void stateChange(adevs::Atomic<double>*,double){}
14          ~CartPID();
15      protected:
16          // OMNET++ method for model initialization
17          void initialize();
18          // Method for processing OMNET++ events
19          void handleMessage(cMessage *msg);
20          void registerDSAP(const char* gate);
21      private:
22          PIDControl *pid; // The PID controller
23          adevs::Hybrid<double> *hysim; // Model of the cart and arm
24          TrajRecorder *traj; // Listener for recording the cart trajectory
25          adevs::SimpleDigraph<double>* top_model; // Holds the PID and cart
26          adevs::Simulator<double> *sim; // Simulator for our model
27          cMessage self_event; // OMNET++ event for our internal events
28          adevs::Bag<adevs::Event<double> > xbag; // Bag for OMNET++ inputs
29          std::ofstream sensor_rx_strm; // Records receipt of sensor msgs
30  };
31
32  #endif
```

_____ ***Source File for the CartPID Class*** _____

```
1   #include "CartPID.h"
2   #include "ByteArrayMessage.h"
3   #include "MACAddress.h"
4   #include "Ieee802Ctrl_m.h"
5   #include <string>
6
7   // Network addresses for the OMNET++ network model
8   static const MACAddress SENSOR_ADDR("999999999999"),
9           CONTROL_ADDR("888888888888");
10  static const int SAP = 9999; // OMNET++ application ID for the cart/PID
11  Define_Module(CartPID); // Make CartPID into an OMNET++ module
12
13  // OMNET++ calls this method at the start of the simulation
14  void CartPID::initialize()
15  {
16      // Create the cart and controller
17      pid = new PIDControl();
18      CartModel *cart = new CartModel();
19      hysim = new adevs::Hybrid<double>(
20          cart,
21          new adevs::corrected_euler<double>(cart,1E-8,0.001),
22          new adevs::linear_event_locator<double>(cart,1E-10)
23          );
```

```
24      traj = new TrajRecorder(cart,hysim);
25      top_model = new adevs::SimpleDigraph<double>();
26      // Models are not coupled because communication is through the
27      // OMNET++ model of the Ethernet.
28      top_model->add(hysim); top_model->add(pid);
29      sim = new adevs::Simulator<double>(top_model);
30      sim->addEventListener(traj);
31      sim->addEventListener(this);
32      // Schedule first internal event
33      if (sim->nextEventTime() < DBL_MAX)
34          scheduleAt(SimTime(sim->nextEventTime()),&self_event);
35      // Register with the OMNET LLC
36      registerDSAP("sensorOut");
37      registerDSAP("controlOut");
38  }
39
40  void CartPID::registerDSAP(const char* gate_name)
41  {
42      Ieee802Ctrl *etherctrl = new Ieee802Ctrl();
43      etherctrl->setDsap(SAP);
44      cMessage *msg =
45          new cMessage("register_DSAP", IEEE802CTRL_REGISTER_DSAP);
46      msg->setControlInfo(etherctrl);
47      send(msg,gate_name);
48  }
49
50  // OMNET++ calls this method when an event occurs at the CartPID model.
51  // These can be self-scheduled events or the arrival of a message
52  // from the network.
53  void CartPID::handleMessage(cMessage *msg)
54  {
55      SimTime timestamp = msg->getArrivalTime();
56      // Internal event
57      if (msg == &self_event) sim->execNextEvent();
58      // External event
59      else {
60          // Cancel any pending self events
61          if (self_event.isScheduled()) cancelEvent(&self_event);
62          // Convert to the expected message type
63          ByteArrayMessage *data = dynamic_cast<ByteArrayMessage*>(msg);
64          assert(data != NULL);
65          // Get the data from the message
66          adevs::Event<double> x;
67          data->copyDataToBuffer(&(x.value),sizeof(double));
68          // Inject a sensor reading into the controller
69          if (std::string(data->getArrivalGate()->getBaseName()) == "sensorIn")
70              x.model = pid;
71          // Control data goes to the cart
72          else x.model = hysim;
```

```
73        // Clean up the message
74        delete data;
75        // Inject the event into the simulator
76        xbag.insert(x);
77        sim->computeNextState(xbag,timestamp.dbl());
78        xbag.clear();
79     }
80     // Process instantaneous responses to the input
81     while (SimTime(sim->nextEventTime()) <= timestamp)
82         sim->execNextEvent();
83     // Schedule the next internal event
84     if (sim->nextEventTime() < DBL_MAX)
85         scheduleAt(SimTime(sim->nextEventTime()),&self_event);
86  }
87
88  // This method is called by our simulator whenever the cart or
89  // controller produces an output event.
90  void CartPID::outputEvent(adevs::Event<double> y, double t)
91  {
92     Ieee802Ctrl *etherctrl = new Ieee802Ctrl();
93     etherctrl->setSsap(SAP);
94     etherctrl->setDsap(SAP);
95     // Sensor output; send it to the controller
96     if (y.model == hysim) {
97         etherctrl->setDest(CONTROL_ADDR);
98         ByteArrayMessage *msg =
99             new ByteArrayMessage("Sensor_data",IEEE802CTRL_DATA);
100        msg->setControlInfo(etherctrl);
101        msg->setDataFromBuffer(&(y.value),sizeof(double));
102        send(msg,"sensorOut");
103     }
104     // Control output; send it to the sensor
105     else {
106         etherctrl->setDest(SENSOR_ADDR);
107         ByteArrayMessage *msg =
108             new ByteArrayMessage("Control_data",IEEE802CTRL_DATA);
109         msg->setControlInfo(etherctrl);
110         msg->setDataFromBuffer(&(y.value),sizeof(double));
111         send(msg,"controlOut");
112     }
113  }
114
115  CartPID::~CartPID()
116  {
117     delete sim; delete top_model; delete traj;
118  }
```

The rest of the integration is done with the OMNeT++ GUI (graphical user interface). Figure 6.4 shows the final configuration of the network. The *controlAndPlant* component contains the *CartPID* model, connecting its output and input to two Ethernet protocol stacks: one stack for the sensor and the other for the controller. The rest of the network is built from existing components.

The network has two parameters that are of interest for our experiment. First is the number of attempts that the MACs in the *CartPID*'s protocol stacks will make to transmit a data packet. By default, this number is 16; this default value is used by the MACs of the models that produce background traffic. By reducing the number of attempts for the controller and cart, however, we hope to improve the robustness of the controller to congestion on the network. The second parameter of interest is the frequency with which the other users attempt to send data. The size of a data packet for these users is fixed at 1000 bytes (8000 bits), and each user produces packets at exponentially distributed intervals (i.e., packet production is modeled by a Poisson arrival process). The mean of the exponential distribution fixes the data rate and, therefore, determines how much of the network's capacity is consumed by these users.

6.1.3 Experiments

When 40% of the network's 10 Mbps is consumed by background traffic, the controller still works admirably with the default number of retransmit attempts. At 50%, however, there is noticeable deterioration, shown in Figure 6.5, and at 75% the controller fails and the pendulum falls over. These two scenarios, therefore, are a good test of the hypothesis that reducing the retry count improves performance.

The most extreme case is a reduction of the maximum number of retransmit attempts from 16 to 0, and doing this helps the controller substantially. Figure 6.6 shows the affect of this adjustment on the trajectories of the pendulum for the same 50% utilization scenario shown in Figure 6.5. Compare these trajectories with Figure 6.2, and the dramatic effect is immediately apparent. The large swings of the pendulum late in the trajectory have been damped, with the oscillations staying nearly inside the $3°$ band seen in the ideal case.

The reason for this tremendous improvement is that old data from the controller and arm angle sensors do not stall the transmission of more recent, more accurate data. Imagine, for instance, that the sensor produces a measurement of $1°$ at $t = 1$. This is inserted into a packet and sent to the MAC device for transmission. If a collision occurs, the MAC device holds onto the data for a short time and then attempts to resend them. While the MAC device waits, the sensor produces a second measurement of, say, $1.35°$ at $t = 1.1$. This newer, more useful data must wait, however, until the old, now useless, data are transmitted. In the 50% utilization scenario, using the default limit on the number of attempts to retransmit, the cart and controller exchange, on average, a total of 248.45 messages, and these are collectively subject to an average of 116 backoffs. So the situation just described occurs in half of the attempted transmissions. By not attempting to retransmit old data, this situation is avoided, and the controller does a better job by always using the most up-to-date information.

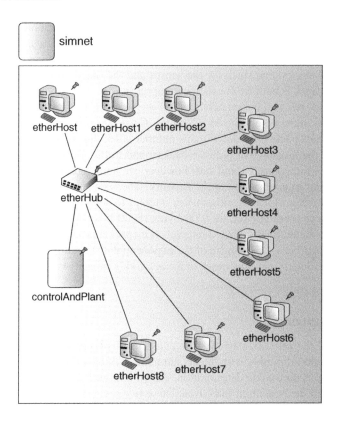

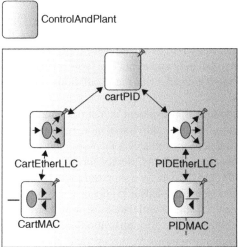

FIGURE 6.4 Diagram of the *CartPID* protocol stack (below) and the Ethernet network (above).

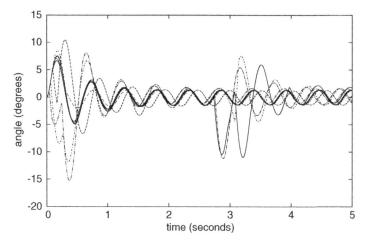

FIGURE 6.5 Plot showing 11 trajectories of the pendulum, each using a separate random-number stream, for a network carrying 50% of its capacity. The maximum number of transmit attempts for the cart and controller is 16.

The results of the same experiment, but conducted with the network carrying 75% of its capacity, are shown in Figure 6.7. When the number of attempts to retry a message are restricted the system is stabilized, but it performs poorly, with the quantization-induced oscillations swinging as far as 10°. Congestion in the network causes a significant loss of data; of an average of 427.45 packets sent, nearly half of those, 212.68 on average, are lost to collisions. Lost data are, in fact, the sole cause

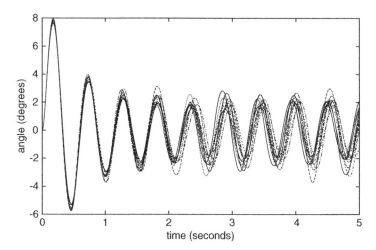

FIGURE 6.6 Plot showing 11 trajectories of the pendulum for a network carrying 50% of its capacity, but with the cart and controller attempting to transmit each packet at most once.

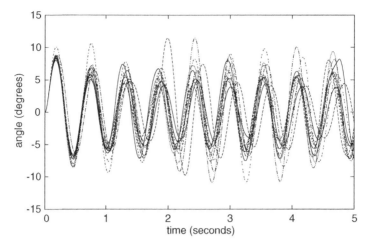

FIGURE 6.7 Plot showing 11 trajectories of the pendulum for a network carrying 75% of its capacity, but with the cart and controller attempting to transmit each packet at most once.

of this poor performance. There are no backoffs, and hence no delays incurred by the MAC protocol.

However, if the number of retransmission attempts is increased to one, there is again a remarkable performance improvement; Figure 6.8 shows the results. Now the initial deflection is dampened substantially and the system oscillates through about 4°. In this case, on average 75.45 packets of the 278.14 sent are lost, so the packet loss rate is 27%, much lower than before. The number of backoffs is correspondingly greater,

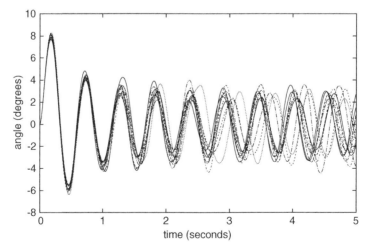

FIGURE 6.8 Plot showing 11 trajectories of the pendulum for a network carrying 75% of its capacity, but with the cart and controller attempting to transmit each packet at most twice.

however, at an average of 134.77, so that nearly half of the messages experience a delay due to collision and queuing.

These experiments support the notion of an optimal setting for the maximum number of attempts to transmit a packet that is conditional on the network utilization; that is, an optimal tradeoff between delay due to backoffs and data lost to collisions. We might even anticipate how the controller will perform as the retry limit is varied around a best choice, and consequently expect, not many, but a single optimal selection. Note first that the number of lost packets increases as the retry limit is shrunk, and decreases as it grows. Let us assume that the change in the packet loss rate is proportional to the change in the retry limit away from its optimum so that

$$\Delta packet\ loss\ rate \propto \Delta retry\ limit$$

Similarly, the delay experienced by each packet that is successfully transmitted decreases as the retry limit shrinks, and increases as it grows. Again, let us assume that the change in the delay is proportional to the change in the retry limit so that

$$\Delta packet\ delay \propto \Delta retry\ limit$$

If the change in the performance metric J, which is to be minized, is the product of these two effects, that is

$$\Delta J \propto \Delta packet\ delay \times \Delta packet\ loss\ rate \propto \Delta retry\ limit^2$$

then about an optimal retry limit our measure of performance will be quadratic and therefore that optimum is unique. Indeed, experiments will bear this out.

To find the optimum, 11 simulations are performed for each selection of the retry limit and network utilization. At each level of network utilization, the performance of the controller as a function of the retry limit is quantified by the total angular deflection over the 5-s observation window. Thus the performance is

$$J(retry\ limit) = \int_0^5 [\omega(t)]^2\ dt \tag{6.3}$$

and our goal is to determine the retry limit that minimizes J for a particular utilization.

Figure 6.9 shows the average J and statistical certainty (99% confidence interval) for the cases where the network is loaded to 50% and 75% of its capacity. In each case, there is a statistically significant decline of J as the retry limit climbs from zero to some best selection and then J gradually increases. For the 75% scenario, the controller becomes unstable when the retry limit is 8 or greater, and the performance numbers for these cases are not shown. For the 50% case, the performance gradually becomes invariant to the retry setting. In all cases, trends in J are reflected in the trend of the statistical uncertainty; greater uncertainty indicates a greater degree of

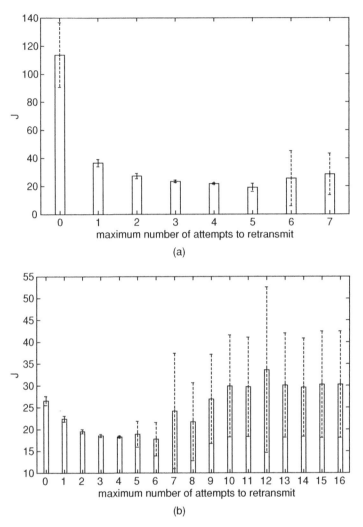

FIGURE 6.9 System performance as a function of the maximum number of transmit attempts: (a) 75%; (b) 50%. Bar show the 99% confidence interval for the mean value of J over 11 trials.

variation in the performance of the system and an intrinsic lack of robustness. The best choices have both a small J and small statistical uncertainty.

We have just seen that the performance of a networked control system can be improved by adapting the network to the controller. In this particular case, there is an optimal selection of the MAC's retry limit. In a more complicated network there will be several parameters at each layer of a network protocol stack that can be tuned for performance. For example, the sizes of the send and receive buffers allocated by the operating system can affect queuing delays and packet losses. When using the Transmission Control Protocol (TCP), jitter and delay can be affected by adjusting the time that a packet's recipient waits to acknowledge its receipt and the time that the sender will wait for an acknowledgment before retransmitting the packet. In many TCP implementations, Nagle's algorithm can be disabled to prevent the bundling of data, which generally increases delays but reduces network utilization, and there are others (see, e.g., Ref. 137). Optimization of the system's performance need not be limited to adjusting parameters of the network protocol; the controller can also be tuned to accommodate the limits of the network (again, see, e.g; Ref. 57). This kind of detailed optimization is a natural application for the simulation technology.

6.2 FREQUENCY REGULATION IN AN ELECTRICAL POWER SYSTEM

Advances in communication and computing technology have reinvigorated interest in the use of electrical load for balancing supply and demand. Simulation has a central place in the evaluation of proposals to use electrical load for frequency regulation and to accommodate unexpected shortfalls in the supply of power (see, e.g., Refs. 3, 39, 56, 59, 65, 98, 108, and 135). Before describing the solution, however, consider the problem. A mismatch in supply and demand causes the rotating machinery in the generators to change, accelerating if there is too much supply and decelerating if there is too much demand. The generator will be damaged if its rotational frequency is not maintained near nominal: 60 Hz in the United States and 50 Hz in much of the rest of the world.

The generators themselves are primarily responsible for frequency control. If the frequency begins to drop, then automatic controls apply more mechanical power to the turbine: steam, water, or whatever is used. This causes the turbine to accelerate, bringing its frequency back to normal, at which time power is reduced slightly to stop the acceleration and maintain the desired frequency. The same actions are taken, but in the opposite direction, if the frequency increases.

A generator is a massive machine with a great deal of inertia, and this limits the rate at which its turbine's speed can be altered. Large, sudden changes in load can cause the frequency to change too rapidly for the automatic controllers to compensate. When this happens, the frequency moves dangerously far from normal, and automatic protection devices disconnect the generator from the electrical network. Loss of the generator exacerbates the mismatch of supply and demand, causing the remaining generators to accelerate still more quickly, overwhelming their automatic controls and forcing them off of the network. If left unchecked, this dynamic causes a widespread blackout.

When supply cannot change quickly enough, demand can be adjusted instead. The idea is simple—if there is excess electrical load, then disconnect it. When the frequency recovers, the load is quickly, but carefully, reconnected. If this is done automatically, then the brief loss of power will be almost unnoticed by customers. This tactic has been employed for decades with the cooperation of industrial consumers of power, with aluminum smelters, skyscrapers, and other facilities agreeing to reduce electricity usage on request in exchange for a reduction in the price of electricity.

Modern communication technology has expanded the possible scope of this idea. With millions of "smart" electrical meters installed in homes and small businesses, large conglomerates of relatively small loads can, in principle, be used to regulate frequency. One mechanism, which is considered in this section, works as follows. Homes and businesses have two electric circuits; one provides uninterrupted power and the other can be disconnected at will by the power company or, possibly, by a load aggregation company that provides regulation services to the power company. Power is supplied through the interruptible circuit at a reduced rate. If, for instance, a water heater is connected to it, then you pay less for hot water in exchange for making the heater available to the power company as a regulation resource.

The power company (or an aggregator) has a communication link to each meter and can send it a request to energize or deenergize the interruptible circuit. The communication system that makes this possible might be owned wholly by the power company. Many companies already own extensive fiberoptic networks, and the last mile to the home can be affordably bridged with wireless technology. This service might also be leased from a communication company (e.g., a phone, cable, or Internet service provider). Regardless, the complete system provides, potentially, for direct control of the electrical load at thousands, perhaps millions, of households and businesses. Significantly, this electrical load can react to a disturbance more quickly than can generators. Thousands of water heaters, for instance, can be turned off in an instant to provide rapid relief from excess load. The major source of delay is the communication network; it must be able to deliver control data in fractions of a second to loads being used for frequency regulation.

Figure 6.10 illustrates the elements of the system that are relevant to this study, which is based loosely on a similar study by Trudnowski et al. [139]. Each generator

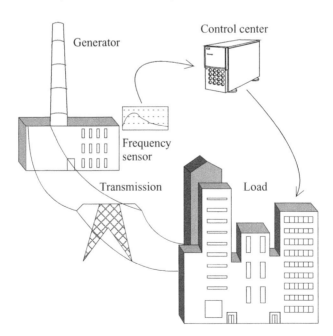

FIGURE 6.10 Elements of the power grid and its subsystem for load control.

transmits to the control center a measurement of its frequency: measurements are sent at points Δf away from the nominal frequency f_{nom}; that is, it transmits a new measurement whenever $f - f_{\text{nom}}$ equals $k \, \Delta f, k = \ldots, -2, -1, 0, 1, 2, \ldots$. The control center maintains the instantaneous average f_{avg} of measurements from all of the generators, and directs the electrical loads to effect a percentage change in demand equal to $K f_{\text{avg}}$, where K is a parameter of the control design.

The most difficult part to model is the communication network, and a very abstract approach is taken here. The movement of data from the generators to the control center to load aggregators is modeled with a first-in first-out server and infinite queue. This simple model lumps the data-processing capabilities of the control center and the aggregator into a component residing at each aggregator. The aggregators are further assumed to be identical, and so one more parameter is added to the model: the data rate R of the communication and control system.

This brings the total number of free parameters to three: K, Δf, and R. The purpose of the model is to determine, for a given electrical network, how these parameters affect the magnitude of the load reduction and frequency at the generators in response to a significant loss of supply. The electrical components of the system are modeled in a generally standard fashion; the details of the generators and transmission lines are described next. These descriptions are brief, highlighting only the necessary mathematical elements. Excellent overviews of the models and underlying theory can be found in textbooks by Nilsson [97] (for sinusoidal steady-state analysis), Glover et al. [52], and Arrillaga and Watson [6].

6.2.1 Generation

The generators are modeled as synchronous machines having six state variables: the deviation of the frequency from nominal, the phase angle, the excitation voltage, the mechanical power that drives the machine, the mechanical power control signal, and the status of the frequency protection breaker.[1] The model has one input variable and one output variable, and these govern its interaction with the transmission system. The input variable is the voltage where the machine connects to the transmission network. The output variable is the current it injects into the network at the same point. Figure 6.11 illustrates the state variables with respect to the physical machine that they model. The model has 10 parameters; these are listed in Table 6.1.

The angular speed of the turbine, ω, is in radians per second; its frequency (in hertz) is

$$f = (2\pi)^{-1}\omega \tag{6.4}$$

The synchronous reactance X_d is a complex impedance, and the terminal voltage V and excitation voltage E are phasors.[2] The state trajectory of the generator is

---

[1] This model is based on Mullen's thesis [152].
[2] Section C.2 in Appendix C gives a brief review of phasors, complex impedances, and their uses in circuit analysis.

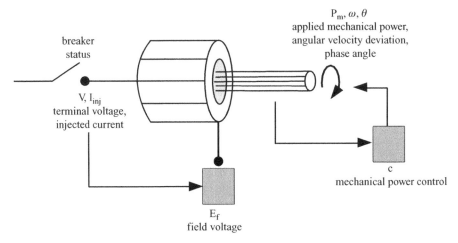

FIGURE 6.11   State variables in the synchronous machine model.

described by the equations

$$E = E_f \angle \theta \qquad \text{(internal machine voltage)} \qquad (6.5)$$

$$I = \frac{E - V}{X_d} \qquad \text{(current flow out of the machine)} \qquad (6.6)$$

$$P_e = \Re\{V I^*\} \qquad \text{(real electrical demand)} \qquad (6.7)$$

$$\dot{\omega} = \frac{P_m - P_e}{M} \qquad \text{(angular acceleration)} \qquad (6.8)$$

$$\dot{\theta} = \omega \qquad \text{(changing phase angle)} \qquad (6.9)$$

$$\dot{c} = -T_1(c + R\omega + A_g\theta) \qquad \text{(speed and phase angle control)} \qquad (6.10)$$

$$\dot{P}_m = T_2(c - P_m + P_s) \qquad \text{(mechanical power adjustment)} \qquad (6.11)$$

TABLE 6.1   Synchronous Machine Parameters

Parameter	Definition
T_1, T_2	Time constants of the speed controller
T_e	Time constant of the excitation controller
$E_{\lim}$	Maximum excitation voltage
M	Angular momentum
R	Gain for the droop control
A_g	Gain of the area generation controller
f_t	Frequency deviation tolerance (in hertz)
X_d	Synchronous reactance
P_s	Output power setpoint

$$\dot{E}_f = \begin{cases} 0 & \text{if } E_f \geq E_{\text{lim}} \wedge |V| < 1 \\ \dfrac{1 - |V|}{T_e} & \text{otherwise} \end{cases} \qquad \text{(excitation control)} \quad (6.12)$$

$$\text{Breaker status} \leftarrow \begin{cases} \text{closed} & \text{if breaker status = closed} \wedge |f| < f_t \\ \text{open} & \text{otherwise} \end{cases} \quad \text{(breaker logic)}$$

$$(6.13)$$

The generator output variable is

$$I_{\text{inj}} = \frac{E}{X_d} \qquad (6.14)$$

6.2.2 Transmission Network and Electrical Loads

The transmission network connects generators and loads. It is modeled with an admittance matrix Y, which is obtained by sinusoidal steady-state analysis. Every load attached to the network is represented by a Norton equivalent circuit: it has an injected current in parallel with an admittance. Passive loads inject no current, and active loads may have a negative or positive injected current. Generators are modeled in the same way, with an injected current calculated by Equation 6.14 and admittance y that is the inverse of the machine's synchronous reactance (i.e., $y = 1/X_d$; see Table 6.1).

Figure 6.12 illustrates the main parts of a model that has generation, load, and transmission. The one line diagram of the two load, two line, single generator system

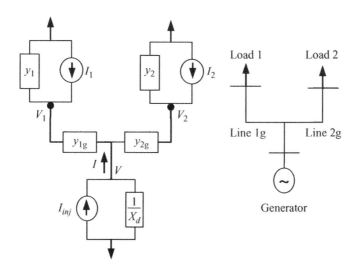

FIGURE 6.12 Circuit diagram and one line drawing of a small power system.

is shown next to its equivalent circuit model. The node voltages and branch currents labeled in the figure are related directly to the input and output variables of the generators, which are described in Section 6.2.1. Specifically, the node voltage V appears in Equations 6.6, 6.7, and 6.12; the generator output current I is derived from its Thevenin equivalent circuit, and the electrical power demand is the product of the output current I and terminal voltage V.

Given the network admittance matrix Y, the load and machine admittances $y_1, \ldots, y_n$, and the injected current vector $\bar{I}_{inj}$, we calculate the voltages $V_1, \ldots, V_n$ appearing at the terminals of loads and generators by

$$\left(Y + \text{diag}(y_1 \ y_2 \ \cdots \ y_n)\right)^{-1} \bar{I}_{inj} = [V_1 \ V_2 \cdots \ V_n]^T$$

This formula is illustrated below using the vectors and matrices for the power system shown in Figure 6.12:

$$\left(\begin{bmatrix} y_{2g} + y_{1g} & -y_{1g} & -y_{2g} \\ -y_{1g} & y_{1g} & 0 \\ -y_{2g} & 0 & y_{2g} \end{bmatrix} + \begin{bmatrix} 1/X_d & 0 & 0 \\ 0 & y_1 & 0 \\ 0 & 0 & y_2 \end{bmatrix} \right)^{-1} \begin{bmatrix} I_{inj} \\ I_1 \\ I_2 \end{bmatrix} = \begin{bmatrix} V \\ V_1 \\ V_2 \end{bmatrix}$$

If a breaker at a generator opens, then the admittance for that generator is zero (i.e., $X_d = \infty$) and I_{inj} is zero. This disconnects the generator from the transmission network. Changes in load are modeled as discrete events that change the load admittance, load current, or both.

6.2.3 Frequency Monitoring and Load Actuation

A generator reports its frequency to the control center at threshold values $k \, \Delta f$, $k \in \mathbb{Z}$; these thresholds are described by event surfaces at $f - k\Delta f = 0$. Reports from the generator are processed at the control center, which keeps the most recent report from each generator. On processing a report, the control center calculates a percentage adjustment for the load and, if the new adjustment differs from the previous one, it tells the loads to change their demands accordingly. The percentage adjustment α is limited to $\pm 30\%$, but within this range is calculated by multiplying the average of the reported frequencies by the control parameter K; in other words, if N generators are connected to the network, the requested adjustment is

$$\alpha = \frac{K}{N} \sum_{j=1}^{N} f_j \tag{6.15}$$

where the f_j is the frequency most recently reported by the jth generator. The new α is then placed into a queue for processing at each load. The loads make adjustments relative to their base demand L to achieve an actual demand $(1 + \alpha)L$. The transmission network closes the control loop; the diagonal elements in Y change discretely as the loads process requests from the control center, thereby changing the electrical demand at the terminals of the generators.

6.2.4 Software Implementation

The transmission network and generators are lumped together in a single model called *ElectricalModel*, which is derived from the *ode_system* class and simulated with a *Hybrid* object. The model comprises a set of differential algebraic equations in the form

$$\dot{\mathbf{x}} = f(\mathbf{x}, \mathbf{V}) \tag{6.16}$$

$$\mathbf{V} = Y^{-1}\mathbf{I} \tag{6.17}$$

where $\mathbf{x}$ is a vector with six state variables for each generator, $\mathbf{I}$ is the current injected by each node into the network, and $\mathbf{V}$ are the node voltages. The entries in the matrix Y change each time a load adjusts its demand or a generator disconnects, and so its inverse must be recalculated at each such event. This can be done with any suitable numerical package; LAPACK was used in this instance.

In addition to its continuous state variables, the *ElectricalModel* has for each generator four state events that are contingent on frequency: one for the overfrequency breaker at $f - f_t = 0$, one for the underfrequency breaker at $f + f_t = 0$, and two for the frequency sensor at $f - (k + 1)\Delta f = 0$ and $f - (k - 1)\Delta f = 0$, where k is the discrete level of f at the last sensor reading. There is one event contingent on E_f, but this is more difficult to handle. Ideally, E_f climbs to E_{lim} and then stops until $1 - |V|$ becomes negative, causing E_f to fall below its limit. If, however, saturation is modeled by $E_f - E_{\text{lim}} = 0$, then the model is illegitimate; on reaching E_{lim} the event condition is always satisfied. The same issue plagues the $1 - |V|$ condition that permits E_f to fall when it is saturated.

Both problems can be solved with a small hysteresis value ϵ. The saturation condition is put a little above E_{lim} at $E_{\text{lim}} + \epsilon$. On reaching this value, E_f stops climbing, and will begin to fall when $|V|$ reaches $1 + \epsilon$. While E_f remains above E_{lim} and below $E_{\text{lim}} + \epsilon$ it may only fall; for $|V| \geq 1$, the derivative of E_f is zero. As soon as $E_f < E_{\text{lim}}$, however, it is allowed to climb again. By labeling these three distinct modes, we can build a state transition diagram for the exciter; this is shown in Figure 6.13. In the state *UNSAT* the excitation voltage may go up or down. From *UNSAT*, the state changes to *SAT* when $E_f = E_{\text{lim}} + \epsilon$. The *SAT* state changes to *FALLING* when $|V| = 1 + \epsilon$. From *FALLING*, it goes back to *SAT* if $|V| = 1$ or to *UNSAT* if $E_f = E_{\text{lim}}$.

The other components of this model are less complicated. The *GenrFail* model starts a scenario by producing an input for the *ElectricalModel* that causes it to disconnect a generator. Outputs from the *ElectricalModel* are sensor readings, and these are fed into the *LoadControl* model, which implements the control logic described in Section 6.2.3. Output from the control center is broadcast to the *Aggregator* models. There is one for each load in the power system. This class models the load aggregator

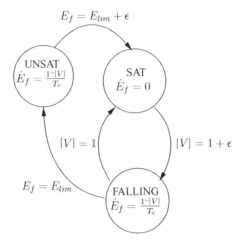

FIGURE 6.13 State transition diagram for the saturating exciter. The initial state is UNSAT with $E_f < E_{\text{lim}}$.

as a server having service time $1/R$ and an infinite queue to hold pending commands. Outputs from the aggregators are new diagonal values for Y, and so become input to the *ElectricalModel*, thereby closing the control loop. The model with all of its parts is illustrated in Figure 6.14, which shows the important classes, and Figure 6.15, which shows how the components are coupled to form the complete system.

6.2.5 Experiments

These experiments are based on the IEEE 118 bus test system,[3] which is illustrated in Figure 6.16. The system has 34 generators, which are assumed to be identical. Their parameters are listed in Table 6.2. The base electrical loads are modeled simply as complex admittances; their values are obtained from the power flow data by assuming a bus voltage $V = 1\angle 0$ so that the bus admittance y is equal to the inverse of its complex power S: $y = 1/S$.[4] Synchronous condensers and capacitor banks at buses are likewise modeled by complex admittances. The model begins in equilibrium, so that $\omega = 0$ at every generator and the other initial conditions are listed by bus number in Table 6.3.

The scenario begins with the generator at bus 79 failing at $t = 1$ s. This removes the largest source of power from the network. Now demand exceeds supply and frequency begins to drop. Without controls beyond those supplied by the generators, all of them are lost, tripping offline within 0.5 s of the initial failure.

---

[3]IEEE test cases are available at http://www.ee.washington.edu/research/pstca/; the data for this study were retrieved in September 2009. For this study, buses with entries in the generation column have generators and buses with entries in the load column are loads; load admittances are calculated from the latter numbers.
[4]This is not a rigorous model of the electrical load (see, e.g., Ref. 111), but it is adequate for our purposes.

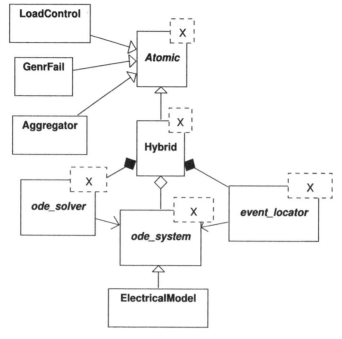

FIGURE 6.14   Class diagram of the model's power and control elements.

Action by the loads can substantially improve this situation. Table 6.4 shows the effects of eight choices for the control parameters. These include large and small values for the network data rates, large and small values for the sensitivity of the frequency sensors, and large and small values for the gain. Each simulation covers 10 s: the 1 s prior to and the 9 s following the loss.

Performance is measured in four ways: First, does the scenario end with the loss of one or more additional generators? Second, what is the largest backlog of messages at the aggregators? Third is the cost J_l of the shed load, which is calculated as the

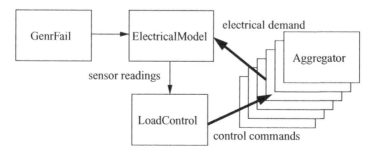

FIGURE 6.15   Coupling of the model's power and control elements.

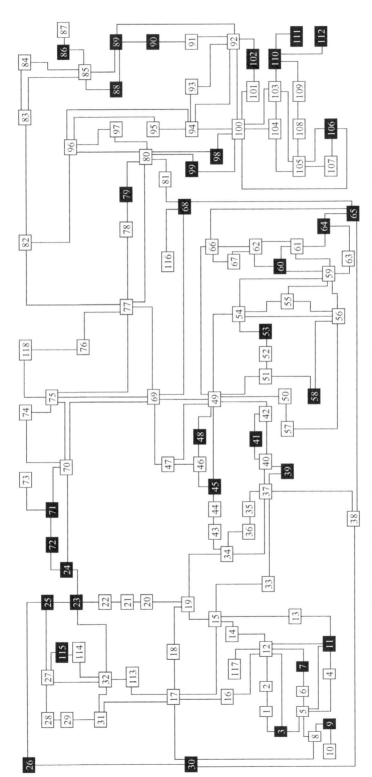

FIGURE 6.16 Diagram of the power system. The black boxes represent buses with a generator.

TABLE 6.2 **Synchronous** **Machine**
Parameters for the 118-Bus Test Case

Parameter	Value
T_1	20
T_2	20
T_e	0.01
$E_{\lim}$	5
M	3
R	50
A_g	200
f_t	0.0025
X_d	$0.001 + j0.01$
P_s	10

time integral of the adjustments requested by the controller; specifically,

$$J_l = \sum_{k=1} |\alpha_{k-1}|(t_k - t_{k-1})$$

where t_k is the time α_k issued by the controller. Fourth is the effectiveness of the controller for damping the generators' movements away from the nominal frequency; this is quantified by the integral sum

$$J_f = \frac{1}{33} \sum_{k=1}^{33} \int_0^{10} (60\omega_k)^2 \, dt$$

where ω_k is the rotational velocity of generator number k (multiplication by 60 converts the per unit rotational velocity to a frequency variation that would be seen in a system where 60 Hz is nominal). This metric is calculated only if no additional generating units are lost.

Table 6.4 highlights the salient features of the system. First, the aggregators must be capable of some minimal data rate to be effective. This minimum is determined by both the sensitivity of the sensors and the magnitude and rate of the frequency excursion. In cases 3 and 4, the slow response of the controller allowed for a large frequency excursion and, due to the fine sensitivity of the sensors, a large backlog in the queues. The backlog in these cases is large enough to prevent the control system from acting in a timely manner, and the result is a blackout, all except one generator is lost and that generator does not supply an acceptable voltage at the loads.

If the data rate is sufficiently high, the controller consistently prevents the loss of a second generator at the cost of a brief interruption for a fraction of the power consumers. The worst case for consumers is cases 8, where a strong response is coupled with fine-grained sensors; the controller is on a hair trigger, but with $K = 12$

TABLE 6.3 Initial Conditions for the Generators

Bus ID	E_f	θ	P_m	c
3	1.00497	0.0432421	1.35158	−8.64842
7	1.00498	0.0460267	0.794661	−9.20534
9	1.00004	0.0492664	0.146725	−9.85327
11	1.01723	0.0366565	2.66869	−7.33131
23	1.00262	0.0477939	0.441222	−9.55878
24	1.00104	0.0484802	0.303956	−9.69604
25	1.00201	0.0483618	0.327631	−9.67237
26	1.00585	0.0437431	1.25137	−8.74863
30	1.00659	0.0440512	1.18976	−8.81024
39	1.00897	0.0431353	1.37295	−8.62705
41	1.00288	0.046637	0.672594	−9.32741
45	1.00404	0.0452297	0.954062	−9.04594
48	1.00879	0.0414223	1.71553	−8.28447
53	1.01405	0.0353373	2.93255	−7.06745
58	1.0158	0.0365551	2.68898	−7.31102
60	1.00331	0.0424173	1.51654	−8.48346
64	1.00344	0.0458577	0.828469	−9.17153
65	1.00278	0.0453248	0.935031	−9.06497
68	1.00917	0.0423695	1.5261	−8.4739
71	1.00069	0.0489407	0.211861	−9.78814
72	1.00337	0.0467811	0.643779	−9.35622
79	1.02359	0.0349618	3.00764	−6.99236
86	1.00163	0.0485503	0.28993	−9.71007
88	1.00904	0.0428412	1.43176	−8.56824
89	1.00514	0.0457476	0.850475	−9.14953
90	1.00054	0.0481395	0.372105	−9.6279
98	0.999622	0.0482093	0.358144	−9.64186
99	1.01192	0.0425017	1.49967	−8.50033
102	1.00541	0.0456922	0.861567	−9.13843
106	1.00428	0.046433	0.713403	−9.2866
110	1.0017	0.0487104	0.257912	−9.74209
111	1.00348	0.0473962	0.52075	−9.47925
112	1.00691	0.0436271	1.27459	−8.72541
115	1.00054	0.0465561	0.688782	−9.31122

lacks the dexterity for making precise adjustments and so tends to overreact. In case 7, however, finely tuned, rapid adjustments give a good response for both the power consumers and power producers. Although consumers might prefer the outcome in case 1, which minimizes the loss of electrical service, the more rapid damping of the frequency excursion in case 7 is indicative of a more robust system and, consequently, yields the greatest benefit for all parties.

The control signal for case 7 is shown in Figure 6.17; it disconnects about 8% of the load for <1.5 s, with load quickly reconnected as the disturbance subsides.

TABLE 6.4 Performance Metrics for Eight-Parameter Sets

Case	R	K	$\Delta f(\times 10^{-3})$	Maximum Message Backlog	$J_l(\times 10^{-2})$	$J_f(\times 10^{-2})$
1	100	2	1.25	6	2.9	3.0
2	100	12	1.25	4	16	4.7
3[a]	100	2	0.125	180	—	
4[a]	100	12	0.125	83	—	—
5	1000	2	1.25	2	3.9	3.1
6	1000	12	1.25	2	13	4.0
7	1000	2	0.125	24	4.8	2.4
8	1000	12	0.125	35	23	2.7

[a]These two cases end in the additional loss of generation and do not report J_l of J_f.

The frequency and mechanical power trajectories for the generators are shown in Figures 6.18 and 6.19. The correspondence between the control signal and frequency excursion is readily apparent. The contingency ends with the generators able to supply sufficient voltage to the majority of the loads, but voltages near the disconnected generator have noticeably sagged: Figure 6.20 shows bus voltages initially and at the end of the scenario. If this model were extended to include voltage regulating transformers at the loads (see, e.g., Ref. 58), these would initiate a second round of corrective actions by creating a greater demand for power (reactive power, in this case) from the generators. This, in turn, could cause nearby generators to reach their E_f limits, instigating a voltage collapse and additional loss of generation. This scenario would make an interesting study.

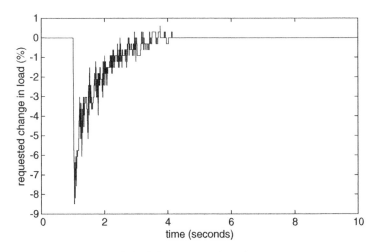

FIGURE 6.17 Control signal in case 7.

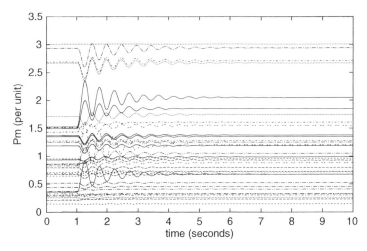

FIGURE 6.18 Mechanical power in case 7.

A final comment should be made about the data Table 6.4. First, observe that the frequency trajectories for case 7 show one generator that barely avoids the disconnect threshold. It is impossible to know whether this is a numerical artifact or a real facet of the model. Regardless, a small perturbation of the model's parameters could push that generator over the edge. So, too, could changes in the floating-point hardware and the numerical algorithms used by the simulator.[5] A thorough analysis of this model

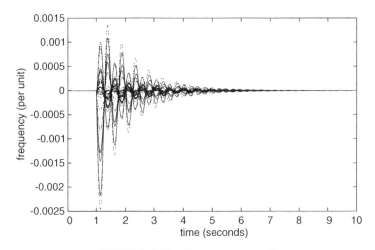

FIGURE 6.19 Frequency in case 7.

[5]The results in this section were calculated using x87 FPU (floating processing unit) instructions for floating-point arithmetic. Using SSE2 instructions, which are common to 64-bit computers, could produce different results in some instances.

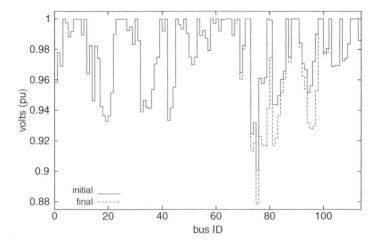

FIGURE 6.20   Initial and final voltage profiles for case 7.

must include a sensitivity study that considers both: this would be an interesting and informative exercise.

6.3 SUMMARY

The examples in this chapter illustrate how the methods developed in Chapter 5 combine the best aspects of two popular and successful techniques for simulating hybrid systems. First, the method of chapter 5 retains the performance benefits of the modular DEVS&DESS [109] and generalized DEVS [50] approaches, and, more specifically, the capability of event-based integrators to avoid unnecessary updates of continuous state variables (see, e.g., Refs. 30, 69, 70, 93, 103, 142, 143, 155, and 158). The tank's interrupt handler, described in Sections 4.1.9 and 4.1.6 (also see Appendix A), concretely illustrates the importance of distinguishing events that directly affect continuous variables from those that do not. Indeed, the relative ease with which the pendulum's stochastic trajectory is sampled is due to the computational simplicity of the events in the Ethernet model; add to each the cost of an integration step, and a sufficient set of samples is impractical to obtain.

Computational efficiency, however, is not the only advantage of the generalized DEVS and the DEVS&DESS approaches. These methods are both derivatives of Zeigler's discrete-event system specification, the topic of Chapter 4, and are therefore well suited for modeling systems with complex, discrete-event dynamics. Because of this, generalized DEVS and DEVS&DESS are applied to many hybrid modeling problems despite the numerical difficulties introduced by the event-based integrators that characterize their implementations.

It is not difficult to overcome these numerical problems, however, once it is recognized that most methods for simulating continuous models can be cast as discrete-event systems. The modeler may easily incorporate into a complex model nearly any method that is suitable for its continuous subsystems. The example of the electrical power system demonstrates the importance of doing this: it is impractical to separate the generators' continuous variables, which are coupled through an admittance matrix that is difficult to invert and that changes with time, into the distinct components required by event-based integrators. More important still, improving the models of the electrical loads will result in a very complex differential algebraic model, and to simulate it will require algorithms that are common to tools for simulating continuous systems but absent from tools for discrete-event simulation.

Lundvall et. al. [78] describe, for example, how the DASRT algorithm is used by the OpenModelica compiler and runtime system to simulate models comprising differential algebraic equations and discrete events. Notably, OpenModelica avoids the numerical difficulties described in Section 5.7, but it suffers from the long execution times inherent to a nonmodular approach.[6] The method of Chapter 5 offers a remedy for the long execution times while retaining both the numerical advantages of the DASRT algorithm and a modeling framework suitable for complex, discrete event systems. Chapter 7 addresses this important possibility.

---

[6] Assuming, of course, that the model contains discrete event components at least as complex as an Ethernet simulator.

CHAPTER 7

THE FUTURE

As computer technology advances, the size and scope of simulations expand. So, too, do the costs of simulation studies, and the idea of simulation as a distinct discipline has appeared, at least in part, as a result of economic forces. Just as the complexity of software reached a crisis in the 1960s (or, more likely, well before this), giving birth to the now well-recognized field of software engineering, the problems posed by large simulation projects are spurring interest in those elements of modeling and simulation that transcend the particular. Software architectures for simulation are one such topic. In this concluding chapter, three other topics are briefly considered; although not conclusive, this short survey includes technologies that are relevant to the construction of simulation software, are being actively pursued at the present, and are likely to have a substantial impact on the future of modeling and simulation.

7.1 SIMULATION PROGRAMMING LANGUAGES

For 40 years, beginning in the 1950s and tapering in the 1990s, simulation programming languages were a major focus of academic and industrial research. Some languages for discrete-event simulation are still widely used, but these appear largely as part of commercial products: SIMAN, MODL, and SLAM, for instance, are the backbones of Arena (Rockwell Automation), Extend (Imagine That!), and Awesim, respectively (see, e.g., Refs. 27, 62, 105, and 112); Raczynsky's PASION (and its more recent variants PSM++ and Bluesss [113]), and the venerable SIMSCRIPT

Building Software for Simulation: Theory and Algorithms, with Applications in C++, By James J. Nutaro
Copyright © 2011 John Wiley & Sons, Inc.

(from CACI, now on version III [116]) persist as well. Nonetheless, many, possibly the majority, of discrete-event models are built with object libraries, like the one developed in this book, and general-purpose, object-oriented programming languages.

This trend began in the 1990s with the widespread adoption of object-oriented programming. The shift is not surprising. Many of the features deemed desirable in a simulation programming language are manifest in modern, objected-oriented languages. Tracing Nance's history of simulation programming languages [95, 96], we find some of the first instances of objects and intrinsic support for sets, lists, and random numbers; these are now commonplace in the standard object libraries for C++, Java, and most other popular languages. Pre- and postprocessing of data, at one time accomplished with the simulation tools themselves, are now done with spreadsheets or numerical software such as R, MATLAB, Scilab, and others.

A significant exception to this rule are languages for modeling and simulation of continuous systems. The diversity of languages has, perhaps, been diminished by the establishment of Modelica as a standard, but extensions to this language are actively developed. The continuing relevance of Modelica, while interest in discrete-event languages fades, can be understood by comparing the problems that these two technologies solve.

Discrete-event simulations tend to be heavy on programming. Abstract data types such as lists, sets, and associative containers are essential in most applications; object-oriented concepts are of paramount importance; and languages for discrete-event systems focused in large part on satisfying these requirements. When these features became intrinsic to mainstream programming languages, the impetus for specialized languages vanished.

Continuous simulations, however, are straightforward in this respect. They deal almost exclusively with relationships between real (or complex) variables. When the equations are in proper form and a suitable numerical algorithm is available, the programming job is simple. Putting a large set of equations into proper form is the major task, and when hundreds or thousands of equations are involved, this task must be automated. That is the purpose of languages for continuous simulation; given a set of differential equations, algebraic constraints, and state event functions, the language compiler performs the algebraic manipulations needed to put these into a simulatable form and generates the necessary simulation code.

The growing importance of hybrid systems is prompting a repetition of history. A small, but substantial, number of researchers are looking for extensions to the Modelica language that will enable it to describe discrete-event systems (see, e.g., Refs. 11, 40, 44, 89, 110, 115, and 124). This is an attempt to re-create the languages that first appeared in the 1970s for combined discrete-event and continuous simulation. The new aspect of the more recent work is modern software technology, which has changed substantially since the 1970s. Reexamining this topic may yield important insights, and certainly it is an intellectual and engineering challenge, but history suggests that new features for modeling discrete event systems must culminate in something like a full-fledged programming language in order to have wide practical value. This development, if followed to its conclusion, will clutter the otherwise simple and very usable Modelica language (or any other language for continuous simulation) with a host of features secondary to its main purpose. Moreover, these features will duplicate capabilities already well developed in other programming languages, and necessarily lag behind the more rapid development of widely used, less specialized tools.

In Chapter 5 it was shown, albeit in a simple form, that a simulator for a continuous model can be embedded in a discrete-event system. This points to a way forward for continuous simulation languages. A Modelica compiler, for instance, could generate automatically the code built by hand for the tank, inverted pendulum, and electrical power system that were used as examples in this book. Taking this approach, extensions to the language itself would aim at making the state variables, state events, and exogenous, discrete trajectories of the continuous model accessible from a discrete-event simulator, with the latter built with a mainstream programming language.

An example of this approach can be found in the M/CD++ compiler, which implements a subset of the Modelica language [30, 143]. M/CD++ uses quantized state integrators and separate components for the distinct elements of the continuous model (see Section 5.7). The compiler transforms its input file to a bond graph, assigns it causality marks, and then creates a network from the causally marked bond graph, with atomic components for each primitive element. The final result is a networked, discrete-event model that is simulated by the CD++ simulation engine.

The advantage of this approach is its reuse of existing software technology. In the particular case of CD++, the implementation language for discrete-event models is C++ and the simulation engine is an object library built with that language. Tools based on this library provide specific, narrowly defined functionality. The CD++ language, for instance, automatically generates couplings for cellular automata; can be used to program simple cells for those models; and the M/CD++ compiler, as we have seen, generates a discrete-event model to approximate a continuous one. The prominence of general-purpose programming languages in discrete-event simulators, and their historical displacement of more specialized languages, suggests that compilers like M/CD++ are a good model for future developments. Continuous system languages with compilers that can create modules for a variety of discrete simulators will have tremendous practical value.

7.2 PARALLEL COMPUTING AND DISCRETE-EVENT SIMULATION

Bigger, more computationally intensive models became possible with every new generation of computers. For 20 years at least, this boost in computing power was essentially free for the software developer; at most, a new compiler was required and possibly a few modifications of the source code to suit some of its quirks. So, with only a modest effort, the new, more powerful computers ran existing models faster or larger models in a reasonable amount of time. This ended when the microscopic parts of the computer could not be made any smaller. Now each new generation of computer contains processors with essentially the same computing capabilities as those of the previous generation; the new computers just have more of them. Parallel computing, once a curiosity for the majority of software developers, is now the only means for better performance.

Algorithms for using parallel computers to simulate discrete-event models have been a topic of intense research since the late 1970s. Like parallel computing in general, this was a topic on the periphery of simulation research when bigger models were a natural consequence of each new generation of computer; and also like parallel computing in general, all except the most trivial (embarrassingly parallel, in the terms of the field) applications of parallel computers to simulation required prodigious, even heroic, effort. Indeed, the performance obtained from a parallel simulator is proportional to its degree of specialization for a particular application. This specialization extends far beyond the code necessary to implement the dynamics of a particular model, and it makes the software more difficult to build and more expensive to maintain.

Simultaneous events are the most easily exploited, but least effective, source of parallelism in a model. This requires no more information than is already available to the simulator, and the parallelized simulation engine is therefore easy to use. Indeed, the necessary modifications to the simulation engine are themselves quite simple; the for loops for computing and routing output and for computing state transitions are parallelized. If there are a very large number of models undergoing changes of state at the same time, if the state transitions are very time-consuming to compute, or both then calculating these in parallel will yield a reduction in the simulator's running time. Unfortunately, this situation is uncommon. In most discrete-event models, simultaneous events are rare and, therefore, very little parallelism can be exploited in this way. So, although this method is simple to apply, it yields benefits for only a small class of models (but these can be significant; see, e.g., Ref. 63).

In some cases, particular events might be both difficult to calculate and amenable to parallel execution. For example, if a continuous model has a very large number of state variables, then its differential functions might be usefully calculated in parallel. The model's state event functions might also be computed in parallel if they are sufficiently complex or numerous. It is better still to parallelize some aspects of the numerical integration and event detection algorithms; this strategy is attractive because, again, it is easy to exploit. The parallelization could even be automated if a continuous simulation language with a suitable compiler were available. The majority of discrete events in a model tend, however, to be fine-grained, requiring very little computation and therefore not susceptible to parallelization. Once again, where the method works, it is likely also to be easy to apply, but these circumstances are exceptional.

The academic research on parallel discrete-event simulation has produced two classes of algorithm, conservative and optimistic, that can use Herculean computers to simulate enormous, complicated models. Different problems are posed by the two classes of algorithm.

Conservative algorithms require a method by which, given the state of a model at time t, its output can be computed to some time $t + \epsilon$ *and* that this can be done without advancing the model's state. The ϵ is called *lookahead*, and large lookahead is essential to good performance. In many cases, lookahead exists in principle, but exploiting it requires carefully crafted, highly specialized code that is difficult to maintain. In Fujimoto's words [44], the software becomes brittle and is prone to breakage when even minor changes to the model's logic are required.

Optimistic algorithms overcome this problem by using speculation to find looka-head automatically. In principle, these algorithms are ideal in two respects: (1) they do not require explicit synchronization points and so are highly scalable; and (2) they automatically exploit any parallelism inherent in the decomposition of the model's state space, that is, in the organization of its atomic components (logical processes, in the terms of the field). Unfortunately, realizing these ideal aspects can be difficult and time-consuming in the extreme.

Among the most challenging problems in practice is to efficiently save and re-store the states of atomic components. If the state of the model is a very simple data structure, occupying just a few words of computer memory, then this is a straight-forward problem to solve. In instances where the state transition function applies small, incremental changes to a large set of state variables, techniques for incre-mental state saving can sometimes be of use (see, e.g., Refs. 37 and 123). This, however, is more difficult and requires intimate knowledge of how the component works. In some circumstances, the state transition function is actually reversible and a near-perfect solution is possible, at least in terms of computational complexity (see, e.g., Refs. 18 and 106). A working implementation, however, can be difficult to construct and maintain. For models with both a complicated state space and ir-reversible dynamics, optimistic algorithms remain an impractical route to parallel execution.

Because of these issues, the most advanced algorithms for parallel discrete-event simulation remain impractical tools for general use, a state of affairs lamented by Fujimoto [43] in 1993, and that persists today. Where they have been successfully applied, it has been through a sustained effort to parallelize the simulation of a particular system; simulations of communication systems and digital circuits are prominent examples (see, e.g., Refs. 49 and 79 and numerous others on VHDL simulations; see also Refs. 45, 76, and 117 as examples of the vast literature on parallel simulations of computer networks). High-performance computing, however, is not the goal of simulations used in engineering, only a means to an end. Model simplification, the other route to reduced execution times, is more attractive when budgets are constrained and deadlines loom.

The existing technology for parallel simulation, therefore, brings the field of modeling and simulation to a kind of crisis. Sequential computers are not getting faster, but in the past this has driven the growth of model-based engineering. Each generation of computers solved larger, more sophisticated problems; however, the programming of these computers did not change radically, at least so far as the end user was concerned. Better performance was, in this sense, only one purchase away.

New computers, however, are not necessarily more powerful than their recent pre-decessors, we have only packed more processors into a single machine. The size and scope of future models will therefore be determined by the degree to which parallel simulation can be made cost-effective. Widespread adoption of parallel simulation algorithms will depend much less on their ability to scale to massive machines, a traditional measure of success, and much more on the cost of use and their general applicability. The latter, therefore, are important topics for future research.

7.3   THE MANY FORMS OF DISCRETE SYSTEMS AND THEIR SIMULATORS

Lackner [72], to whom the classical worldviews of event scheduling, process orientation, and activity scanning are frequently attributed [35, 95], was among the first to consider a discrete-event system as something distinct from its incarnation in a computer program. It was not until the 1970s, however, that analysis methods other than simulation received sustained attention, and from these ruminations emerged a variety of mathematical structures for modeling and reasoning about discrete-event dynamics: Zeigler's discrete-event system specification (DEVS), the numerous flavors of Petri nets, and asynchronous cellular automata are examples.

Many, if not most, of these mathematical structures were developed independently of one another and, just as often, proceeded with their developers generally unaware of mutually reinforcing concepts. Duplication is therefore rife, fundamental discoveries are often repeated, and simulation technology is reinvented whenever the scope of a burgeoning field exceeds the bounds of pencil-and-paper analysis. This variety of thought and form is essential to healthy growth, but its benefits can be realized only when mutual awareness leads to cross-fertilization.

Unfortunately, fractured development has produced a misconception in some instances that the vast host of analysis and programming tools represent fundamentally different approaches to the study of discrete-event systems. In most instances, this simply isn't true. Two particular cases were illustrated in this book: the general subsumption of discrete-time systems by discrete-event systems, and the alternative representations of asynchronous cellular automata as hybrid automata and as DEVS models. An appreciation of these similarities is essential for building models of complex systems, in which practical necessity requires the different parts to be expressed in different forms. If, indeed, these separate expressions were incompatible, then combined models would be impossible to build.

The study of relationships between model representations is a relatively undeveloped, but critically important, area of research. Its most practical outcome is the construction of modeling methods and simulation tools in which models having different forms can be meaningfully and more easily combined. It remains a matter of opinion as to whether this is best accomplished by combining simulation algorithms (e.g., the approach taken by the Ptolemy project [34]), by the mathematical transformation of models into a common structure (e.g., the approach taken by the AToM3 tool [33, 92, 141]), or by some intermediate means (e.g., see Refs. 85, 126, and 148).

Regardless, repeatable methods for combined modeling and a broader understanding of commonalities in the multitudinous forms of discrete-event systems are essential. Diversity in particular must be tempered by an improved understanding of shared elements; without this, fundamental concepts are lost in a morass of technical detail. This problem, therefore, is of both academic and practical interest, and its unraveling will have a consequential and transformational effect on the theory and practice of modeling and simulation.

7.4   OTHER FACETS OF MODELING AND SIMULATION

Modeling and simulation has many dimensions; software design and programming are two of these and are certainly important for building simulators. Two other facets are discussed above: (1) simulation tools, which include special programming languages and (2) the many theories of discrete-event systems, which link simulation models with other methods of analysis. The list of important topics does not end here, however. Truncer Ören [104], Rogers [119], and Mielke et al. [87], in their expositions of education in modeling and simulation and the emerging body of knowledge for modeling and simulation (referred to by the acronym MSBOK), identify a host of topics that are important to the field and its applications; these include

1. The design of experiments
2. Methods for the analysis of input and output data
3. Methods for validation and verification of models
4. Numerical analysis and mathematical topics relevant to understanding and simulating dynamic systems
5. Management of engineering projects
6. Computer graphics, artificial intelligence, computer networking, and other topics related to the construction of virtual environments
7. Modeling methods

This list might also include systems theory, a variety of model representations and their simulation techniques (e.g., algorithms and data structures for programming the classical worldviews of discrete-event simulation), and systems with dynamic structures (see, e.g., Refs. 89, 140, 154, and 156). Textbooks on modeling and simulation cover many of these aspects (see, e.g., Refs. 19, 41, 42, 73, and 143), but a broader education is required to accumulate all of the fundamental skills.

Recognition of this fact has recently (at the time of this writing) spawned several PhD and master's degree programs in modeling and simulation. These are offered by several institutions, including the University of Central Florida, the MOVES Institutes at the Naval Postgraduate School, and the Virginia Modeling, Analysis and Simulation Center (VMASC) at Old Dominion University (where an undergraduate degree might also be offered in the near future). Prompting this interest in modeling and simulation education is, at least in part, the huge investment in modeling and simulation technology by the US Department of Defense, the consequent recognition that large modeling and simulation projects are major engineering endeavors, and a hard-won realization that success requires teams of engineers with a diverse, but particular, mix of skills. It remains to be seen whether "simulation engineer" will emerge with recognition equaling that of electrical, mechanical, and the other established engineering disciplines. Regardless, affordable simulations and robust software architectures will remain inseparable for the foreseeable future.

APPENDIX A

DESIGN AND TEST OF SIMULATIONS

Simulation software can persist for as long as the system it models, supporting design at first, and later test, operations, maintenance, and the design of the system's replacement. Some models are built to satisfy specific, short-term needs, and these are designed, constructed, and tested with little or no concern for long-term maintenance. Large models, however, or families of models that will provide service for years, must be treated like any large software project. An appropriate lifecycle model, with careful attention to documentation, testing, and version control, are fundamental to success.

The composition of the development team is also important, and there are two roles that every simulation project must fill in some measure. Domain experts who understand the system that is being modeled are an obvious necessity. Software engineers conversant with simulation techniques—numerical analysis, discrete-event simulation, and the other topics addressed in this book—are also needed. Models for engineering often require analysts, who (perhaps surprisingly) are not necessarily domain experts, to prepare input for and process output from the model; this is particularly important when the model has substantial random elements and, consequently, statistical rigor is needed to use it effectively.

The concern of the software engineer is chiefly with the design, construction, and maintenance of the simulation program. The modular modeling framework that we have developed, and its supporting simulation architecture, encourages a piecewise approach to the design and construction of a model. After the interface to a module is established, its internal workings can be designed, refined, tested, and maintained in isolation. Modules are combined from the bottom up, thereby limiting the scope of

Building Software for Simulation: Theory and Algorithms, with Applications in C++, By James J. Nutaro
Copyright © 2011 John Wiley & Sons, Inc.

integration at each stage to a few thoroughly tested components. Likewise, the scope of change is controlled as requirements evolve.

A.1   DECOMPOSING A MODEL

As a general rule, an atomic component should be small enough that its dynamic behavior is easily understood. A simple model can be verified by inspection, its response to input easily anticipated, and manual simulation used to construct test cases. Often, a design begins from the top and works its way down. The model is initially conceived in terms of its largest parts and their interconnections. The modeler then looks for an atomic representation of these parts.

Sometimes one can be constructed easily. More often, the state space of a subsystem is too large or the dynamics too intricate, and an atomic representation is futile. The modeler then looks for a way to break the complicated subsystem into parts that, when interacting, will produce the desired behavior. This proceeds as before, with the decomposition being conceived in its largest parts. Atomic models are found for these or, that being intractable, the subsystems are further decomposed. Eventually, a fine enough decomposition is found and atomic models are built. Going back up the hierarchy of decomposed systems, successively more complicated pieces are combined to realize the original goal.

A.1.1   Bottom–Up Testing

One advantage of building a complicated model from simpler atomic pieces is that testing can be done as the components are integrated. Code inspections, inspection of design documents (state transition diagrams, phase diagrams, event graphs, etc.), and small simulations that can be verified by hand calculations are all very effective ways of uncovering errors. The small simulations deserve particular attention; *keep these small programs and build a script to run them and check their output.*

As the model develops, you should acquire a collection of test cases that are run often to help uncover a host of problems, including unintended interactions between components, problems introduced during code optimization, and to guarantee that adding new behavior to an atomic model does not alter its old behavior in an unintended way. As the model evolves, the suite of test cases must evolve with it.

The set of test cases can also be used to pinpoint problems in ways that a debugger cannot. When a coupled model exhibits an unusual, unexpected, and undesired behavior, it is usually a consequence of one of two factors: (1) the component interconnections have been improperly coded or (2) some subcomponent is not behaving as expected. Factor 1 can be checked by inspecting the network's routing method. In many cases, if the coupling expressed in the code is translated into a drawing on paper, then the source of the problem becomes apparent. Complicated routing functions may require the simulation to print a trace of source–destination pairs that is (tediously) examined for unintended interactions. Try these methods first, and resort to more drastic measures, such as stepping through the code with a debugger, only if simpler techniques fail to identify a coupling problem and you are quite sure of the behavior of the subcomponents.

Confidence in the subcomponents is gained chiefly by extensive testing. In decomposing a large model, the designer necessarily imagines the interactions that will occur between its components. Test cases are constructed from these anticipated interactions by building small simulations that supply a component with likely input trajectories. Initially, the set of test cases is small: simple trajectories and the few tricky cases that the designer believes are likely to occur. New trajectories are added to address new behavior or to understand and fix problems discovered by actual use.

The semigroup property can be exploited to construct test cases for the latter purpose. Knowing the time of the failure, the state of the model at some point immediately prior to it and the subsequent input trajectory are recorded during a regular simulation run. A test case is then built that puts the model into the recorded state and feeds it the recorded input trajectory. Now the component can be debugged. When the problem is solved, this new test case is added to the test suite and the regression tests are run to make sure that no new problems were introduced.

A.1.2 Invariants and Assertions

Bouncing balls cannot pass through the floor, the total energy in a closed system is nonincreasing, and the quantity of material in a container must be nonnegative and less than its capacity; these are examples of invariant rules that a correct simulation does not violate. When a system changes state or produces output, these invariants can be checked to ensure that they are satisfied. If they are not, then something is broken.

The robotic tank has several examples of simple invariants. The *PacketProcessing* model (Section 4.4) produces an output only if it has a packet in its queue; this constraint is checked by an assertion in the output function. Likewise, the model does not produce output when it is interrupted; this, too, is checked with an assertion. Another example is in the *TankPhysicsEqns*, where the rotational velocity must be zero if the tank is not turning; this is checked when the differential functions are calculated.

Constraints on input and output trajectories can also be checked with assertions. For example, the *Xor* model in Section 3.2.3 expects two values in its input bag. An assertion in its state transition function checks whether this constraint is satisfied. The *TankPhysicsEqns* and *InterruptHandler* contain similar checks on the types of the input objects that they receive.

A.2 INPUT AND OUTPUT OBJECTS

Early in the design of a simulator it is necessary to decide how input and output events will be implemented. The solution will depend a great deal on the programming language that is used, and C++ offers a greater variety of solutions than do many other languages. Three strategies are common in practice: using simple structures and primitive types, constructing a hierarchy of event classes, and using the union type to create a simple structure that carries several kinds of events. Inevitably, these strategies will become mixed up in a large model, making it is necessary to glue them together. There is a useful strategy for this problem as well.

A.2.1 Simple Structures

Primitive types—doubles, ints, and chars—are an obvious choice for models that do not require much variety in their input and output. The *Machine* model from Section 4.2.4 uses integers to communicate the number of parts given to and produced by a machine. Using primitive types is advantageous because they are quickly and automatically created and destroyed in the method's stack space. This gives good performance and avoids problems managing memory: the *gc_output* method does nothing for the *Machine* class.

Simple data structures are a step beyond primitive types, permitting models to exchange more data while avoiding explicit memory management. This works well if the data structures are not too complicated. They are copied and destroyed repeatedly by the simulator, however, and a severe performance penalty can be accrued if too many data are crammed into these objects. The *IO_Type* structure used by the *CellularAutomaton* model in Section 3.5 is an example of a simple object being used for input and output.

A.2.2 Unions

Unions can cram several different types of events into a simple structure. This approach is used by the simulator for the robotic tank. Each input and output is a *SimEvent* structure that contains two fields: a type and the event data. The data can be contained in one of five structures, each part of a union and, therefore, overlaid in memory. The implementation of the *SimEvent* is listed below.

This solution retains the advantages of using a simple data structure and adds flexibility; besides, it also introduces a new opportunity for error. To use the data correctly, the data recipient must check the type code and then access the data in the proper way. If, for example, the type is SIM_MOTOR_VOLTAGE, then the data must be accessed using the *simMotorVoltage* method to interpret them properly as a *SimMotorVoltage* structure. Any other interpretation will produce junk. The *TankPhysicsEqns* and *InterruptHandler* models can accept only a single type of event, and so they contain assertions to ensure the type is correct before using the data. The *PacketProcessing* model can accept both SIM_PACKET and SIM_INTERRUPT events, and it always checks the event type before interpreting and processing the data. In a large model, incompatible components may unwittingly be coupled together, and if proper checks and assertions are omitted, then the error may go undetected and lead to mysterious failures.

___ *Definition of the Simulation Events Used in the Tank Simulator* ___

```
1   #ifndef Events_h_
2   #define Events_h_
3
4   // Enumeration of simulation event types.
5   typedef enum {
6      SIM_MOTOR_VOLTAGE, // Tank motor voltage
7      SIM_TANK_POSITION, // Tank position
8      SIM_INTERRUPT, // Interrupt handler start/end
9      SIM_PACKET, // Packet from the network
10     SIM_MOTOR_ON_TIME, // Motor on time
11     SIM_NO_EVENT // No assigned type
12  } SimEventType;
13  // Motor voltage data
14  struct SimMotorVoltage { double el, er; };
15  // Tank position data
16  struct SimTankPosition { double x, y, theta; };
17  // On-time settings for the interrupt handler.
18  struct SimMotorOnTime
19  {
20     unsigned char left, right;
21     bool reverse_left, reverse_right;
22  };
23  // A network packet
24  struct SimPacket { float left_power, right_power; };
25  // The I/O type for all models in the tank simulator
26  class SimEvent
27  {
28  public:
29     SimEvent():type(SIM_NO_EVENT){}
30     // Create a specific type of event
31     SimEvent(SimEventType type):type(type){}
32     // Create a SIM_MOTOR_VOLTAGE event
33     SimEvent(SimMotorVoltage event):
34        type(SIM_MOTOR_VOLTAGE) { data.volts = event; }
35     // Create a SIM_TANK_POSITION event
36     SimEvent(SimTankPosition event):
37        type(SIM_TANK_POSITION) { data.pos = event; }
38     // Create an event to set the motor on-time counters
39     SimEvent(SimMotorOnTime event):
40        type(SIM_MOTOR_ON_TIME) { data.ontime = event; }
41     // Create a SIM_PACKET event
42     SimEvent(SimPacket event):type(SIM_PACKET) { data.packet = event; }
43     // Get the event type
44     SimEventType getType() const { return type; }
45     // Get the motor voltage data
46     const SimMotorVoltage& simMotorVoltage() const { return data.volts; }
47     // Get the tank position data
```

```
48      const SimTankPosition& simTankPosition() const { return data.pos; }
49      // Get the motor settings
50      const SimMotorOnTime& simMotorOnTime() const { return data.ontime; }
51      // Get the network packet
52      const SimPacket& simPacket() const { return data.packet; }
53      // The STL needs this operator
54      bool operator<(const SimEvent& b) const { return type < b.type; }
55  private:
56      SimEventType type;
57      union
58      {
59          SimMotorVoltage volts;
60          SimTankPosition pos;
61          SimMotorOnTime ontime;
62          SimPacket packet;
63      } data;
64  };
65
66  #endif
```

A.2.3   Pointers and Hierarchies of Events

When simple data structures and unions are insufficient, the designer almost invariably resorts to pointers. Now the output of a model can be an arbitrarily complex object to which the recipients of the event receive a pointer. In many ways, using pointers for input and output is a necessary evil; all variations on this theme have considerable drawbacks. The need for explicit memory management is most immediately apparent; this issue, along with the *gc_output* method for addressing it, were discussed in Section 3.1.5.

There are other, more subtle and far-reaching, impacts that pointers have on the design of the simulator. In fact, it is not a problem with using pointers, but a more general difficulty arising from the use of indirection to move events from source to destination. Suppose that we construct a hierarchy of classes, such as the one shown in Figure A.1, for the types of events in the simulation. The base class contains information common to all events: a virtual method for printing the event data to a log, a pointer to the source of the event, and maybe a type code to help with debugging. Each derived class contains information that is pertinent to a specific type(s) of event.

The input–output type of the *Atomic*, *Network*, and *Simulator* classes is a pointer to the base class X. The route method carries this pointer from the *output_func* of the originating model to the *delta_ext* and *delta_conf* methods of the receiving models. The models, however, need the classes *EventA* and *EventB* that are derived from X. The simulator cannot provide these because the type information is lost when the event is routed.

Runtime type identification is used at the event's destination to recover the lost type information and downcast the object accordingly. The downcast is done with the

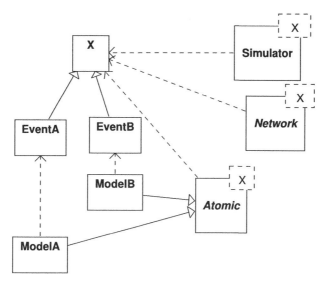

FIGURE A.1   A notational class hierarchy for input and output events, its relationship to the *Simulator* and *Network*, and to models derived from the *Atomic* class.

dynamic_cast operator.[1] Given a pointer to an event of type A that we want to cast as the derived type B, the dynamic cast returns a pointer to B if the cast was successful and NULL otherwise. This operation usually appears in the loop that processes items in the bag of input; an example is shown below.

———— *Using* dynamic_cast *in a Model with Many Event Types* ————

```
1  void SomeModel::delta_ext(double e, const Bag<A*>& xb)
2  {
3      Bag<A*>::const_iterator iter;
4      for (iter = xb.begin(); iter != xb.end(); iter++) {
5          B* x = dynamic_cast<B*>(*iter);
6          if (x != NULL) {
7              ...
8          }
9          ...
10     }
11 }
```

This solution is similar to the use of unions described above, but is more robust when a simulation has many types of events. Nonetheless, there is, like with a union, an implicit dependence between communicating components; specifically, the

[1] The dynamic_cast operator can be used only with polymorphic types that is, with classes that have a virtual method. A virtual destructor is sufficient.

component that generates an event must produce a type that is compatible with the expectations of the receiver. Violations of this implicit agreement will cause an error.

A more insidious problem with exchanging pointers is that the output object is shared by its producer and all of its recipients. If any of these modify the object while calculating their state transition, that modification will be visible to all the models that share the object and appear later in the *Simulator*'s iteration through imminent and active objects. In effect, the shared object becomes a hidden channel for communication, and its effects can be unpredictable, are generally undesirable, and the root cause can be difficult to pin down. This problem is avoided by treating input objects as read-only, and permitting modification of the object only in the scope of the *output_func* of the model that created it.

A.2.4 Mixing Strategies with Model Wrappers

It is sometimes desirable to connect two models that, although otherwise compatible, differ in the type of object that they use for input and output. The problem is illustrated in Figure A.2, where model M_A that operates on events of type A is connected to M_B that operates on events of type B. The *Simulator*, which is designed for use as a component within a larger model, offers a simple solution. It is illustrated in Figure A.3.

One of the models, M_B in this instance, and its simulator are contained in a *ModelWrapper*, which is derived from the *Atomic* class and implements the *EventListener* interface. The input and output types of the *ModelWrapper* are compatible with M_A, and the class has a virtual method *translateInput* for converting a *Bag* of events of type A into a *Bag* of events of type B. This method is called by the external and confluent transition functions, which subsequently inject the converted inputs into M_B by using the *computeNextState* method of the encapsulated *Simulator*. The *gc_input* method disposes of the input events in a way that is compatible with the memory management strategy used by model M_A.

The conversion of outputs from M_B to a type acceptable by M_A is more complicated; the essential steps are illustrated in Figure A.4. Output from M_B is calculated with the *Simulator*'s *computeNextOutput*, which is called by the *output_func* of the *ModelWrapper*. The output events are intercepted by the *ModelWrapper*'s

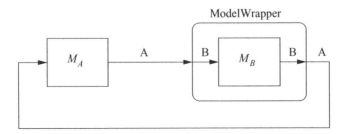

FIGURE A.2 Using a model wrapper to couple two models with different types for input and output.

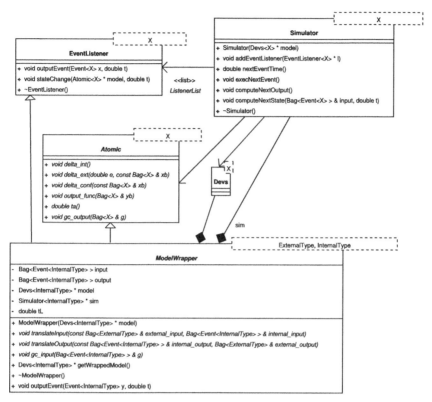

FIGURE A.3   Class diagram showing the *ModelWrapper* and its relationship to the *Simulator* and *Atomic* classes.

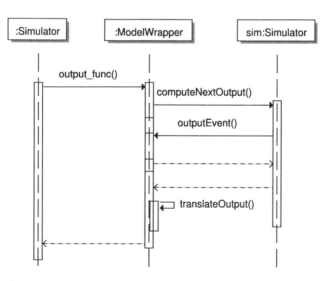

FIGURE A.4   Sequence diagram showing how the *ModelWrapper* converts output objects.

outputEvent method and stored in a bag for use when *computeNextOutput* returns. The *translateOutput* method converts this collection of output objects of type B into a collection of objects of type A, and these are subsequently copied into the output bag that was provided to the *ModelWrapper*'s *output_func* method.

The time advance of the *ModelWrapper* is the difference between its next event time, determined by the *nextEventTime* method of the *Simulator*, and its last event time, which is maintained as a state variable. Finally, the internal transition function is implemented with the *Simulator*'s *computeNextState* method.

The code that implements the *ModelWrapper* is listed below. It has two template parameters: the first is for the type of object used by M_A, and the second is for the type used by M_B. The virtual methods *gc_input*, *translateOutput*, *translateInput*, and *gc_output* are implemented by derived classes.

_____ *Implementation of the ModelWrapper* _____

```
1   #ifndef __adevs_wrapper_h_
2   #define __adevs_wrapper_h_
3   #include "adevs_models.h"
4
5   namespace adevs
6   {
7       template <typename ExternalType, typename InternalType>
8       class ModelWrapper:
9           public Atomic<ExternalType>, public EventListener<InternalType>
10      {
11          public:
12              // Create a wrapper for the supplied model. The ModelWrapper
13              // takes ownership of the model and deletes it when the
14              // ModelWrapper itself is deleted.
15              ModelWrapper(Devs<InternalType>* model);
16              // This method is used to translate incoming input objects into
17              // input objects for the wrapped model. Put these new input
18              // objects into the internal_in bag. The external_in
19              // bag contains the input values supplied to the wrapper's
20              // transition function.
21              virtual void translateInput(const Bag<ExternalType>& external_in,
22                  Bag<Event<InternalType> >& internal_in) = 0;
23              // This method is used to translate output from the model
24              // into objects that the ModelWrapper can produce. The
25              // internal_out bag contains all the output events
26              // produced by the wrapped model. The external_out bag
27              // should be filled with objects of type ExternalType, and
28              // these will become output from the ModelWrapper.
29              virtual void translateOutput(
30                  const Bag<Event<InternalType> >& internal_out,
31                  Bag<ExternalType>& external_out) = 0;
32              // This method is for garbage collection of input events created
33              // by the wrapper for its model. It is called when the wrapper
```

```
34        // is finished using the events created by the translateInput
35        // method. The bag 'g' contains the objects to be cleaned up.
36        virtual void gc_input(Bag<Event<InternalType> >& g) = 0;
37        // Get the wrapped model
38        Devs<InternalType>* getWrappedModel() { return model; }
39        // These methods are inhereted from the Atomic class
40        void delta_int();
41        void delta_ext(double e, const Bag<ExternalType>& xb);
42        void delta_conf(const Bag<ExternalType>& xb);
43        void output_func(Bag<ExternalType>& yb);
44        double ta();
45        void outputEvent(Event<InternalType> y, double t);
46        // The destructor destroys the wrapped model too.
47        ~ModelWrapper();
48     private:
49        // Bag of events created by the input translation method
50        Bag<Event<InternalType> > input;
51        // Output from the wrapped model
52        Bag<Event<InternalType> > output;
53        // The wrapped model
54        Devs<InternalType>* model;
55        // Simulator for driving the wrapped model
56        Simulator<InternalType>* sim;
57        // The time of the last event
58        double tL;
59    };
60
61  template <typename ExternalType, typename InternalType>
62  ModelWrapper<ExternalType,InternalType>::
63  ModelWrapper(Devs<InternalType>* model):
64     Atomic<ExternalType>(),EventListener<InternalType>(),
65     model(model),tL(0.0)
66  {
67     sim = new Simulator<InternalType>(model);
68     sim->addEventListener(this);
69  }
70
71  template <typename ExternalType, typename InternalType>
72  void ModelWrapper<ExternalType,InternalType>::delta_int()
73  {
74     // Update the internal clock
75     tL = sim->nextEventTime();
76     // Execute the next autonomous event for the wrapped model
77     sim->execNextEvent();
78  }
79
80  template <typename ExternalType, typename InternalType>
81  void ModelWrapper<ExternalType,InternalType>::
82  delta_ext(double e, const Bag<ExternalType>& xb)
```

```
83  {
84      // Update the internal clock
85      tL += e;
86      // Convert the external inputs to internal inputs
87      translateInput(xb,input);
88      // Apply the input
89      sim->computeNextState(input,tL);
90      // Clean up
91      gc_input(input);
92      input.clear();
93  }
94
95  template <typename ExternalType, typename InternalType>
96  void ModelWrapper<ExternalType,InternalType>::
97  delta_conf(const Bag<ExternalType>& xb)
98  {
99      // Update the internal clock
100     tL = sim->nextEventTime();
101     // Convert the external inputs to internal inputs
102     translateInput(xb,input);
103     // Apply the input
104     sim->computeNextState(input,tL);
105     // Clean up
106     gc_input(input);
107     input.clear();
108 }
109
110 template <typename ExternalType, typename InternalType>
111 double ModelWrapper<ExternalType,InternalType>::ta()
112 {
113     if (sim->nextEventTime() < DBL_MAX) return sim->nextEventTime()-tL;
114     else return DBL_MAX;
115 }
116
117 template <typename ExternalType, typename InternalType>
118 void ModelWrapper<ExternalType,InternalType>::
119 output_func(Bag<ExternalType>& yb)
120 {
121     // Compute the output events;
122     // this causes the outputEvent method to be called
123     sim->computeNextOutput();
124     // Translate the internal outputs to external outputs
125     translateOutput(output,yb);
126     // Clean up; note that the contents of the output bag
127     // are deleted by the wrapped model's gc_output method
128     output.clear();
129 }
130
131 template <typename ExternalType, typename InternalType>
```

```
132  void ModelWrapper<ExternalType,InternalType>::
133  outputEvent(Event<InternalType> y, double t)
134  {
135    // Save the events for processing by the output_func
136    output.insert(y);
137  }
138
139  template <typename ExternalType, typename InternalType>
140  ModelWrapper<ExternalType,InternalType>::~ModelWrapper()
141  {
142    delete sim; delete model;
143  }
144
145  } // end of namespace
146
147  #endif
```

A.3 REDUCING EXECUTION TIME

Code optimization takes time away from essential activities: model validation, model refinement, and experimentation. Moreover, carefully tuned code can still fail to give adequate performance, but code optimization has, at least, a clear goal. Model simplification, which is the only option when code optimization fails, trades away information for execution time, and is therefore difficult in both its technical challenges and its compromise of purpose.

Before time and effort are expended on a faster simulator, ask first whether the simulator is fast enough already. If it produces all of the needed data at a rate that is adequate for their intended use, then don't bother with performance improvements; time can be better spent elsewhere. For interactive simulations, the data rate is measured in frames per second; for batch simulations it is usually runs per hour or some similar figure. Whatever the metric, the decision to undertake an optimization should be made in its light, and an acceptable level of performance must be defined so that code improvement can end when the target is reached.[2]

Two things are needed for success: a set of test cases and a code profiler. The test cases should be part of a test suite that is run whenever the code is changed. Performance improvement is largely a matter of trial and error, and as adjustments are made and unmade, the code will break. Unless tests are run often, it will be impossible to know when a fault is introduced and, just as important, which change created the problem.

A profiler measures the execution time of the different sections of code. Automatic profilers, like the gprof tool that is part of the GNU compiler collection, provide

---

[2]Michael Abrash's collection *Graphics Programming Black Book* [2], though it discusses dated technology, still contains excellent, practical, and relevant advise on how to approach the problem of optimizing code to improve execution time.

measurements for the individual functions and methods in a program. This information shows which parts of the code consume the majority of the execution time and, consequently, can benefit most from careful attention to performance. Sometimes this coarse-grained information is enough for making significant improvements. If more precision is needed, timers can be placed manually around specific sections of code that are thought to be problematic.

To demonstrate the benefits of using a profiler, consider again the performance problem caused by the tank's interrupt handler. The problem was described in Section 4.1.6; when the interrupt handler produced a new voltage value at every interrupt, it caused the continuous motion of the tank to be updated at an unmanageable rate and prevented the model from being used interactively. The performance problem was immediately obvious, but a profiler was needed to find its cause. The culprit in this instance was the output function of the interrupt handler. That section of code before the change is listed below.

######## *Problematic Output Method for the InterruptHandler* _____

```
1   void InterruptHandler::output_func(Bag<SimEvent>& yb)
2   {
3       // If this is the start of an interrupt, send the motor voltage
4       // and an interrupt indicator
5       if (phase == OUTPUT) {
6           // Send the voltage
7           SimMotorVoltage volts;
8           volts.el = left_v;
9           volts.er = right_v;
10          yb.insert(SimEvent(volts));
11          // Send the interrupt indicator
12          yb.insert(SimEvent(SIM_INTERRUPT));
13      }
14      // If this is the start of an interrupt, then send an interrupt indicator
15      else if (phase == WAIT) {
16          yb.insert(SimEvent(SIM_INTERRUPT));
17      }
18  }
```

Note that the output function sends the voltage values at each interrupt, which is quite often when the interrupt frequency is high. The gross effect can be seen in the execution time of the experiment, described in Section 2.4, to determine power lost in the motors as a function of the interrupt frequency. Using the output function above, 3 min 40 s are needed to produce the data shown in Figure 2.12. The same experiment conducted with the optimized output function requires two minutes and forty six seconds: a substantial improvement.

The GNU C++ compiler instruments code automatically when the '-pg' option is passed to it and the linker. When the instrumented code is run, it produces a profile showing, among other things, time spent executing each function and method in the simulation. The profile data in Tables A.1 and A.2 were created from the loss of

TABLE A.1   Flat Profile (Abridged) Generated by Loss of Power Experiment

```
...
Each sample counts as 0.01 seconds.
%    cumulative
time ... calls ... name
45.86 ... 491887 ... adevs::rk45<SimEvent>::trial_step(double)
32.33 ... 2951322 ... TankPhysicsEqns::der_func(double const*, double*)
3.76 ... 492244 ... adevs::Simulator<SimEvent>::computeNextState(adevs::Bag<adevs::Event<SimEvent> >&, double)
3.76 ... 328212 ... adevs::rk45<SimEvent>::integrate(double*, double)
2.26 ... 492095 ... adevs::Simulator<SimEvent>::inject_event(adevs::Atomic<SimEvent>*, SimEvent&)
1.50 ... 984341 ... adevs::Schedule<SimEvent, double>::schedule(adevs::Atomic<SimEvent>*, double)
1.50 ... 492098 ... adevs::Atomic<SimEvent>::typeIsAtomic()
1.50 ... 164181 ... adevs::improved_interval_halving<SimEvent>::find_events(bool*, double const*, double*,
                                                    adevs::ode_solver<SimEvent>*, double)
1.50 ... 164031 ... adevs::Hybrid<SimEvent>::delta_ext(double, adevs::Bag<SimEvent> const&)
0.75 ... 984338 ... adevs::Simulator<SimEvent>::clean_up(adevs::Atomic<SimEvent>*)
0.75 ... 492244 ... adevs::Simulator<SimEvent>::route(adevs::Network<SimEvent>*, adevs::Devs<SimEvent>*, SimEvent&)
0.75 ... 492243 ... adevs::Simulator<SimEvent>::computeNextOutput()
0.75 ... 492243 ... adevs::Schedule<SimEvent, double>::getImminent(adevs::Bag<adevs::Atomic<SimEvent>*>&, unsigned int) const
0.75 ... 492093 ... InterruptHandler::output_func(adevs::Bag<SimEvent>&)
0.75 ... 328362 ... TankPhysicsEqns::state_event_func(double const*, double*)
....
```

293

TABLE A.2 Call Graph (Abridged) Generated by Loss of Power Experiment

index	% time	self	children	called	name
					......
[3]	85.7	0.02	1.12	164031	adevs::Hybrid<SimEvent>::delta_ext(double, adevs::Bag<SimEvent> const&) [3]
		0.02	0.52	164031/328212	adevs::rk45<SimEvent>::integrate(double*, double) [4]
		0.00	0.54	164031/164031	adevs::rk45<SimEvent>::advance(double*, double) [6]
		0.02	0.01	164031/164181	adevs::improved_interval_halving<SimEvent>::find_events(bool*, double const*, double*, adevs::ode_solver<SimEvent>*, double) [11]
		0.00	0.00	164031/164031	TankPhysicsEqns::external_event(double*, double, adevs::Bag<SimEvent> const&) [42]
		0.00	0.00	164031/164181	TankPhysicsEqns::time_event_func(double const*) [38]
		0.00	0.00	1/328212	TankPhysics::TankPhysics(TankPhysicsEqns*) [22]
		0.00	0.00	149/328212	adevs::Hybrid<SimEvent>::delta_int() [21]
		0.02	0.52	164031/328212	adevs::rk45<SimEvent>::advance(double*, double) [6]
		0.02	0.52	164031/328212	adevs::Hybrid<SimEvent>::delta_ext(double, adevs::Bag<SimEvent> const&) [3]
[4]	82.0	0.05	1.04	328212	adevs::rk45<SimEvent>::integrate(double*, double) [4]
		0.61	0.43	491887/491887	adevs::rk45<SimEvent>::trial_step(double) [5]
					......

power experiment run at half throttle with a signal frequency of 7000 Hz. The *Hybrid* class now shows up clearly as a performance problem, consuming almost half of the execution time in its *trial_step* method.

The *trial_step* method is called only when an event occurs in the *Hybrid* class. Looking a little further into the profile, the *delta_ext* method of the *Hybrid* class appears at the ninth spot in the list. This suggests that a large number of trial steps are being executed in response to input events received by the *TankPhysics*, which is the only *Hybrid* object in our simulation. The call graph for the *delta_ext* method seems to confirm this. The relevant portions of the profile are shown in the tables.

The cumulative time spent in the *delta_ext* method and its children amounts to 85.7% of the total execution time. Of the methods that it calls, the most time consuming is the *integrate* method, using up 82% of the total execution time, which in turn calls the culprit at the top of Table A.1: *trial_step*. Each input to the *Hybrid* model causes the integration step to be performed, and this is degrading the performance of the simulation.

From here, it is easy to deduce that frequent voltage events arriving from the *InterruptHandler* are the root of the problem. Fortunately, most of these events do not actually change the voltage value, and so there is a simple remedy for the performance problem. The modified output function is shown below. It produces an event only when the voltage actually changes. This cuts the execution time by roughly $\frac{1}{3}$, and now the model works admirably as part of the interactive tank simulation. Such a substantial performance improvement with so simple a change is unusual, but the ease with which the problematic section of code was identified shows the tremendous benefits of using a profiler.

_____ *Optimized Output Method for the InterruptHandler* _____

```
1   void InterruptHandler::output_func(Bag<SimEvent>& yb)
2   {
3       // If this is the start of an interrupt, send the motor voltage
4       // and an interrupt indicator
5       if (phase == OUTPUT) {
6           // If the voltage changed, then send the new values
7           if (last_left_v != left_v || last_right_v != right_v) {
8               SimMotorVoltage volts;
9               volts.el = left_v;
10              volts.er = right_v;
11              yb.insert(SimEvent(volts));
12          }
13          // Send the interrupt indicator
14          yb.insert(SimEvent(SIM_INTERRUPT));
15      }
16      // If this is the start of an interrupt, then send an indicator for it
17      else if (phase == WAIT) {
18          yb.insert(SimEvent(SIM_INTERRUPT));
19      }
20  }
```

APPENDIX B

PARALLEL DISCRETE-EVENT SIMULATION

A parallel computer is used most effectively and with least difficulty to produce large numbers of statistically independent samples of a stochastic process. This application of parallel computing is vitally important for drawing meaningful conclusions from models that include random numbers, and is therefore very common in practice.

Amdahl's law explains why this use of parallel computers is so attractive, and conversely why other uses pose such devilish difficulties. Suppose that we must add a large column of numbers. This is a simple but tedious task for a single person. If there are two people, each sums half the numbers and then one of them combines the two sums to get the final result: this last step cannot be done in parallel. If the column is large, there is probably enough work for two people to stay very busy, and the time needed to combine the result is relatively insignificant. If we add a third person, then each has less to do and relatively more time is spent combining their results. Adding more people further reduces the individual workload while increasing the effort to coordinate their labor.

Every job requires some work that cannot be split up, and the number of computers, human or otherwise, that can be usefully employed is therefore limited. Let T_s be the time needed finish a job with a single computer, T_p be the time to solve it with N computers, and α be the fraction of a job that can be done in parallel. These are related by the equation

$$T_p = T_s(1 - \alpha + \alpha/N) \tag{B.1}$$

Building Software for Simulation: Theory and Algorithms, with Applications in C++, By James J. Nutaro
Copyright © 2011 John Wiley & Sons, Inc.

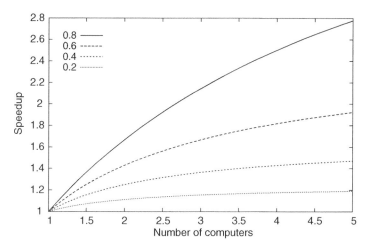

FIGURE B.1 Amdahl's law for several values of α.

The speedup S obtained by perfect employment of the N computers is

$$S = \frac{T_s}{T_p} = \frac{N}{(1 - \alpha)N + \alpha} \tag{B.2}$$

Equation B.2 is Amdahl's law.

If we want to use a simulation to generate a number of independent datasets much larger than N, then $\alpha \approx 1$ because these independent calculations need not be coordinated in any way. The speedup is perfect: using N computers gives a result N times faster. As α shrinks, the potential for speedup vanishes: Figure B.1 shows the diminishing returns. At the same time, the code becomes more difficult to parallelize. This is a very gloomy picture of parallel computing, but it tempers our expectations.

Amdahl's law shows a limit to the amount of computing power that can be brought to bear on a problem. As the size of the problem grows, however, so does the number of the computers that can be usefully employed; this is Gustafson's law. It is based on the observation that α tends not to be fixed, but grows along with the size of the problem. Suppose that a particular problem consists of a serial part that takes T_{seq} units of time to finish and a parallel part that N computers complete in T_{par} units of time, so that the total execution time is $T_{\text{seq}} + T_{\text{par}}$. The same job executed by a single computer requires $T_{\text{seq}} + N T_{\text{par}}$. As before, T_{seq} accounts for a fraction $1 - \alpha$ of the total time; but T_{par}, not $N T_{\text{par}}$, is the remaining α. In this model, α grows at T_{par} grows; that is, the larger the job, the greater the potential for parallelism. Hence, the speedup obtained by the N computers is

$$S = \frac{T_{\text{seq}} + N T_{\text{par}}}{T_{\text{seq}} + T_{\text{par}}} = \frac{1 - \alpha + N\alpha}{(1 - \alpha) + \alpha} = 1 - \alpha(1 - N) \tag{B.3}$$

Gustafson's law is illustrated in Figure B.2.

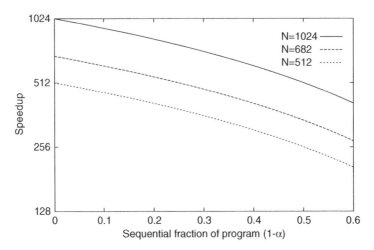

FIGURE B.2   Gustafson's law for a fixed number of computers and decreasing α.

These two laws show that big computers are used for solving big problems; do not expect to solve small problems a little bit faster. This lesson is particularly important for discrete-event simulations, which are notoriously difficult to parallelize.[1] Nonetheless, given a model of sufficient size and complexity, parallel computers can be used very effectively to reduce the running time of a simulation. Fujimoto [44] gives an excellent overview of the very broad field of parallel discrete-event simulation. This chapter focuses on a particular algorithm that is relatively simple to implement and use while still performing well for many models when simulating on multicore and multiprocessor workstations.

B.1 A CONSERVATIVE ALGORITHM

There are three types of algorithms for using parallel computers to simulate discrete-event models. The simplest, but often least effective, calculate simultaneous events in parallel. The output function and event-routing calculations for the set of imminent models can be done in parallel, and so can the calculation of the next states for imminent and activated models. Amdahl's law, however, dooms this approach. In general, there are few simultaneous events in an iteration, and these are processed very quickly. This keeps α small; the overhead for coordinating access to input bags, starting and joining teams of threads, and other tasks overshadow the small benefit of computing a few output and state transition functions in parallel. Worse, Gustafson's law does not hold because α tends to remain fixed; only a handful of models are active in each iteration regardless of how many components the model actually has.

---

[1]Fujimoto's remarks on this subject are insightful and still relevant [43].

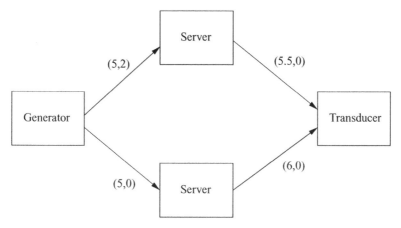

FIGURE B.3   A discrete-event model with parallelism that can be exploited by conservative and optimistic simulation algorithms. The servers and transducer can process their inputs in parallel if the servers have a lookahead of at least 1.

Optimistic and conservative algorithms are the two other options. Both work on essentially the same principle, which is illustrated in Figure B.3. In this illustration there are four atomic models. The first model is an input-free generator, the next two are servers with a queue and fixed service time, and the last measures throughput, turnaround time, and other performance statistics for the system. The generator produces jobs for the servers at regular intervals of one unit of time. These are assigned roundrobin to the servers, which need between one and two units of time to complete the work. The transducer is output-free, merely collecting jobs and recording statistics.

Each model is assigned to one processor of the parallel computer. The processor with the generator can compute its output trajectory without concern for the activity of any other component in the system. As it produces output, these are timestamped and sent to the processors that have the servers. The simulators for the servers keep inputs from the generator in the order of their timestamps, processing the events as quickly as possible and sending the results on to the transducer. The two servers can be simulated in parallel. The transducer, just like the servers, keeps its input events in sorted order and processes them as quickly as possible.

Here is the difficult part—before the transducer advances its state to time t, it must know the output trajectories of both servers to time t. Having received an input at time $(5.5, 0)$ from the upper server and input at time $(6, 0)$ from the lower server, the transducer can advance only to time $(5.5, 1)$. Otherwise it risks omitting future inputs from the upper server that might influence its evolution.

The solution to this problem is what differentiates conservative and optimistic algorithms. An optimistic algorithm saves the state of the transducer and then continues to advance its state under the assumption that the known inputs are complete and correct. If, having advanced to time t, the simulator receives an input at $t' < t$, then the saved state is restored and the simulation restarted from t'. When this works, it works very well; but optimistic simulations are mind-bogglingly difficult to implement. Every atomic model must provide special code to save and restore its state, each simulation process needs a tremendous amount of machinery to cancel incorrect outputs and restore saved states, and all of this must work quickly and efficient.

The need for efficient state saving and restoration is the greatest obstacle in practice. While the simulation engine can be reused from application to application, the code for managing state is special for every model, and when the state of a model has lists, maps, priority queues, and other complicated data structures, it is almost impossible to save and restore quickly. Consequently, optimistic algorithms remain primarily a subject for research, and have not yet had a significant impact on modeling and simulation in practice.

Conservative algorithms use knowledge of each model's particular, dynamic behavior to avoid calculations that may be incorrect and require undoing. Referring again to Figure B.3, if we know that the upper server will not produce another output until time $(5.5 + \epsilon_1, 0)$, and the lower server until time $(6 + \epsilon_2, 0)$, then the state of the transducer can be advanced to time $(\min\{5.5 + \epsilon_1, 6 + \epsilon_2\}, 1)$ while the servers progress to their next output. If the servers and transducers have much to do in the intervening time, then a great deal of useful parallel computing can take place.

B.1.1 Lookahead

The defining characteristic of a causal system is that its output is a function of its present state and past and present input. The response function ρ of a system gives its output trajectory when begun in an initial state q and stimulated with an input trajectory x. The state transition and output function define ρ by

$$\rho(q, x[t_i, t_f)) = y[t_i, t_f) \iff (\forall \tau \in [t_i, t_f))(y(\tau) = \Lambda(\Delta(q, x[t_i, \tau]))) \quad \text{(B.4)}$$

Consider two input trajectories $x_1[t_i, t_f)$ and $x_2[t_i, t_f)$ that are equal to time t'; that is, $(\forall t \in [t_i, t'))(x_1(t) = x_2(t))$. The output trajectories of a causal system that result from these two inputs will be equal up to time t'. Specifically, if $y_1 = \rho(q, x_1)$ and $y_2 = \rho(q, x_2)$, then $(\forall t \in [t_i, t'))(y_1(t) = y_2(t))$. Of course, for $t \geq t'$ the trajectories need not agree. All of the systems studied in this text, and all systems of practical interest, are causal.

A system is *strongly* causal if there is some time $t'' > t'$ such that the output to t'' is the same even if the input is not. Specifically, $(\forall t \in [t_i, t''))(y_1(t) = y_2(t))$, where, y_1 and y_2 are as before. In this case, there is a short time ϵ separating t' and t'' in which the output of the system appears insensitive to its input.[2] This ϵ is called *lookahead*.

Every discrete-event system has a lookahead of $(0, 1)$, just as every discrete-time system has a lookahead of 1. These lookaheads, however, are not particularly useful for parallel computing. Rather, a discrete-event system with *real* lookahead ϵ has a

---

[2]This definition is good enough for our purposes, but in fact ϵ may be infinitesimal. See the textbook by Mesarovic and Takahara [86] for a more general treatment.

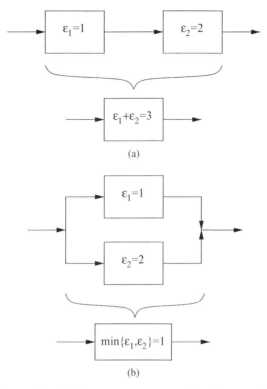

FIGURE B.4 Lookahead of components connected in series (a) and in parallel (b).

response function that satisfies $y_1(t' \triangleright (\epsilon, 0)) = y_2(t' \triangleright (\epsilon, 0))$, where t' is the same described above. So, if the input trajectory is known to time t, then the output is fixed to, but not at, time $t \triangleright (\epsilon, 0)$.[3]

Lookahead in an atomic model is found by a careful study of its dynamics. An atomic model whose autonomous actions are always separated by some positive, real interval of time has a lookahead equal to that interval. The machine model from Section 4.2.3 has this property; it has a lookahead equal to its processing time. The tank's *PacketProcessing* model has this property as well; its lookahead is equal to the packet processing time.

The lookahead of a network model can be found from the lookaheads of its components. The combined lookahead of models connected in series is equal to the sum of their individual lookaheads, a fact derived easily from the definition. Referring to Figure B.4, the response of the first component to $x[t, t')$ is known to time $t' \triangleright (\epsilon_1, 0)$. Consequently, the input to the second component is known to this

---

[3]A more restrictive definition of lookahead is found in most of the literature on conservative parallel simulation; standard definitions can be found, for example, in the textbook by Fujimoto [44]. Our definition allows a model to produce output in the interval spanned by its lookahead; other definitions permit this only in special cases.

time, and so its output is known to time $(t' \rhd (\epsilon_1, 0)) \rhd (\epsilon_2, 0)$. Let $t' = (\tau, c)$, and we have

$$((\tau, c) \rhd (\epsilon_1, 0)) \rhd (\epsilon_2, 0) = (\tau + \epsilon_1, 0) \rhd (\epsilon_2, 0) = (\tau + \epsilon_1 + \epsilon_2, 0)$$

and so the lookahead of the series is $\epsilon_1 + \epsilon_2$.

The combined lookahead of models in parallel is just as easily deduced from the parallel configuration shown in Figure B.4; the lookahead of the resultant is equal to the smaller of the lookahead of its components. This is a consequence of the resultant's output at any time t being the bag union of the output of each component at t.

Feedback connections within a network do not contribute to its lookahead because the feedforward connections are the quickest means for input to affect output. This observation and the two rules above imply that the lookahead of a network is the shortest path by which an input to the network can influence its output. For small networks, like the one shown in Figure B.5, the lookahead can be found by inspection.

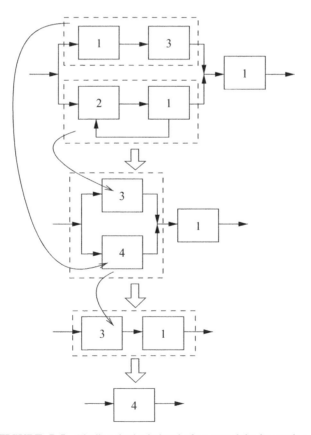

FIGURE B.5   Finding the lookahead of a network by inspection.

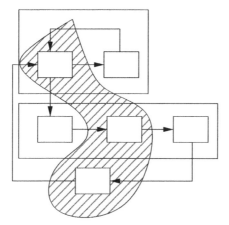

FIGURE B.6   Partitioning a model for parallel simulation with two processors. Atomic models (shown as solid white blocks) in the striped area are assigned to processor number 1; the remainder to processor number 2. Partitions can cut across the boundaries of the network models.

To create the lookahead graph, each node is labeled with its lookahead. Serially connected nodes are reduced to a single node with lookahead equal to the sum of its constituents. Nodes connected in parallel are replaced with a single node having the smallest of the component lookaheads. This process ends when a single node remains; its lookahead is the network's lookahead.

B.1.2   The Algorithm

The atomic component's of the model are assigned to the processors of the parallel computer. The components assigned to each processor are constituted into a single network model, and this network is reduced to its atomic equivalent. This reorganization and reduction will in fact be accomplished automatically by careful use of the *Simulator* developed in Chapter 4. The operation of the algorithm can therefore be considered for the relatively simple case of a network of atomic components, as shown in Figure B.6.

Each processor has five things: the model itself, an *earliest input time* denoted *eit*, an *earliest output time* denoted *eot*, a time-sorted list of events that is the known input trajectory for the model, and a queue of received messages that have not been examined. The *eit*s and *eot*s are initially $(0, 0)$. A surprisingly simple procedure is executed by each processor:

1. Advance the state of the model until its next event time is greater than or equal to *eit*, sending timestamped output events to the model's influencees as we go. These output events are inserted at the back of the recipients the message queue.

2. If the next event time is equal to *eit*, then send the output for that time.

3. Find the smaller of *eit* ▷ (ϵ, 0) and, if output was sent at *eit*, *eit* ▷ (0, 1) or, if not, the time of the next autonomous event. If this calculated value is larger than the present value of *eot*, then set *eot* to the calculated value and send that in a message to the model's influencees.

4. Process the contents of the message queue from front to back. Messages carrying input events are placed into the time-sorted list. The largest message timestamp received from each processor is retained as a local estimate of its earliest output time.

5. Calculate *eit* as the smaller of the stored earliest output times.

6. Repeat these steps until the simulation is finished.

This algorithm extracts parallelism from the model by allowing some groups of components to advance their states independently of other groups. An input-free model, for example, has $eit = \infty$ and so moves ahead in time independently of all other components, even those for which it provides input. These models advance at whatever rate the supplier sustains.

Feedback arrangements, however, can be quite restrictive. Although the output of a model is insensitive to input received in the interval spanned by its lookahead, the state is not, and to produce the model's output requires advancing its state. Therefore, parallelism is restricted to the simultaneous production of output by the model with the smaller *eot* and its consumption by the model with the larger *eot*.

B.2   IMPLEMENTING THE ALGORITHM WITH OpenMP

OpenMP consists of compiler pragmas and a small library of functions that are used to write programs for shared memory, parallel computers (see, e.g., Chapman et al.'s *Using OpenMP* [21]). It is standardized, portable across operating systems, and supported by most modern C and C++ compilers. Just two of OpenMP's features and C's obscure, but standard, volatile type are necessary to build a conservative parallel simulation engine.

B.2.1   Pragmas, Volatiles, and Locks

OpenMP uses compiler pragmas to guide its automatic parallelization of a program. The most important of these is the parallel pragma that spawns N threads to execute in parallel N copies of a code block. This pragma has the form

```
#pragma omp parallel
{
    // execute this code in parallel
}
```

At the start of the block following the pragma, OpenMP spawns a group of threads. The exact number is determined by the OpenMP system, but can usually be specified by setting the OMP_NUM_THREADS environment variable. Each thread executes the body of code inside the block and then waits for the other threads to finish. When every thread has completed its work, all except the main thread of execution terminate and the program continues.

Variables that are declared outside the parallel block are shared by all of the threads. Variables declared within the block are local to each thread. When two threads modify the same shared variable, there is no way of knowing the order in which those thread will make their adjustments. This wreaks havoc with data structures such as lists, queues, and maps when two threads try, for instance, to remove the first element in a linked list. OpenMP provides locks for solving this problem.

A lock is a shared variable of type *omp_lock_t*. The lock is created with *omp_init_lock*, acquired and released with *omp_set_lock* and *omp_unset_lock*, respectively, and destroyed with *omp_destroy_lock*. Only one thread can own the lock at any time. If a thread tries to acquire a lock that is already owned, then that thread will stall on *omp_set_lock* until the owning thread calls *omp_unset_lock*. When the lock has been released, the stalled thread acquires the lock and resumes execution. OpenMP guarantees that a lock will never be owned by more than a single thread at any given time. Therefore, the code inside a lock/unlock pair will never be executed by more than a single thread at any time.

The program listed below shows how the parallel pragma and lock are used to implement a "Hello world!" program. In this example, a lock controls access to the shared variable *thread_num* and the C++ *cout* stream, which does not usually support simultaneous access by multiple threads. The program starts some number of threads that take turns incrementing the *thread_num* variable and writing a message to *cout*.

_____ Using the Pragma Parallel and a Lock in an OpenMP Program _____

```
1   #include <omp.h> // Include the OpenMP functions
2   #include <iostream>
3   using namespace std;
4
5   int main()
6   {
7       int thread_num = 0; // A shared variable
8       // Create a lock for controlling access to cout and thread_num
9       omp_lock_t lock;
10      omp_init_lock(&lock);
11      // Start a group of threads. Each will execute the block of code
12      #pragma omp parallel
13      {
14          omp_set_lock(&lock); // Acquire the lock
15          // Print our message and increment the shared variable
16          cout << "Hello from thread " << thread_num++ << endl;
```

```
17      cout.flush();
18      omp_unset_lock(&lock); // Release the lock
19    } // Wait for all of the threads to finish executing
20    return 0;
21  }
```

Running this program with OMP_NUM_THREADS set to 3 gives the result shown below.

```
$ export OMP_NUM_THREADS=3; ./a.out
Hello from thread 0
Hello from thread 1
Hello from thread 2
$
```

In this example, all of the code in the parallel block is protected by a lock, and so the threads don't do anything concurrently. The next example eliminates the shared *thread_num* variable and thereby exhibits real parallelism. Here, each thread obtains its thread ID from OpenMP and stores it in a local (i.e., not shared) variable. A global variable that is read-only holds the total count of threads. Each thread takes turns with *cout* to print its thread ID. The code is listed below.

———— *Using a Thread-Local Variable in an OpenMP Program* ————

```
1   #include <omp.h> // Include the OpenMP functions
2   #include <iostream>
3   using namespace std;
4
5   int main()
6   {
7     // Store the number of threads used by OpenMP in a shared variable
8     int max_threads = omp_get_max_threads();
9     // Create a lock for controlling access to cout
10    omp_lock_t lock;
11    omp_init_lock(&lock);
12    // Start a group of threads. Each will execute the block of code
13    #pragma omp parallel
14    {
15      // Store the thread ID in a local variable. Every thread has its
16      // own thread_num variable which is not shared
17      int thread_num = omp_get_thread_num();
18      omp_set_lock(&lock); // Acquire the lock
19      // Print our message
20      cout << "Hello from thread " << thread_num <<
21        " of " << max_threads << endl;
22      cout.flush();
23      omp_unset_lock(&lock); // Release the lock
```

```
24      } // Wait for all of the threads to finish executing
25      return 0;
26  }
```

This program run with three threads gives the result shown below.

```
$ ./a.out
Hello from thread 1 of 3
Hello from thread 2 of 3
Hello from thread 0 of 3
$
```

In the first program, the *thread_num* variable is incremented sequentially by each thread in turn, and the output from the program is predictable. In the second program, the threads print their identifiers in whatever order they happen to acquire access to standard output.

When a thread modifies a shared variable, its new value is not, in general, immediately available for the other threads in the program. The modifying thread may keep the variable in a register or its local memory cache, and it could be quite some time before that new value migrates to the main memory and the memory caches of the other threads. For this reason, variables modified inside a locked section of code receive special treatment by OpenMP. When *omp_set_lock* is called, the calling thread synchronizes its local memory and the global shared memory, thereby ensuring a consistent view of any shared variables. This is done again when *omp_unset_lock* is called so that changes made by the thread to shared variables become globally visible.

Because of these and other necessary actions, acquiring and releasing a lock can take a long time. In some rare cases, however, shared variables can be used without explicit synchronization. The volatile type is an important tool in these instances. By declaring a variable to be volatile,[4] the compiler is advised that it may change in ways that are not under the control of the program. Therefore, access to this variable should not be optimized by, for example, storing it in a register or keeping it in a fast memory cache. Changes made to a volatile type will be visible almost immediately to other threads in the program, and extra instructions to flush the thread's local memory are thereby avoided.

The code listed below uses a volatile integer to implement a shared token. The value of the token is set to the identifier of the thread that owns it. When a thread acquires the token, it prints a message to the screen. Only one thread can have the token at any time, and threads without the token spin until they acquire it. Observe that *the token variable is set only by the owning thread*. All other threads treat it as read-only. This ensures that writes occur in an immutable sequence.

---

[4]This use of volatile is specific to C and C++. Other languages may provide a volatile type, but there is no guarantee that it can be used in the same way.

_____ ***Using a Volatile Variable in an OpenMP Program*** _____

```
1   #include <omp.h> // Include the OpenMP functions
2   #include <iostream>
3   using namespace std;
4
5   int main()
6   {
7       // These are shared variables
8       int num_threads = omp_get_max_threads();
9       volatile int token_owner = 0;
10      // Start a group of threads
11      #pragma omp parallel
12      {
13          // Get the ID of the thread
14          int thread_num = omp_get_thread_num();
15          // Pass the token around twice
16          for (int i = 0; i < 2; i++)
17          {
18              while (token_owner != thread_num); // Wait for the token
19              // Print our message
20              cout << "Thread " << thread_num << " has the token" << endl;
21              cout.flush();
22              token_owner = (thread_num+1)%num_threads; // Pass the token
23          }
24      } // Wait for all of the threads to finish executing
25      return 0;
26  }
```

Executing this code shows clearly how the threads take turns with the token. If, however, the volatile specifier for the shared variables were removed, this code could deadlock when the token changes hands.

```
$ ./a.out
Thread 0 has the token
Thread 1 has the token
Thread 2 has the token
Thread 0 has the token
Thread 1 has the token
Thread 2 has the token
$
```

B.2.2 Overview of the Simulator

Using the simulator from Chapter 4, a collection of atomic models can be manipulated as though it were a single system. The *computeNextState* method computes the collective state transition function; the *computeOutput* method, the output function;

and the *nextEventTime* method, the time advance. To accommodate the arbitrary partitioning of a model across processors, the simulation engine is modified in four ways:

1. An attribute is added to the *Atomic* class to indicate the thread it is assigned to.
2. To the *Simulator* is added a pointer to a *LogicalProcess* object that handles interthread events. The *LogicalProcess* has the ID of its thread and a method for sending events to other *LogicalProcess*es. This method is used by the *Simulator*'s *route* method when it encounters an *Atomic* model that is not assigned to it.
3. A method is added to the *Simulator* for assigning it a model. This method places the atomic components of the model into the *Simulator*'s schedule.
4. The *Simulator* is derived from the new *AbstractSimulator* class, which defines a common interface for the parallel and sequential simulators and encompasses the *EventListener* callbacks that are common to both.

The new methods, attributes, and classes for the simulation engines are shown in Figure B.7. Four new classes constitute the parallel simulator: the *MessageQ*, the *LogicalProcess*, the *ParSimulator*, and the *AbstractSimulator*. The *AbstractSimulator* serves two purposes: (1) it provides a common interface for both the *Simulator* and *ParSimulator*, which is a convenience for users of the simulation engine; and (2) it contains and exposes the management of *EventListeners* so that the *outputEvent* and *stateChange* callbacks produced by the *Simulator* can be intercepted by the *LogicalProcess* and passed on to the *ParSimulator*, which ultimately informs its registered listeners.

B.2.3   The *LogicalProcess*

The *LogicalProcess* class coordinates events that traverse thread boundaries with events that are internal to the *Simulator*.[5] A parallel simulation has one *LogicalProcess* for each thread, and one thread for each physical processor on the computer. Each *LogicalProcess* executes the algorithm described in Section B.1.2.

The *LogicalProcess*es communicate by putting messages into one anothers' *MessageQ*, which serve as first in, first out communication channels. Two types of messages are exchanged: EIT (earliest input time) messages and OUTPUT messages. On receiving any type of message, the *LogicalProcess* stores the message timestamp in a table. This table records the earliest time at which an input might be received from

---

[5]The literature on parallel discrete-event simulation is focused largely on transforming a sequential, event-oriented simulation program into a parallel, event-oriented simulation program. The sequential program is, in essence, treated as an atomic model that encompasses the entirety of the system being modeled. To simulate this model in parallel, it is necessary to partition the system's state variables into modular units; these units are called *logical processes*. The *LogicalProcess* class fills this same role of managing the state variables local to a process, which in this case are contained in the *Atomic* models assigned to the local *Simulator*.

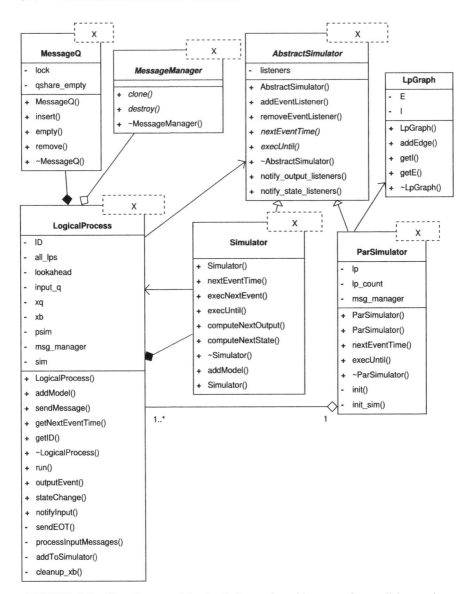

FIGURE B.7   Class diagram of the simulation engine with support for parallel execution.

the adjacent *LogicalProcess*es. The minimum of these times is the earliest input time for the model. EIT messages are discarded after their timestamp is recorded, and OUTPUT messages are put in the time-sorted list of input events.

Unlike the sequential simulator, the parallel simulator does not coordinate iterations of the simulation loop in each thread. It is therefore necessary to code time as an explicit pair, with c at each *LogicalProcess* being incremented following each iteration of the simulation loop that does not advance the real time t. Messages between threads carry the complete timestamp (t, c).

The *LogicalProcess* can execute events, internal and external, that occur at times shorter than the earliest input time. The *Simulator*'s *computeNextState* method is used to advance the state of the model, injecting inputs and computing internal events for as long as their occurrence times are smaller than *eit*. At each internal event, the *Simulator* calls the *notifyInput* method of its *LogicalProcess* whenever an *Atomic* residing in another thread receives input. These events become OUTPUT messages for the corresponding *LogicalProcess*.

There is one special case that occurs when the time of the next internal event is equal to the earliest input time. Recall that the output at time (t, c) is completely determined by the input up to, but not including (t, c). Therefore, although a state transition at the earliest input time must be deferred, the output can be sent safely.

Having advanced the state of the model to the earliest input time, and sent its output trajectory up to and including this time, the *LogicalProcess* updates its earliest output time and sends this to its influencees. Now the simulation procedure repeats. The *LogicalProcess* extracts all of its messages from the input queue, updating its earliest input time and putting input events into the time-sorted list. Then it again advances its state and output trajectory. Eventually, the state trajectory will be advanced to the specified stopping time, and the simulation procedure returns.

Three problems emerge in the course of implementing the procedure described above:

1. Determining the lookahead of the *LogicalProcess* when it does not know how the models assigned to it are connected. The conservative, but safe, solution is to assume that the components are connected in parallel. The *addModel* method does just this, calculating the lookahead as the minimum of the assigned components. Observe also that if a *Network* is added to the *LogicalProcess*, then all of its components are also adopted; this is necessary to ensure that the lookahead obtained from the *Network* gives a valid lower bound on the timestamps of messages that will exit the *LogicalProcess*.

2. The related problem of determining how the logical processes are connected. This information is provided to the *LogicalProcess* in an *LpGraph* object which encodes a directed graph. If the edge (A,B) is in the graph, then the logical process A sends output to logical process B; if (B,A) is also in the graph, then A and B are connected in a feedback arrangement. The *getI* method of the *LpGraph* returns the logical processes that influence its argument. Similarly, the *getE* method returns the logical processes that its argument influences.

3. A problem that is specific to C++ (and languages in general that do not provide garbage collection): determining how to free output objects that traverse a thread boundary. The *Simulator* will call the *gc_output* method of the object's originator as soon as the *computeNextState* method returns. However, when this occurs, the object is likely to be residing in the input queue of another thread, still waiting to be processed. Deleting the object would therefore be disastrous.

A solution to this problem is to have the model builder provide methods for copying and deleting output objects. When a separate copy of an object is made for each thread that receives it, the garbage collection problem remains local to each thread and can, therefore, be dealt with just as in the single-threaded case. The *MessageManager* class serves this purpose. It has two virtual methods: *clone*, which creates a copy of its argument, and *destroy*, which frees the memory occupied by the copy. Objects are cloned in the *notifyInput* method of the *LogicalProcess* just before being sent to another thread. Cloned objects are deleted after they have been used to compute a state transition.

The code that implements the *LogicalProcess* is listed below. Its relative brevity is due to reuse of the *Simulator*. This is yet another example of reuse; the *Simulator*, by supplying an interface that exposes the state transition function and output function of a model's resultant, allows the *LogicalProcess* to be implemented as though it were operating on an atomic model. The required modifications to the *Simulator*, described in Section B.2.2, are trivial and do not fundamentally change the abstraction; they merely provide a means of assigning different parts of the resultant's state space (i.e., its atomic models) to distinct physical processors.

Implementation of the LogicalProcess

```
1   #include "adevs_time.h"
2   #include "adevs_message_q.h"
3   #include "adevs_msg_manager.h"
4   #include "adevs_abstract_simulator.h"
5   #include "object_pool.h"
6   #include "adevs_simulator.h"
7   #include <omp.h>
8   #include <iostream>
9   #include <vector>
10  #include <list>
11  #include <map>
12  #include <queue>
13  #include <limits.h>
14  #include <cassert>
15
16  namespace adevs
17  {
18
19  template <class X> class LogicalProcess: public EventListener<X>
20  {
21    public:
22      // The constructor assigns 1) an ID, 2) the set I of influencers,
23      // 3) the set E of influencees, 4) an array of pointers to the other
24      // logical processes in the simulator; the array is indexed by ID,
25      // 5) a pointer to an AbstractSimulator that is used to notify
26      // registered EventListeners, and 6) a MessageManager to manage
27      // memory associated with events that leave the LogicalProcess.
28      LogicalProcess(int ID, const std::vector<int>& I,
```

```
29          const std::vector<int>& E, LogicalProcess<X>** all_lps,
30          AbstractSimulator<X>* sim, MessageManager<X>* msg_manager);
31      // Assign a model to this logical process.
32      void addModel(Devs<X>* model);
33      // Send a message to the logical process
34      void sendMessage(Message<X>& msg) { input_q.insert(msg); }
35      // Get the time of the next internal event for the logical process
36      Time getNextEventTime() { return sim.nextEventTime(); }
37      // Get the ID given to the logical process
38      int getID() const { return ID; }
39      // The destructor leaves the models intact.
40      ~LogicalProcess();
41      // Run the main simulation loop until time t_stop
42      void run(double t_stop);
43      // Notify EventListeners of output and changes in state
44      void outputEvent(Event<X> x, double t)
45      {
46          psim->notify_output_listeners(x.model,x.value,t);
47      }
48      void stateChange(Atomic<X>* model, double t)
49      {
50          psim->notify_state_listeners(model,t);
51      }
52      // The sequential simulator calls this method when an event
53      // needs to be received by an atomic model attached to
54      // a remote logical process (i.e. not this one)
55      void notifyInput(Atomic<X>* model, X& value);
56  private:
57      const int ID; // ID of this logical process
58      const std::vector<int> E, I; // List of influencees and influencers
59      LogicalProcess<X>** all_lps; // All of the logical processes
60      double lookahead; // Lookahead of this logical process
61      std::map<int,Time> eit_map; // Earliest possible input times
62      MessageQ<X> input_q; // Incoming messages
63      std::priority_queue<Message<X> > xq; // Input sorted by timestamp
64      Bag<Event<X> > xb; // Bag for injecting input into the Simulator
65      // Earliest input and output times, and the time of the next
66      // internal event
67      Time eit, eot, tSelf;
68      // Abstract simulator for notifying EventListeners
69      AbstractSimulator<X>* psim;
70      MessageManager<X>* msg_manager; // To manage inter-thread events
71      // Simulator for computing local state transitions and outputs
72      Simulator<X> sim;
73      // Compute and send the logical processes earliest output time
74      void sendEOT(Time tStop);
75      // Update eit and move input events from input_q to xq
76      void processInputMessages();
77      // Attach a model to the sequential simulator
```

```
78      void addToSimulator(Devs<X>* model);
79      // Cleanup output messages that left the logical process
80      void cleanup_xb();
81   };
82
83   template <typename X>
84   LogicalProcess<X>::LogicalProcess(int ID, const std::vector<int>& I,
85        const std::vector<int>& E, LogicalProcess<X>** all_lps,
86        AbstractSimulator<X>* psim, MessageManager<X>* msg_manager):
87      ID(ID),E(E),I(I),all_lps(all_lps),psim(psim),
88      msg_manager(msg_manager),sim(this)
89   {
90      tSelf = eot = eit = Time(0.0,0); // Safe guesses are 0
91      all_lps[ID] = this; // Add ourself to the set of logical processes
92      lookahead = DBL_MAX; // No models, so infinite lookahead to start
93      for (typename std::vector<int>::const_iterator iter = I.begin();
94           iter != I.end(); iter++)
95        if (*iter != ID) eit_map[*iter] = Time(0.0,0); // Safe guess
96      // Register to receive output produced by the sequential simulator
97      sim.addEventListener(this);
98   }
99
100  template <typename X>
101  void LogicalProcess<X>::addModel(Devs<X>* model)
102  {
103     // Assume models are connected in parallel
104     lookahead = std::min(model->lookahead(),lookahead);
105     assert(lookahead > 0.0); // Better be positive, or something is wrong
106     // Attach it to the sequential simulator and set the thread assignment
107     addToSimulator(model);
108  }
109
110  template <typename X>
111  void LogicalProcess<X>::addToSimulator(Devs<X>* model)
112  {
113     model->setProc(ID); // Assign the model to this process
114     // Atomic models are attached directly to the sequential simulator
115     // by inserting them into the event schedule
116     Atomic<X>* a = model->typeIsAtomic();
117     if (a != NULL)
118     {
119        sim.addModel(a); // Schedule the model
120        // Get the time of the next internal event
121        tSelf.t = sim.nextEventTime();
122     }
123     // Decompose a network model and assign its components to ourself
124     else
125     {
126        // Get the set of components
```

```
127        Set<Devs<X>*> components;
128        model->typeIsNetwork()->getComponents(components);
129        // Add them to ourself
130        typename Set<Devs<X>*>::iterator iter = components.begin();
131        for (; iter != components.end(); iter++) addToSimulator(*iter);
132    }
133 }
134
135 template <typename X>
136 void LogicalProcess<X>::notifyInput(Atomic<X>* model, X& value)
137 {
138    assert(model->getProc() != ID); // This had better not be ours
139    // Create a message carrying a copy of the event object
140    Message<X> msg(msg_manager->clone(value));
141    msg.t = tSelf; // Set the timestamp
142    msg.src = this; // Note the process that produced the message
143    msg.target = model; // The target is the atomic model getting the input
144    msg.type = Message<X>::OUTPUT; // It is an OUTPUT from an atomic model
145    all_lps[model->getProc()]->sendMessage(msg); // Send the message
146 }
147
148 template <typename X>
149 void LogicalProcess<X>::sendEOT(Time tStop)
150 {
151    Message<X> msg; // Create a message to carry the EOT update
152    msg.target = NULL; // This is not an input for an atomic model
153    msg.type = Message<X>::EIT;
154    msg.src = this; // Note the process that produced the message
155    // Calculate our EOT estimate. Note that tStop contains the smaller
156    // of the earliest input time and the simulation end time
157    msg.t = tStop;
158    msg.t.t += lookahead; msg.t.c = 0; // Add the lookahead
159    // msg now carries the time to which our output is fixed. If this time
160    // is larger than our next event time, then our next output will
161    // actually occur sooner than this.
162    if (tSelf <= msg.t)
163    {
164       msg.t = tSelf; // In this case, tSelf is our EOT
165       // Recall that every discrete event model has a lookahead of (0,1)
166       // and so if tSelf is actually at eit then we have already sent
167       // the corresponding outputs. Hence, our next output can occur
168       // at the earliest in the next discrete instant.
169       if (tSelf == eit) msg.t.c += 1;
170    }
171    assert(msg.t.c >= 0); // c must not be negative
172    // Our next event time can shrink, but EOT is strictly increasing. So
173    // don't do anything if the calculated EOT is smaller than the last
174    // eot that we transmitted.
175    if (msg.t <= eot) return;
```

```
176        else eot = msg.t; // Otherwise, save the new EOT
177        // Send it to all of our influencees
178        for (std::vector<int>::const_iterator iter = E.begin();
179                iter != E.end(); iter++)
180           if (*iter != ID) all_lps[(*iter)]->sendMessage(msg);
181    }
182
183    template <typename X>
184    void LogicalProcess<X>::processInputMessages()
185    {
186        while (!input_q.empty()) // Process all pending messages
187        {
188           Message<X> msg(input_q.remove()); // Extract the message
189           eit_map[msg.src->getID()] = msg.t; // Update eit for the source
190           if (msg.type == Message<X>::OUTPUT) // Save input to the atomic models
191               xq.push(msg);
192        }
193        // Update our earliest input time
194        eit = Time::Inf();
195        for (std::map<int,Time>::iterator iter = eit_map.begin();
196                iter != eit_map.end(); iter++)
197           eit = std::min((*iter).second,eit);
198    }
199
200    template <typename X>
201    void LogicalProcess<X>::run(double t_stop)
202    {
203        while (true)
204        {
205           bool tstop_reached = false;
206           // Make sure we stop at t_stop
207           Time tStop(eit);
208           if (Time::Inf() <= tStop || tStop.t > t_stop)
209           {
210               tStop = Time(t_stop,UINT_MAX);
211               tstop_reached = true;
212           }
213           // The main simulation loop runs until all pending events are
214           // scheduled for after the simulation end time
215           while (tSelf <= tStop || (!xq.empty() && xq.top().t <= tStop))
216           {
217               // Find the time of the next event
218               Time tN(tSelf); // Time of the internal event
219               // Is the next input event earlier that this?
220               if (!xq.empty() && xq.top().t < tN) tN = xq.top().t;
221               // If the next internal event is before or at the next event time,
222               // then calculate and send the model's output
223               if (tSelf == tN) sim.computeNextOutput();
224               // If the next event is at EIT, then we don't have all of the
```

```
225          // input for time tN and must wait to compute the next state
226          // of the model
227          if (tN == eit) { assert(!tstop_reached); break; }
228          // Otherwise inject the input for time tN
229          while (!xq.empty() && xq.top().t <= tN)
230          {
231              Message<X> msg(xq.top()); // Get the message
232              xq.pop(); // Remove it from the pending queue
233              assert(msg.target->getProc() == ID); // Better be for us
234              // Add the input to the bag of events that will be injected
235              // into the sequential simulator
236              Event<X> input_event(msg.target,msg.value);
237              xb.insert(input_event);
238          }
239          assert(tN.t < DBL_MAX); // The simulator should not be passive
240          sim.computeNextState(xb,tN.t); // Compute the state at tN
241          // Use the message manager to delete input received from foreign
242          // logical processes
243          cleanup_xb();
244          // Calculate the time of our next internal event
245          tSelf = tN; // Set next event to the time of the last event
246          if (tSelf.t < sim.nextEventTime()) // If it is in the real future
247          {
248              tSelf.t = sim.nextEventTime(); // Set the real part
249              tSelf.c = 0; // The discrete part becomes zero
250          }
251          else tSelf.c++; // Otherwise just increment the discrete part
252      }
253      // Calculate and send our earliest output time
254      sendEOT(tStop);
255      if (tstop_reached) return; // Exit if we are done
256      processInputMessages(); // Otherwise process any waiting messages
257   }
258 }
259
260 template <class X>
261 void LogicalProcess<X>::cleanup_xb()
262 {
263    // Use the MessageManager to delete the copied objects
264    // that were received from foreign logical processes
265    typename Bag<Event<X> >::iterator iter = xb.begin();
266    for (; iter != xb.end(); iter++)
267        msg_manager->destroy((*iter).value);
268    xb.clear();
269 }
270
271 template <class X>
272 LogicalProcess<X>::~LogicalProcess()
273 {
```

```
274     // Delete objects received from the other logical processes.
275     // Note that the Simulator does not delete its models
276     // and neither does this destructor, so they are still available
277     // after the simulation ends
278     while (!xq.empty())
279     {
280         Message<X> msg(xq.top());
281         xq.pop();
282         Event<X> input_event(msg.target,msg.value);
283         xb.insert(input_event);
284     }
285     cleanup_xb();
286 }
287
288 } // end of namespace
```

B.2.4 The *MessageQ*

The *MessageQ* is used for communication between threads. It functions as a first-in/first-out queue that can be accessed simultaneously by multiple senders and a single receiver, the queue's owner. A message is inserted into the back of the queue by calling the *insert* method, and the message at the front of the queue is removed by calling the *remove* method. The state of the queue, empty or full, is discovered by calling the *empty* method. In a parallel simulation where each thread stays busy processing events, a *LogicalProcess* will find a message in the queue every time it looks. Consequently, there is no provision for halting until a message becomes available. Instead, a *LogicalProcess* spins on the *empty* method if it cannot progress without a message and no message has yet become available.

Two lists are used to implement the *MessageQ*. One of these is the *safe list*, and it is accessed only by the *LogicalProcess* that owns the *MessageQ*. The other is the *shared list*, into which messages are inserted. The status of the shared list is kept in a volatile Boolean variable that is true if the shared list is empty and false otherwise. Because the several threads may attempt to access the shared list at the same time, it is protected by a lock.

To insert a message into the *MessageQ*, the caller acquires the lock, pushes the message onto the back of the shared list, sets the Boolean variable that indicates the list's status to false (i.e., not empty), and releases the lock.

Only the owning *LogicalProcess* can extract a message from the *MessageQ*. To do this, it first checks the status of the safe list. If this list is not empty, then the first message is extracted from it. Otherwise, the lock for the shared list is acquired, the shared list and safe list are swapped, the status of the shared list is set to true (i.e., empty), and the lock is released. Now the safe list, which was formerly the shared list, contains at least one message and the first one is extracted.

Of course, a message can be extracted from the list only if it is not empty. Before calling *remove*, the owning thread checks to see whether (1) the safe list is not empty or (2) the shared list is not empty. If either of these conditions is true, then a message can be obtained from the *MessageQ*. The implementation of the *MessageQ* is listed below.

───────────────── ***Implementation of the MessageQ*** ─────────────────

```
1   #ifndef __adevs_message_q_h_
2   #define __adevs_message_q_h_
3   #include "adevs_models.h"
4   #include "adevs_time.h"
5   #include <omp.h>
6   #include <list>
7   #include <cassert>
8
9   namespace adevs
10  {
11
12  // Early declaration for use as the Message source.
13  // The LogicalProcess is defined elsewhere.
14  template <typename X> class LogicalProcess;
15  // These are the messages exchanged by LogicalProcesses
16  template <typename X> struct Message
17  {
18      typedef enum { OUTPUT, EIT } msg_type_t;
19      Time t; // Message timestamp
20      LogicalProcess<X> *src; // Logical process that produced the message
21      Devs<X>* target; // Model that is the target for the message's value
22      X value; // Value of the input to the target
23      msg_type_t type; // The type of the message (OUTPUT or EIT)
24      Message():value(){} // Default constructor
25      // Create a message with a particular value
26      Message(const X& value):value(value){}
27      // Copy constructor
28      Message(const Message& other):
29          t(other.t),src(other.src),target(other.target),
30          value(other.value),type(other.type) {}
31      // Assignment operator
32      const Message<X>& operator=(const Message<X>& other)
33      {
34          t = other.t;
35          src = other.src;
36          target = other.target;
37          value = other.value;
38          type = other.type;
39          return *this;
40      }
41      // Sort by timestamp, smallest timestamp first in the STL priority_queue
42      bool operator<(const Message<X>& other) const { return other.t < t; }
43  };
```

```
44    // This is the buffer used by LogicalProcesses for their incoming Messages
45    template <class X> class MessageQ
46    {
47      public:
48        // Create an empty message queue
49        MessageQ()
50        {
51            omp_init_lock(&lock); // Create the lock that protects qshare
52            qshare_empty = true; // qshare is initially empty
53            qsafe = &q1; // Point to the shared and safe message lists
54            qshare = &q2;
55        }
56        // Put a message at the back of the list
57        void insert(const Message<X>& msg)
58        {
59            omp_set_lock(&lock); // Acquire the lock
60            qshare->push_back(msg); // Message to the back of the shared list
61            qshare_empty = false; // The shared list is not empty now
62            omp_unset_lock(&lock); // Release the lock and return
63        }
64        // Is the message buffer empty? This works without a lock because
65        // qsafe is accessed only by the owning LogicalProcess and
66        // qshare_empty is volatile
67        bool empty() const { return qsafe->empty() && qshare_empty; }
68        // Get the message at the front of the list
69        Message<X> remove()
70        {
71            // If the safe list is empty, then we must get the message
72            // from the shared list
73            if (qsafe->empty())
74            {
75                // Swap the shared and safe lists
76                std::list<Message<X> > *tmp = qshare;
77                omp_set_lock(&lock); // Get the lock
78                qshare = qsafe; // Make the safe list into the shared list
79                qshare_empty = true; // The shared list is now empty
80                omp_unset_lock(&lock); // Release the lock
81                qsafe = tmp; // Finish the swap
82            }
83            // There is a message in the safe list; extract the first one
84            Message<X> msg(qsafe->front());
85            qsafe->pop_front();
86            return msg; // Return it
87        }
88        ~MessageQ()
89        {
90            // Just destroy the lock; the content of the messages are owned
91            // by the LogicalProcess
92            omp_destroy_lock(&lock);
```

```
93      }
94   private:
95      omp_lock_t lock; // Lock to protect qshare and qshare_empty
96      std::list<Message<X> > q1, q2; // The lists themselves
97      std::list<Message<X> > *qsafe, *qshare; // Roles for q1 and q2
98      volatile bool qshare_empty; // Is qshare empty?
99   };
100
101   } // end of namespace
102
103   #endif
```

B.2.5 The *ParSimulator*

The *ParSimulator* class hides the parallel simulation algorithm behind an interface that closely resembles the *Simulator* interface. The user can register an *EventListener* to be notified when output is produced by and state changes occur in the component models; the constructor accepts a *Devs* model whose components are assigned to specific logical processes in accordance with the user preferences, and the *execUntil* method runs the parallel algorithm until a specified end time. The implementation of this class is listed below.

The assignment of components to *LogicalProcess*es is one of the main functions of the *ParSimulator*. Each *Devs*, atomic and network, has a *setProc* method that is used by the modeler to assigned it to a specific thread. Valid assignments are in the range of 0 to *omp_get_max_threads*-1. By default, a model is unassigned and this is indicated by a thread number of −1. Models are attached to processors depth first. A *Network* with a valid assignment is given to the appropriate *LogicalProcess*, which adopts its and all of its components. If the *Network* does not have a valid assignment, then the *ParSimulator* looks at the assignments of its children. Again, *Network*s with a valid assignment are given to the appropriate *LogicalProcess*; those without a valid assignment are expanded. An *Atomic* model, however, is always assigned to some *LogicalProcess*; if the atomic model has an invalid assignment, then a *LogicalProcess* is selected at random. This assignment process is illustrated in Figure B.8.

_____ *Implementation of the ParSimulator* _____

```
1   #ifndef __adevs_par_simulator_h_
2   #define __adevs_par_simulator_h_
3   #include "adevs_abstract_simulator.h"
4   #include "adevs_msg_manager.h"
5   #include "adevs_lp.h"
6   #include "adevs_lp_graph.h"
7   #include <cassert>
8   #include <cstdlib>
9   #include <iostream>
10  #include <vector>
```

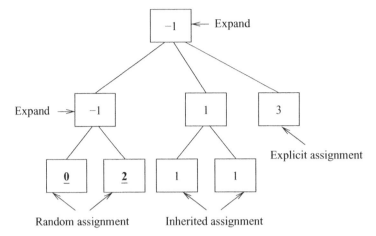

FIGURE B.8 An assignment of a network model to a set of logical processes. Each block in the tree is a model; the leaves are atomic and intermediates are networks. The labels are processor assignments; underlining indicates a −1 that was altered during the assignment process.

```
11
12   namespace adevs
13   {
14
15   template <class X> class ParSimulator: public AbstractSimulator<X>
16   {
17       public:
18           // Create a simulator for the model. This constructor assumes that
19           // the logical processes are all connected to each other
20           ParSimulator(Devs<X>* model, MessageManager<X>* msg_mngr = NULL);
21           // This constructor accepts a directed graph whose edges tell the
22           // simulator which processes feed input to which other processes.
23           ParSimulator(Devs<X>* model, LpGraph& g,
24               MessageManager<X>* msg_mngr = NULL);
25           // Get the model's next event time
26           double nextEventTime();
27           // Run the simulator until the next event time is greater
28           // than the specified value.
29           void execUntil(double stop_time);
30           // Delete the simulator, but leave the model intact
31           ~ParSimulator();
32       private:
33           LogicalProcess<X>** lp; // Pointers to the logical processes
34           int lp_count; // Number of logical processes in lp
35           MessageManager<X>* msg_manager; // For managing inter-lp events
36           void init(Devs<X>* model);
37           void init_sim(Devs<X>* model, LpGraph& g);
38   };
```

```
39
40   template <class X>
41   ParSimulator<X>::ParSimulator(Devs<X>* model, MessageManager<X>* msg_mngr):
42     AbstractSimulator<X>(),msg_manager(msg_mngr)
43   {
44     // Create an all to all coupling of logical processes in place of
45     // the LpGraph not provided by the user
46     lp_count = omp_get_max_threads();
47     LpGraph g;
48     for (int i = 0; i < lp_count; i++)
49     {
50       for (int j = 0; j < lp_count; j++)
51       {
52         if (i != j)
53         {
54           g.addEdge(i,j);
55           g.addEdge(j,i);
56         }
57       }
58     }
59     init_sim(model,g); // Initialize the simulator
60   }
61
62   template <class X>
63   ParSimulator<X>::ParSimulator(Devs<X>* model, LpGraph& g,
64       MessageManager<X>* msg_mngr):
65     AbstractSimulator<X>(),msg_manager(msg_mngr)
66   {
67     init_sim(model,g); // Initialize the simulator
68   }
69
70   template <class X>
71   void ParSimulator<X>::init_sim(Devs<X>* model, LpGraph& g)
72   {
73     // Create a default manager if one was not provided
74     if (msg_manager == NULL) msg_manager = new NullMessageManager<X>();
75     lp_count = omp_get_max_threads(); // One logical process per thread
76     lp = new LogicalProcess<X>*[lp_count]; // Allocate the lp array
77     // Create the logical processes; IDs are the array positions
78     for (int i = 0; i < lp_count; i++)
79       lp[i] = new LogicalProcess<X>(i,g.getI(i),g.getE(i),lp,
80             this,msg_manager);
81     init(model); // Partition the model for simulation by the processes
82   }
83
84   template <class X>
85   double ParSimulator<X>::nextEventTime()
86   {
87     // Calculate the time of the next event as the smaller of the
```

```
88      // next event times of the logical processes
89      Time tN = Time::Inf();
90      for (int i = 0; i < lp_count; i++)
91      {
92          if (lp[i]->getNextEventTime() < tN)
93              tN = lp[i]->getNextEventTime();
94      }
95      return tN.t;
96  }
97
98  template <class X>
99  ParSimulator<X>::~ParSimulator<X>()
100 {
101     for (int i = 0; i < lp_count; i++)
102         delete lp[i]; // Delete the logical processes
103     delete [] lp; // Delete the array that held them
104     delete msg_manager; // Delete the message manager
105 }
106
107 template <class X>
108 void ParSimulator<X>::execUntil(double tstop)
109 {
110     // Create a separate thread for each logical process and execute
111     // until the simulation stop time is reached
112     #pragma omp parallel
113     {
114         lp[omp_get_thread_num()]->run(tstop);
115     }
116 }
117
118 template <class X>
119 void ParSimulator<X>::init(Devs<X>* model)
120 {
121     // If the model wants a process that exists, then do the assignment
122     if (model->getProc() >= 0 && model->getProc() < lp_count)
123     {
124         lp[model->getProc()]->addModel(model);
125         return;
126     }
127     // Otherwise, try to place it
128     Atomic<X>* a = model->typeIsAtomic();
129     if (a != NULL) // Atomic models are assigned at random
130     {
131         int lp_assign = a->getProc();
132         if (lp_assign < 0 || lp_assign >= lp_count)
133             lp_assign = ((long int)a)%lp_count;
134         lp[lp_assign]->addModel(a);
135     }
136     // The components of a network model are recursively assigned
```

```
137    else
138    {
139       Set<Devs<X>*> components;
140       model->typeIsNetwork()->getComponents(components);
141       typename Set<Devs<X>*>::iterator iter = components.begin();
142       for (; iter != components.end(); iter++) init(*iter);
143    }
144  }
145
146  } // End of namespace
147
148  #endif
```

B.3   DEMONSTRATION OF GUSTAFSON'S AND AMDAHL'S LAWS

The conservative algorithm works best when the model is partitioned such that information flows forward. The connections between processes ideally form a tree with data originating at the root and flowing down to the leaves. With this arrangement, each branch of the tree can be executed as quickly as the upstream process provides input to it. Feedback, by which a process at a lower level in the tree feeds information to its parent, limits the exploitable parallelism to simultaneous state transitions.

For example, consider just two models connected in a feedback arrangement. Beginning at time zero, suppose that the first model has a lookahead ϵ_1 and time advance of Δt_1 and the second model of ϵ_2 and Δt_2, respectively. The first act of each processor is to send the smaller of its Δt and ϵ to its neighbor and thereby establish the earliest input times.

Consider first what happens if $\epsilon_1 < \Delta t_1$ and $\epsilon_2 < \Delta t_2$. Neither process can do anything useful; each merely updates its estimate of the earliest input time by the ϵ of its neighbor. This happens again and again until the accumulated ϵs reach the smaller of the Δts and the first event finally occurs. Clearly, no useful work is done in parallel and substantial time is wasted while the processors agree on the time of the next executable event. This is the worst-case scenario.

In the best circumstances, $\Delta t_1 < \epsilon_1$ and $\Delta t_2 < \epsilon_2$. In this case, the processes exchange their next event times and if, say, $\Delta t_2 < \Delta t_1$, the internal event at the second processor and external event at the first processor are executed in parallel. Some small amount of parallelism is exploited, but any benefit is likely overwhelmed by time lost to the exchange of estimates for the earliest output times and the output values themselves.

With this in mind, the benchmark model embodies the ideal case where models feed information forward. With careful attention to how the model is partitioned for parallel simulation, this ideal can often be realized in practice. Manufacturing problems provide a good example. Raw material enters a plant and is processed in stages. Specific stages may send defective parts back for reprocessing, and the stages connected by feedback loops are incorporated into a single logical process. The

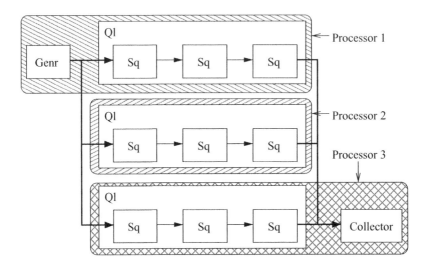

FIGURE B.9   The benchmark model with nine servers in three lines and its partitioning for three processors. The box labels indicate the model's class.

remaining stages constitute serial or parallel flows of material. Doing this necessarily restricts the number of processors that can be usefully exploited, and the benchmark reflects this fact. We will consider a small number of processors and a relatively large problem, an ideal circumstance for showing Gustafson's law applied to simulations executing on a multicore workstation.

The benchmark model is a queuing network constructed from atomic models that contain a queue and server with a first-come, first-served policy. The servers have a processing time of $1 + \mathbf{r}$ seconds, where $\mathbf{r}$ is exponentially distributed with a mean of one second. These form N serial arrangements of Q servers each. The lines of servers are fed by a single generator that produces a new job every $2/N$ seconds and chooses at random one of the N lines of servers to process it. This ensures that, on average, each line of queues receives a job every two seconds. The output from the lines of servers arrive at a collector, which counts the finished jobs as they arrive. The model is illustrated in Figure B.9.

The model is partitioned for P processors in the following way. The generator and $\lfloor N/P \rfloor$ of the lines of servers are assigned to the first processor. Processors $2, \ldots, P - 1$ each get $\lfloor N/P \rfloor$ lines of servers, and processor P gets the collector and the lines of servers that remain. With this partitioning, processor 1 provides input to $2, \ldots, P$, and processors $1, \ldots, P - 1$ provide input to P. A partitioning of three lines of servers is illustrated in Figure B.9. The generator, which is input-free, and the collector, which is output-free, each have infinite lookahead. The individual servers have a lookahead of 1, and each line of Q servers therefore has a lookahead of Q. The lines are arranged in parallel, and so each processor can conservatively estimate its lookahead as Q. In fact, the first processor, which has the generator, has infinite lookahead and likewise the last processor, which contains the collector.

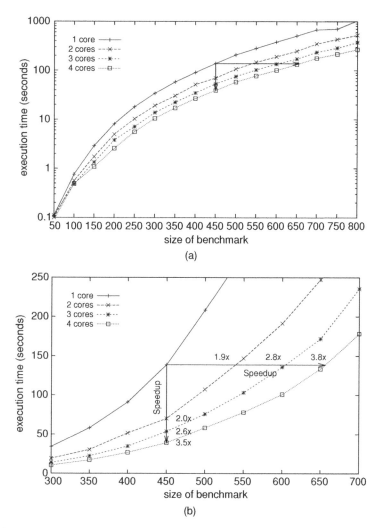

FIGURE B.10 Execution time of the benchmark as a function of size and the number of processors used: (a) execution times; (b) closeup view of part (a) illustrating Gustafson's and Amdahl's laws.

The servers with queues, the lines of servers, the generator, and the collector differ only minimally from the discrete-event models that we have seen so far; they are implemented by the *Sq*, *Ql*, *Genr*, and *Collector* classes, respectively. The *Qn* class, which connects these components and assigns them to processors, and the *main* function, which creates and executes the parallel simulator, show how the new elements of the simulation engine are used. The code for these is listed below.

This benchmark can be scaled in three dimensions: the number N of lines of servers, the number Q of queues and servers in each line; and the simulation ending time T. In this instance, the model is set up with $N = Q$ and $T = 3N$; so a problem of size 100 has $N = Q = 100$ and $T = 300$. The choice of $N = Q$ is arbitrary. Using $T = 3N$ ensures that some of the jobs arrive at the collector before the simulation terminates. What is important is that, as Gustafson's law requires, the parallel part of the simulation grows with its size while the serial part remains essentially unchanged. Therefore, as the size of the model grows, we can maintain a reasonable execution time by using a larger computer.

Figure B.10 confirms our expectations. These results were produced with a four-core Intel processor. A critical feature of this plot is the horizontal line connecting equal execution times using one, two, three, and four cores. The parallel fraction of the program grows with the size of the problem, and the trend predicted by Gustafson's law is unmistakable: the speedup, although not ideal, is steady when the number of processors matches the size of the problem. Amdahl's law can also be seen in this plot: the vertical line connecting the execution times for a fixed-size simulation shows diminishing returns. This experiment reinforces the argument with which the chapter began. Parallel computers are marginally useful for speeding up small problems but are very good for maintaining a reasonable execution time as the simulation grows.

_____ *Main Function for the Benchmark Program* _____

```
1   #include "Qn.h"
2   #include "adevs_par_simulator.h"
3   #include <iostream>
4   using namespace adevs;
5   using namespace std;
6
7   int main(int argc, char** argv)
8   {
9       if (argc < 4) {
10          cerr << "Need # queues, # lines, and end time" << endl;
11          return 0;
12      }
13      if (argc == 5)
14          cout << "Using " << omp_get_max_threads()<< " threads" << endl;
15      int queues = atoi(argv[1]);
16      int lines = atoi(argv[2]);
17      double tend = atof(argv[3]);
18      LpGraph lpg;
19      Qn* model = new Qn(queues,lines,lpg);
20      AbstractSimulator<int>* sim;
21      if (argc == 5) sim = new ParSimulator<int>(model,lpg);
22      else sim = new Simulator<int>(model);
23      sim->execUntil(tend);
24      delete sim; delete model;
25      return 0;
26  }
```

--------------- *Qn Class for the Benchmark Program* ---------------

```
1   #ifndef _Qn_h_
2   #define _Qn_h_
3   #include "adevs.h"
4   #include "Genr.h"
5   #include "Sq.h"
6   #include <iostream>
7
8   class Qn: public adevs::Network<int>
9   {
10     public:
11       // Create a model with s lines of q servers. The arrangement
12       // of the logical processes is returned via the supplied LpGraph.
13       Qn(int q, int s, adevs::LpGraph& lpg):
14           adevs::Network<int>(),qcount(s),ql(new Ql*[s]),
15           genr((double)s/2.0),collect()
16       {
17           int thrds = omp_get_max_threads(); // Get the number of threads
18           genr.setParent(this); // The generator goes to process zero
19           genr.setProc(0);
20           collect.setParent(this); // Collector goes on the last process
21           collect.setProc(thrds-1);
22           // The queues are split among all the processes
23           for (int i = 0; i < qcount; i++)
24           {
25               ql[i] = new Ql(q);
26               ql[i]->setParent(this);
27               ql[i]->setProc(i%thrds);
28           }
29           // Add 0->[1,thrds) to the LpGraph. This connects the
30           // generator to everyone.
31           for (int i = 1; i < thrds; i++) lpg.addEdge(0,i);
32           // Add [0,thrds-1)->thrds-1 to the LpGraph. This connects
33           // everyone to the collector.
34           for (int i = 0; i < thrds-1; i++) lpg.addEdge(i,thrds-1);
35       }
36       void getComponents(adevs::Set<adevs::Devs<int>*>& c)
37       {
38           for (int i = 0; i < qcount; i++) c.insert(ql[i]);
39           c.insert(&genr); c.insert(&collect);
40       }
41       void route(const int &value, adevs::Devs<int> *model,
42           adevs::Bag<adevs::Event<int> > &r)
43       {
44           if (model == &genr)
45               r.insert(adevs::Event<int>(ql[value%qcount],value));
46           else r.insert(adevs::Event<int>(&collect,value));
47       }
```

```
48      ~Qn()
49      {
50          // Delete the components of the model
51          for (int i = 0; i < qcount; i++) delete ql[i];
52          delete [] ql;
53      }
54  private:
55      const int qcount;
56      Ql** ql;
57      Genr genr;
58      Collector collect;
59  };
60
61  #endif
```

APPENDIX C

MATHEMATICAL TOPICS

C.1 SYSTEM HOMOMORPHISMS

A *morphism* is a mapping from one system to another. When such a mapping exists, one system, the "big" system, is capable of doing all the essential work of another system, the "small" system. If the mapping is reversible, so that the small and big systems can change places, then the two systems are in fact identical except for the renaming and, possibly, a reversible recombination of their input, output, and state variables. A *homomorphism* is a mapping from big system to a small system that loses some information about the big system. The small system, in this case, does less than the big system, and the mapping is not reversible. If the mapping is reversible, then it is an isomorphism and the systems involved are interchangeable.

A trivial example will introduce the idea in an intuitive way. Consider first a discrete-time system (see Chapter 3) with a single state, single input, and single output; call this system A. Any other discrete-time system, call it B, is capable of mimicking A as follows. Let the entire set of states of B be mapped to the single state of A, and likewise with B's set of outputs. A's single input is mapped to any input of B, which in particular does not matter. Now the input for A is fed, via the mapping, into B. In response, B changes state and produces an output, and this action, observed through the lens of the morphism, looks exactly like the response of A: B remains in its single state (as seen through the mapping) and produces its single output (again, as seen through the mapping). This is a trivial example of a homomorphism. If B has only a single state, input, and output to begin with, then A and B are trivially isomorphic.

Building Software for Simulation: Theory and Algorithms, with Applications in C++, By James J. Nutaro
Copyright © 2011 John Wiley & Sons, Inc.

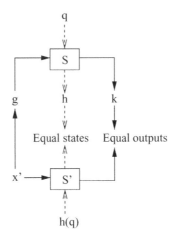

FIGURE C.1   Illustration of a homomorphisms from big system S to small system S'.

More generally, a system morphism from a big system with set of states Q, inputs X, outputs Y, time base T, state transition function Δ, and output function Λ to a small system described by Q', X', Y', T', Δ', and Λ' comprises three functions

$$g :< X', T' > \to < X, T >$$
$$h : \bar{Q} \to_{onto} Q', \text{ where } \bar{Q} \subseteq Q$$
$$k : Y \to_{onto} Y'$$

that satisfy

$$h(\Delta(q, g(x'))) = \Delta'(h(q), x') \tag{C.1}$$
$$k(\Lambda(q)) = \Lambda'(h(q)) \tag{C.2}$$

where $q \in \bar{Q}$ and $x' \in X'$. The function g transforms an input trajectory for the small system into an input trajectory for the big system. The function h transforms a subset of the states of the big system to states of the small system in such a way that all of the small system's states are covered (i.e., the function h is onto). The function k does the same thing as h, but for the sets of output.

Equations C.1–C.2 are illustrated in Figure C.1. The idea is that the following two procedures produce identical results:

1. Provide to the big system a suitably transformed input for the small system, compute the resulting state of the big system, and transform this into a state of the small system.
2. Transform the initial state of the big system into a state for the small system and apply the same input as above to compute a new state for the small system.

A useful fact is that if the trajectories are decomposable into generator segments, then a homomorphism constructed on that set of generators implies a homomorphism of the complete system (see, e.g., Ref. 157). The primitive segments for discrete-time and discrete-event systems satisfy this requirement. For instance, every trajectory of a discrete-time system can be constructed by concatenating trajectories of unit length. Hence, these constitute generators for the system. The functions h and g can now be applied to the single-step transition function δ as follows, where x' is now a generator segment:

$$h(\delta(q, g(x'))) = \delta'(h(q), x') \tag{C.3}$$

Equation C.3 implies Equation C.1 and is often a more practicable tool for constructing homomorphisms.

C.2 SINUSOIDAL STATE-STEADY ANALYSIS

Changes in the speed, output power, and excitation voltage of an electric generator occur much more slowly than do changes in voltages and currents in transmission wires, capacitor banks, and other electrical equipment. It is therefore convenient in the analysis of generator dynamics to avoid dynamic models of purely electrical devices and use instead simpler algebraic models. For this purpose, it is assumed that these devices always see a sinusoidal voltage and current characterized by $A \sin(\omega t + \theta)$. The amplitude A and phase angle θ may vary with time, but the frequency ω is fixed. Justification for these assumptions can be found in almost any textbook on power systems engineering or the analysis of electric circuits (see, e.g., Ref. 52 or 97). This assumption simplifies the calculation of currents and voltages in the transmission network by considering only instantaneous changes in amplitudes and phase angles. We proceed as follows:

1. Each sinusoidal source is replaced by a *phasor* $A \cos \theta + j A \sin \theta$. With a slight abuse of notation, this is abbreviated $A \angle \theta$.[1]
2. Inductors L, resistors R, and capacitors C are replaced with complex impedances $j\omega L$, $(j\omega C)^{-1}$, and R, respectively. This produces a network containing only complex impedances Z that satisfy Ohm's law when the currents I and voltages V are phasors: $V = I Z$. The complex power at a device is $S = V I^*$. The real part of S is called *real power* and the imaginary part, *reactive power*.
3. Voltages at nodes and currents in branches are calculated using the mesh current or node voltage method.

---

[1] In fact, $A \angle \theta = A \cos(\omega t + \theta)$ and $A \cos \theta + j A \sin \theta$ is the phasor transform of that sinusoid. In most cases, the use of $A \angle \theta$ for the phasor does not cause confusion.

There is a slight incongruence when using this method of analysis in conjunction with dynamic models of the generators. The transmission system model is constructed by assuming that the power signal has a fixed frequency. However, the synchronous machine model has a frequency that varies. In fact, frequency variation at the generators appears on the transmission lines and everywhere else, but they are ignored when calculating line currents and node voltages. Change in the generator frequencies cannot be similarly eliminated because it drives change in the machines' phase angles, and these phase angles determine how power flows from the generators to the loads. Nonetheless, this method of calculation is very practical and widely used.

REFERENCES

1. *IEEE Standard for Distributed Interactive Simulation—Application Protocols*, IEEE Standard 1278.1a-1998, Aug. 1998.

2. M. Abrash, *Michael Abrash's Graphics Programming Black Book*, Special ed., Coriolis Group Books, 1997.

3. F. L. Alvarado, Is system control entirely by price feasible? *Proc. 36th Annual Hawaii Int. Conf. System Sciences*, Jan. 2003, pp. 6–9.

4. A. Ames, A. Abate, and S. Sastry, Sufficient conditions for the existence of zeno behavior, *Proc. 44th IEEE Conf. Decision and Control and European Control (ECC 2005)*, Dec. 2005.

5. A. D. Ames, *A Categorical Theory of Hybrid Systems*, PhD thesis, Dept. Electrical Engineering and Computer Sciences, Univ. California, Berkeley, 2006.

6. J. Arrillaga and N. R. Watson, *Computer Modelling of Electrical Power Systems*, Wiley, 2001.

7. W. R. Ashby, *An Introduction to Cybernetics*, Chapman & Hall, 1956.

8. F. J. Barros, Dynamic structure discrete event system specification: A new formalism for dynamic structure modeling and simulation, *Proc. 27th Winter Simulation Conf. (WSC '95)*, 1995, pp. 781–785.

9. F. J. Barros, Modeling formalisms for dynamic structure systems, *ACM Trans. Model. Comput. Simulation* 7(4):501–515 (1997).

10. C. Barz, R. Göpffarth, P. Martini, and A. Wenzel, A new framework for the analysis of simultaneous events, *Proc. 2003 Summer Computer Simulation Conf. (SCSC'03)*, July 2003.

Building Software for Simulation: Theory and Algorithms, with Applications in C++, By James J. Nutaro
Copyright © 2011 John Wiley & Sons, Inc.

11. T. Beltrame, *Design and Development of a Dymola/Modelica Library for Discrete Event-Oriented Systems Using DEVS Methodology*, Master's thesis, ETH Zürich, Dept. Computer Science, Inst. Computational Science, 2006.

12. F. T. Bergmann and H. M. Sauro, Comparing simulation results of SBML capable simulators, *Bioinformatics* **24**(17):1963–1965 (2008).

13. H. Bersini and V. Detour, Asynchrony induces stability in cellular automata based models, in R. A. Brooks and P. Maes, eds., *Artificial Life IV*, MIT Press, 1994, pp. 382–387.

14. F. P. Brooks, *The Mythical Man-Month and Other Essays on Software Engineering*, Dept. Computer Science, Univ. North Carolina at Chapel Hill, 1975.

15. R. Brown, Calendar queues: A fast 0(1) priority queue implementation for the simulation event set problem, *Commun. ACM* **31**(10):1220–1227 (1988).

16. W. Cai, F. B. S. Lee, and L. Chen, An auto-adaptive dead reckoning algorithm for distributed interactive simulation, *Proc. 13th Workshop on Parallel and Distributed Simulation (PADS '99)*, 1999, pp. 82–89.

17. L. P. Carloni, R. Passerone, A. Pinto, and A. L. Sangiovanni-Vincentelli, Languages and tools for hybrid systems design, *Found. Trends Electron. Design Automation* **1**(1/2):1–193 (2006).

18. C. D. Carothers, K. S. Perumalla, and R. M. Fujimoto, Efficient optimistic parallel simulations using reverse computation, *ACM Trans. Model. Comput. Simulation* **9**(3):224–253 (1999).

19. F. E. Cellier, *Continuous System Modeling*, Springer, 1991.

20. F. E. Cellier and E. Kofman, *Continuous System Simulation*, Birkhauser, 2005.

21. B. Chapman, G. Jost, and R. van der Pas, *Using OpenMP: Portable Shared Memory Parallel Programming*, MIT Press, 2007.

22. R. N. Charette, Why software fails, *IEEE Spectrum* **42**(9):42–49 (Sept. 2005).

23. Y. K. Cho, B. P. Zeigler, and H. S. Sarjoughian, Design and implementation of distributed real-time DEVS/CORBA, *Proc. 2001 IEEE Int. Conf. Systems, Man, and Cybernetics*, 2001, Vol. 5, pp. 3081–3086.

24. Y. K. Cho, J. H. Kim, and T. G. Kim, DEVS framework for component-based modeling/simulation of discrete event systems, *Proc. 2002 Summer Computer Simulation Conf.*, July 2002, pp. 210–215.

25. A. C. Chow, B. P. Zeigler, and D. H. Kim, Abstract simulator for the parallel DEVS formalism, *Proc. 5th Annual Conf. AI, Simulation, and Planning in High Autonomy Systems*, 1994, pp. 157–163.

26. A. Chung, H. Chow, and B. P. Zeigler, Parallel DEVS: A parallel, hierarchical, modular, modeling formalism, *Proc. 26th Winter Simulation Conf.*, 1994, pp. 716–722.

27. J. R. Clymer, *Simulation-Based Engineering of Complex Systems*, 2nd ed., Wiley, 2009.

28. D. Cornforth, D. G. Green, D. Newth, and M. Kirley., Do artificial ants march in step? Ordered asynchronous processes and modularity in biological systems, in *Artificial Life VIII*, MIT Press, 2002, pp. 28–32.

29. B. A. Cota and R. G. Sargent, A modification of the process interaction world view, *ACM Trans. Model. Comput. Simulation* **2**(2):109–129 (1992).

30. M. C. D'Abreu and G. A. Wainer, M/CD++: Modeling continuous systems using Modelica and DEVS, *Proc. 13th IEEE Int. Symp. Modeling, Analysis, and Simulation of Computer and Telecommunication Systems (MASCOTS '05)*, 2005, pp. 229–238.

31. T. Daum and R. G. Sargent, Experimental frames in a modern modeling and simulation system, *IIE Trans.* **33**(3):181–192 (March 2001).

32. P. K. Davis and R. H. Anderson, *Improving the Composability of Department of Defense Models and Simulations*, RAND Corp., 2003.

33. J. de Lara and H. Vangheluwe, AToM3: A tool for multi-formalism and meta-modelling, *Proc. 5th Int. Conf. Fundamental Approaches to Software Engineering (FASE '02)*, 2002, pp. 174–188.

34. J. Eker, J. W. Janneck, E. A. Lee, J. Liu, X. Liu, J. Ludvig, S. Neuendorffer, S. Sachs, and Y. Xiong, Taming heterogeneity—the Ptolemy approach, *Proc. IEEE* **91**(1):127–144 (Jan. 2003).

35. E. H. Page, Jr., *Simulation Modeling Methodolgy: Principles and Etiology of Decision Support*, PhD thesis, Dept. Computer Science, Virginia Polytechnic Inst., Blacksburg, VA, 1994.

36. J. M. Esposito and V. Kumar, An asynchronous integration and event detection algorithm for simulating multi-agent hybrid systems, *ACM Trans. Model. Comput. Simulation* **14**(4):363–388 (2004).

37. T. H. Feng and E. A. Lee, Incremental checkpointing with application to distributed discrete event simulation, *Proc. 38th Winter Simulation Conf. (WSC '06)*, 2006, pp. 1004–1011.

38. L. Feng-Li, J. Moyne, and D. Tilbury, Network design consideration for distributed control systems, *IEEE Trans. Control Syst. Technol.* **10**(2):297–307 (March 2002).

39. Federal Energy Regulatory Commission (FERC), *Assessment of Demand Response and Advanced Metering*, Staff report, Docket AD06-2-000, Aug. 2006.

40. J. A. Ferreira and J. P. E. de Oliveira, Modelling hybrid systems using state charts and modelica, *Proc. 7th IEEE Int. Conf. Emerging Technologies and Factory Automation*, 1999, Vol. 2, pp. 1063–1069.

41. G. S. Fishman, *Discrete-Event Simulation: Modeling, Programming, and Analysis*, Springer, 2001.

42. P. A. Fishwick, *Simulation Model Design and Execution: Building Digital Worlds*, Prentice Hall, 1995.

43. R. M. Fujimoto, Parallel discrete event simulation: Will the field survive? *ORSA J. Comput.* **5**(3):213–230 (1993).

44. R. M. Fujimoto, *Parallel and Distributed Simulation Systems*, Wiley-Interscience, 1999.

45. R. M. Fujimoto, K. S. Perumalla, and G. F. Riley, *Network Simulation*. Morgan & Claypool, 2006.

46. D. Färnqvist, K. Strandemar, K. H. Johansson, and J. P. Hespanha, Hybrid modeling of communication networks using modelica, *Proc. 2nd Int. Modelica Conf.* March 2002, pp. 209–213.

47. E. Gamma, R. Helm, R. Johnson, and J. M. Vlissides, *Design Patterns: Elements of Reusable Object-Oriented Software*, Addison-Wesley, 1995.

48. M. Gardner, The fantastic combinations of John Conway's new solitaire game: Life, *Sci. Am.* **223**:120–123 (1970).

49. S. Ghosh, P2EDAS: Asynchronous, distributed event driven simulation algorithm with inconsistent event preemption for accurate execution of VHDL descriptions on parallel processors, *IEEE Trans. Comput.* **50**(1):28–50 (2001).

50. N. Giambiasi, Bruno Escude, and S. Ghosh, GDEVS: A generalized discrete event specification for accurate modeling of dynamic systems, *Simulation* **17**(3):120–134 (2000).

51. E. Glinsky and G. Wainer, New parallel simulation techniques of DEVS and cell-DEVS in CD++, *Proc. 39th Annual Simulation Symp. (ANSS '06)*, 2006, pp. 244–251.

52. J. D. Glover, M. S. Sarma, and T. Overbye, *Power Systems Analysis and Design*, 4th ed., Cengage Learning, 2008.

53. A. Goderis, C. Brooks, I. Altintas, E. A. Lee, and C. Gobel, Heterogeneous composition of models of computation, *Future Generation Comput. Syst.* **25**(5):552–560, (May 2009).

54. R. Siow. M. Goh, and I. L.-J. Thng, MList: An efficient pending event set structure for discrete event simulation, *Int. J. Simulation* **4**(5–6):66–77 (Dec. 2003).

55. D. Green, D. Newth, D. Cornforth, and M. Kirley, On evolutionary processes in natural and artificial systems, *Proc. 5th Australia-Japan Joint Workshop on Intelligent and Evolutionary Systems*, 2001, pp. 1–10.

56. D. J. Hammerstrom, R. Ambrosio, T. A. Carlon, J. G. DeSteese, G. R. Horst, R. Kajfasz, L. Kiesling, P. Michie, R. G. Pratt, M. Yao, J. Brous, D. P. Chassin, R. T. Guttromson, O. M. Järvegren, S. Katipamula, N. T. Le, and T. V. O. S. Thompson, *Pacific Northwest GridWise Testbed Demonstration Projects*, Technical Report PNNL-17167, Pacific Northwest National Laboratory, Richland, WA, Oct. 2007.

57. J. P. Hespanha, P. Naghshtabrizi, and Xu Yonggang, A survey of recent results in networked control systems, *Proc. IEEE* **95**(1):138–162 (Jan. 2007).

58. I. A. Hiskens and M. A. Pai, Hybrid systems view of power system modelling, *Proc. 2000 IEEE Int. Symp. Circuits and Systems (ISCAS 2000)*, May 2000, Vol. 2, pp. 228–231.

59. S. Hoffman, R. Renner, S. Drenker, L. Carmicheal, and J. Flood, Taking advantage of real-time pricing, *IEEE Power Eng. Rev.*, **17**(9):9–12 (Sept. 1997).

60. N. M. Josuttis, *C++ Standard Library, The: A Tutorial and Reference*, Addison-Wesley Professional, 1999.

61. D. C. Karnopp, D. L. Margolis, and R. C. Rosenberg, *System Dynamics: A Unified Approach*, 2nd ed., Wiley, 1990.

62. W. D. Kelton, R. P. Sadowski, and D. T. Sturrock, *Simulation with ARENA*, 4th ed., McGraw-Hill, 2007.

63. D. H. Kim and B. P. Zeigler, Orders-of-magnitude speedup with DEVS representation and high-performance simulation, *Enabling Technol. Simulation Sci.* **3083**(1):232–243 (1997).

64. Y. J. Kim and T. G. Kim, A heterogeneous simulation framework based on the DEVS bus and the high level architecture, *Proc. 1998 Winter Simulation Conf.*, 1998, pp. 421–428.

65. B.J. Kirby, Load response fundamentally matches power system reliability requirements, *Proc. 2007 IEEE Power Engineering Society General Meeting*, June 2007, pp. 1–6.

66. J. F. Klingener, Combined discrete-continuous simulation models in ProModel for Windows, *Proc. 27th Conf. Winter Simulation (WSC '95)*, 1995, pp. 445–450.

67. J. F. Klingener, Programming combined discrete-continuous simulation models for performance, *Proc. 28th Conf. Winter Simulation conference (WSC '96)*, 1996, pp. 833–839.

68. G. J. Klir, *An Approach to General Systems Theory*, Van Nostrand Reinhold, 1969.

69. E. Kofman, M. Lapadula, and E. Pagliero, *PowerDEVS: A DEVS-Based Environment for Hybrid System Modeling and Simulation*, Technical Report LSD0306, School of Electronic Engineering, Univ. Nacional de Rosario, Rosario, Argentina, 2003.

70. E. Kofman. Discrete event simulation of hybrid systems, *SIAM J. Sci. Comput.* **25**(5):1771–1797 (2004).

71. E. Kreyszig, *Advanced Engineering Mathematics*, 7th ed., Wiley, 1993.

72. M. R. Lackner, *Digital Simulation and Systems Theory*, Technical Report SDC SP-1612, System Development Corp., Santa Monica, CA, April 1964.

73. A. M. Law, *Simulation Modeling and Analysis*, 4th ed., McGraw-Hill, 2001.

74. A. T. Le, *Modelling and Control of Tracked Vehicles*, PhD thesis, Dept. of Mechanical and Mechatronic Engineering, Univ. Sydney Jan. 1999.

75. E. A. Lee and H. Zheng, *Operational Semantics of Hybrid Systems*, Vol. 3414 of *Lecture Notes in Computer Science*, Springer, Berlin/Heidelberg, 2005, pp. 25–53.

76. S. Lee, J. Leaney, T. O'Neill, and M. Hunter, Performance benchmark of a parallel and distributed network simulator, *Proc. 19th Workshop on Principles of Advanced and Distributed Simulation (PADS '05)*, 2005, pp. 101–108.

77. M. Lu, S.-C. Lau, and E. K. Y. Chan, Combined simulation modeling using simplified discrete event simulation approach: A mining case study, *Proc. 2007 Summer Computer Simulation Conf. (SCSC'07)*, 2007, pp. 421–428.

78. H. Lundvall, P. Fritzson, and B. Bachmann, *Event Handling in the OpenModelica Compiler and Runtime System*. Technical Report 2, Dept. Computer and Information Science, Linköping Univ., 2008.

79. D. Lungeanu and C. J. R. Shi. Parallel and distributed VHDL simulation, *Proc. Conf. Design, Automation and Test in Europe (DATE '00)*, 2000, pp. 658–662.

80. N. Lynch, R. Segala, and F. Vaandrager, Hybrid I/O automata, *Inform. Comput.* **185**(1):105–157 (2003).

81. R. Madhoun and G. Wainer, Studying the impact of web-services implementation of distributed simulation of DEVS and Cell-DEVS models, *Proc. 2007 Spring Simulation Multiconf.*, 2007, Vol. 2, pp. 267–278.

82. O. Maler, Z. Manna, and A. Pnueli, From timed to hybrid systems, *Proc. REX Workshop "Real-Time: Theory in Practice,"* Vol. 600 of *Lecture Notes in Computer Science*, Springer-Verlag, 1992, pp. 447–484.

83. Z. Manna and A. Pnueli, Verifying hybrid systems, in *Hybrid Systems*, Vol. 736 of *Lecture Notes in Computer Science*, Springer, 1993, pp. 4–35.

84. A. S. Matveev and A. V. Savkin, *Qualitative Theory of Hybrid Dynamical Systems*, Birkhauser, 2000.

85. G. R. Mayer and H. S. Sarjoughian, Complexities of simulating a hybrid agent-landscape model using multi-formalism composability, *Proc. 2007 Spring Simulation Multiconf. (SpringSim '07)*, 2007, pp. 161–168.

86. M. C. Mesarovic and Y. Takahara, *Abstract Systems Theory*, Springer, 1989.

87. R. R. Mielke, M. W. Scerbo, K. T. Gaubatz, and G. S. Watson, A multidisciplinary model for M&S graduate education, *Proc. 2008 Spring Simulation Multiconf. (SpringSim '08)*, 2008, pp. 763–769.

88. S. Mittal, J. Risco, and B. P. Zeigler, DEVS-based simulation web services for net-centric T&E, *Proc. 2007 Summer Computer Simulation Conf.*, 2007, pp. 357–366.

89. P. Mosterman, M. Otter, and H. Elmqvist, Modeling Petri nets as local constraint equations for hybrid systems using modelica, *Proc. 1998 Summer Computer Simulation Conf.*, July 1998.

90. P. J. Mosterman, A hybrid modeling and simulation methodology for dynamic physical systems, *Simulation* **78**(1):5–17 (2002).

91. P. J. Mosterman and G. Biswas, A comprehensive methodology for building hybrid models of physical systems, *Artificial Intell.* **121**(1–2):171–209 (2000).

92. P. J. Mosterman and H. Vangheluwe, Computer automated multi-paradigm modeling: An introduction, *Simulation* **80**(9):433–450 (2004).

93. A. Muzy, A. Aiello, P.-A. Santoni, B. P. Zeigler, J. J. Nutaro, and R. Jammalamadaka, Discrete event simulation of large-scale spatial continuous systems, *Proc. 2005 IEEE Int. Conf. Systems, Man and Cybernetics*, Oct. 2005, Vol. 4, pp. 2991–2998.

94. A. Muzy, E. Innocenti, A. Aiello, J.-F. Santucci, and G. Wainer, Specification of discrete event models for fire spreading, *Simulation* **81**(2):103–117 (2005).

95. R. E. Nance, A history of discrete event simulation programming languages, *Proc. HOPL-II: 2nd ACM SIGPLAN Conf. History of Programming Languages*, 1993, pp. 149–175.

96. R. E. Nance, Simulation programming languages: An abridged history, *Proc. 27th Winter Simulation Conf. (WSC '95)*, 1995, pp. 1307–1313.

97. J. W. Nilsson, *Electric Circuits*, 4th ed., Addison-Wesley, 1993.

98. J. Nutaro and V. Protopopescu, The impact of market clearing time and price signal delay on the stability of electric power markets, *IEEE Trans. Power Syst.* **24**(3):1337–1345 (Aug. 2009).

99. J. Nutaro, A second order accurate Adams-Bashforth type discrete event integration scheme, *Proc. 21st Int. Workshop on Principles of Advanced and Distributed Simulation (PADS'07)*, June 2007, pp. 25–31.

100. J. Nutaro, Discrete event simulation of continuous systems, in P. A. Fishwick, ed., *Handbook of Dynamic System Modeling*, Chapman & Hall, CRC, 2007, Chap. 11.

101. J. Nutaro and P. Hammonds, Combining the model/view/control design pattern with the DEVS formalism to achieve rigor and reusability in distributed simulation, *J. Defense Model. Simulation* **1**(1):19–28 (April 2004).

102. J. Nutaro, T. Kuruganti, and M. Shankar, Seamless simulation of hybrid systems with discrete event software packages, *Proc. 40th Annual Simulation Symp. (ANSS '07)*, 2007, pp. 81–87.

103. J. J. Nutaro, B. P. Zeigler, R. Jammalamadaka, and S. R. Akerkar, Discrete event solution of gas dynamics within the DEVS framework, in P. M. A. Sloot, D. Abramson, A. V. Bogdanov, J. Dongarra, A. Y. Zomaya, and Y. E. Gorbachev, eds., *Proc. Int. Conf. Computational Science*, Vol. 2660 of *Lecture Notes in Computer Science*, Springer, June 2003, pp. 319–328.

104. T. I. Ören, Toward the body of knowledge of modeling and simulation (M&SBOK), *Proc. Interservice/Industry Training and Simulation Conf. (I/ITSEC)*, Nov. 2005, pp. 1–19.

105. C. D. Pegden, R. E. Shannon, and R. P. Sadowski, *Introduction to Simulation Using Siman*, McGraw-Hill, 1995.

106. K. S. Perumalla, Parallel and distributed simulation: Traditional techniques and recent advances, *Proc. 38th Winter Simulation Conf. (WSC '06)*, 2006, pp. 84–95.

107. P. Peschlow and P. Martini, Efficient analysis of simultaneous events in distributed simulation, *Proc. 11th IEEE Int. Symp. Distributed Simulation and Real-Time Applications (DS-RT 2007)*, Oct. 2007.

108. M. A. Piette, *Development and Evaluation of Fully Automated Demand Response in Large Facilities*, Technical Report CEC-500-2005-013, Lawrence Berkeley National Laboratory/California Energy Commission/Demand Response Research Center, Berkeley, CA, Jan. 2005.

109. H. Praehofer, System theoretic formalisms for combined discrete-continuous system simulation, *Int. J. General Syst.* **19**(3):226–240 (1991).

110. V. S. Prat, A. Urquia, and S. Dormido, ARENALib: A Modelica library for discrete-event system simulation, *Proc. 5th Int. Modelica Conf. (Modelica 2006)*, Sept. 2006, Vol. 2, pp. 539–548.

111. W. W. Price, H. D. Chiang, H. K. Clark, C. Concordia, D. C. Lee, J. C. Hsu, S. Ihara, C. A. King, C. J. Lin, Y. Mansour, K. Srinivasan, C. W. Taylor, and E. Vaahedi, Load representation for dynamic performance analysis [of power systems], *IEEE Trans. Power Syst.* **8**(2):472–482 (May 1993).

112. A. B. Pritsker and J. J. O'Reilly, *Simulation with Visual SLAM and Awesim*, Wiley, 1999.

113. S. Raczynski, *Modeling and Simulation: The Computer Science of Illusion*, Wiley, 2006.

114. A. Ralston and P. Rabinowitz, *A First Course in Numerical Analysis*, 2nd ed., Dover Publications, 2001.

115. M. A. P. Remelhe, Combining discrete event models and modelica—general thoughts and a special modeling environment, *Proc. 2nd Int. Modelica Conf.*, March 2002, pp. 203–207.

116. S. V. Rice, H. M. Markowitz, A. Marjanski, and S. M. Bailey, The SIMSCRIPT III programming language for modular object-oriented simulation, *Proc. 37th Winter Simulation Conf. (WSC '05)*, 2005, pp. 621–630.

117. G. F. Riley, M. H. Ammar, R. M. Fujimoto, A. Park, K. Perumalla, and D. Xu, A federated approach to distributed network simulation, *ACM Trans. Model. Comput. Simulation* **14**(2):116–148 (2004).

118. D. J. Roberts and P. M. Sharkey, Maximising concurrency and scalability in a consistent, causal, distributed virtual reality system whilst minimising the effect of network delays, *Proc. 6th Workshop on Enabling Technologies on Infrastructure for Collaborative Enterprises (WET-ICE '97)*, 1997, pp. 161–166.

119. R. V. Rogers, What makes a modeling and simulation professional? The consensus view from one workshop, *Proc. 29th Winter Simulation Conference (WSC '97)*, 1997, pp. 1375–1382.

120. T. Rohaly, Answer to "what is the maximum transfer rate (kbytes/sec) i can expect using sockets over the tini 10baset interface?" (online posting, March 5, 2001, at http://www.jguru.com/faq/view.jsp?EID=344126).

121. R. Rönngren, J. Riboe, and R. Ayani, Lazy queue: An efficient implementation of the pending-event set, *Proc. 24th Annual Symp. Simulation*, 1991, pp. 194–204.

122. R. Rönngren and M. Liljenstam, On event ordering in parallel discrete event simulation, *Proc. 13th Workshop on Parallel and Distributed Simulation (PADS '99)*, 1999, pp. 38–45.

123. R. Rönngren, M. Liljenstam, R. Ayani, and J. Montagnat, Transparent incremental state saving in time warp parallel discrete event simulation, *Proc. 10th Workshop on Parallel and Distributed Simulation (PADS '96)*, 1996, pp. 70–77.

124. V. Sanz, A. Urquia, and S. Dormido, Introducing messages in modelica for facilitating discrete-event system modeling, *Proc. 2nd Int. Workshop on Equation-Based Object-Oriented Languages and Tools*, July 2008, pp. 83–94.

125. R. G. Sargent, Some recent advances in the process world view, *Proc. 36th Conf. Winter Simulation (WSC '04)*, 2004, pp. 293–299.

126. H. S. Sarjoughian, Model composability, *Proc. 38th Winter Simulation Conf. (WSC '06)*, 2006, pp. 149–158.

127. H. S. Sarjoughian and B. P. Zeigler. DEVS and HLA: Complementary paradigms for modeling and simulation, *Trans. Soc. Comput. Simulation Int.* **17**(4):187–197 (2000).

128. R. J. Schilling, *Fundamentals of Robotics: Analysis and Control*, Prentice-Hall, 1990.

129. B. Schönfisch and A. de Roos, Synchronous and asynchronous updating in cellular automata, *Biosystems* **51**(3), 1999.

130. T. J. Schriber and D. T. Brunner, Inside discrete-event simulation software: How it works and why it matters, *Proc. 30th Winter Simulation Conf.* 1998, pp. 77–86.

131. L. Schruben, Simulation modeling with event graphs, *Commun. ACM* **26**(11):957–963 (Nov. 1983).

132. S. Schulz, T. C. Ewing, and J. W. Rozenblit, Discrete event system specification (DEVS) and StateCharts equivalence for embedded systems modeling, *Proc. 7th IEEE Int. Conf. Workshop on the Engineering of Computer-Based Systems*, April 2000, pp. 308–316.

133. R. A. Serway, *Physics for Scientists and Engineers*, 3rd ed., updated version, Saunders College Publishing, 1992.

134. R. W. Stark and W. H. Hughes, Asynchronous, irregular automata nets: The path not taken, *Biosystems* **55**(1–3) (2000).

135. R. H. Staunton, J. D. Kueck, B. J. Kirby, and J. Eto, Demand response: an overview of enabling technologies, *Public Util. Fortnight.* **139**(20) (Nov. 2001).

136. G. Strang, *Linear Algebra And Its Applications,* 3rd ed., Brooks Cole, 1988.

137. A. S. Tanenbaum, *Computer Networks*, 3rd ed., Prentice-Hall, 1996.

138. Y. Tang, K. Perumalla, R. Fujimoto, H. Karimabadi, J. Driscoll, and Y. Omelchenko, Parallel discrete event simulations of physical systems using reverse computation, *Proc. ACM/IEEE/SCS Workshop on Principles of Advanced and Distributed Simulation (PADS)*, June 2005.

139. D. Trudnowski, M. Donnelly, and E. Lightner, Power-system frequency and stability control using decentralized intelligent loads, *Proc. 2005/2006 IEEE PES Transmission and Distribution Conf. and Exhibition*, May 2006, pp. 1453–1459.

140. A. M. Uhrmacher, Dynamic structures in modeling and simulation: A reflective approach, *ACM Trans. Model. Comput. Simulation* **11**(2):206–232(2001).

141. H. Vangheluwe and J. de Lara, Foundations of multi-paradigm modeling and simulation: Computer automated multi-paradigm modelling: Meta-modelling and graph transformation, *Proc. 35th Conf. Winter Simulation (WSC '03)*, 2003, pp. 595–603.

142. G. A. Wainer and N. Giambiasi, Cell-DEVS/GDEVS for complex continuous systems, *Simulation* **81**(2):137–151 (Feb. 2005).

143. G. A. Wainer, *Discrete-Event Modeling and Simulation: A Practitioner's Approach (Computational Analysis, Synthesis, and Design of Dynamic Models)*, CRC Press, 2009.

144. Y. -H. Wang and B. P. Zeigler, Extending the DEVS formalism for massively parallel simulation, *Discrete Event Dyn. Syst.* **3**(2–3) (July 1993).

145. M. A. Weiss, *Data Structures and Algorithm Analysis in C*, Benjamin/Cummings, 1992.

146. F. Wieland, The threshold of event simultaneity, *Simulation* **72**(3):149 (1999).

147. S. Wolfram, *A New Kind of Science*, Wolfram Media, 2002.

148. T. Wutzler and H. S. Sarjoughian, Interoperability among parallel DEVS simulators and models implemented in multiple programming languages, *Simulation* **83**(6):473–490 (2007).

149. A. W. Wymore, *A Mathematical Theory of Systems Engineering—The Elements*, Wiley, 1967.

150. A. W. Wymore, *Model-Based Systems Engineering*, CRC Press, 1993.

151. S. Yakowitz and F. Szidarovszky, *An Introduction to Numerical Computations*, 2nd ed., Macmillan, 1989.

152. B. P. Zeigler, *Theory of Modeling and Simulation*, Wiley-Interscience, 1976.

153. S. Mullen, Power system simulator for smart grid development, Master thesis, University of Minnesota, May 2006.

154. B. P. Zeigler, *Multifacetted Modelling and Discrete Event Simulation*, Academic Press, 1984.

155. B. P. Zeigler, Embedding DEV&DESS in DEVS, *Proc. DEVS Integrative M&S Symp.* (DEVS'06), April 2006.

156. B. P. Zeigler, T. G. Kim, and C. Lee, Variable structure modelling methodology: An adaptive computer architecture example, *Trans. Soc. Comput. Simulation Int.* **7**(4):291–318 (1990).

157. B. P. Zeigler, T. G. Kim, and H. Praehofer, *Theory of Modeling and Simulation*, 2nd ed., Academic Press, 2000.

158. B. P. Zeigler, H. Sarjoughian, and H. Praehofer, Theory of quantized systems: DEVS simulation of perceiving agents, *Cybernet. Syst.* **31**(6):611–647 (Sept. 2000).

159. B. P. Zeigler, H. S. Song, T. G. Kim, and H. Praehofer, DEVS framework for modelling, simulation, analysis, and design of hybrid systems, *Proc. HSAC*, 1996, pp. 529–551.

160. J. Zhang, K. H. Johansson, J. Lygeros, and S. Sastry, Zeno hybrid systems, *Int. J. Robust Nonlinear Control* **11**:435–451 (2001).

161. H. Zheng, *Operational Semantics of Hybrid Systems*, PhD thesis, Univ. California, Berkeley, May 2007.

162. S. Zhou, W. Cai, B. -S. Lee, and S. J. Turner, Time-space consistency in large-scale distributed virtual environments, *ACM Trans. Model. Comput. Simulation* **14**(1):31–47 (2004).

INDEX

adevs, web site, 5
Admittance matrix, 259–260, 270
Amdahl's law, 296–298, 327–328
  defined, 296
Assembly line, 129–131, 137–141, 165–168.
  See also Press and drill
Assertion, 281–282
Asynchronous cellular automata, *see* Cellular
  automata, asynchronous
Atomic model (defined), 8, 32–33, 39, 101
  simulation algorithm, 38, 104–105

Bag, 40, 42, 63
  defined, 40
  implementation, 153–156
  systems with, 42, 114
Bond graph, 8, 13–15, 273
Breaker (over- and under- frequency), 257–261

Cart, *see* Pendulum
Categorical hybrid systems, 236
Causal system, 300
CD++, 229, 273
Cellular automata, 6, 91, 93, 98–99, 273, 276
  asynchronous, 176–178, 276
  are differential automata, 229–232

Circuit
  example of hybrid system, 195–197, 208–210
  one-line drawing of a power system, 259
  speed control of motor, 10, 14
Code inspection, 280
Code optimization, 280, 291
Combined modeling, 276
Communication network, 226, 237, 256–257
Conservative algorithm, 274, 298–301, 304, 311,
  325
  earliest input time, 303, 309–311, 315–316, 325
  earliest output time, 303–304, 311, 313, 317,
  325
  feedback, 302, 304, 311, 325
  partition, 303, 309, 325–326
Continuous input, 186
Control center, 256–257, 260–261

Dead reckoning, 225–226
Debugger, 280
DEVS, 5, 101, 225, 269, 276
  &DESS, 236, 269
  generalized (GDEVS, Giambiasi), 225, 269
  graph, 21
Differential automata, 229–230, 232, 236. *See also*
  Cellular automata, are differential automata

Printed and bound by CPI Group (UK) Ltd, Croydon, CR0 4YY

27/10/2024

14580259-0001